Mixx Manga Premium Edition
Volume 4

MAGIC KNIGHT

RAYEARTH

by CLAMP

Mixx Entertainment Presents
Rayearth 4 by CLAMP
Mixx Manga Premium Edition is an imprint of Mixx Entertainment, Inc.
ISBN: 1-892213-43-5
First Printing July 2000

10   9   8   7   6   5   4   3   2   1

This volume contains the RAYEARTH installments from TOKYOPOP Magazine Volumes
No.3:5 through No.3:10 in their entirety.

Translator - Anita Sengupta. Retouch Artist - Wilbert Lucana. Graphic Assistant - Steve Kindernay.
Graphic Designer - Akemi Imafuku. Associate Editor - Jake Forbes. Editor - Mary Coco.
Production Coordinator - Fred Lui. Director of Publishing - Henry Kornman.

Email: info@mixxonline.com
Come visit us at www.TOKYOPOP.com.

Mixx Entertainment, Inc.
Los Angeles - Tokyo

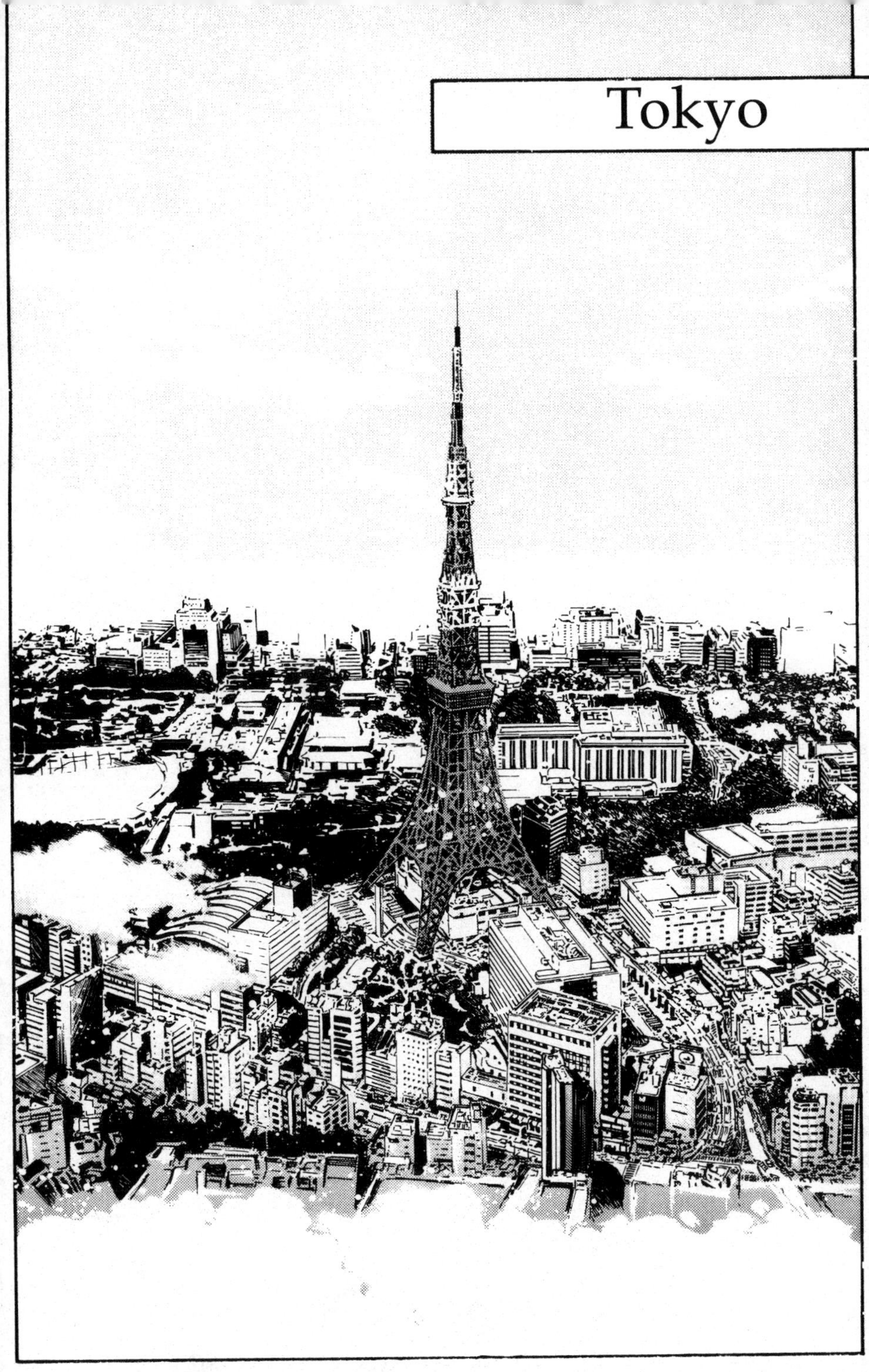
Tokyo

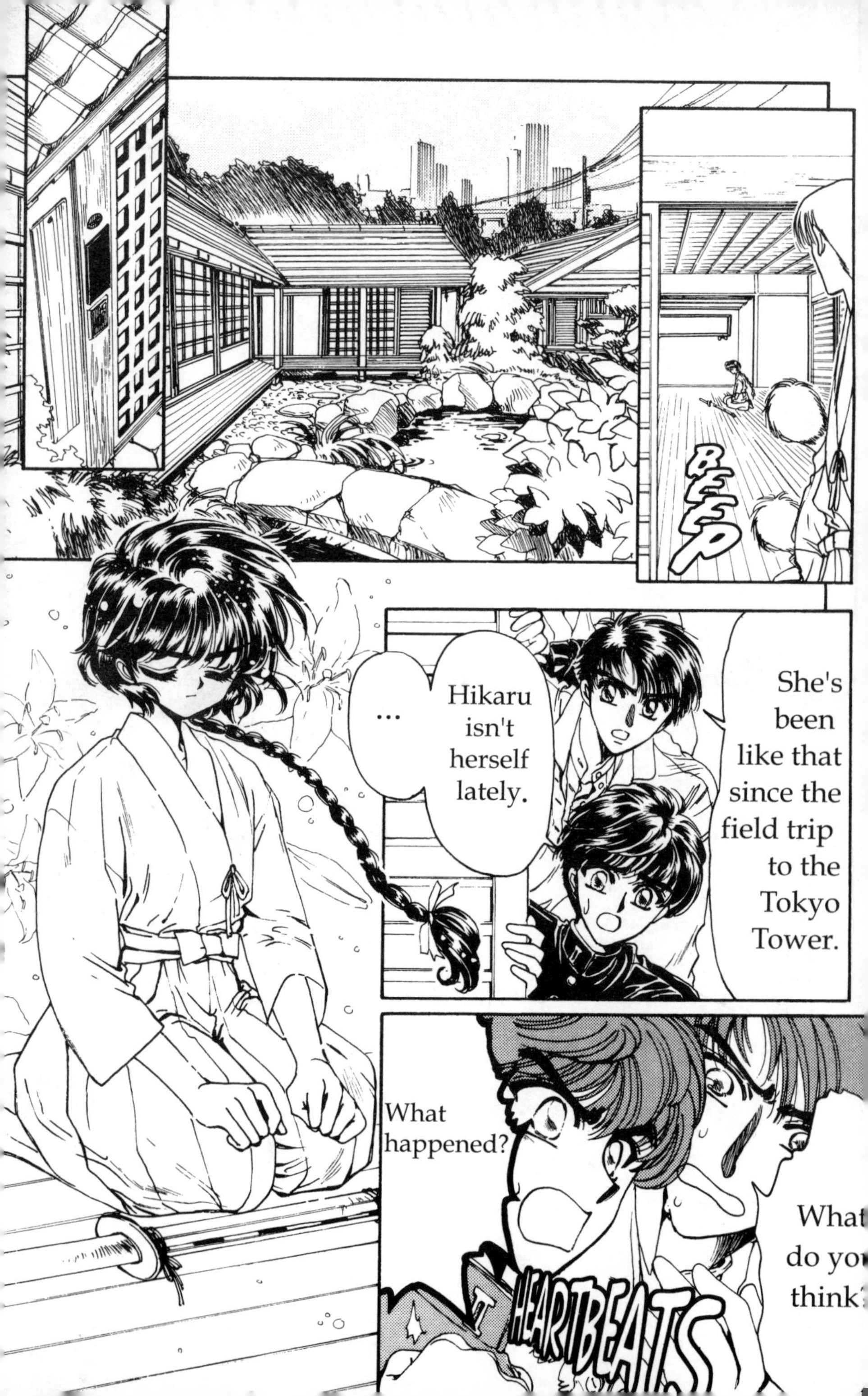
BEEP
She's been like that since the field trip to the Tokyo Tower.
... Hikaru isn't herself lately.
What happened?
HEARTBEATS

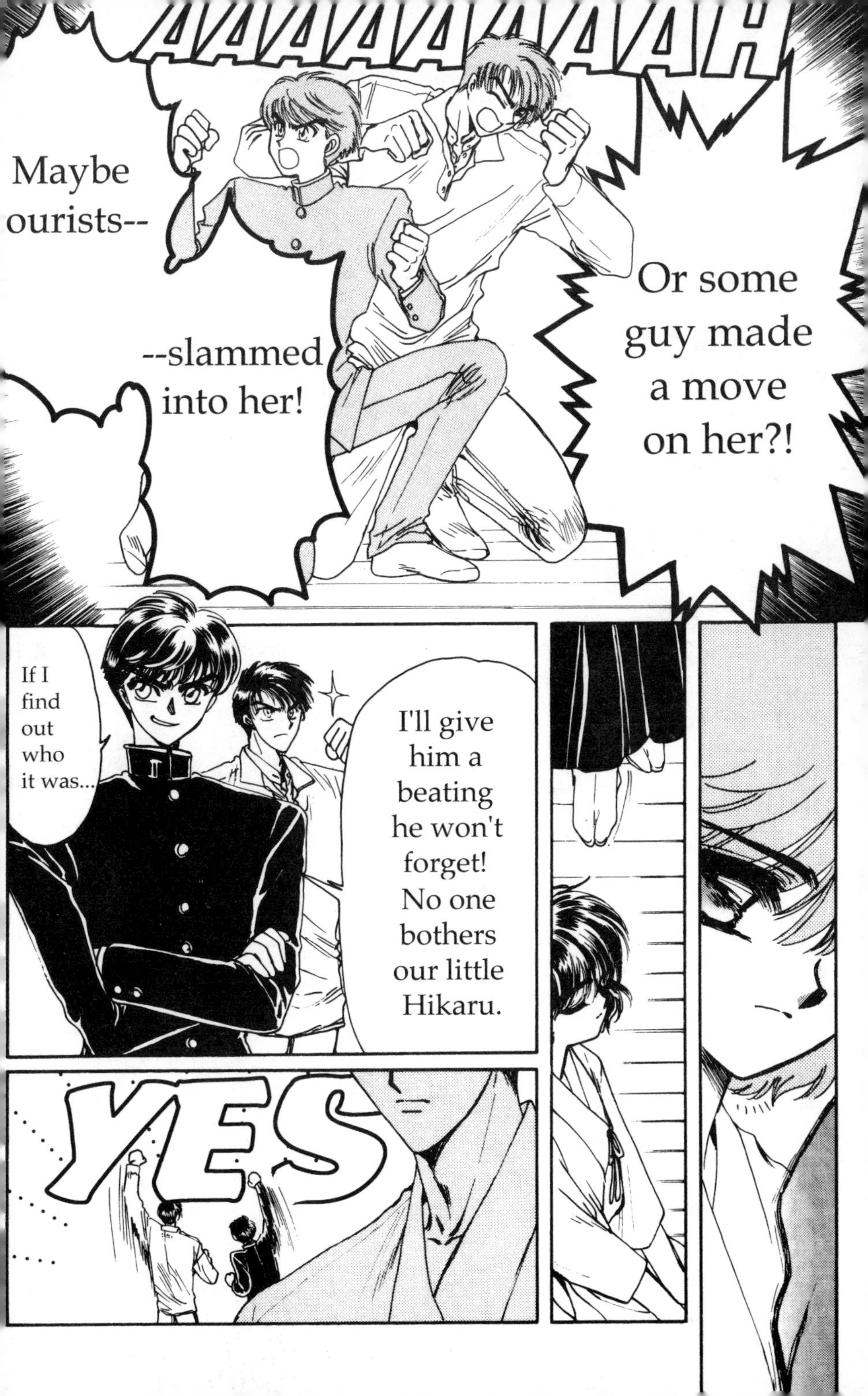

AAAAAAAAAAAH
Maybe ourists--
--slammed into her!
Or some guy made a move on her?!
If I find out who it was...
I'll give him a beating he won't forget! No one bothers our little Hikaru.
YES

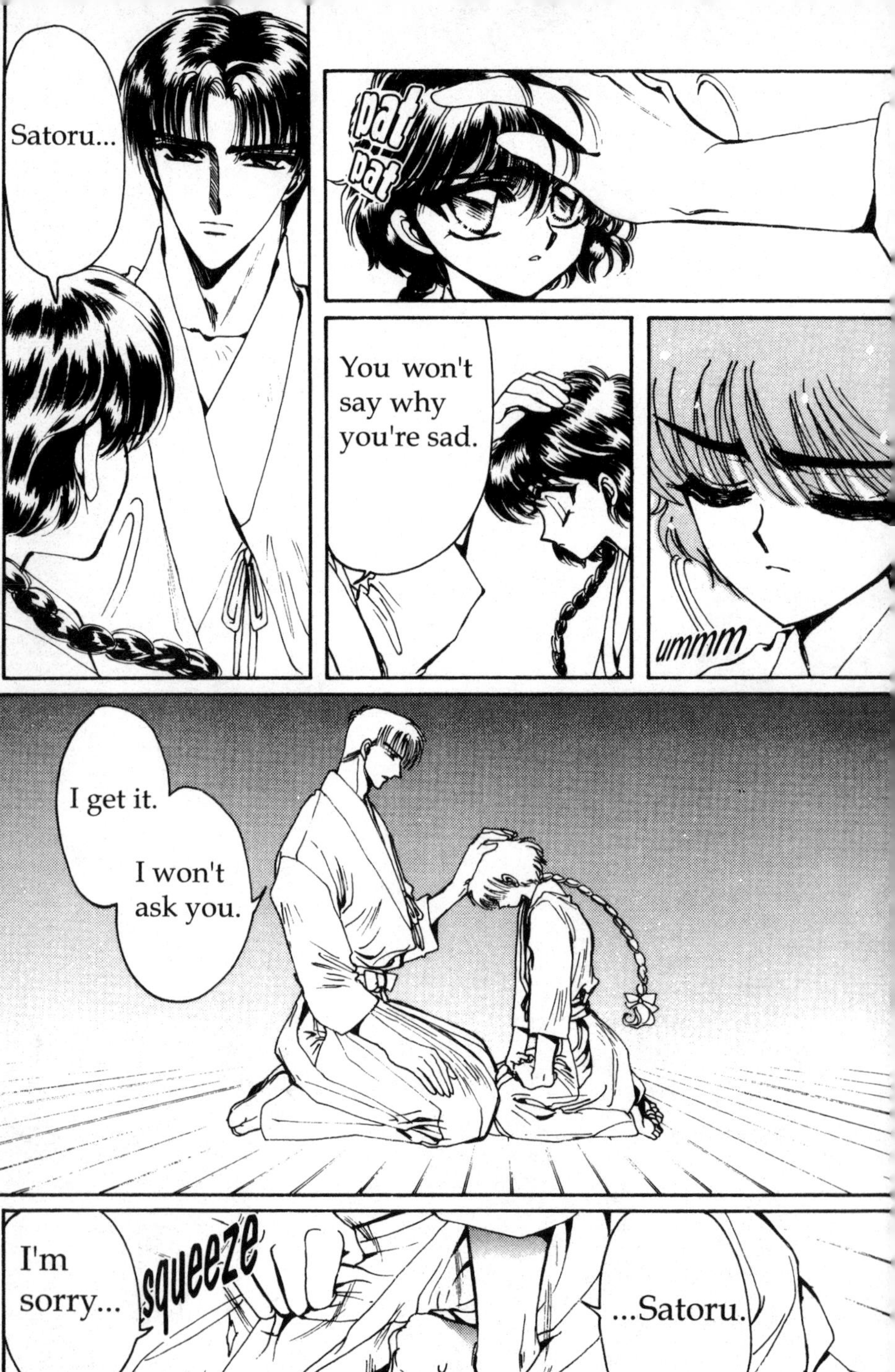
Satoru...
pat pat
You won't say why you're sad.
ummm
I get it.
I won't ask you.
I'm sorry...
squeeze
...Satoru.

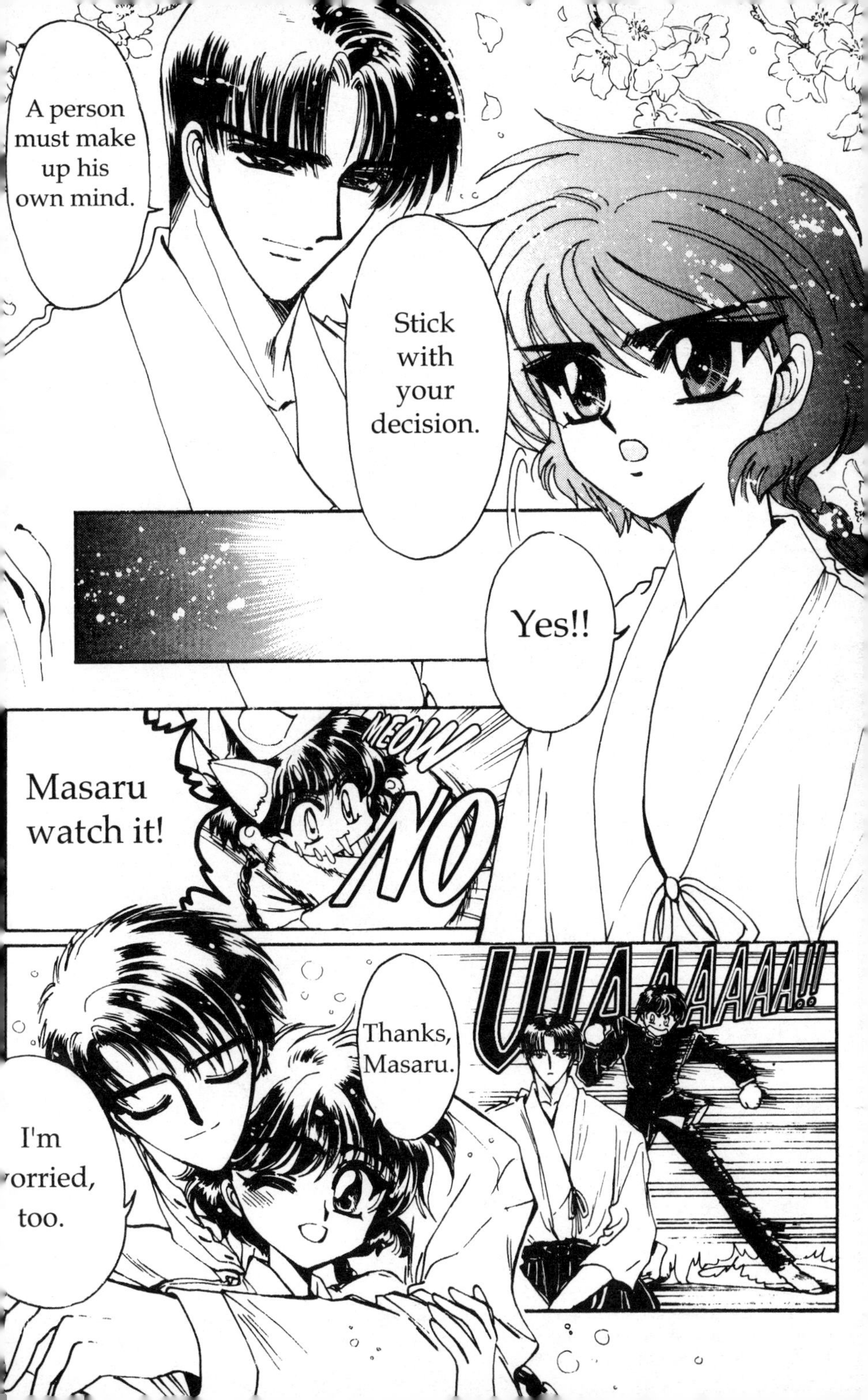
A person must make up his own mind.
Stick with your decision.
Yes!!
Masaru watch it!
MEOW
NO
UUAAAAAAA!!
Thanks, Masaru.
I'm orried, too.

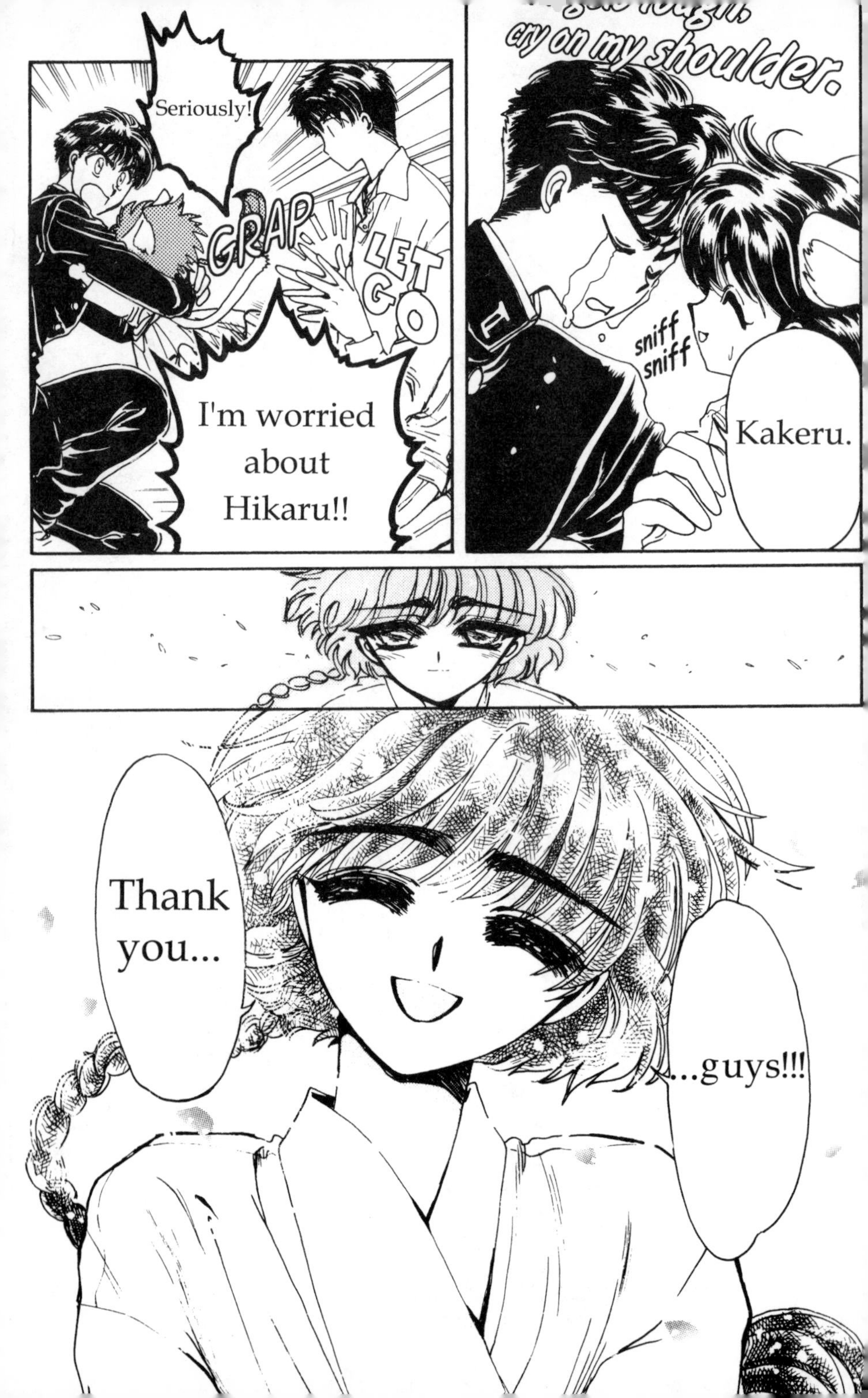

cry on my shoulder.
sniff sniff
Kakeru.
Seriously!
GRAP
LET GO
I'm worried about Hikaru!!
Thank you...
...guys!!!

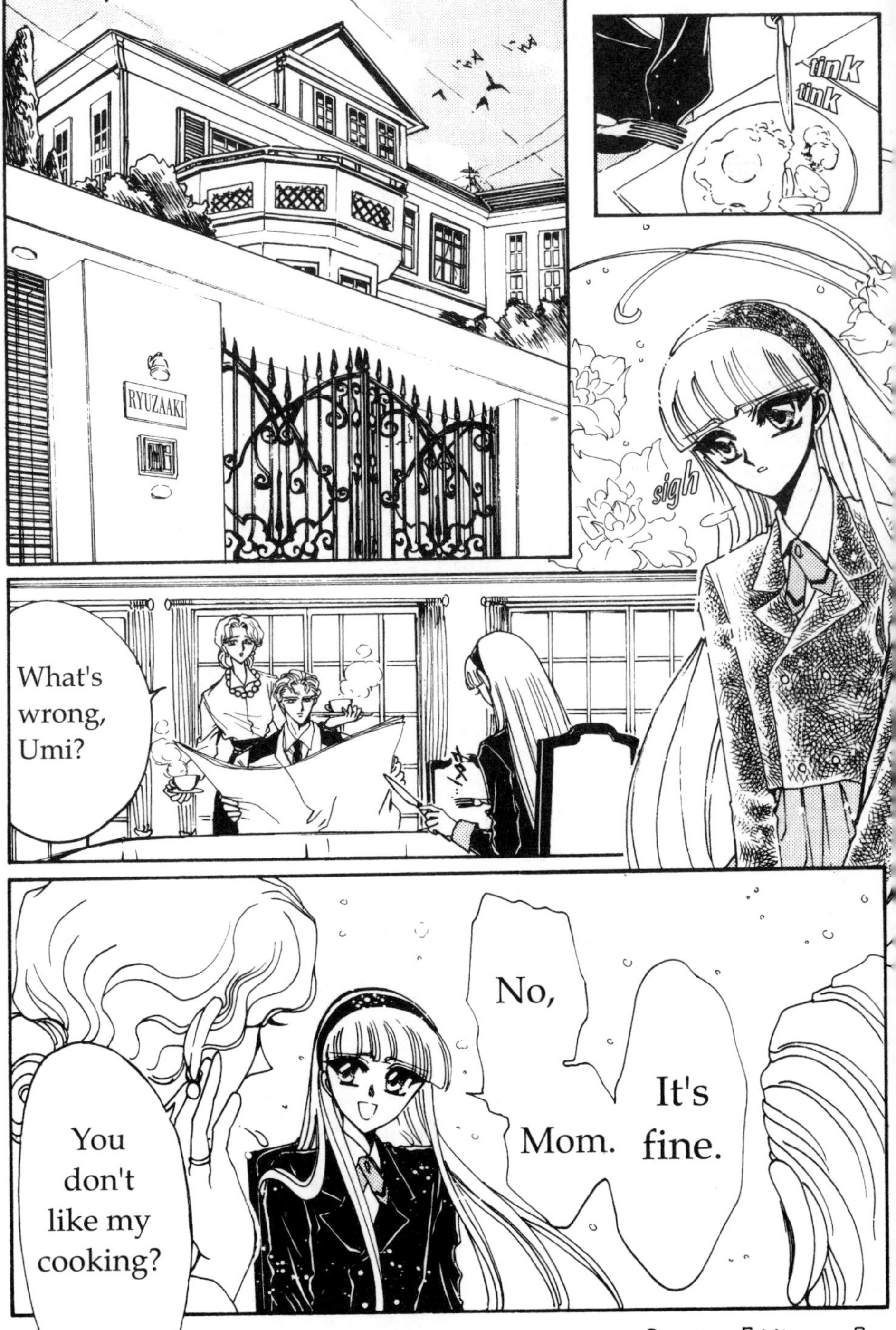
RYUZAAKI
tink
tink
sigh
What's wrong, Umi?
You don't like my cooking?
No, Mom.
It's fine.

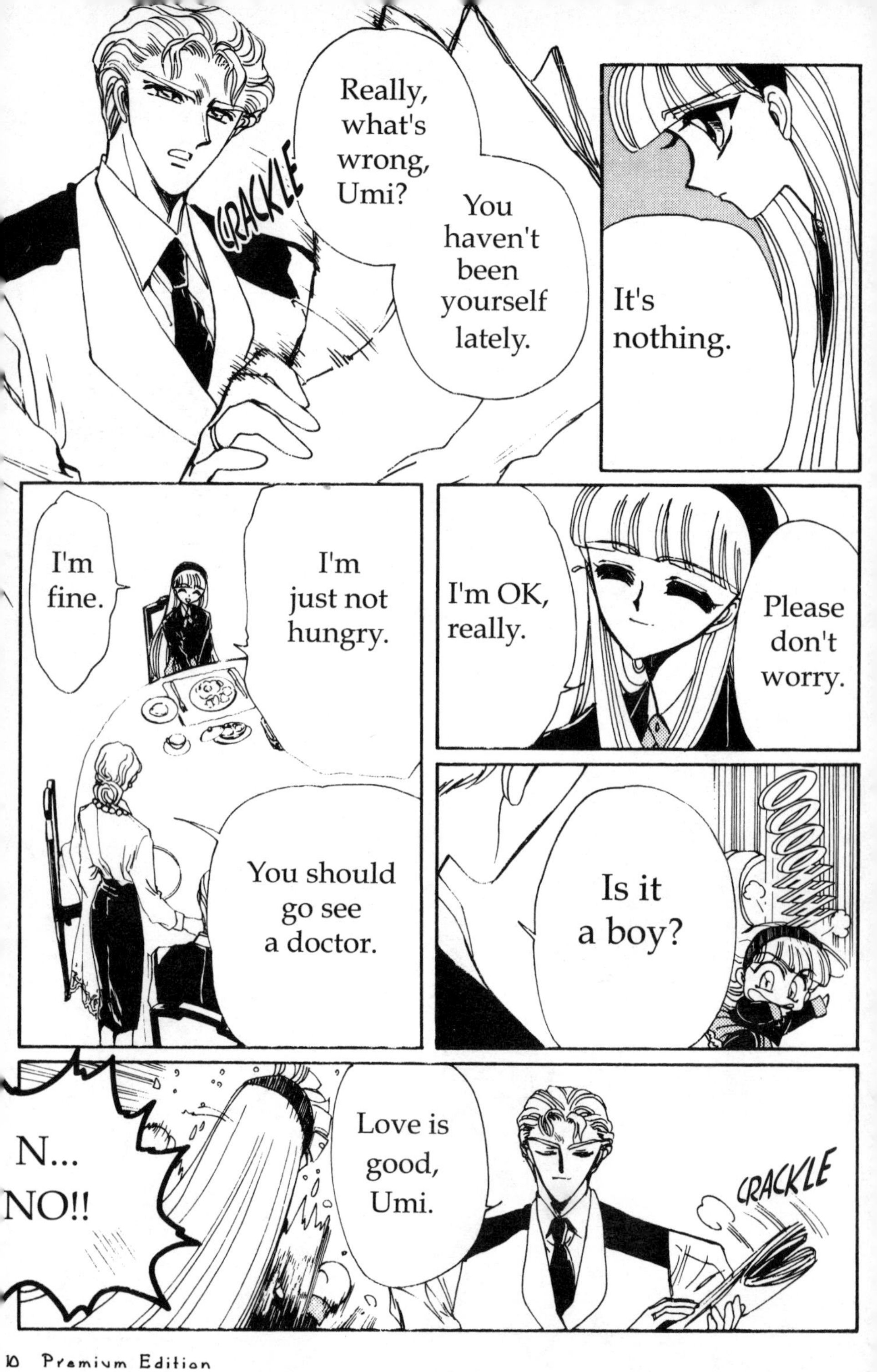
Really, what's wrong, Umi?
CRACKLE
You haven't been yourself lately.
It's nothing.
I'm fine.
I'm just not hungry.
You should go see a doctor.
I'm OK, really.
Please don't worry.
Is it a boy?
N... NO!!
Love is good, Umi.
CRACKLE

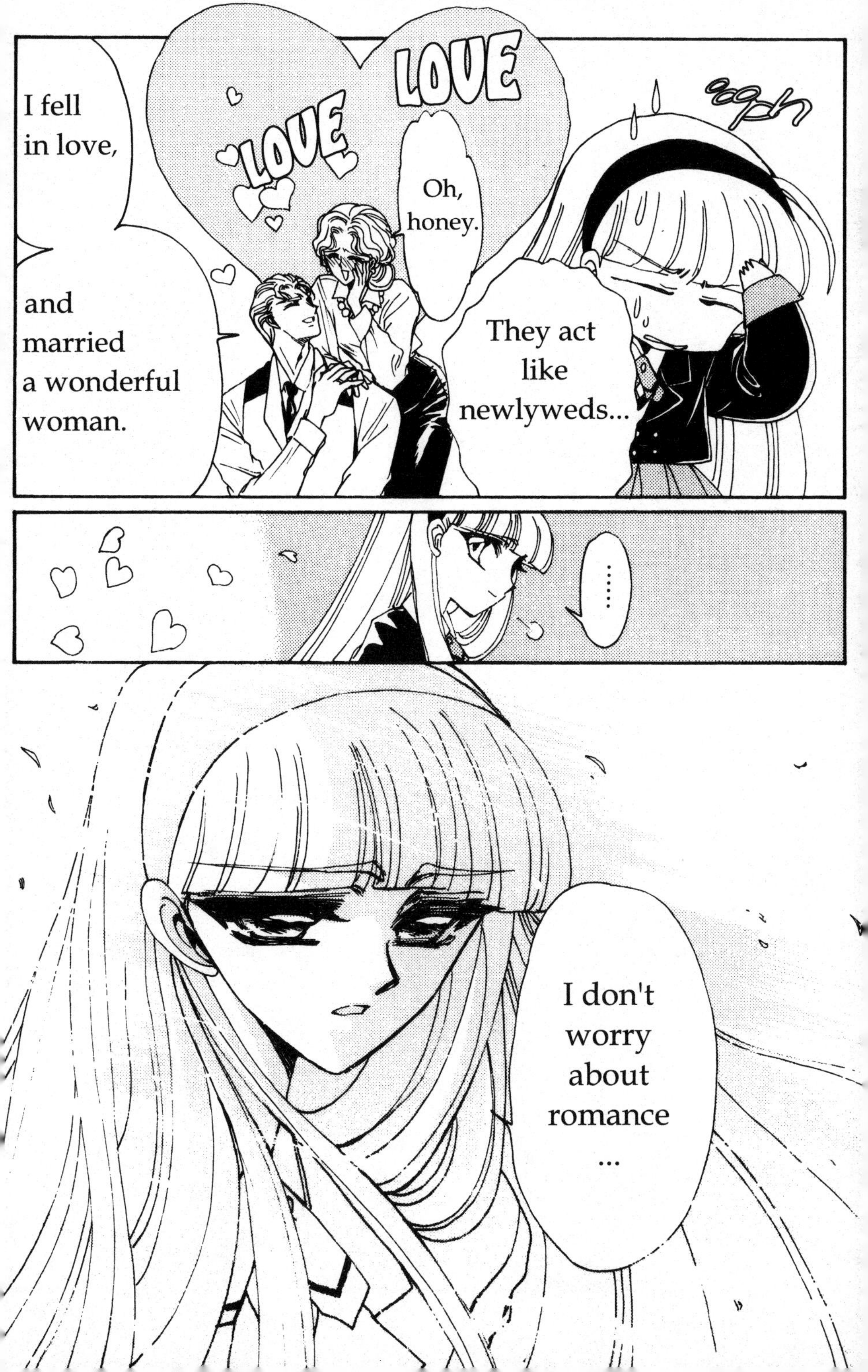
I fell in love,
and married a wonderful woman.
LOVE
LOVE
Oh, honey.
ooph
They act like newlyweds...
......
I don't worry about romance ...

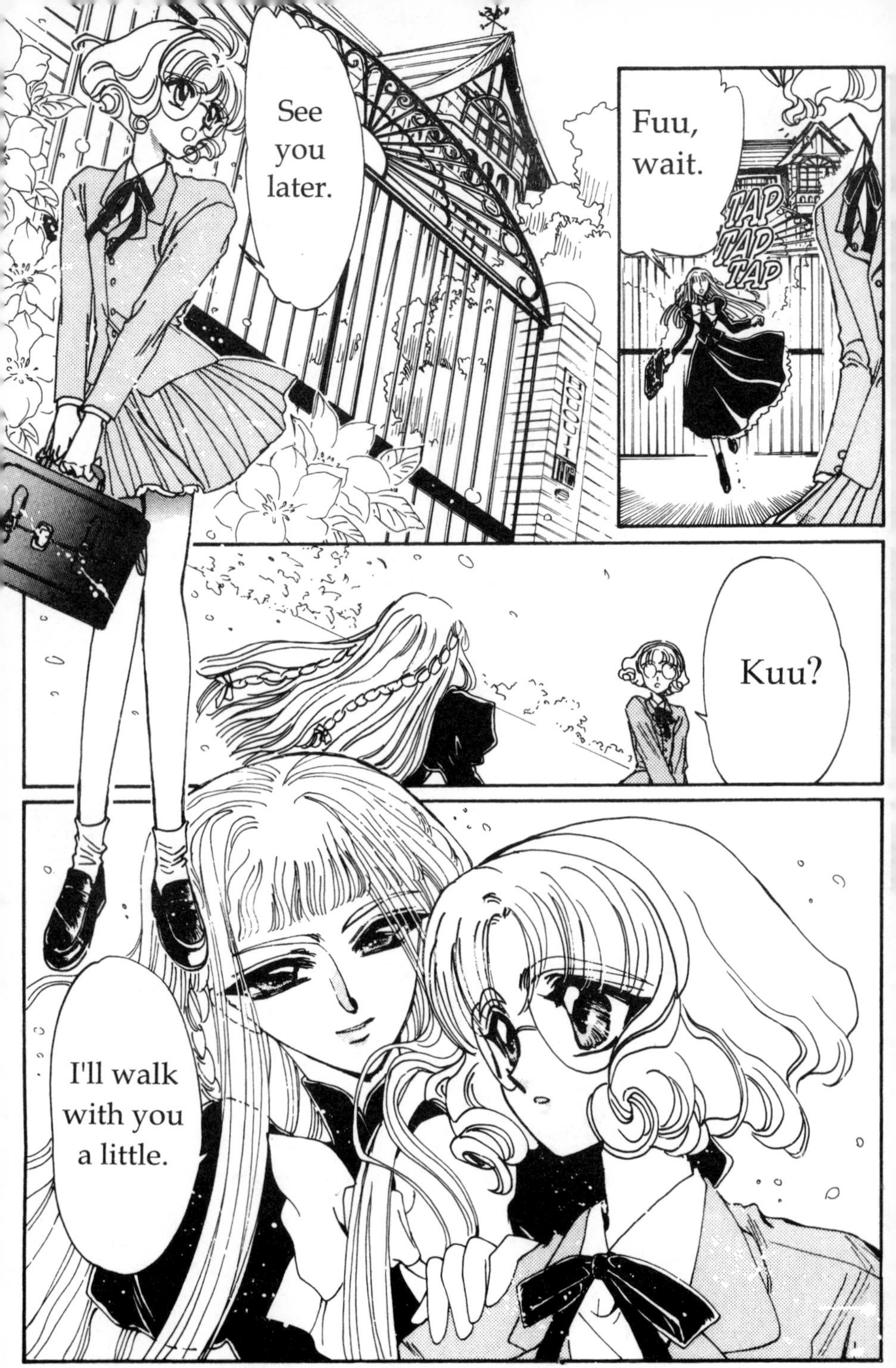
See you later.
Fuu, wait.
TAP TAP TAP
Kuu?
I'll walk with you a little.

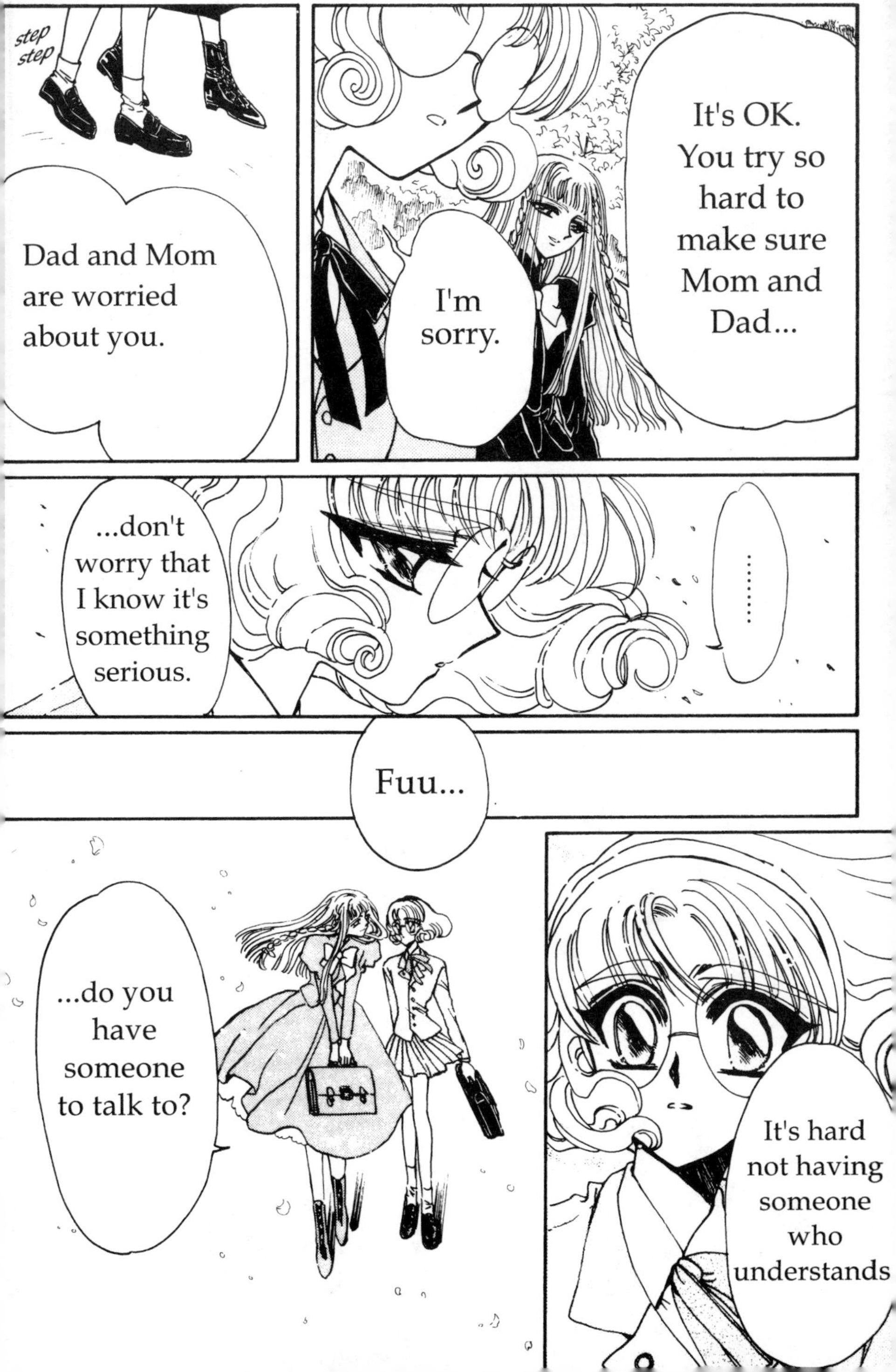
step
step
Dad and Mom are worried about you.
I'm sorry.
It's OK. You try so hard to make sure Mom and Dad...
...don't worry that I know it's something serious.
....
Fuu...
...do you have someone to talk to?
It's hard not having someone who understands

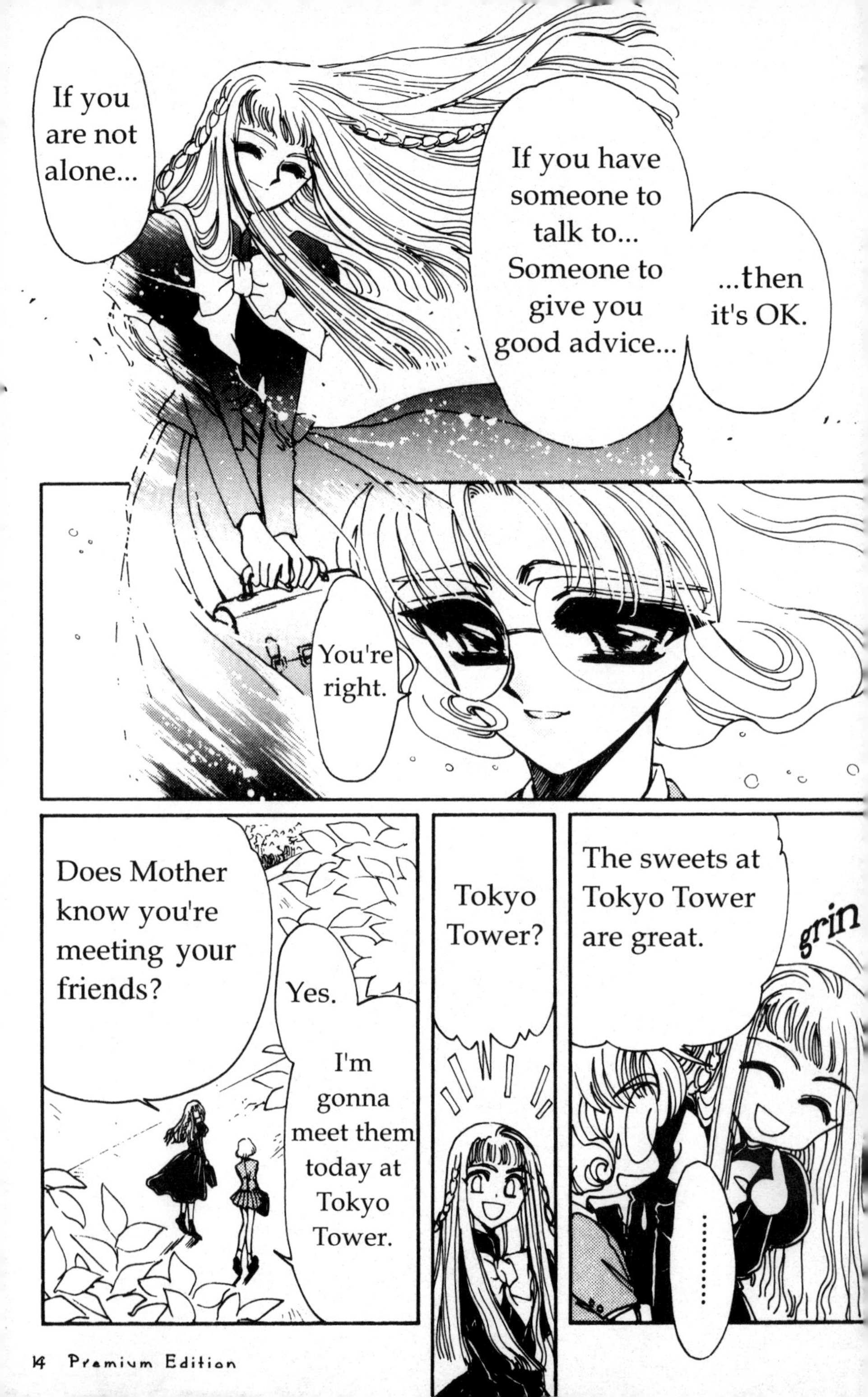
If you are not alone...
If you have someone to talk to... Someone to give you good advice...
...then it's OK.
You're right.
Does Mother know you're meeting your friends?
Yes.
I'm gonna meet them today at Tokyo Tower.
Tokyo Tower?
The sweets at Tokyo Tower are great.
grin
....

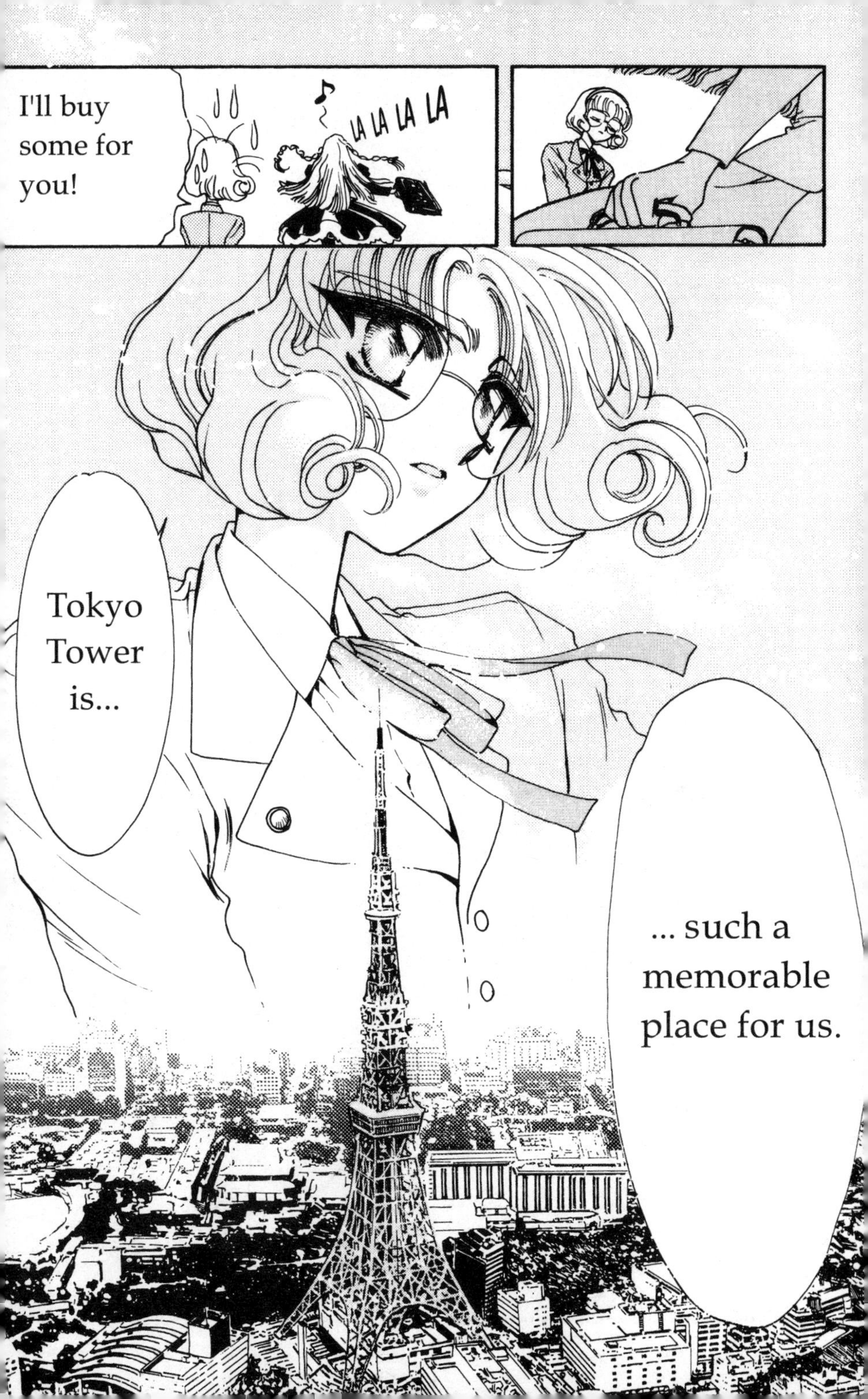
I'll buy some for you!
LA LA LA LA
Tokyo Tower is...
... such a memorable place for us.

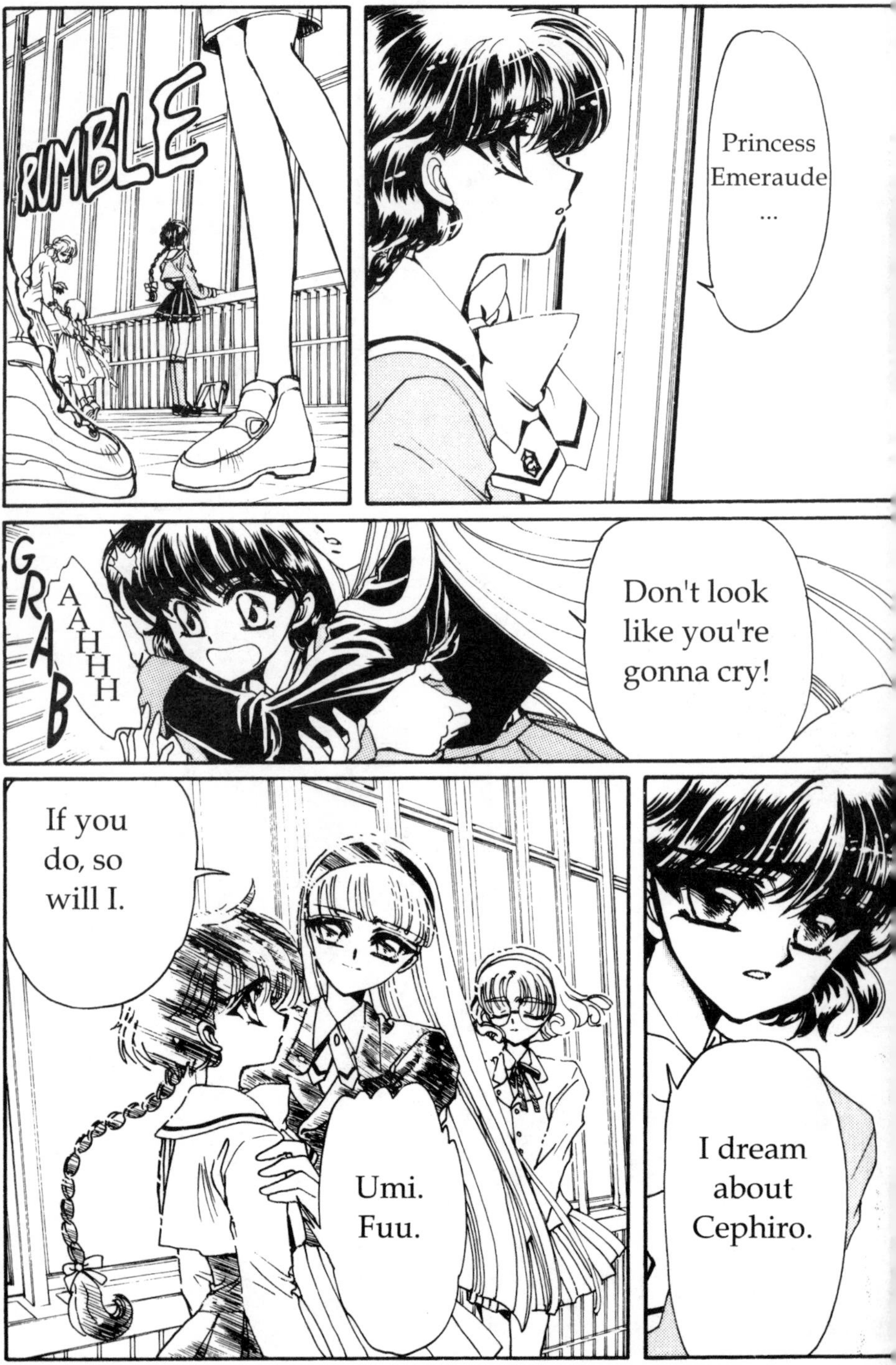
RUMBLE
Princess Emeraude ...
GRAB
AAHHH
Don't look like you're gonna cry!
If you do, so will I.
Umi. Fuu.
I dream about Cephiro.

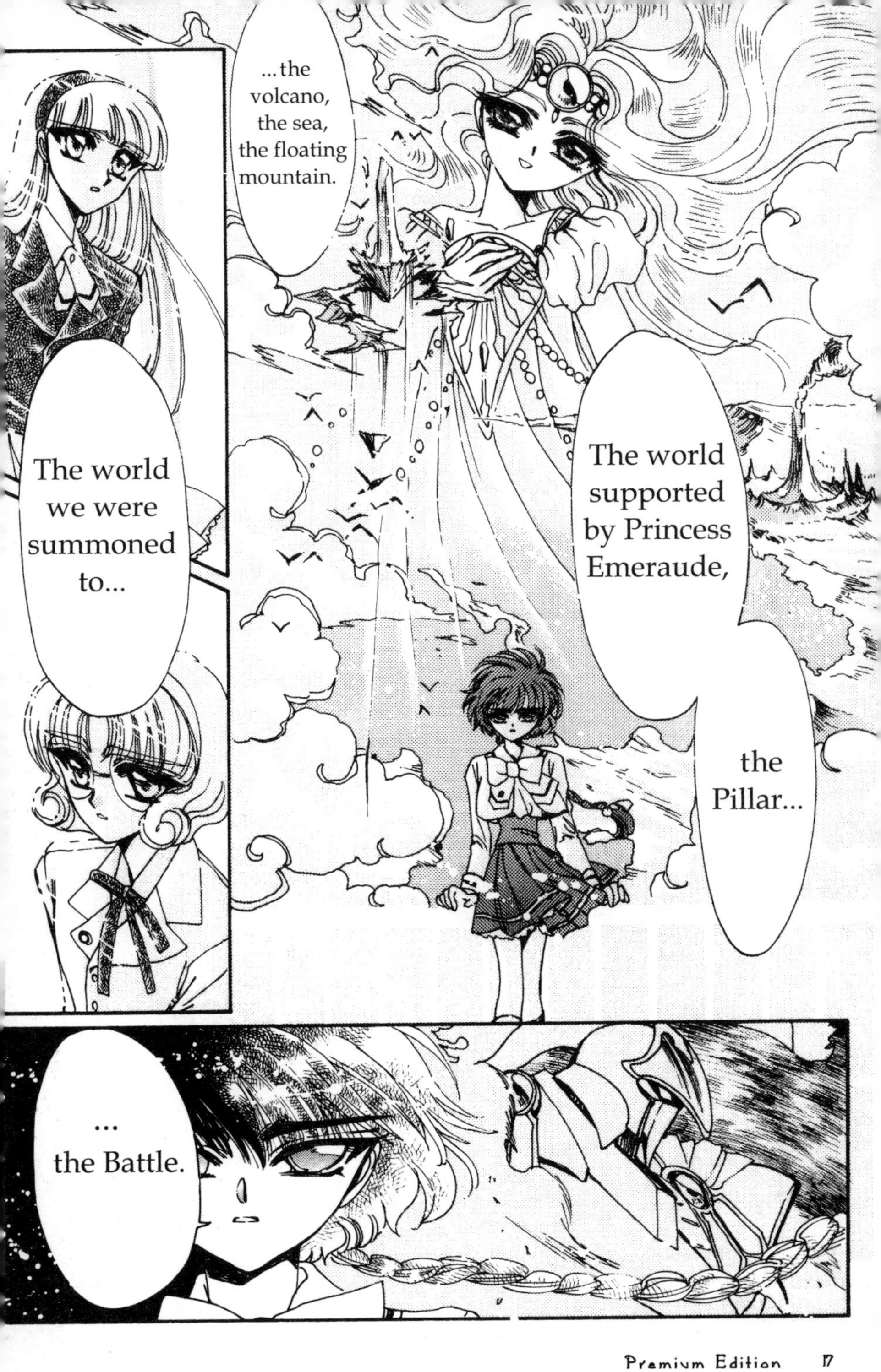

The world supported by Princess Emeraude,
the Pillar...
...the volcano, the sea, the floating mountain.
The world we were summoned to...
... the Battle.

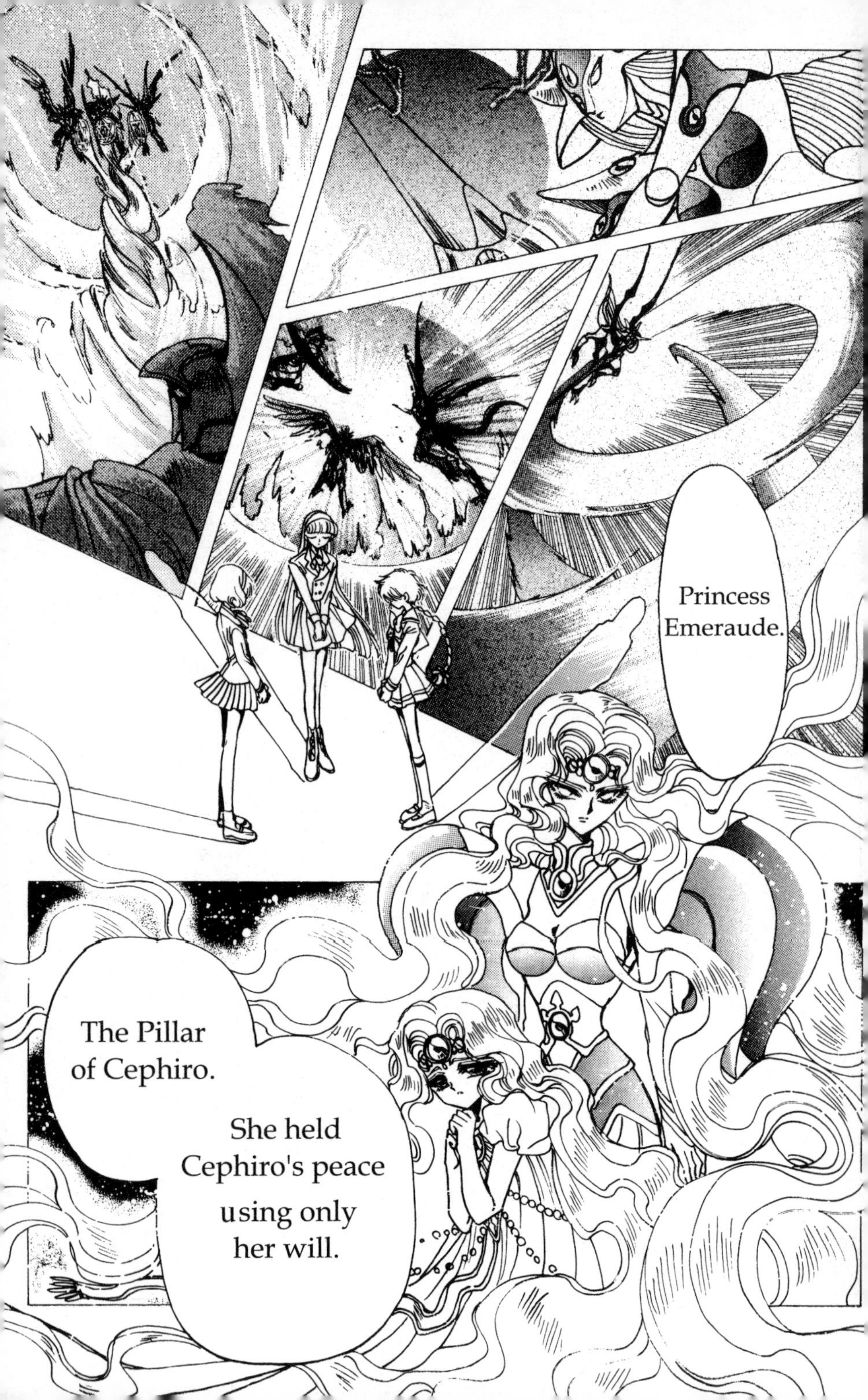
Princess Emeraude.
The Pillar of Cephiro.
She held Cephiro's peace using only her will.

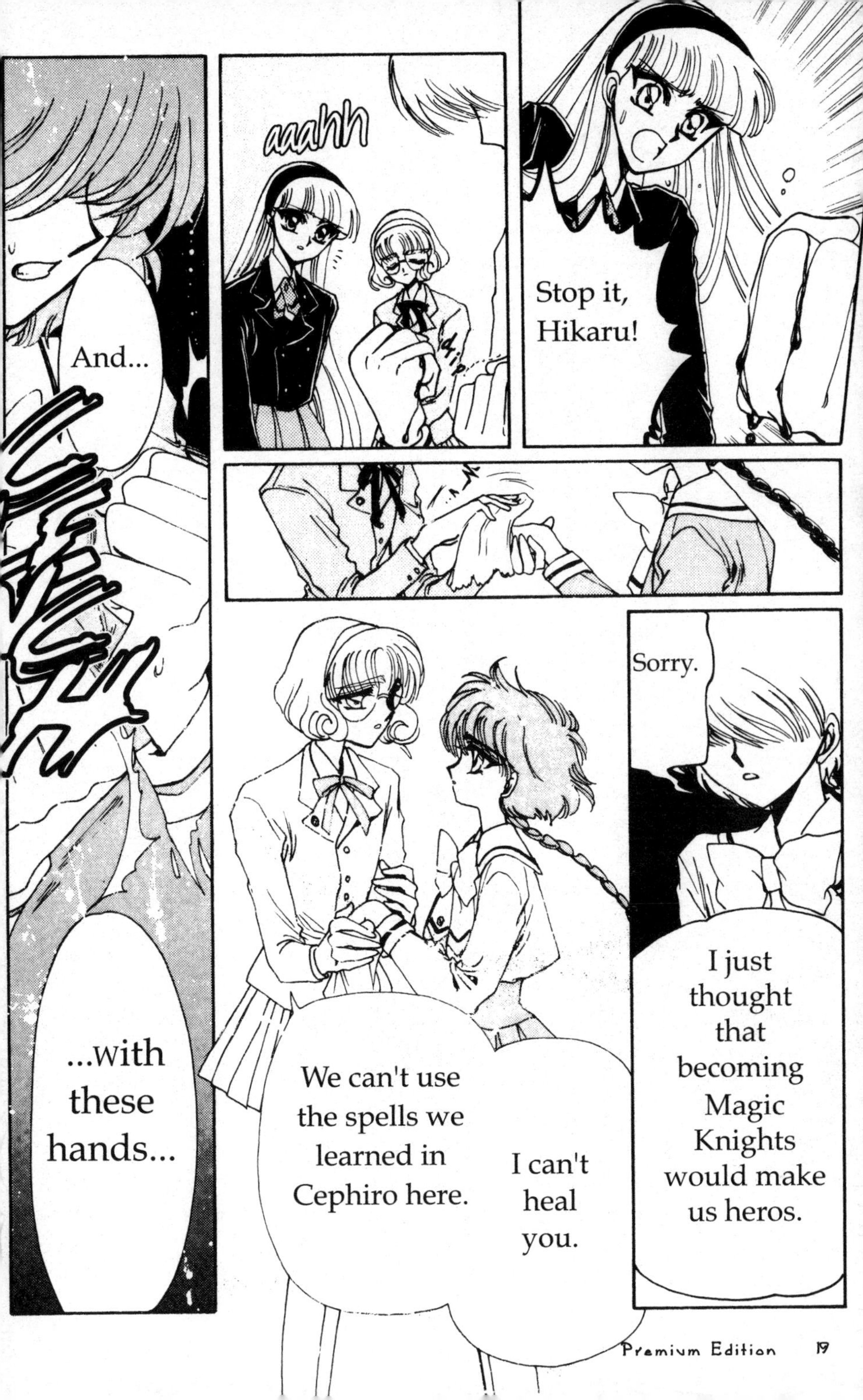
And...
...with these hands...
aaahh
Stop it, Hikaru!
We can't use the spells we learned in Cephiro here.
I can't heal you.
Sorry.
I just thought that becoming Magic Knights would make us heros.

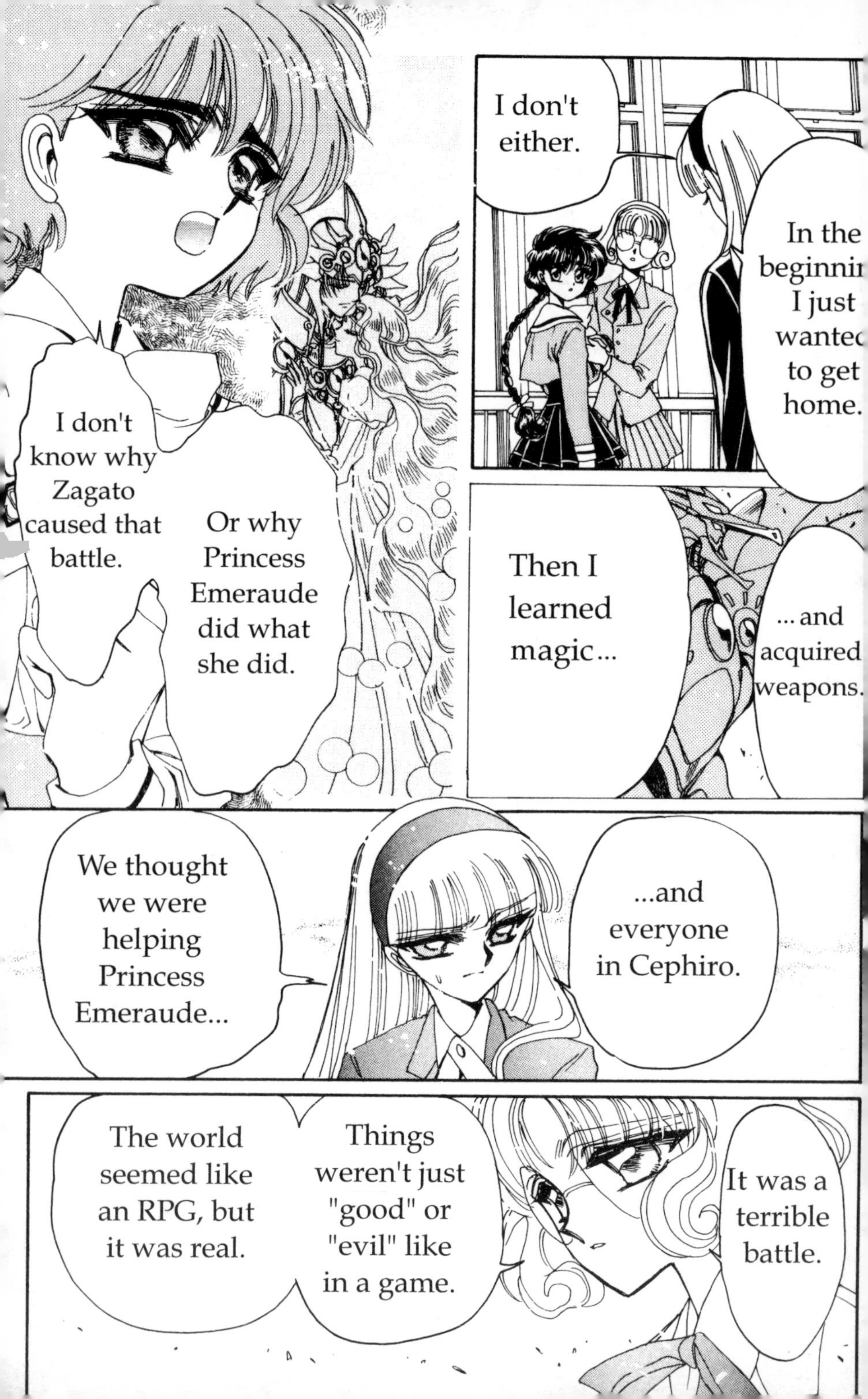
I don't know why Zagato caused that battle.
Or why Princess Emeraude did what she did.
I don't either.
In the beginnin I just wante to get home.
Then I learned magic...
... and acquired weapons.
We thought we were helping Princess Emeraude...
...and everyone in Cephiro.
The world seemed like an RPG, but it was real.
Things weren't just "good" or "evil" like in a game.
It was a terrible battle.

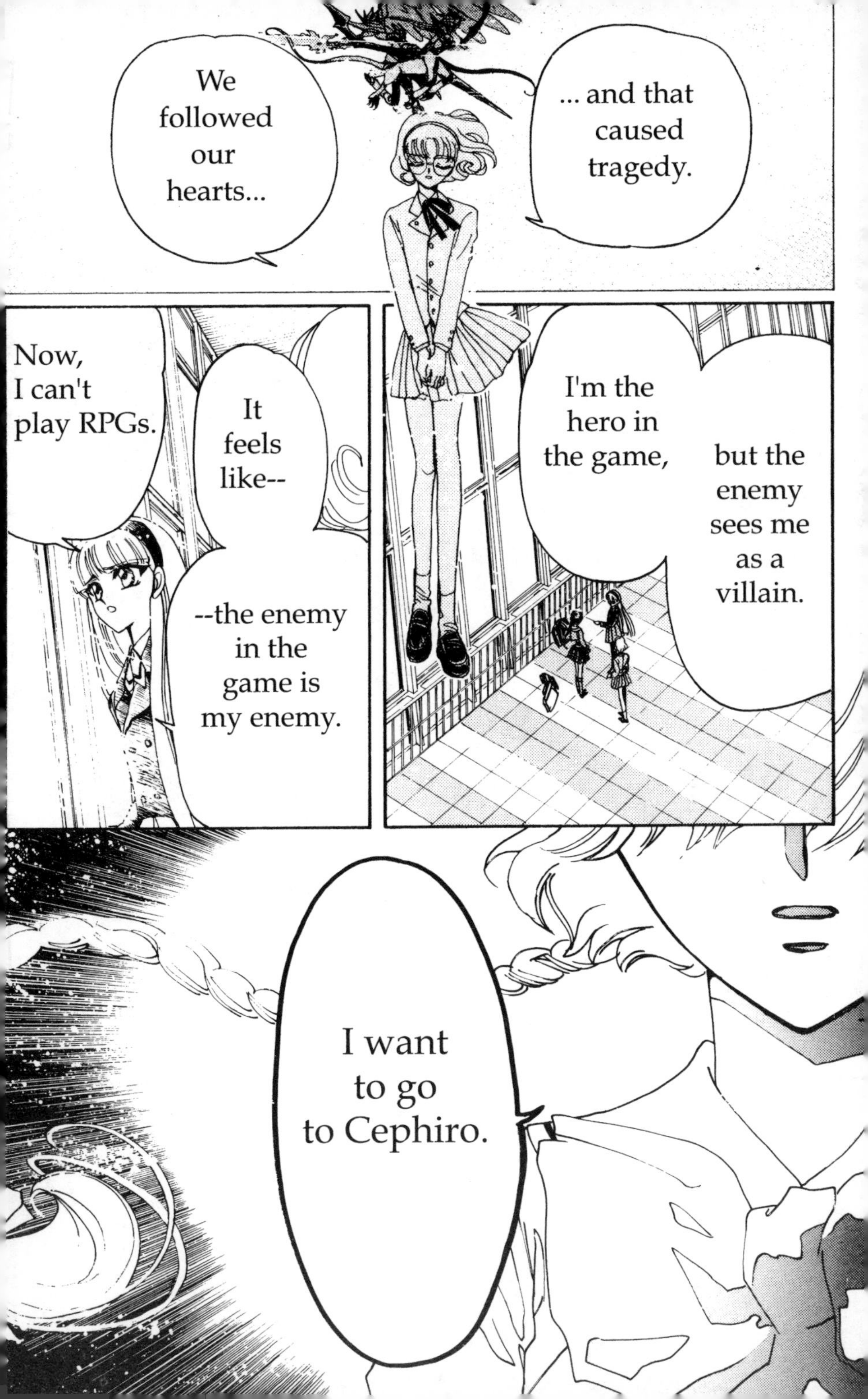
We followed our hearts...
... and that caused tragedy.
Now, I can't play RPGs.
It feels like--
--the enemy in the game is my enemy.
I'm the hero in the game,
but the enemy sees me as a villain.
I want to go to Cephiro.

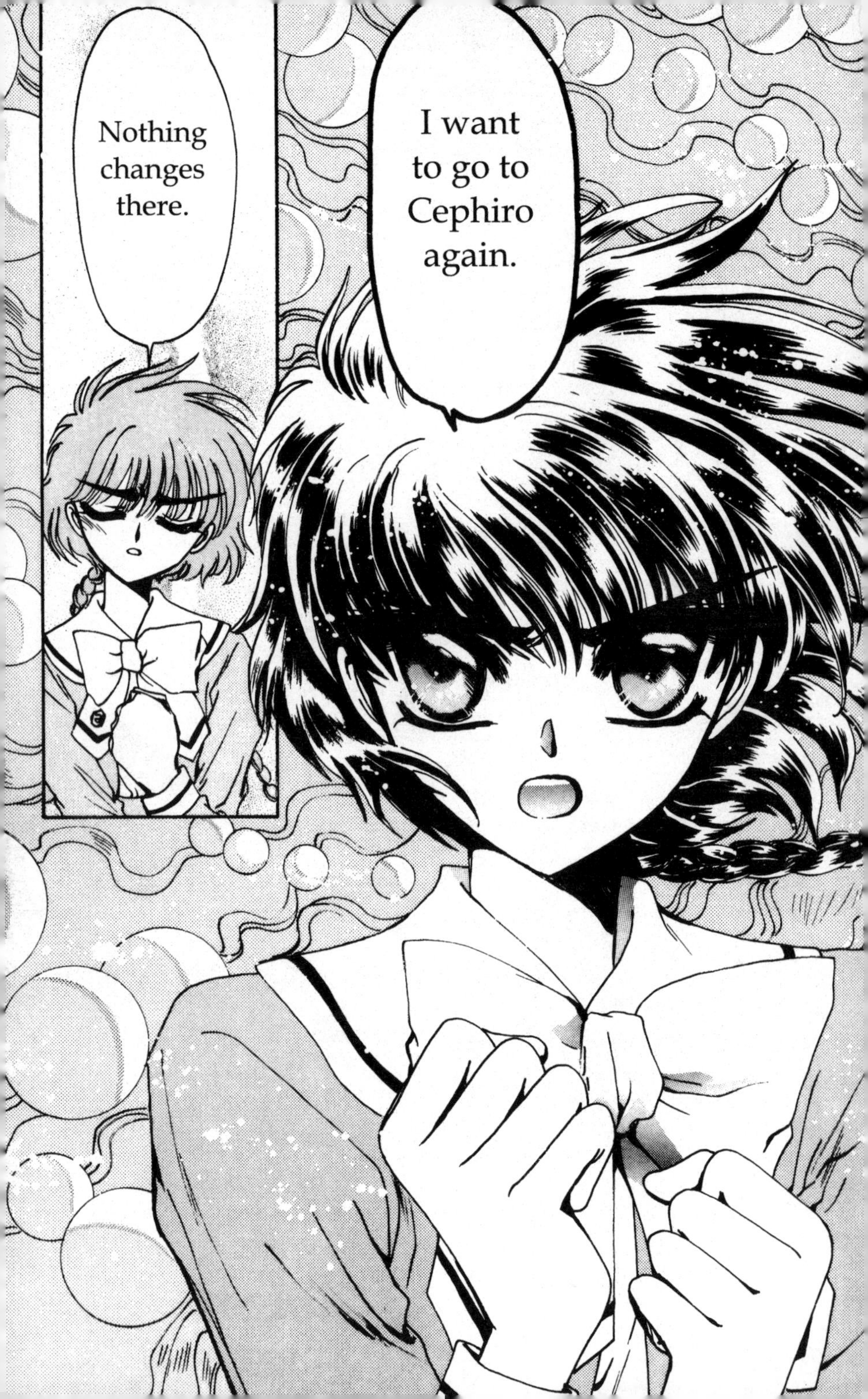
I want to go to Cephiro again.
Nothing changes there.

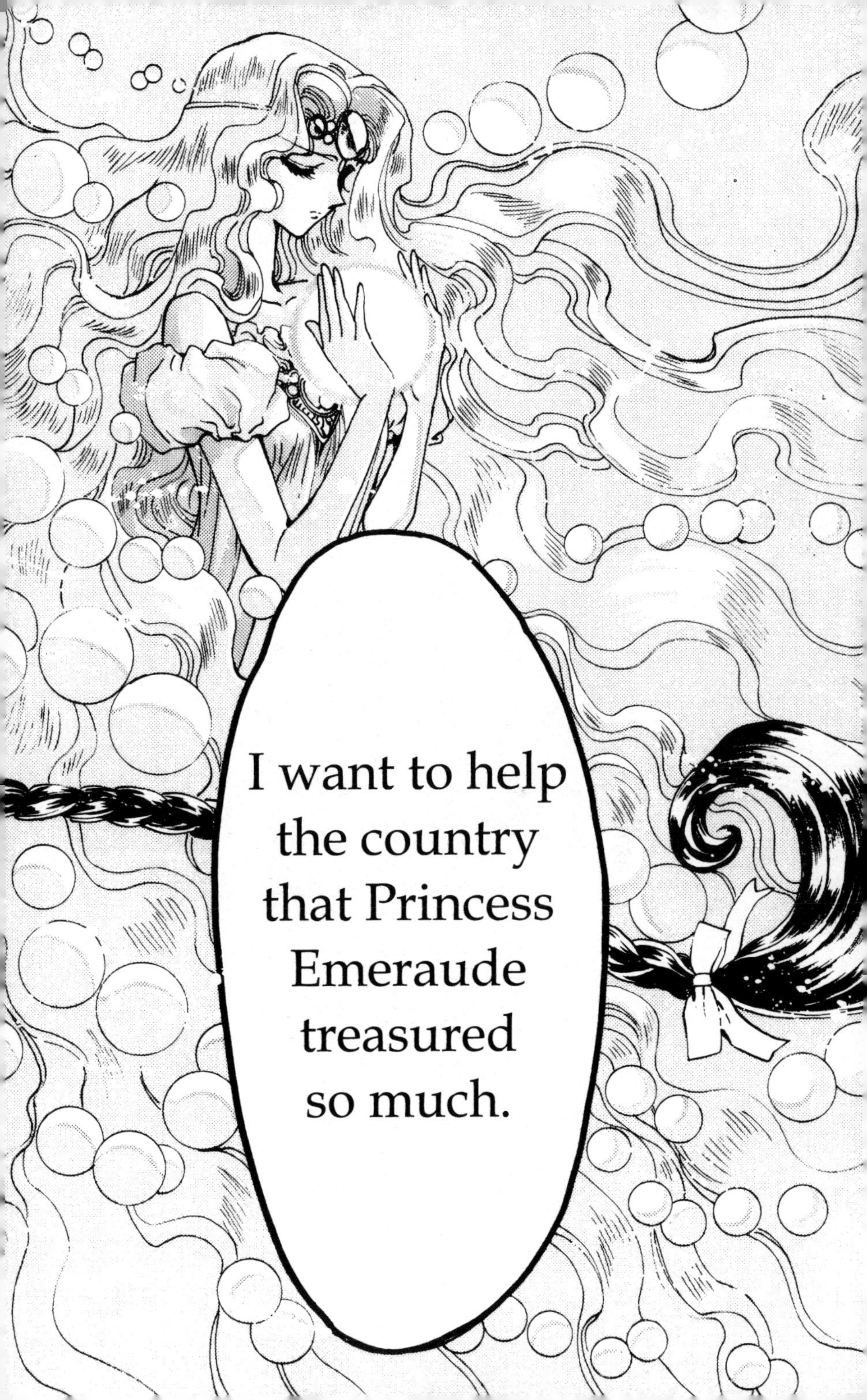
I want to help the country that Princess Emeraude treasured so much.

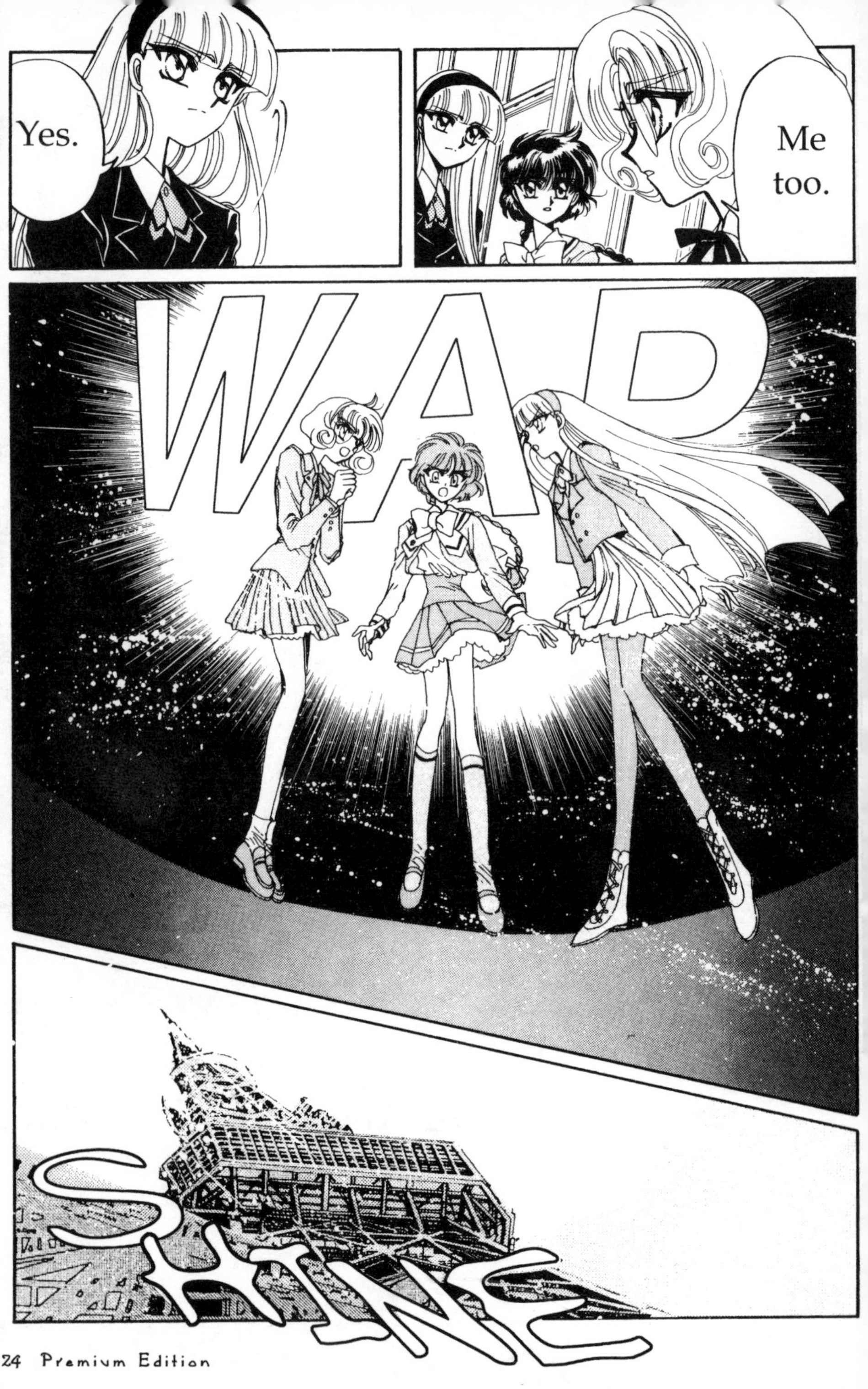
Me too.
Yes.
WAP
SHING

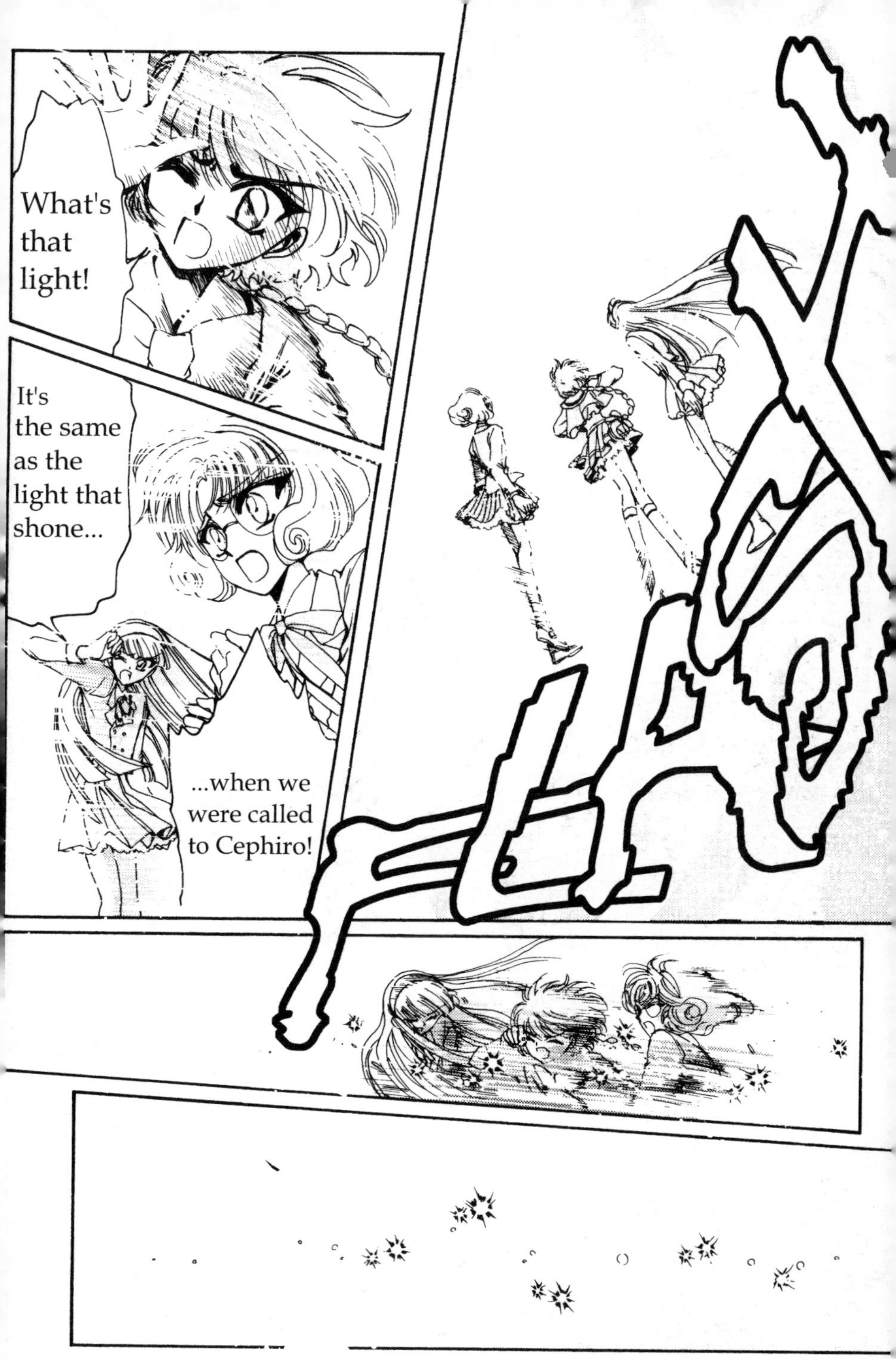
What's that light!
It's the same as the light that shone...
...when we were called to Cephiro!

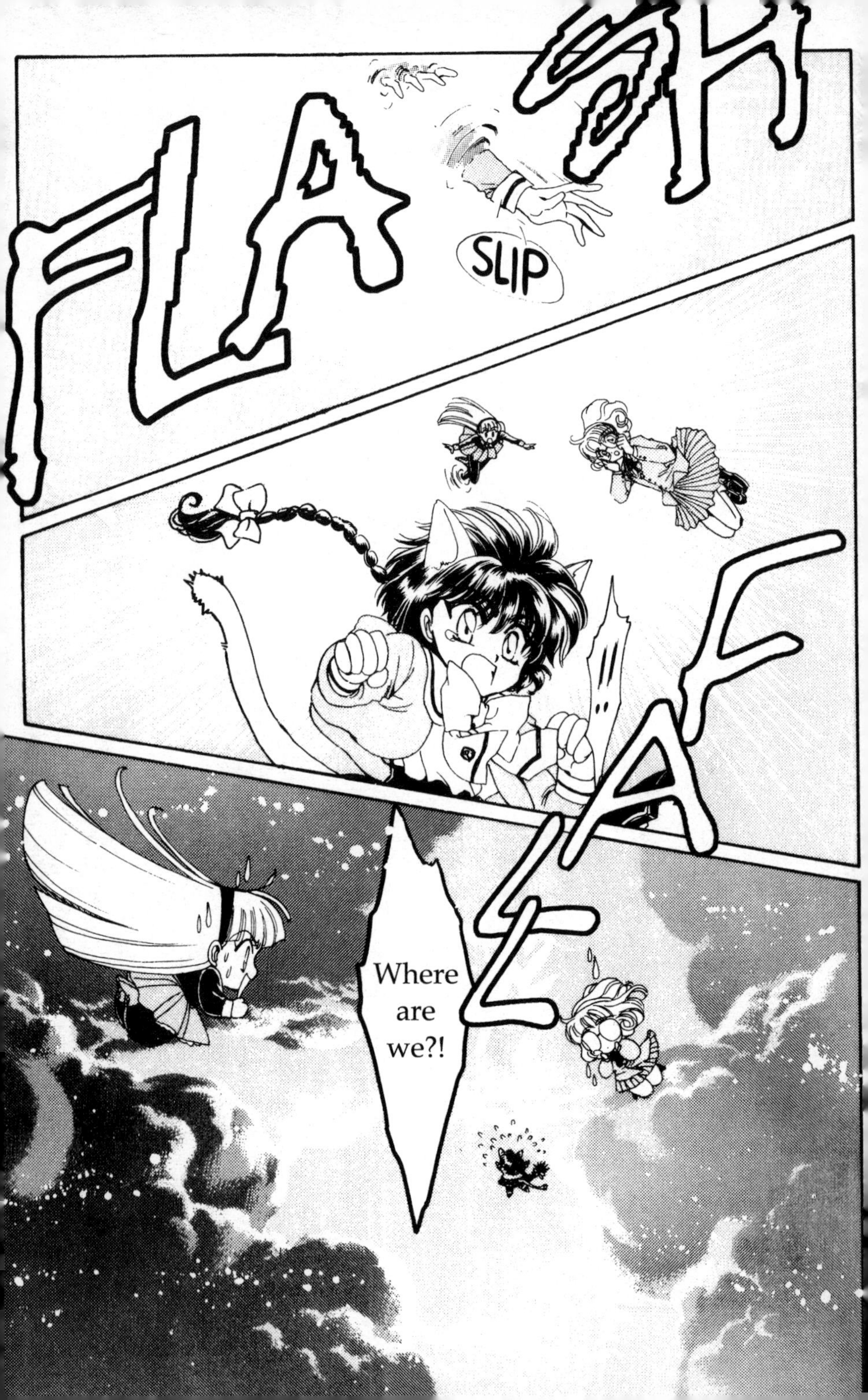
FLASH
SLIP
ZAAZ
Where are we?!

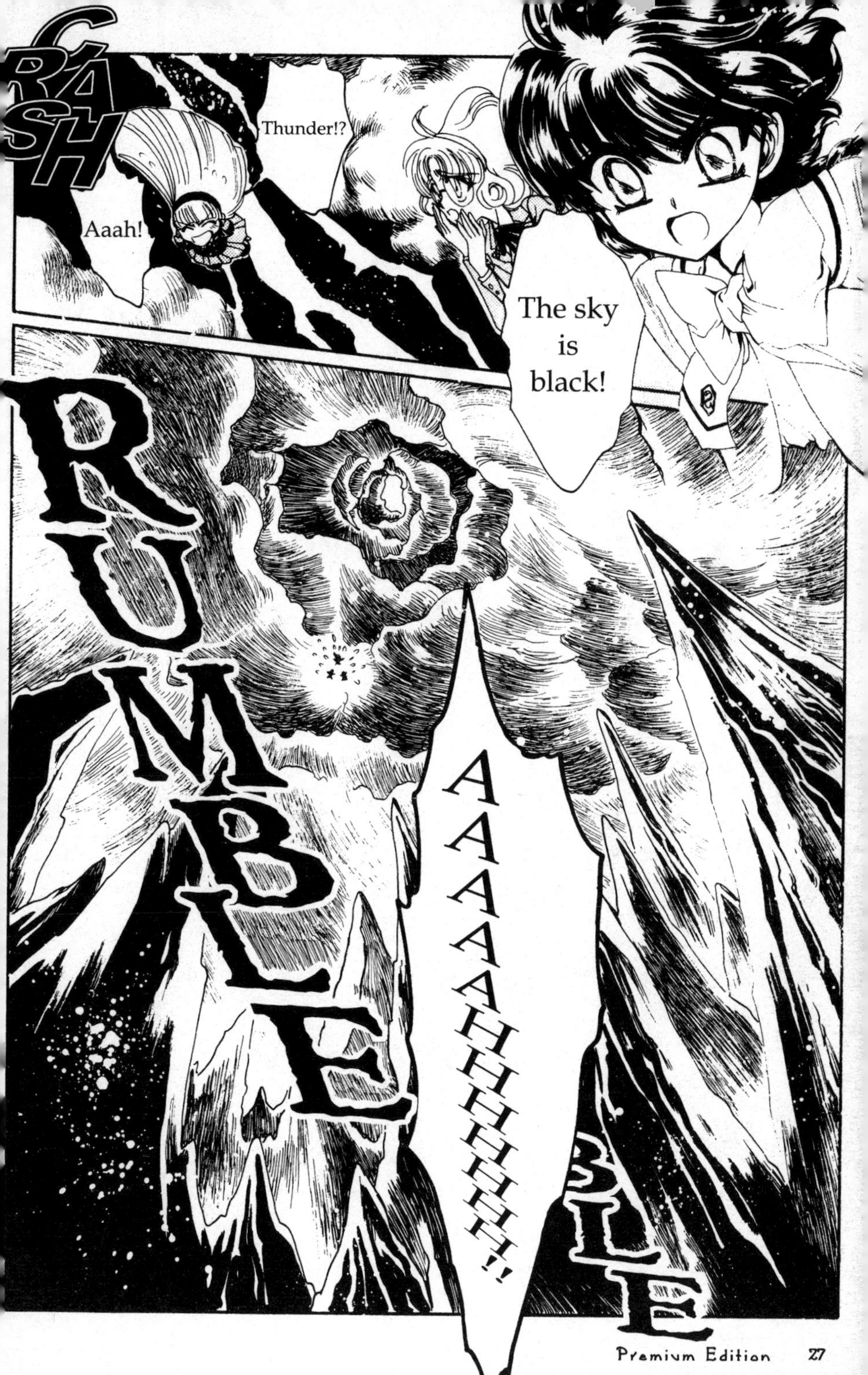
CRASH
Thunder!?
Aaah!
The sky is black!
RUMBLE
AAAAAHHHHHHH!!
BLE

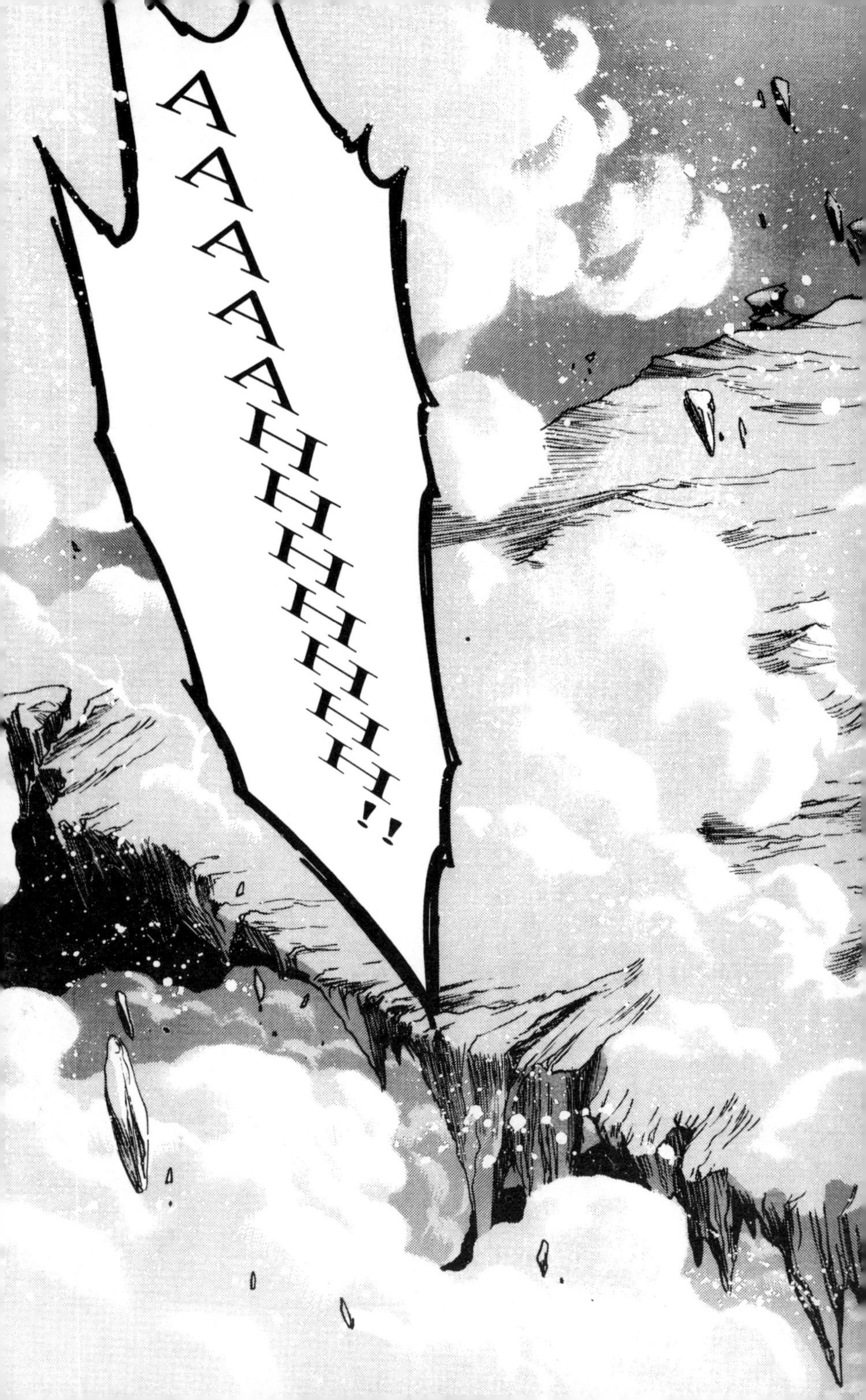
AAAAAHHHHHHH!!

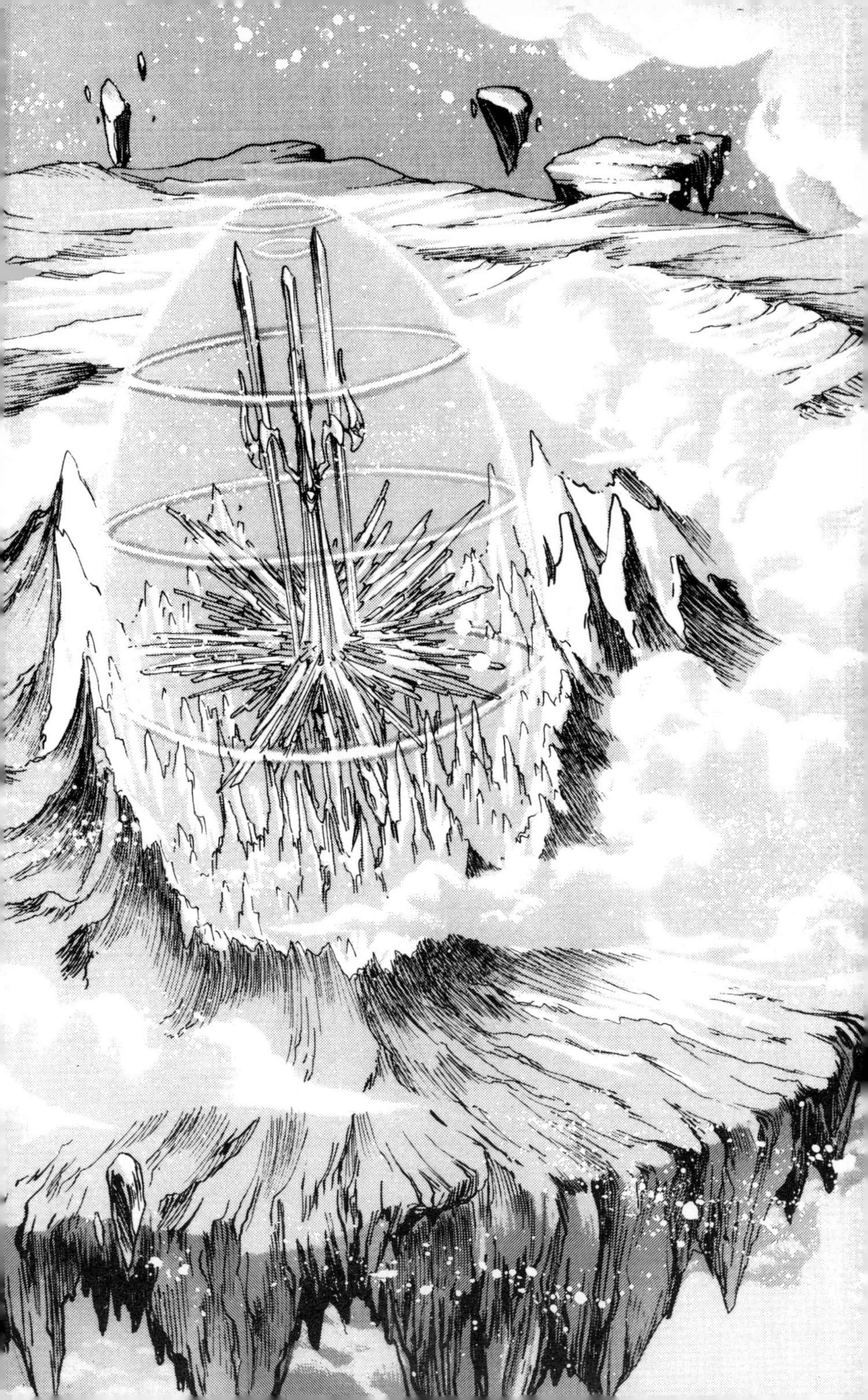

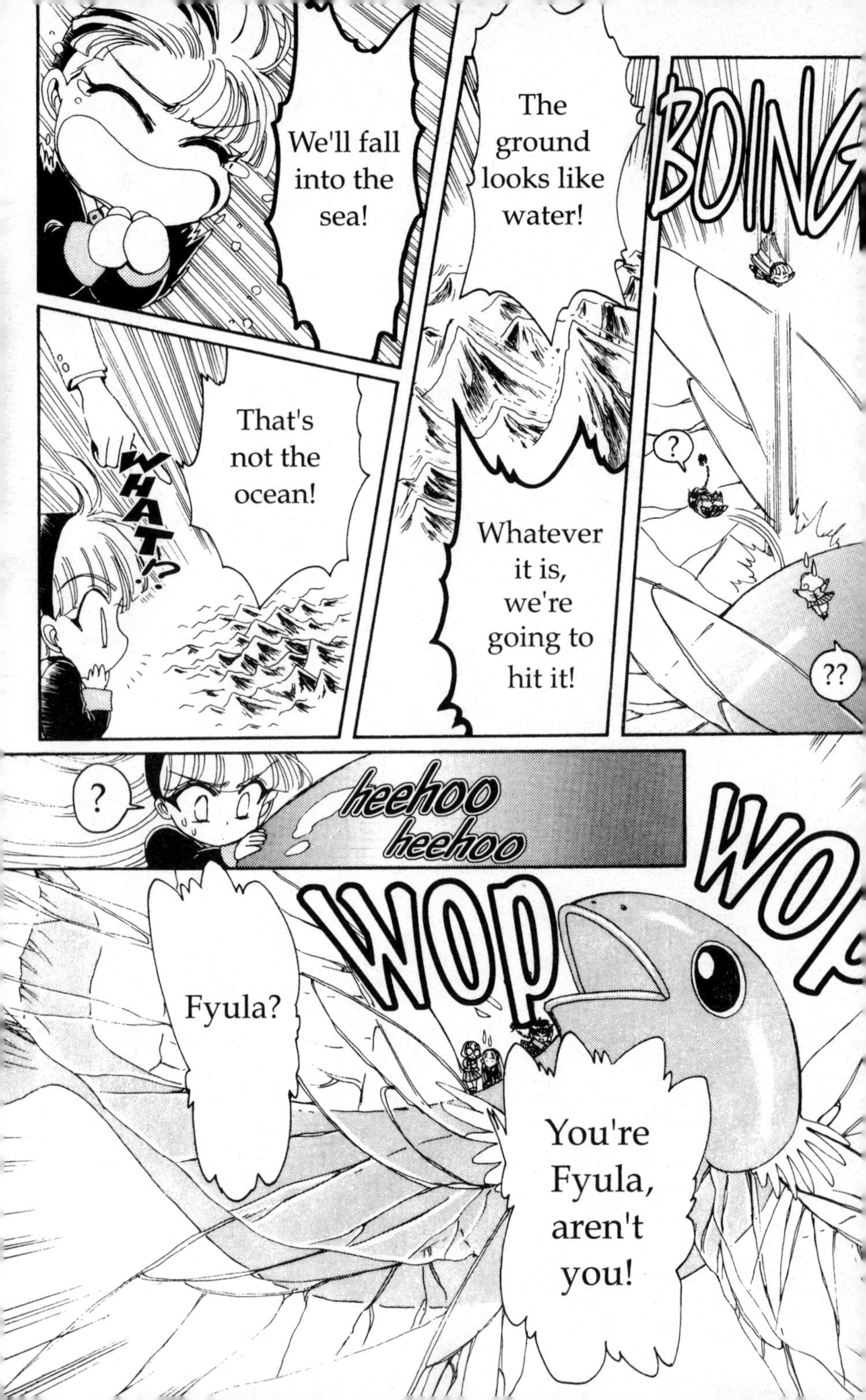
We'll fall into the sea!
That's not the ocean!
WHAT!?
The ground looks like water!
Whatever it is, we're going to hit it!
BOING
?
??
?
heehoo heehoo
WOP
WOP
Fyula?
You're Fyula, aren't you!

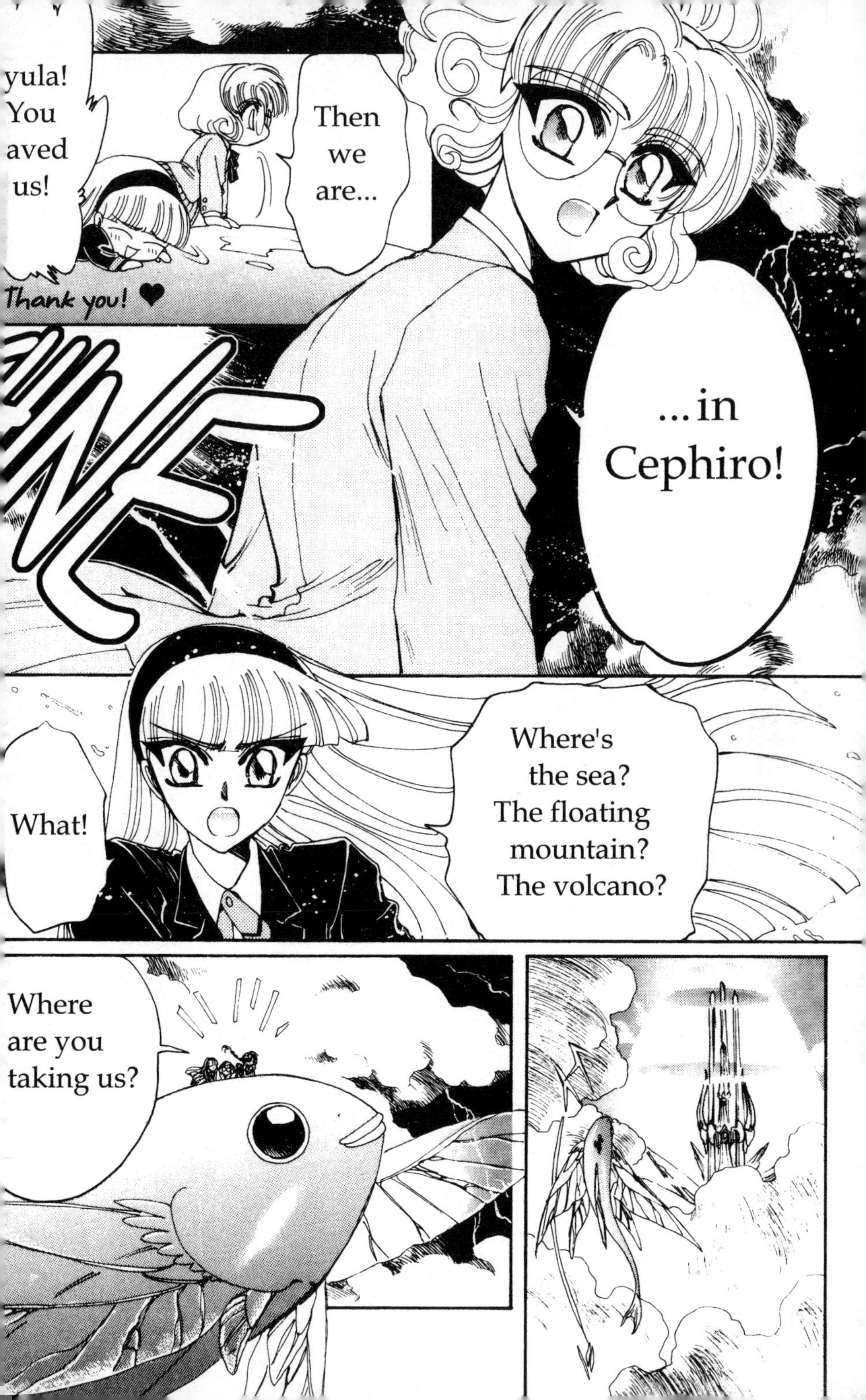
yula! You aved us!
Thank you!
Then we are...
...in Cephiro!
What!
Where's the sea? The floating mountain? The volcano?
Where are you taking us?

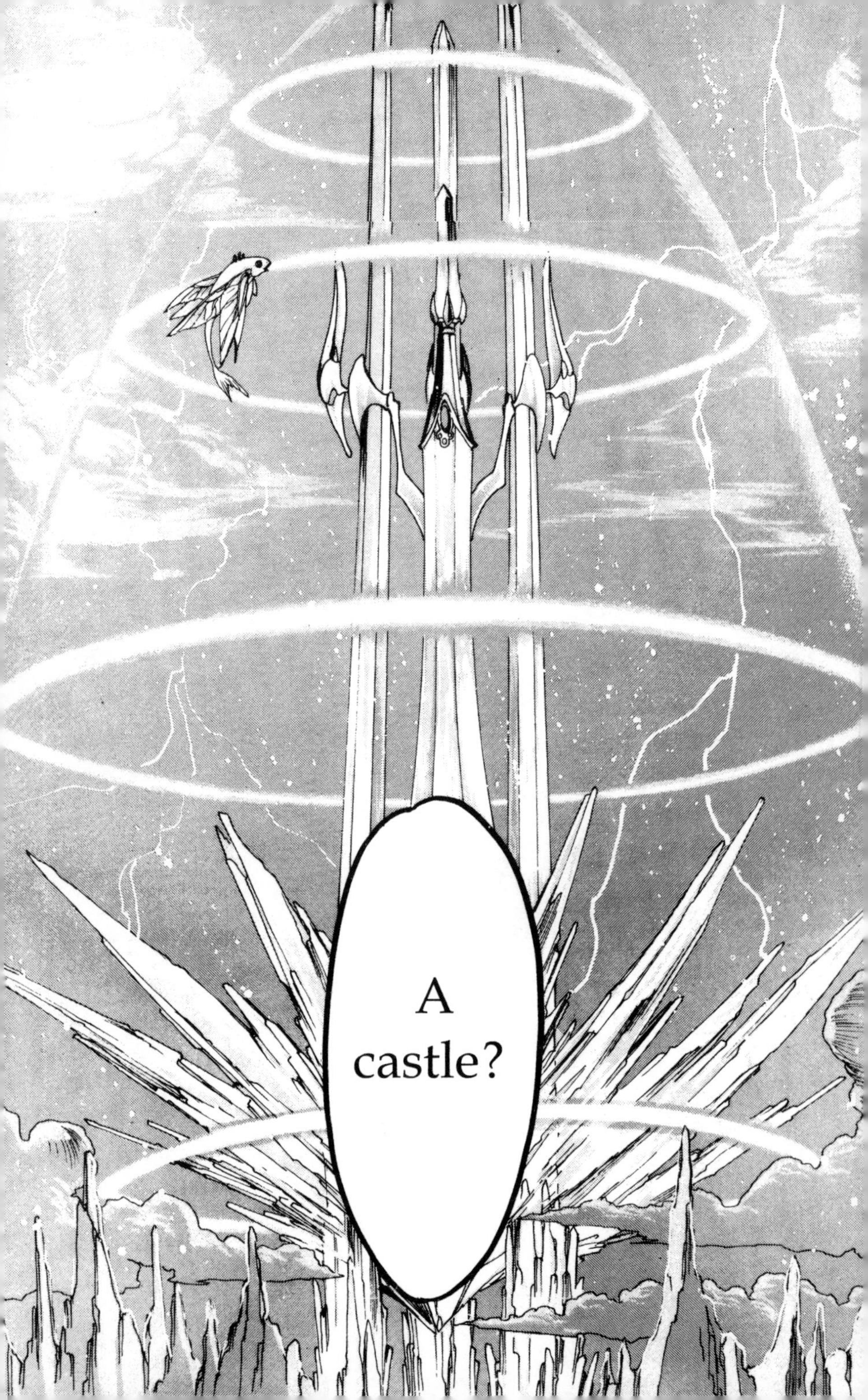
A castle?

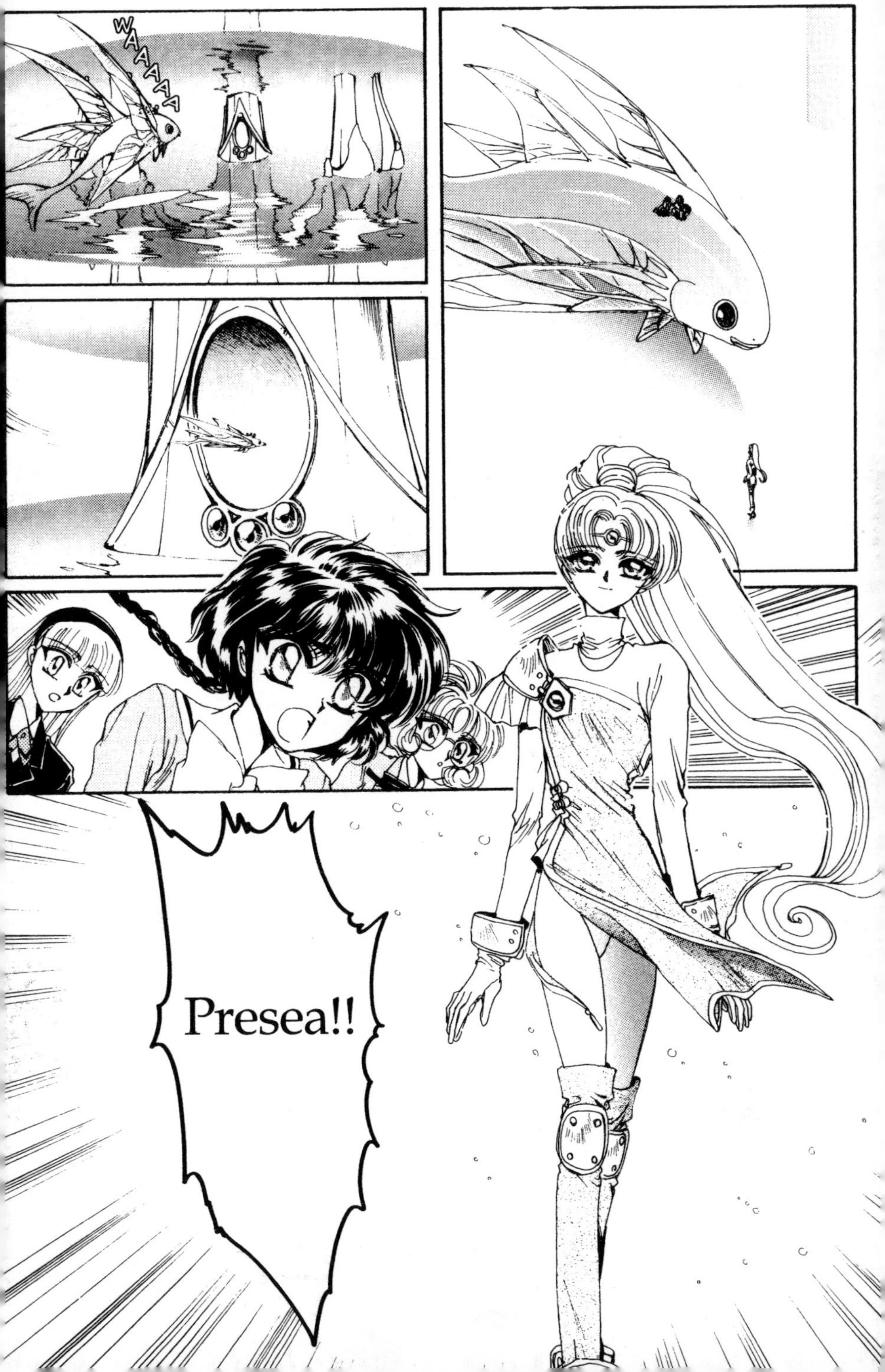
WAAAAAA
Presea!!

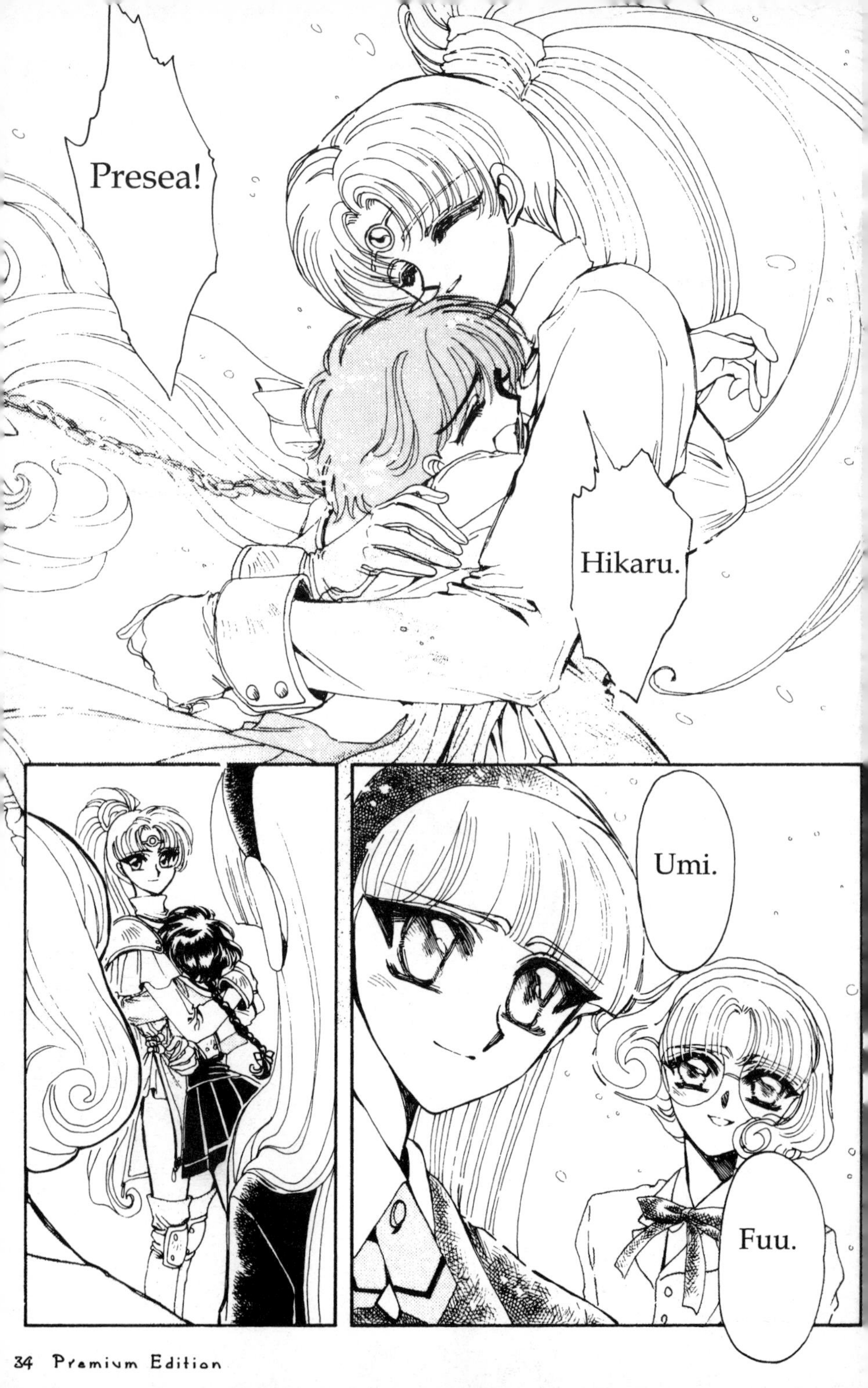
Presea!
Hikaru.
Umi.
Fuu.

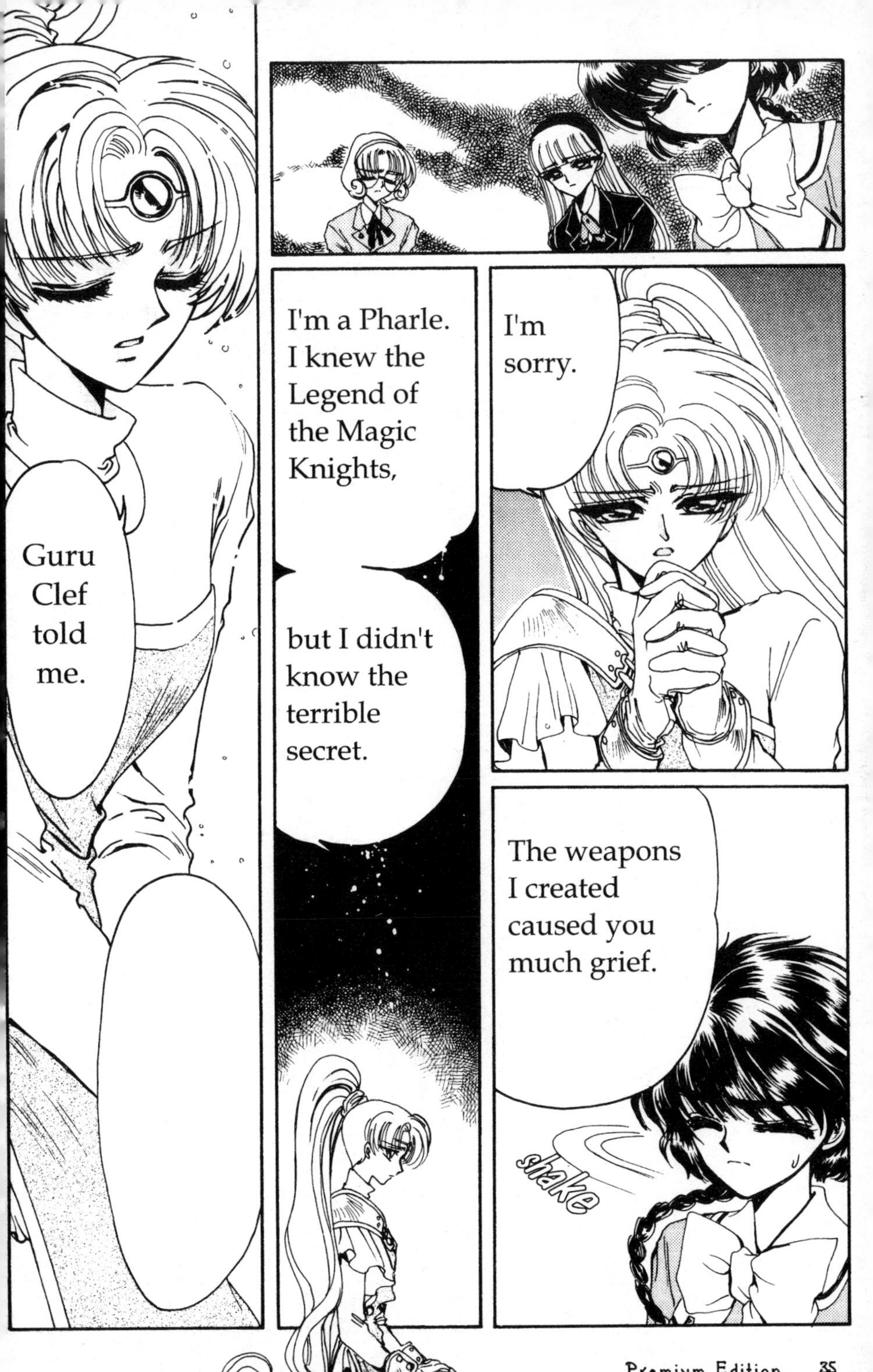
I'm sorry.
The weapons I created caused you much grief.
I'm a Pharle. I knew the Legend of the Magic Knights,
but I didn't know the terrible secret.
shake
Guru Clef told me.

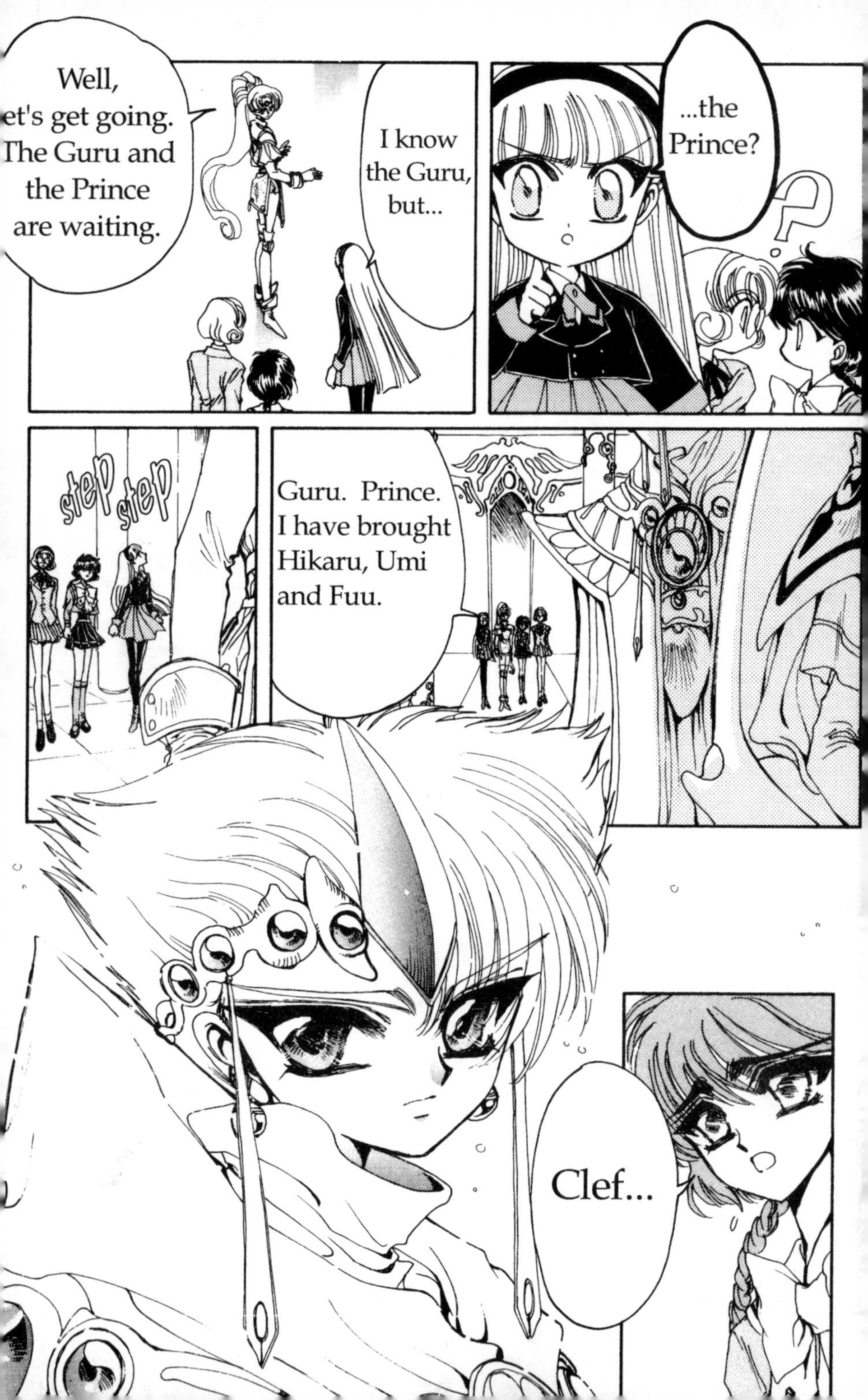
...the
Prince?
I know
the Guru,
but...
Well,
et's get going.
The Guru and
the Prince
are waiting.
Guru. Prince.
I have brought
Hikaru, Umi
and Fuu.
step step
Clef...

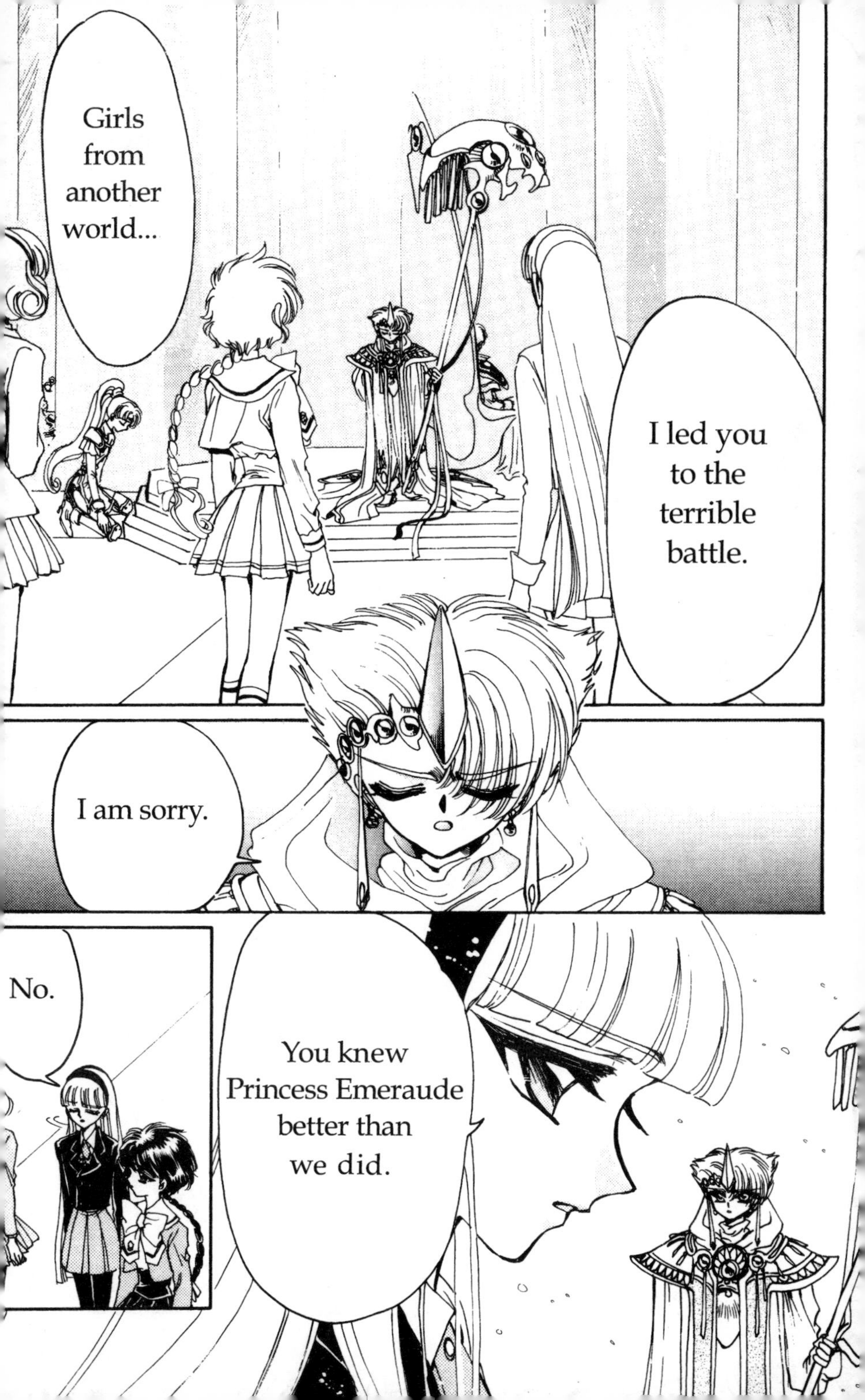
I led you to the terrible battle.
Girls from another world...
I am sorry.
You knew Princess Emeraude better than we did.
No.

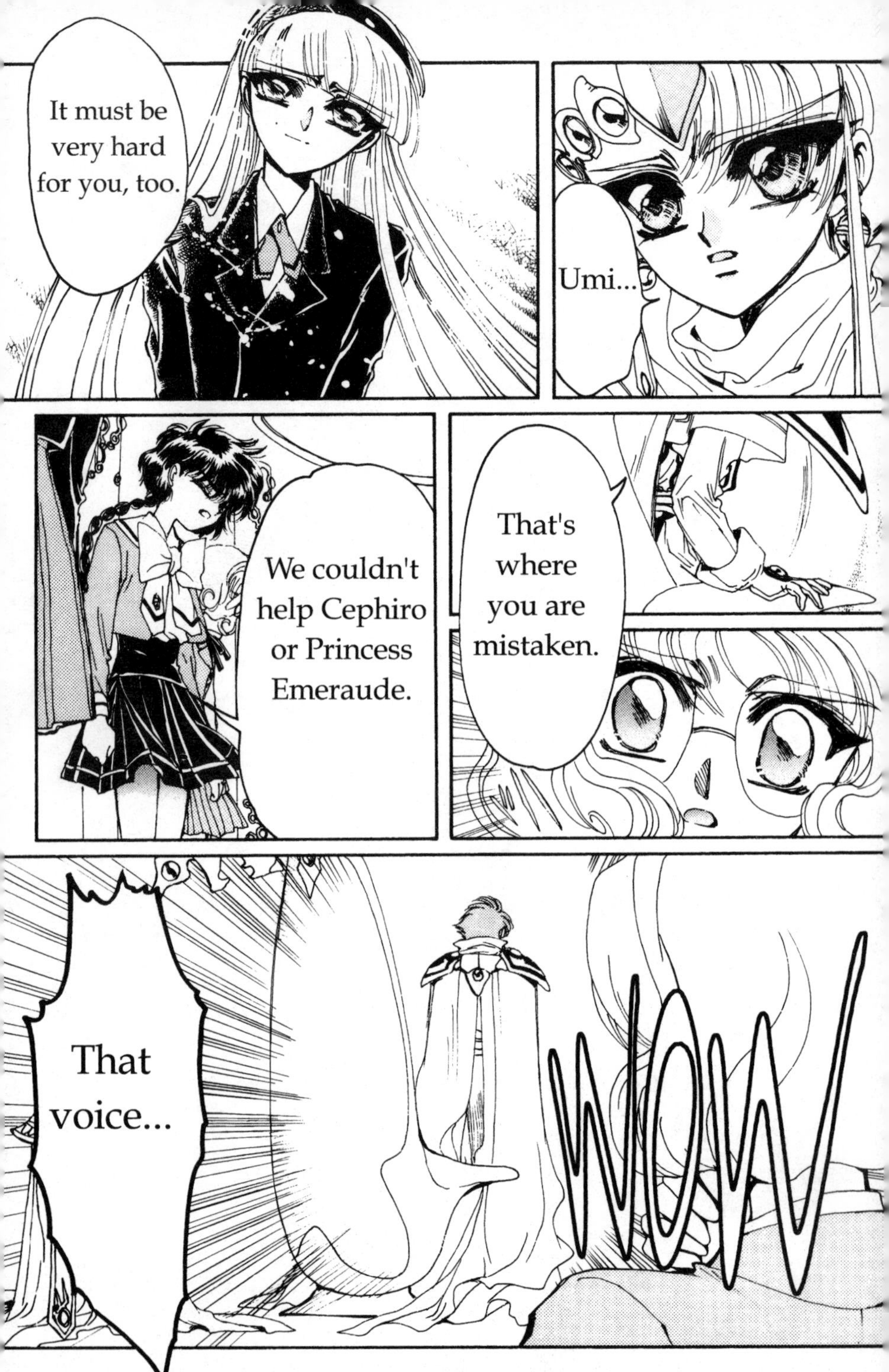

It must be very hard for you, too.
Umi...
That's where you are mistaken.
We couldn't help Cephiro or Princess Emeraude.
That voice...
WOW

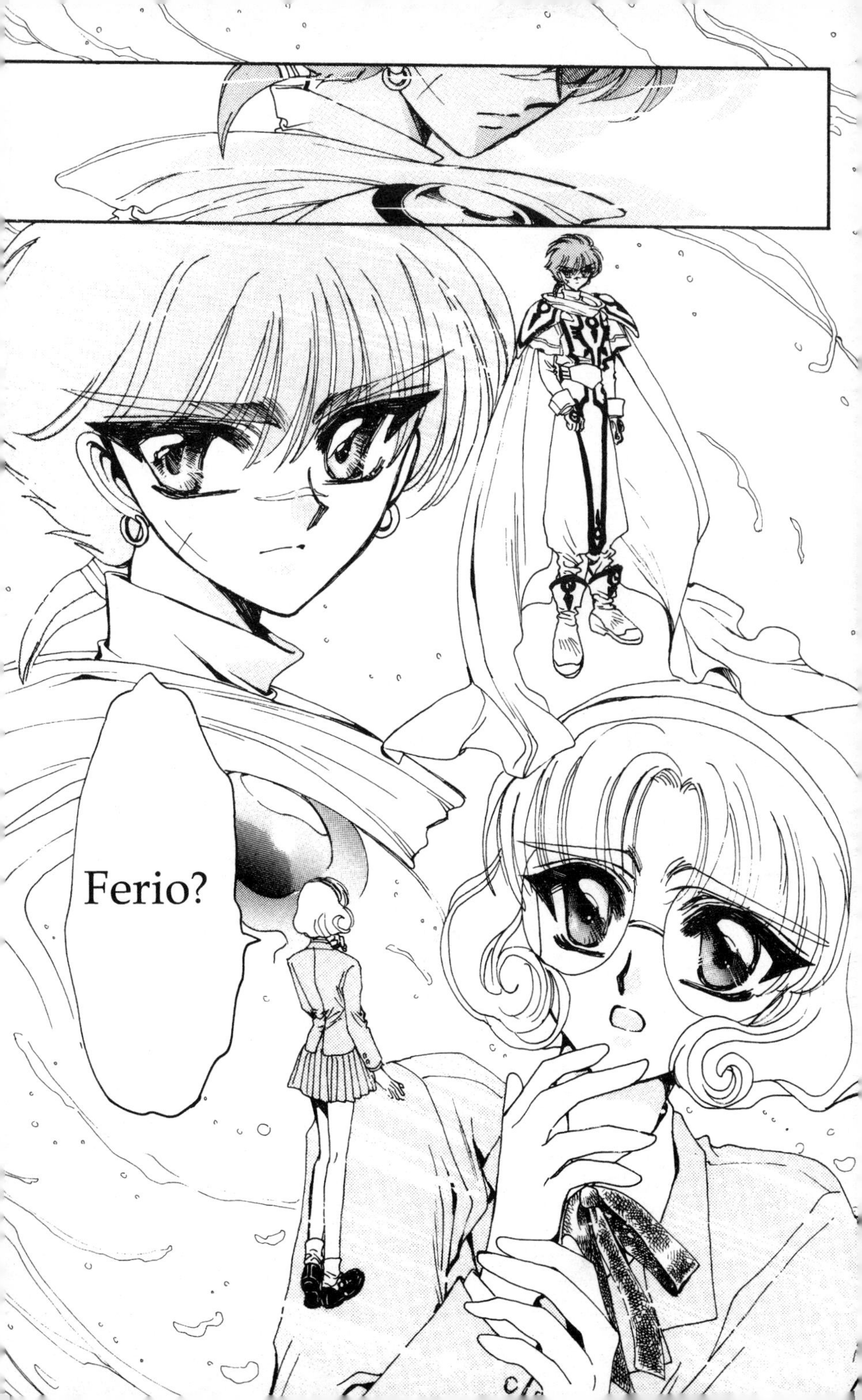
Ferio?

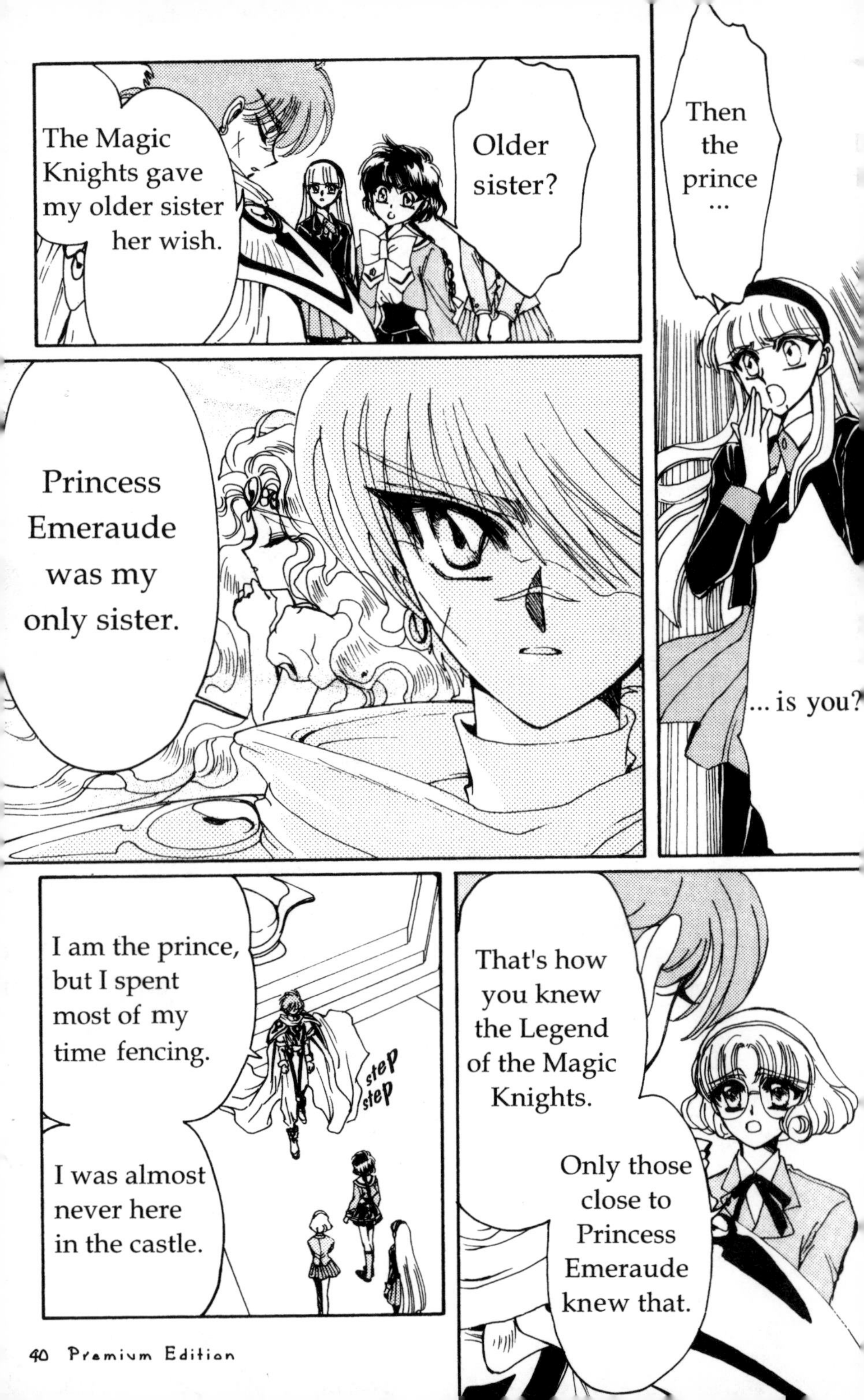
The Magic Knights gave my older sister her wish.
Older sister?
Then the prince ...
Princess Emeraude was my only sister.
... is you?
I am the prince, but I spent most of my time fencing.
step step
I was almost never here in the castle.
That's how you knew the Legend of the Magic Knights.
Only those close to Princess Emeraude knew that.

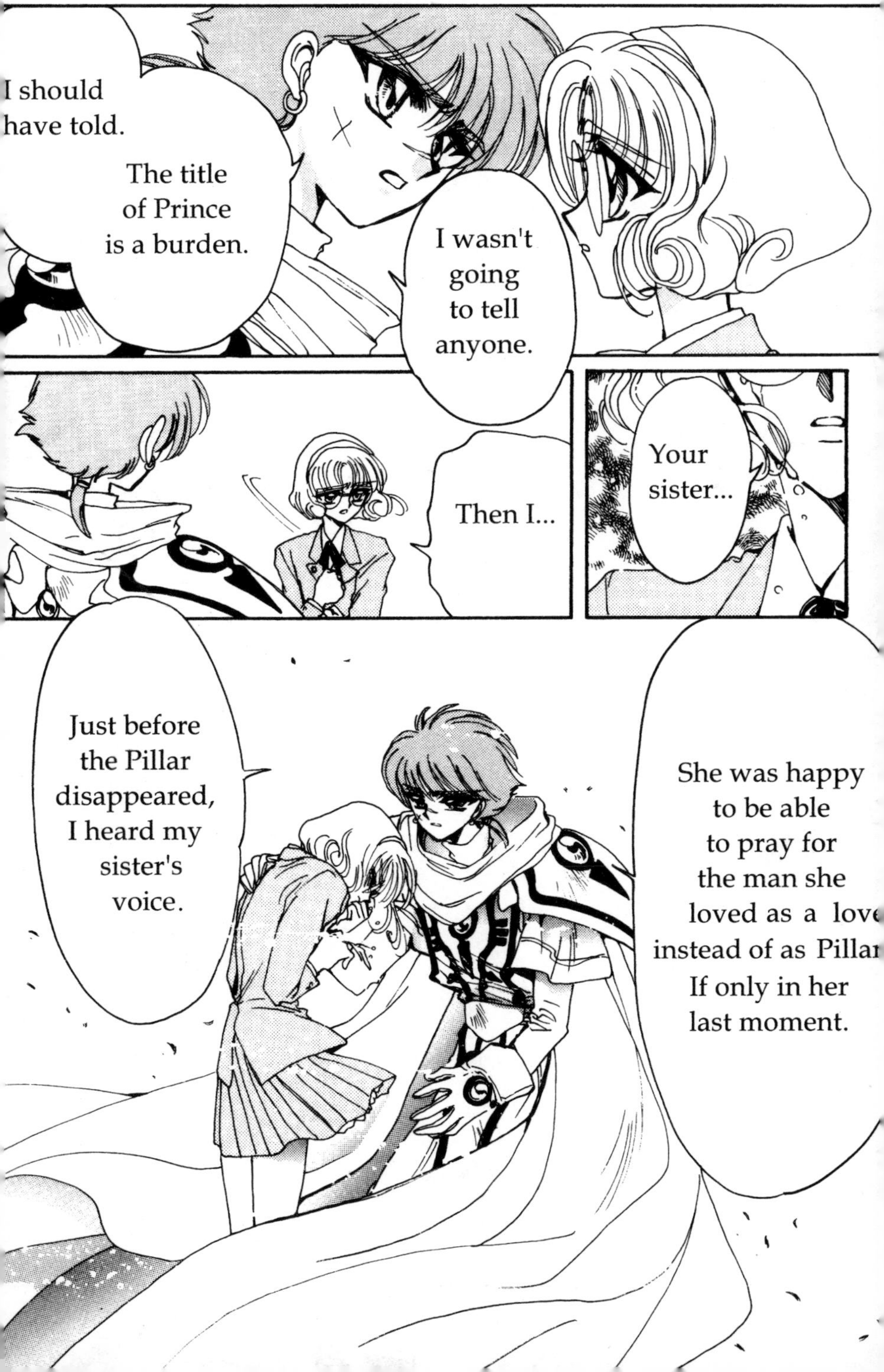
I should have told.
The title of Prince is a burden.
I wasn't going to tell anyone.
Then I...
Your sister...
Just before the Pillar disappeared, I heard my sister's voice.
She was happy to be able to pray for the man she loved as a love instead of as Pillai If only in her last moment.

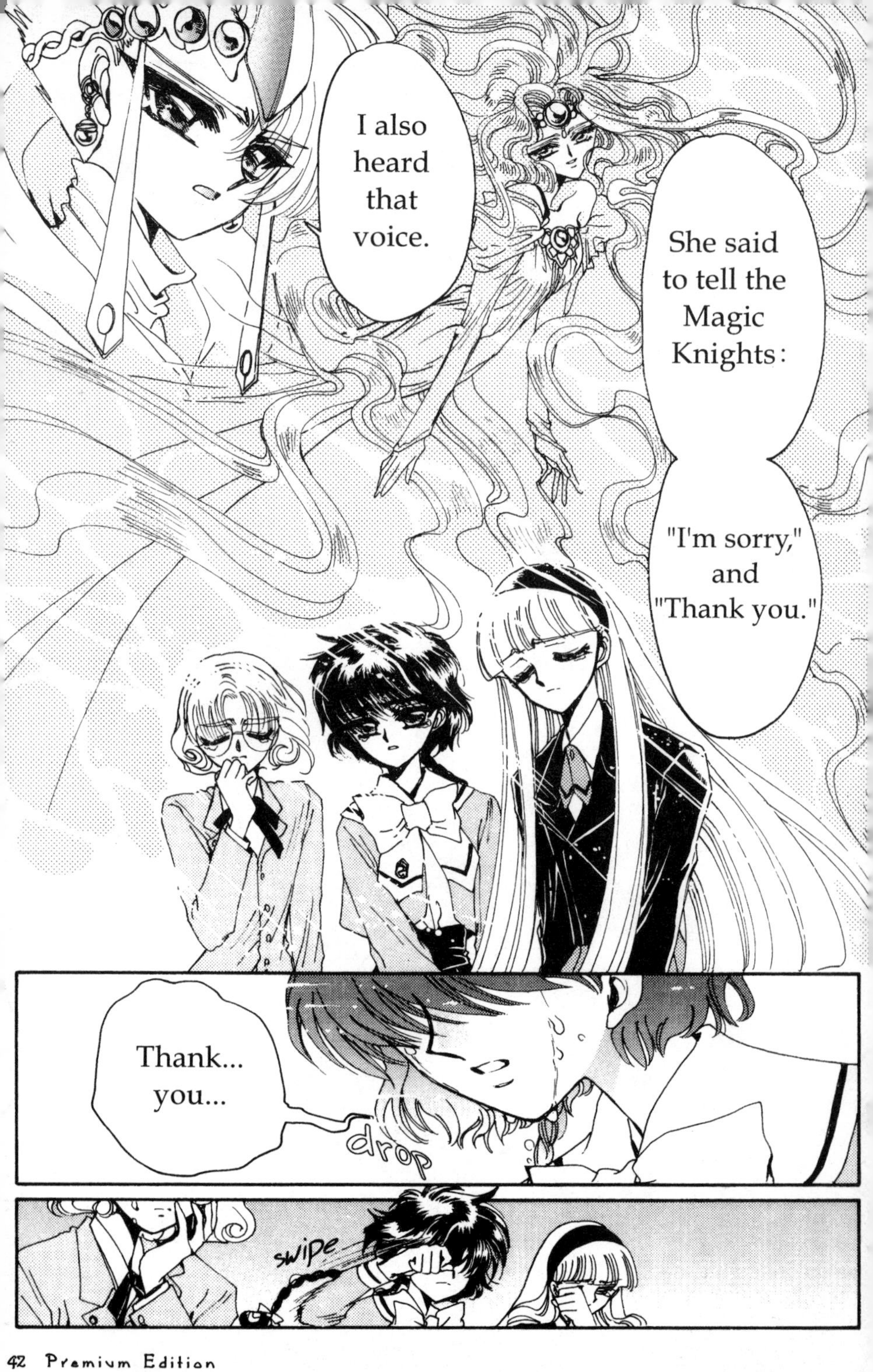
I also heard that voice.
She said to tell the Magic Knights:
"I'm sorry," and "Thank you."
Thank... you...
drop
swipe

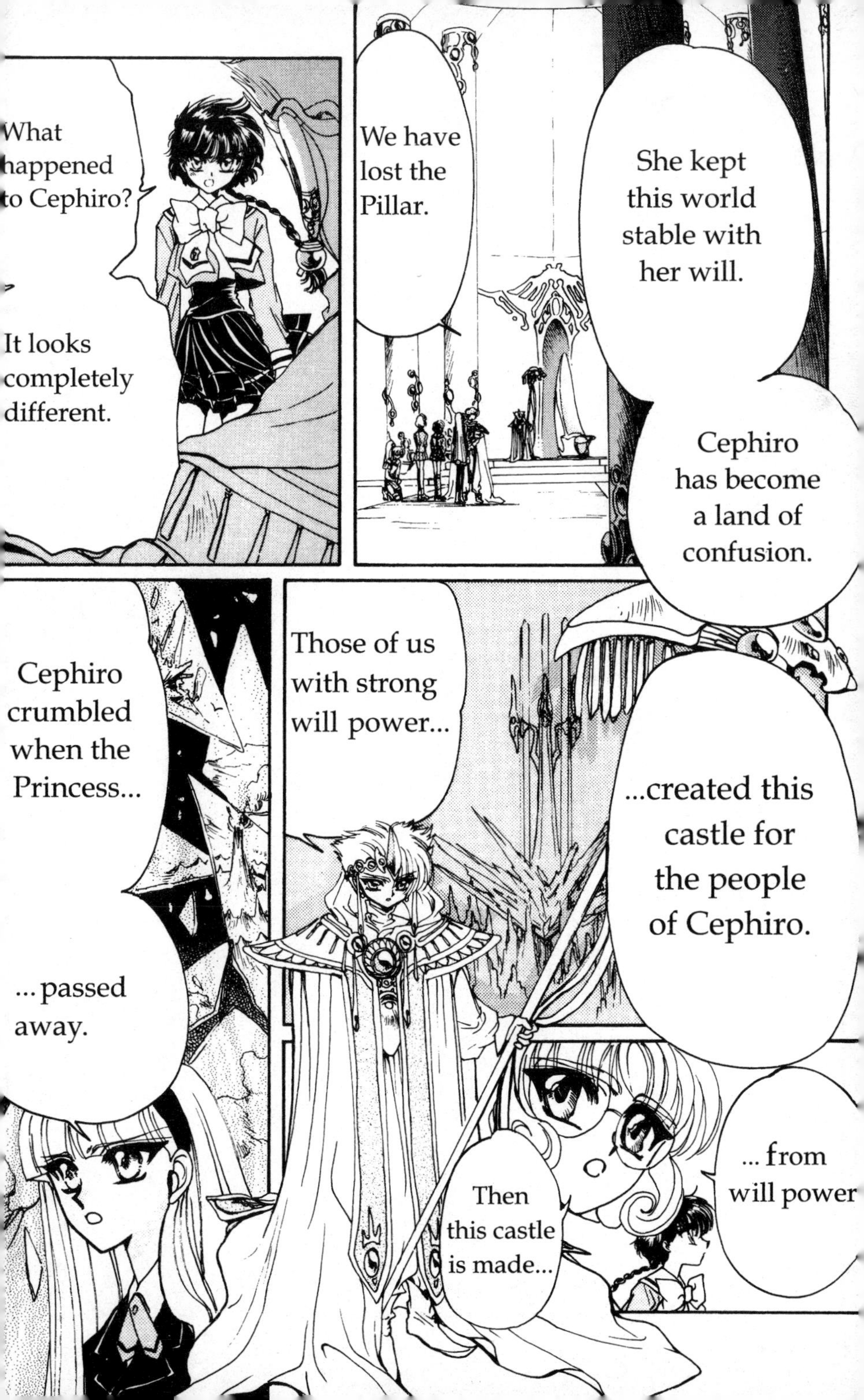
What happened to Cephiro?
It looks completely different.
We have lost the Pillar.
She kept this world stable with her will.
Cephiro has become a land of confusion.
Cephiro crumbled when the Princess...
... passed away.
Those of us with strong will power...
...created this castle for the people of Cephiro.
Then this castle is made...
... from will power

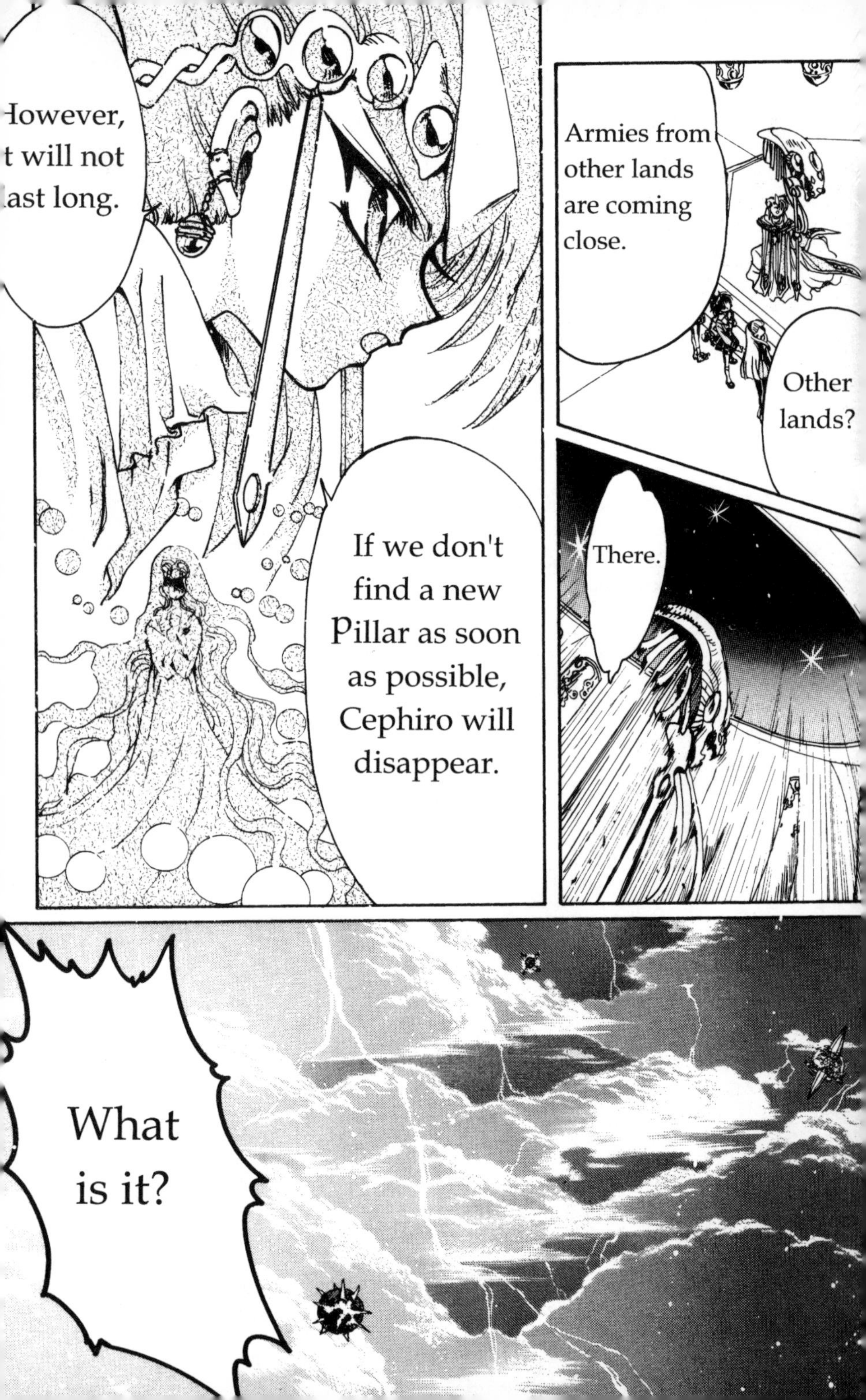
However, it will not last long.
If we don't find a new Pillar as soon as possible, Cephiro will disappear.
Armies from other lands are coming close.
Other lands?
There.
What is it?

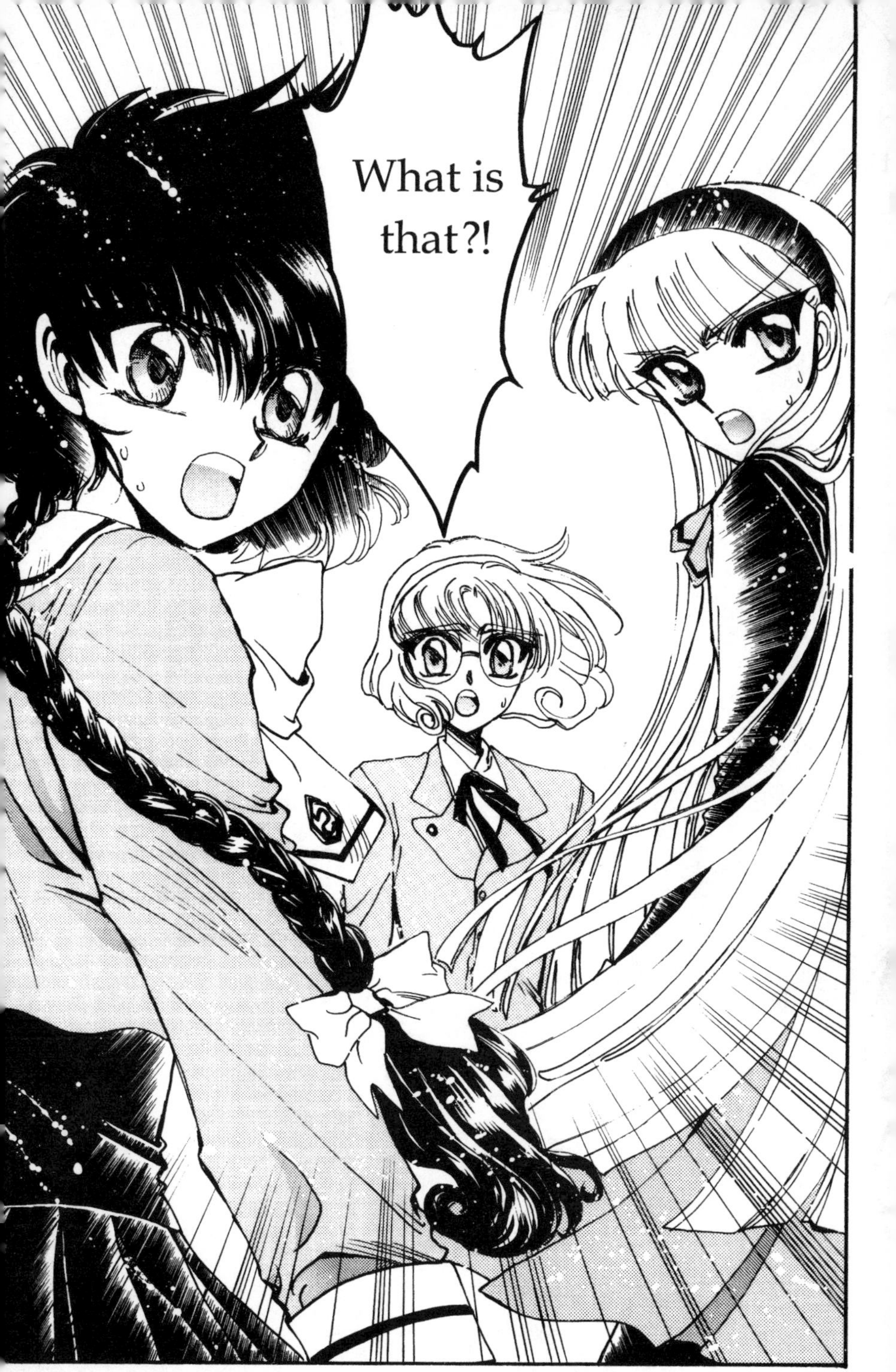
What is that?!

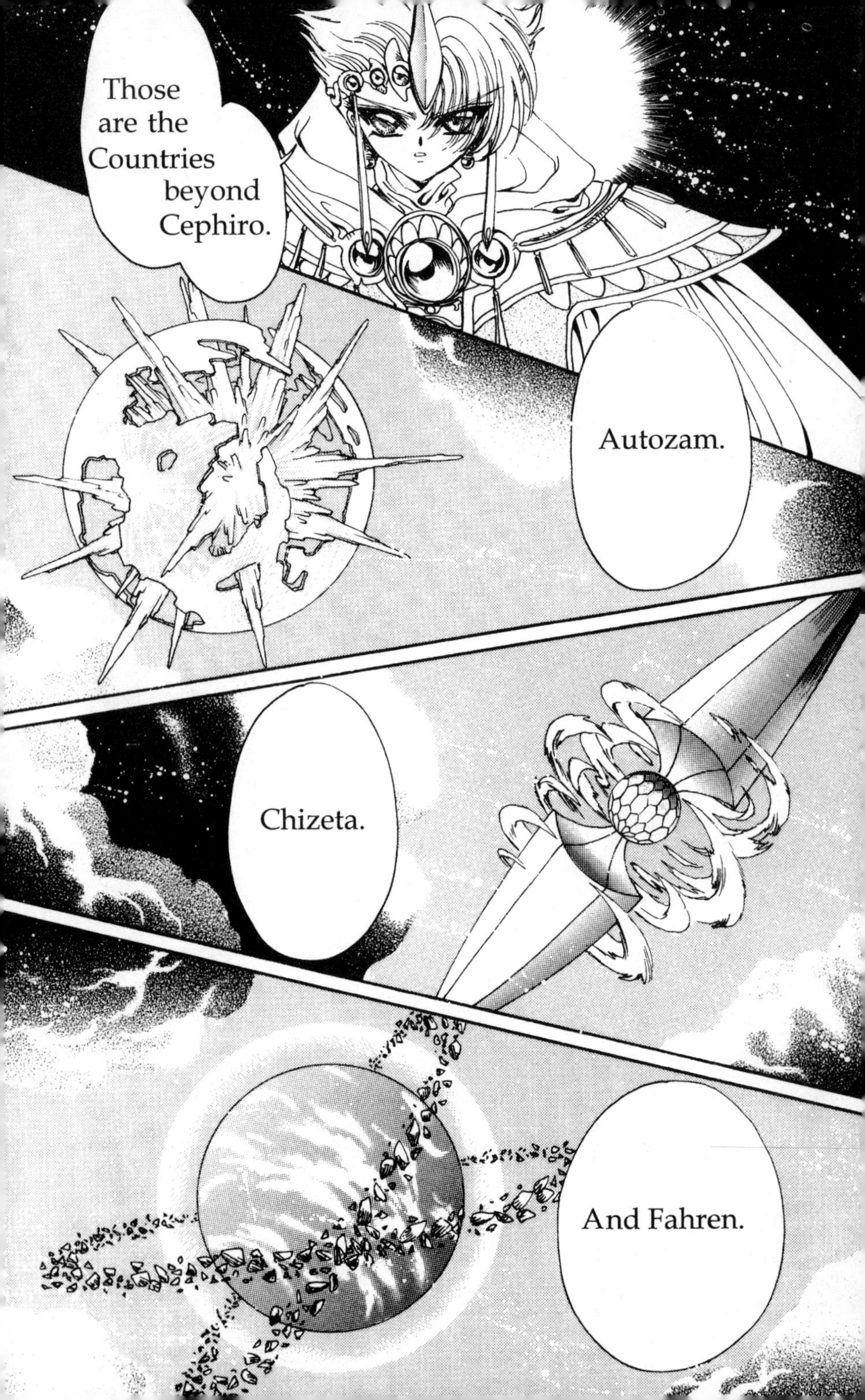
Those are the Countries beyond Cephiro.
Autozam.
Chizeta.
And Fahren.

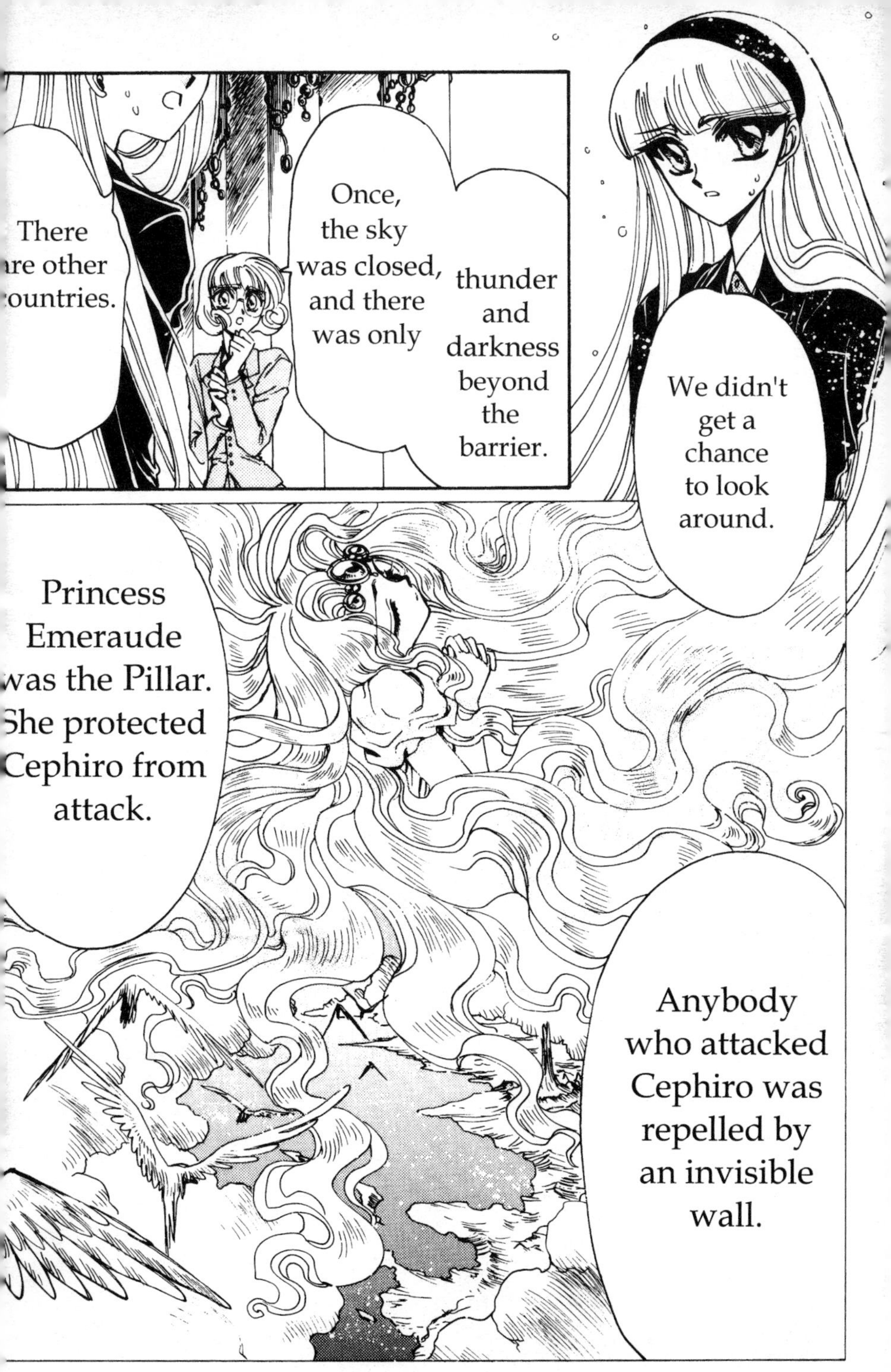
We didn't get a chance to look around.
There re other ountries.
Once, the sky was closed, and there was only
thunder and darkness beyond the barrier.
Princess Emeraude was the Pillar. She protected Cephiro from attack.
Anybody who attacked Cephiro was repelled by an invisible wall.

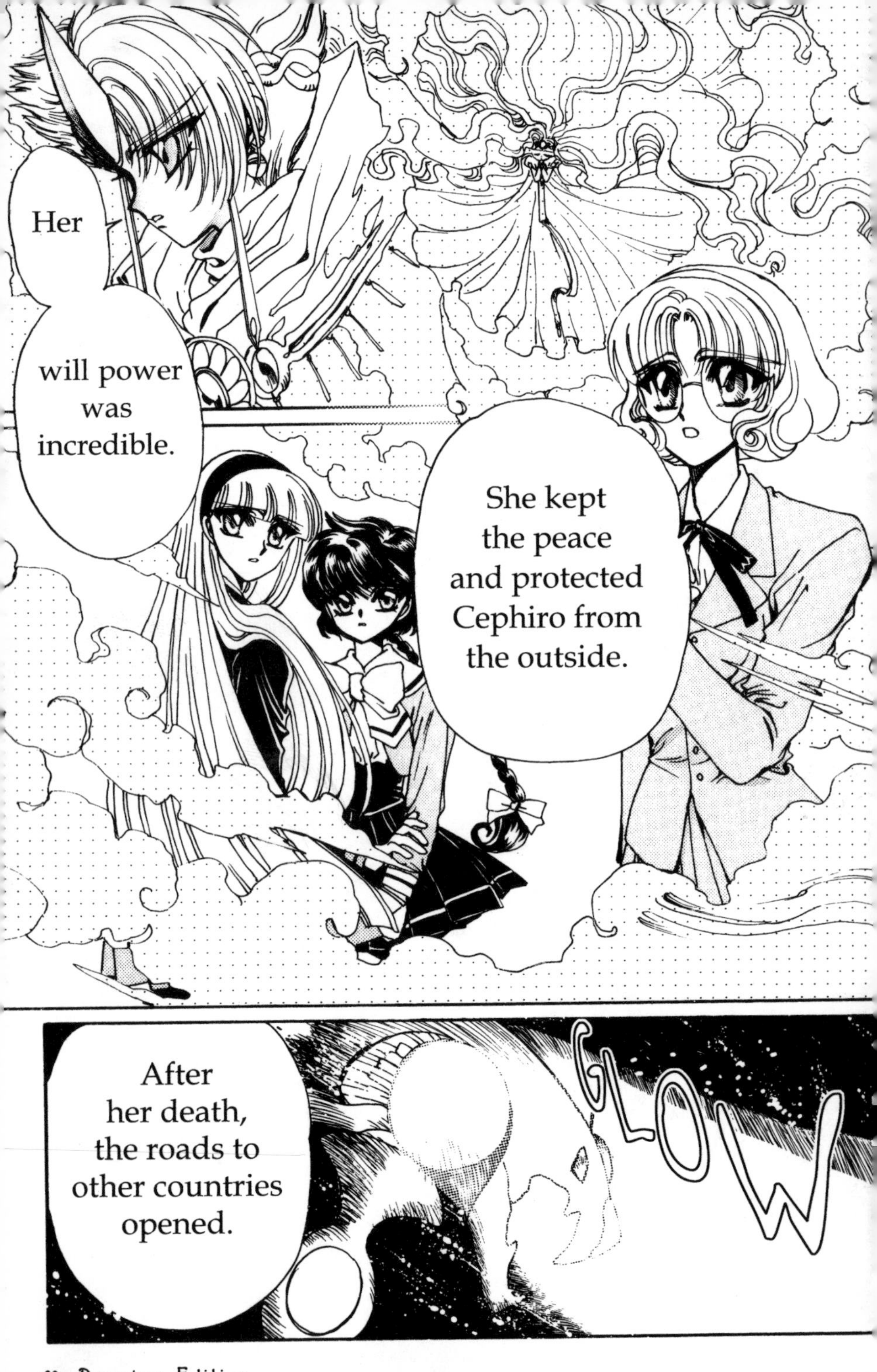
Her
will power was incredible.
She kept the peace and protected Cephiro from the outside.
After her death, the roads to other countries opened.
GLOW

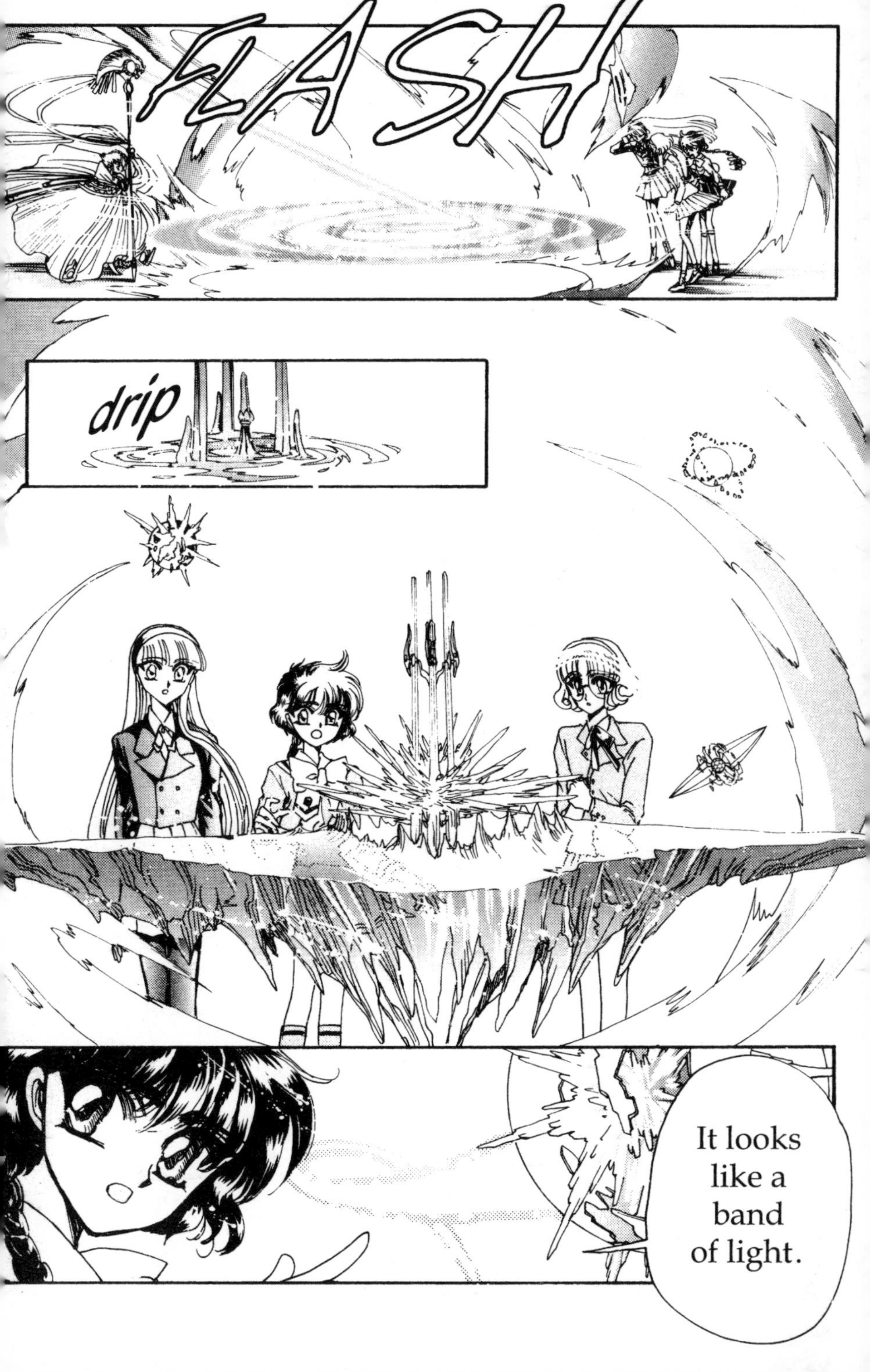
FLASH
drip
It looks like a band of light.

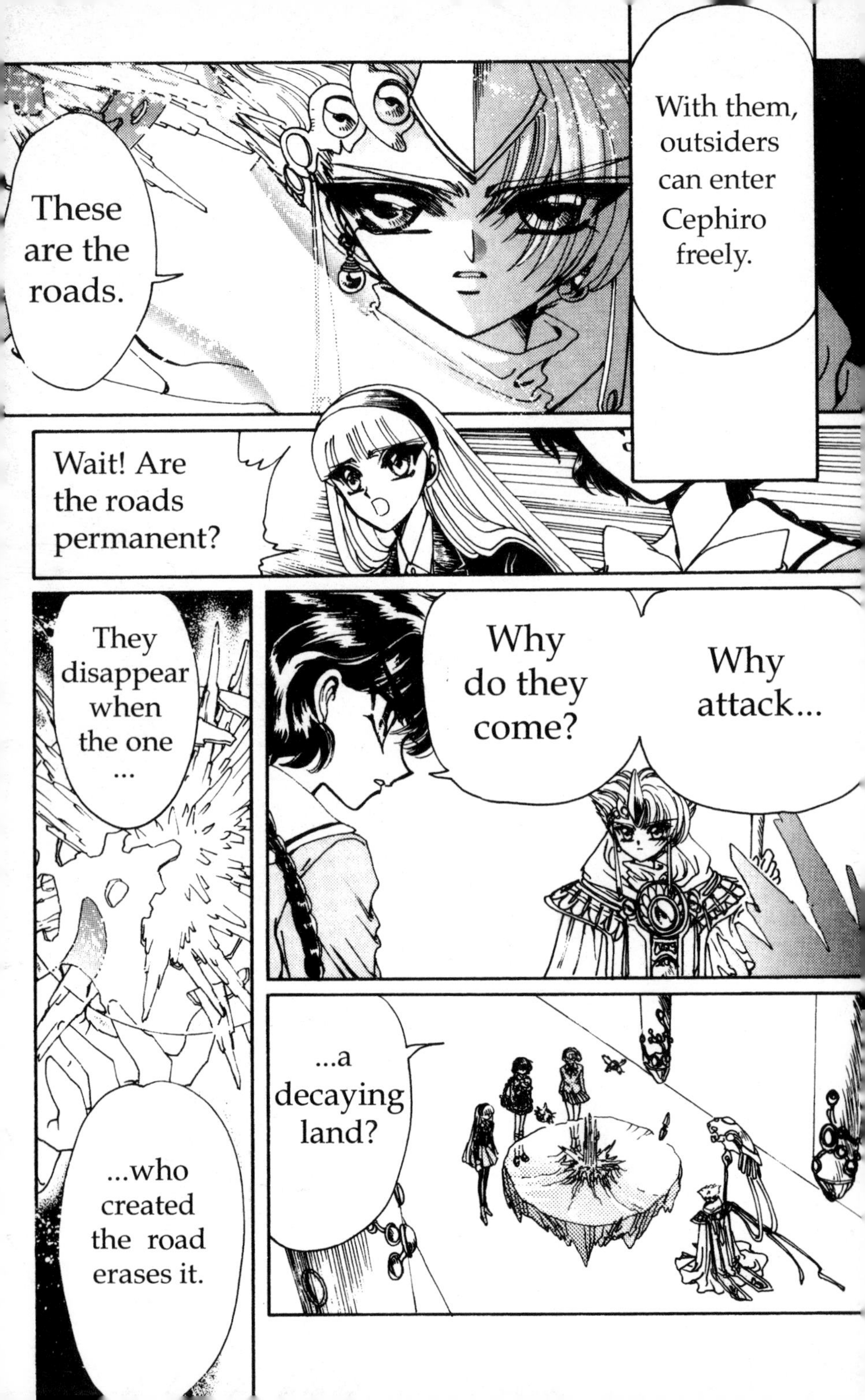
These are the roads.
With them, outsiders can enter Cephiro freely.
Wait! Are the roads permanent?
They disappear when the one ...
...who created the road erases it.
Why do they come?
Why attack...
...a decaying land?

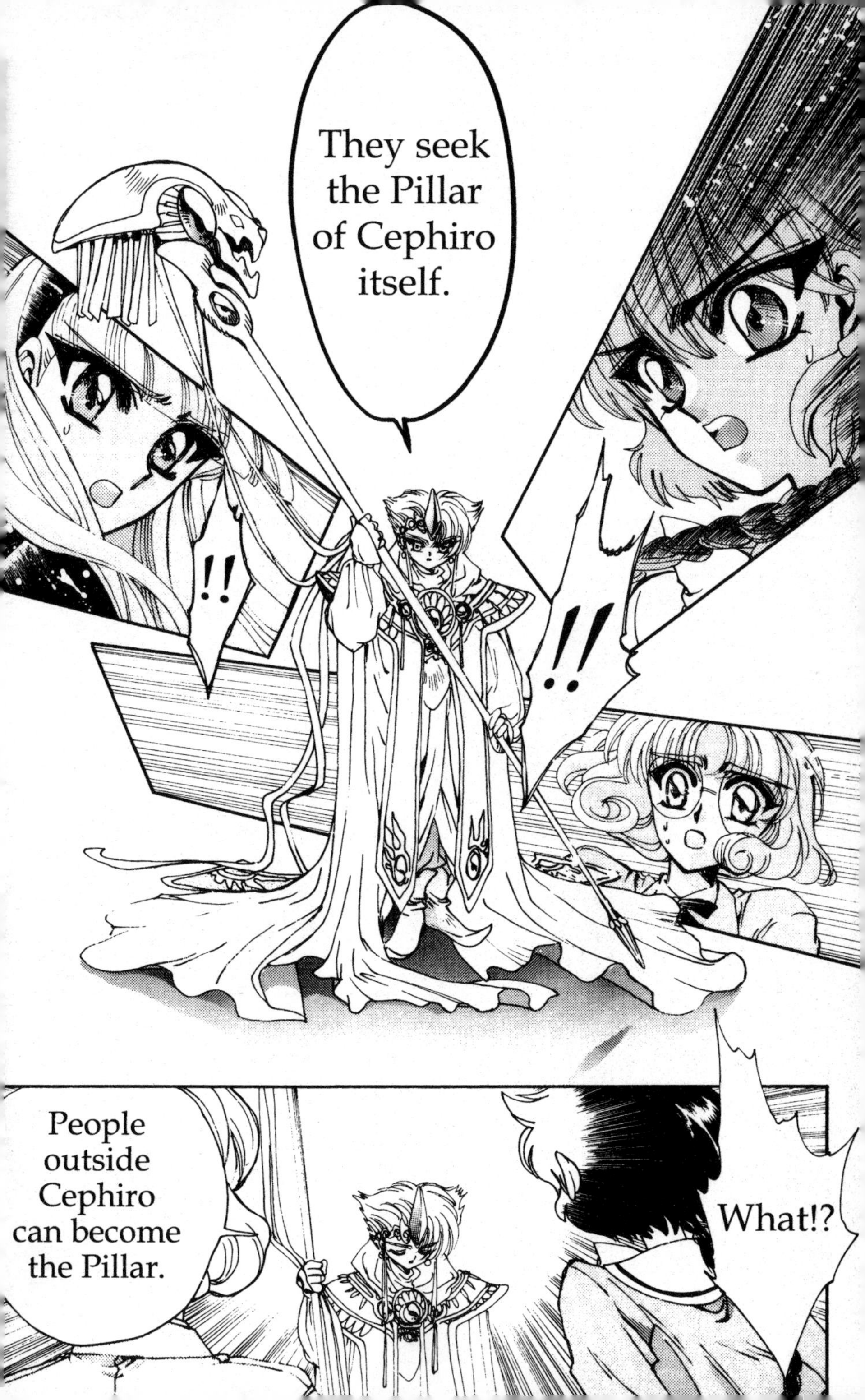
They seek the Pillar of Cephiro itself.
!!
!!
What!?
People outside Cephiro can become the Pillar.

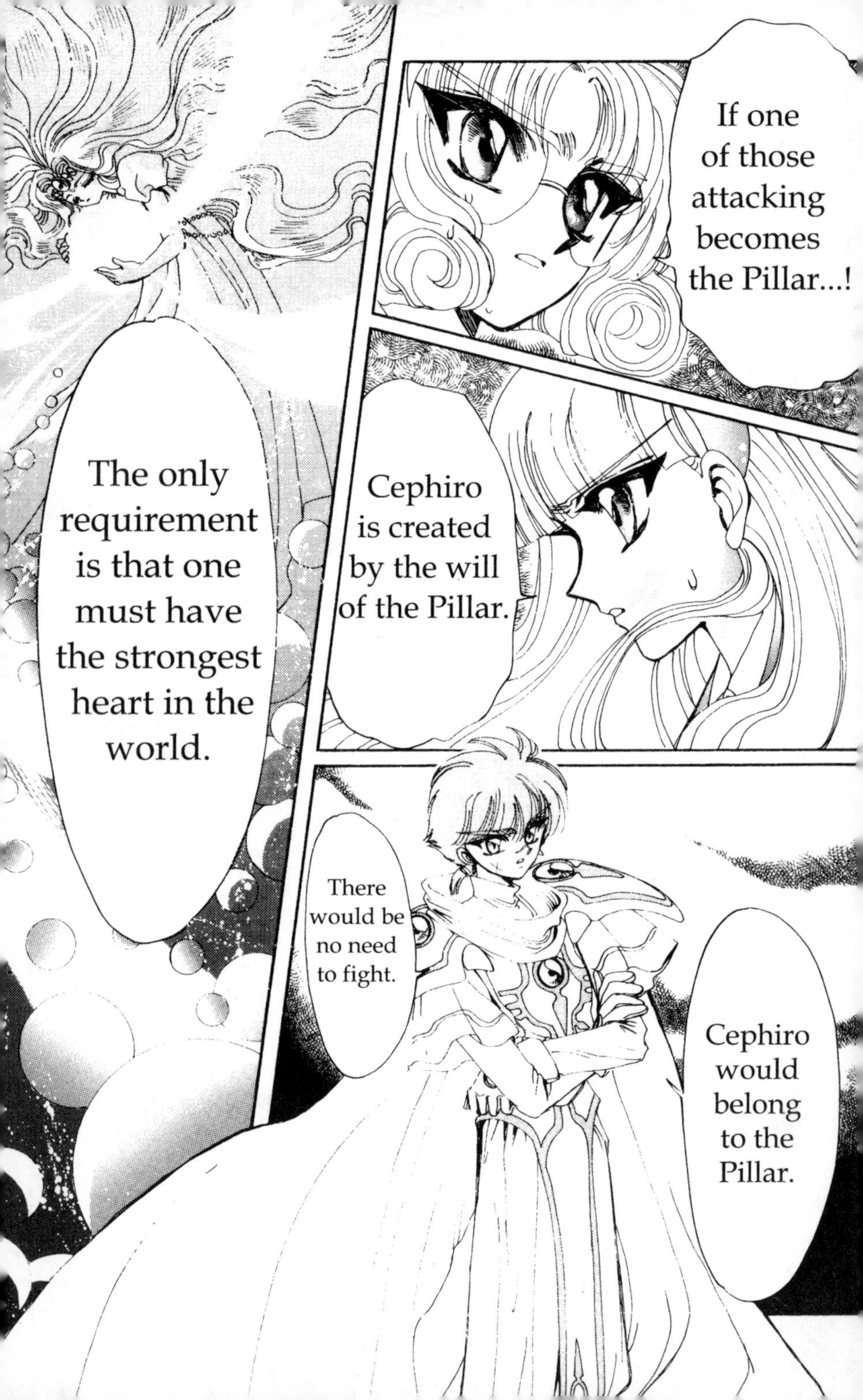
If one of those attacking becomes the Pillar...!
Cephiro is created by the will of the Pillar.
The only requirement is that one must have the strongest heart in the world.
Cephiro would belong to the Pillar.
There would be no need to fight.

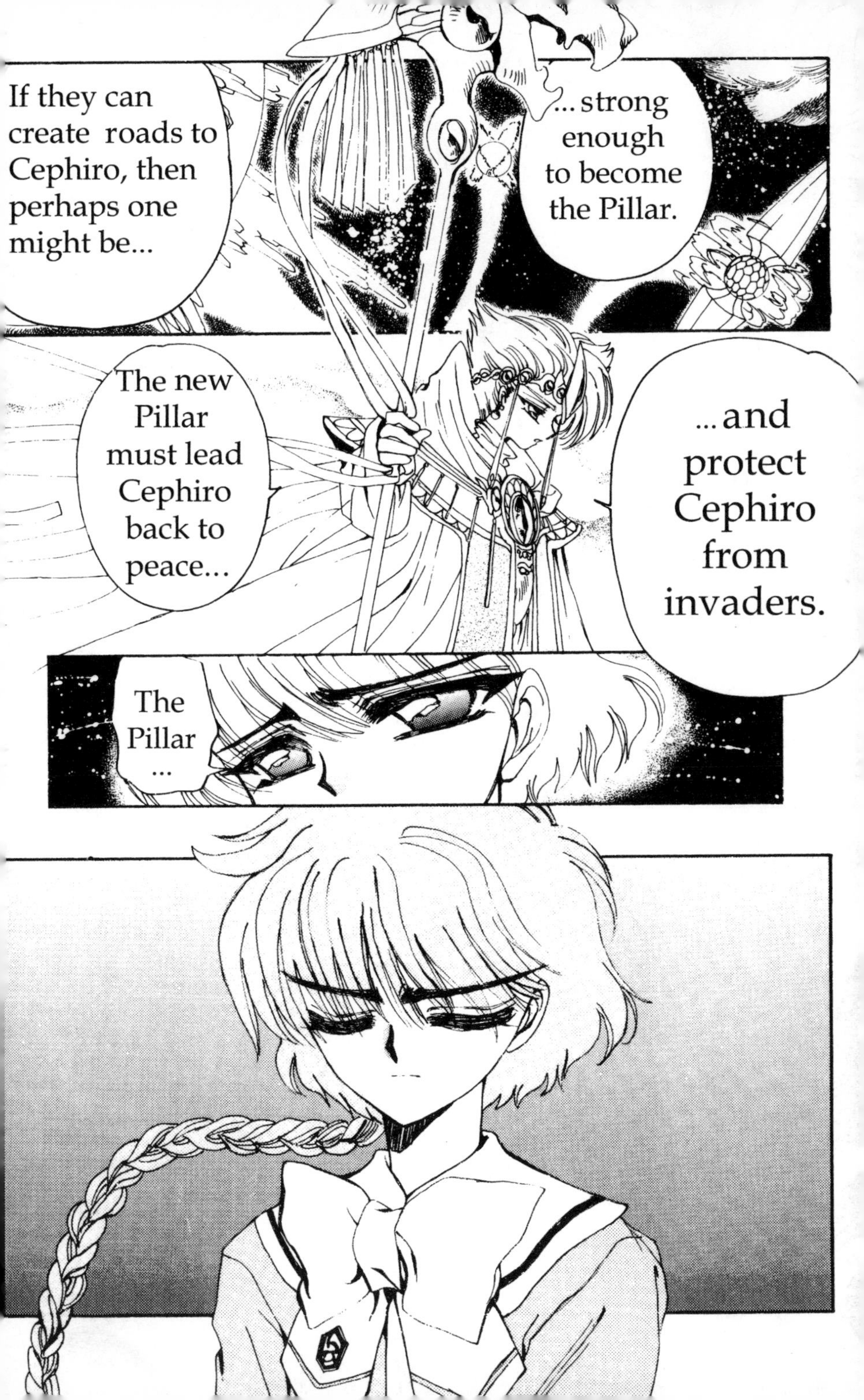
If they can create roads to Cephiro, then perhaps one might be...
... strong enough to become the Pillar.
The new Pillar must lead Cephiro back to peace...
... and protect Cephiro from invaders.
The Pillar ...

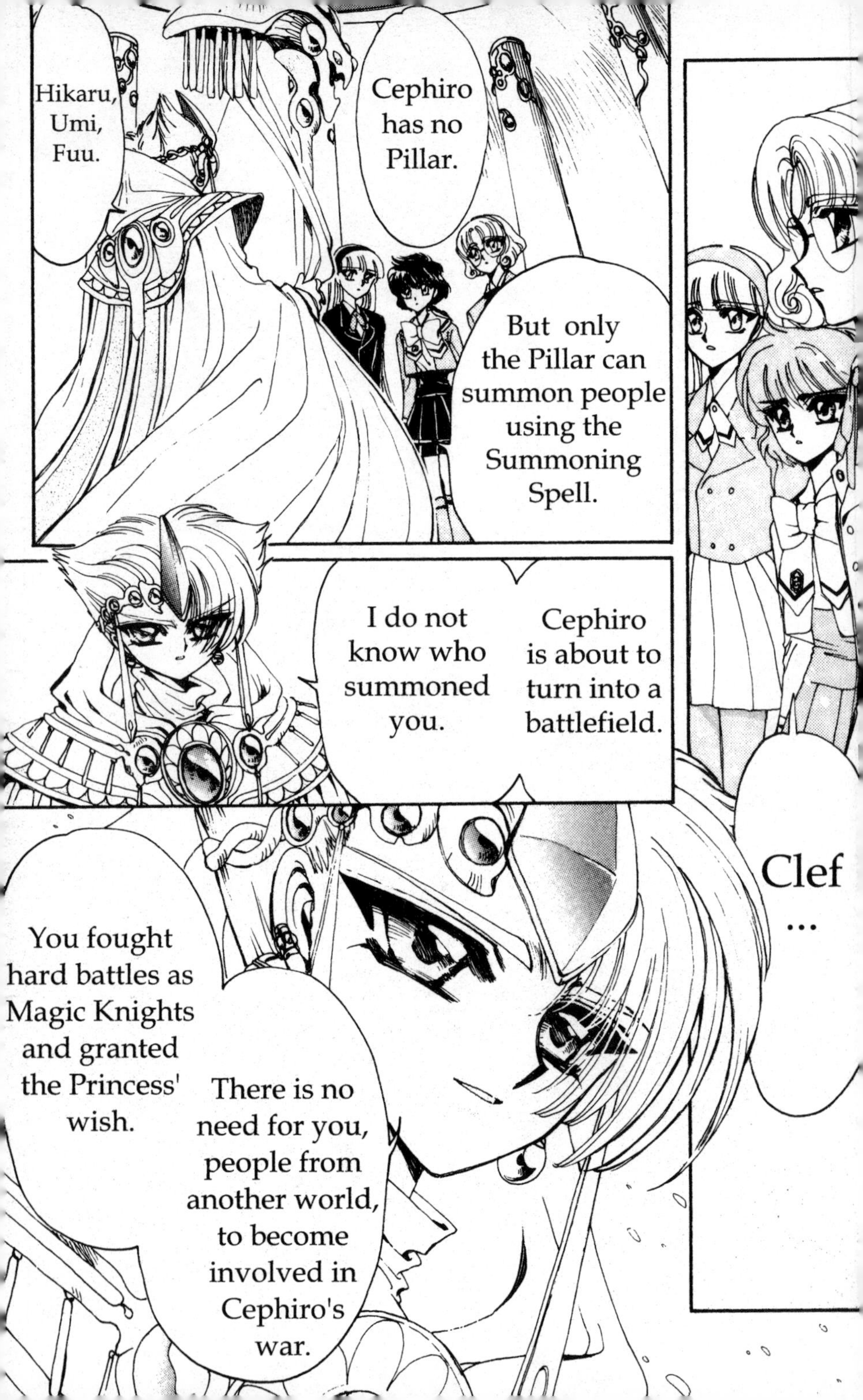
Hikaru, Umi, Fuu.
Cephiro has no Pillar.
But only the Pillar can summon people using the Summoning Spell.
I do not know who summoned you.
Cephiro is about to turn into a battlefield.
You fought hard battles as Magic Knights and granted the Princess' wish.
There is no need for you, people from another world, to become involved in Cephiro's war.
Clef ...

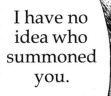

I have no idea who summoned you.

But someone in Cephiro has a heart strong enough to summon from other worlds.

We will find the new Pillar.

That's all I can do for this country which Princess Emeraude gave her life for.

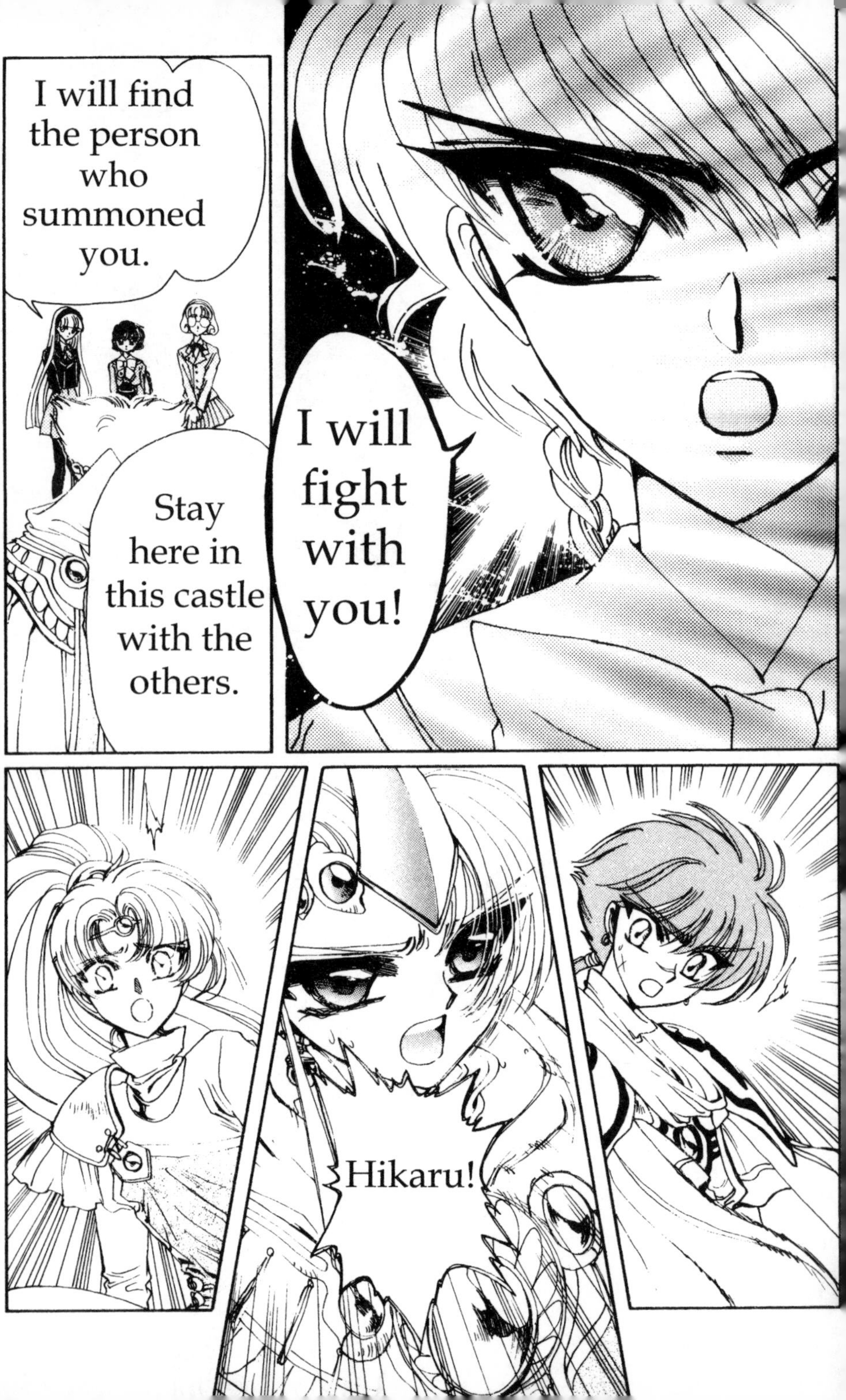
I will find the person who summoned you.
Stay here in this castle with the others.
I will fight with you!
Hikaru!

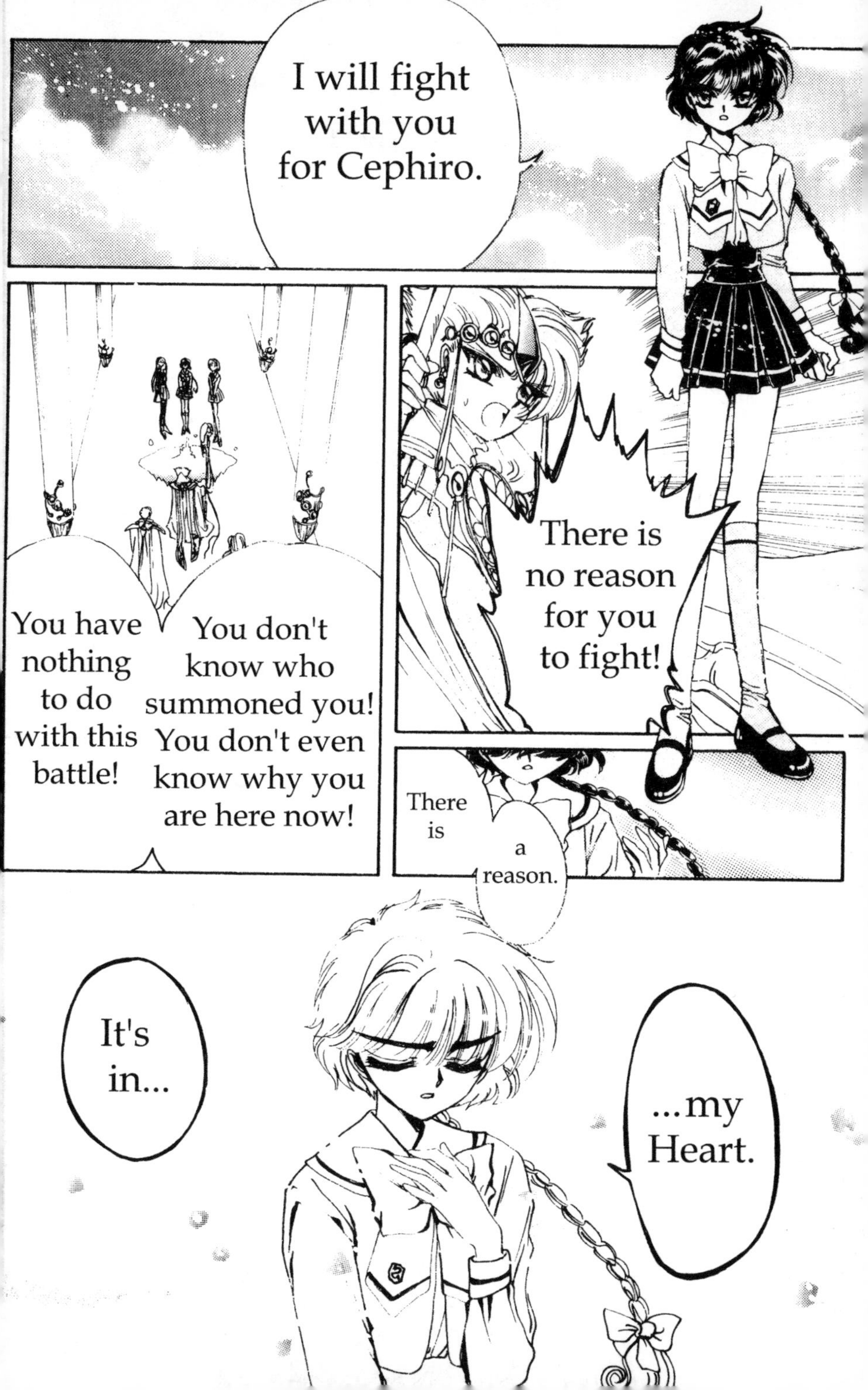
I will fight with you for Cephiro.
You have nothing to do with this battle!
You don't know who summoned you! You don't even know why you are here now!
There is no reason for you to fight!
There is a reason.
It's in...
...my Heart.

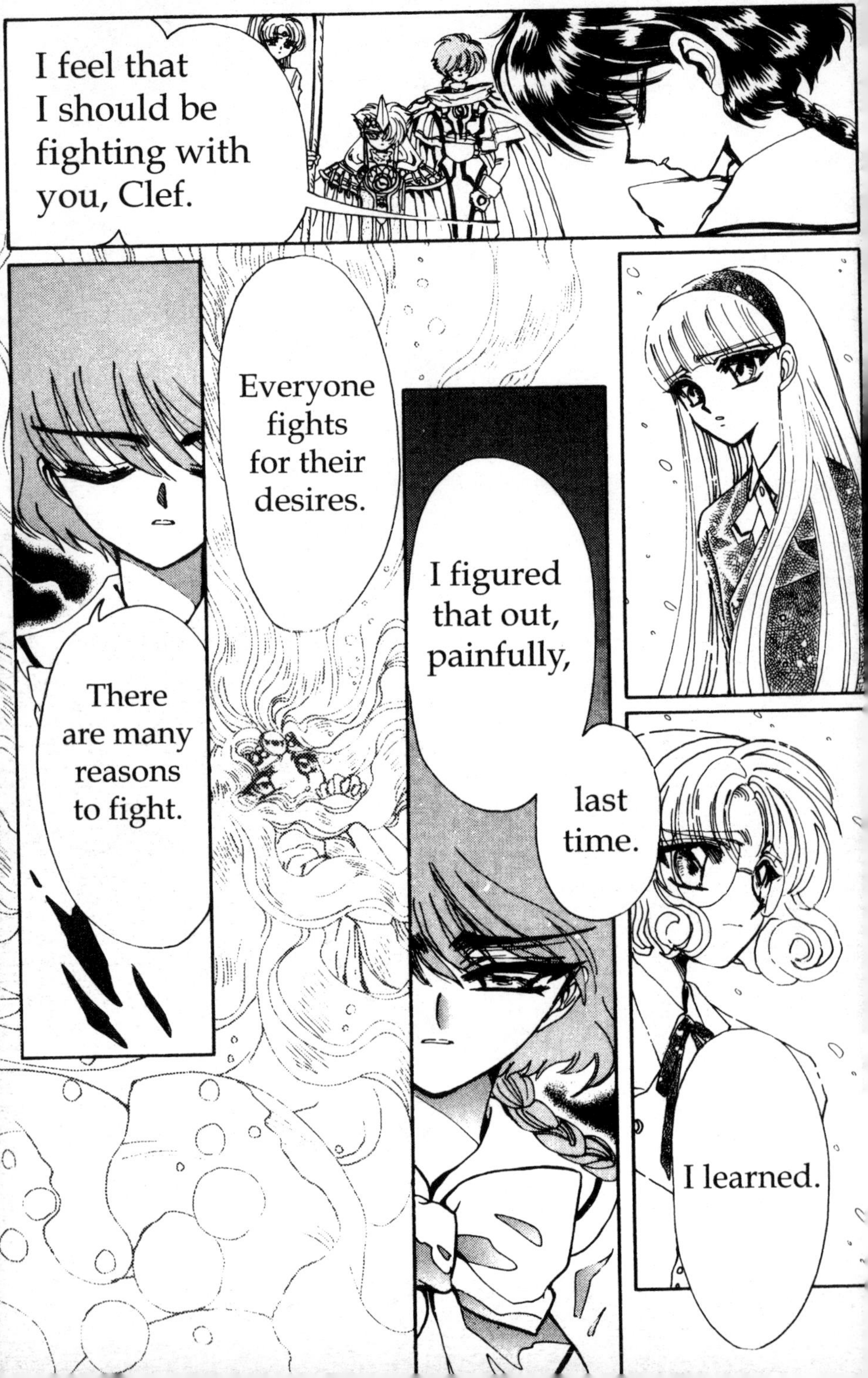
I feel that I should be fighting with you, Clef.
Everyone fights for their desires.
There are many reasons to fight.
I figured that out, painfully,
last time.
I learned.

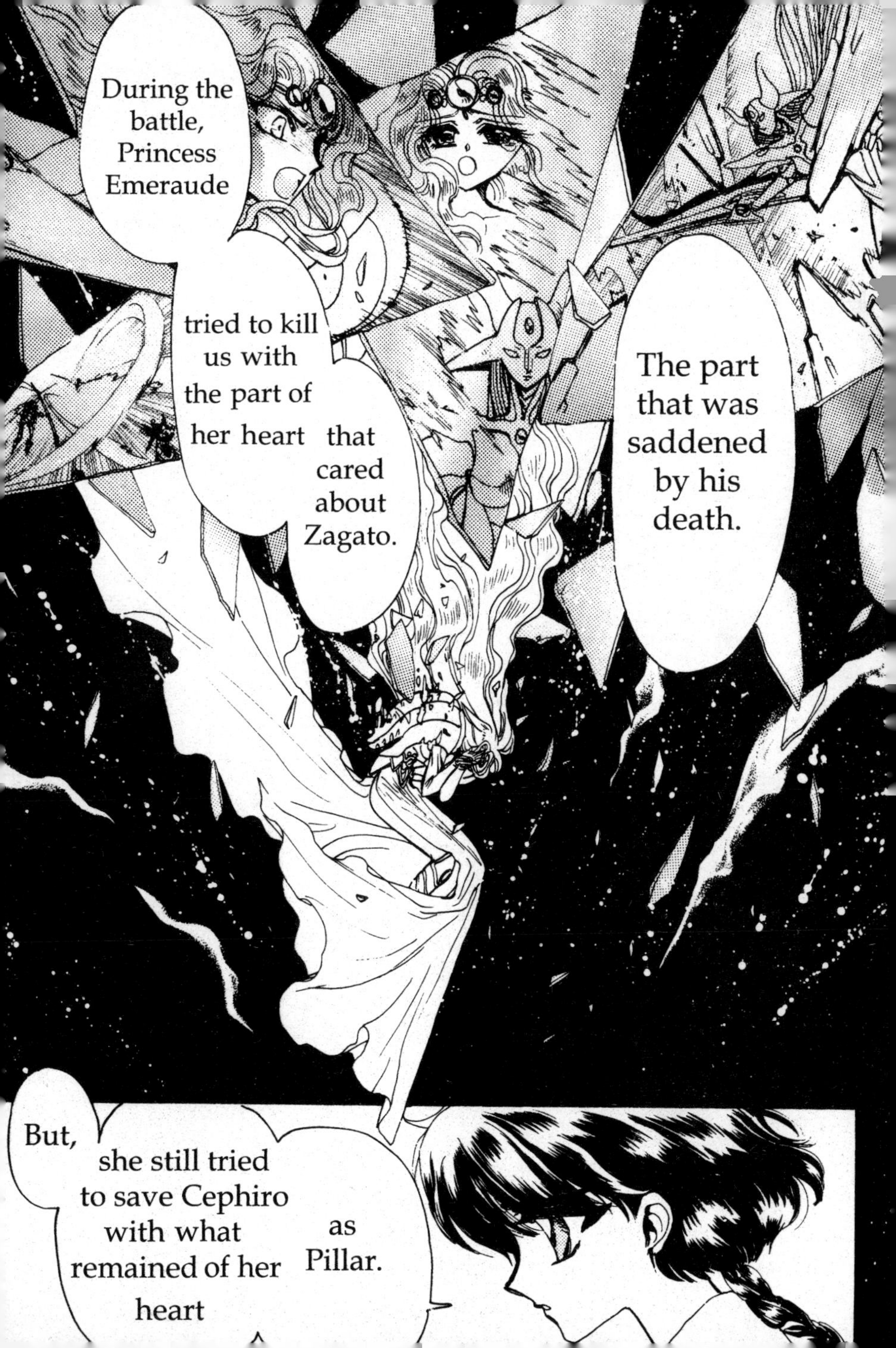
During the battle, Princess Emeraude
tried to kill us with the part of her heart that cared about Zagato.
The part that was saddened by his death.
But, she still tried to save Cephiro with what remained of her heart as Pillar.

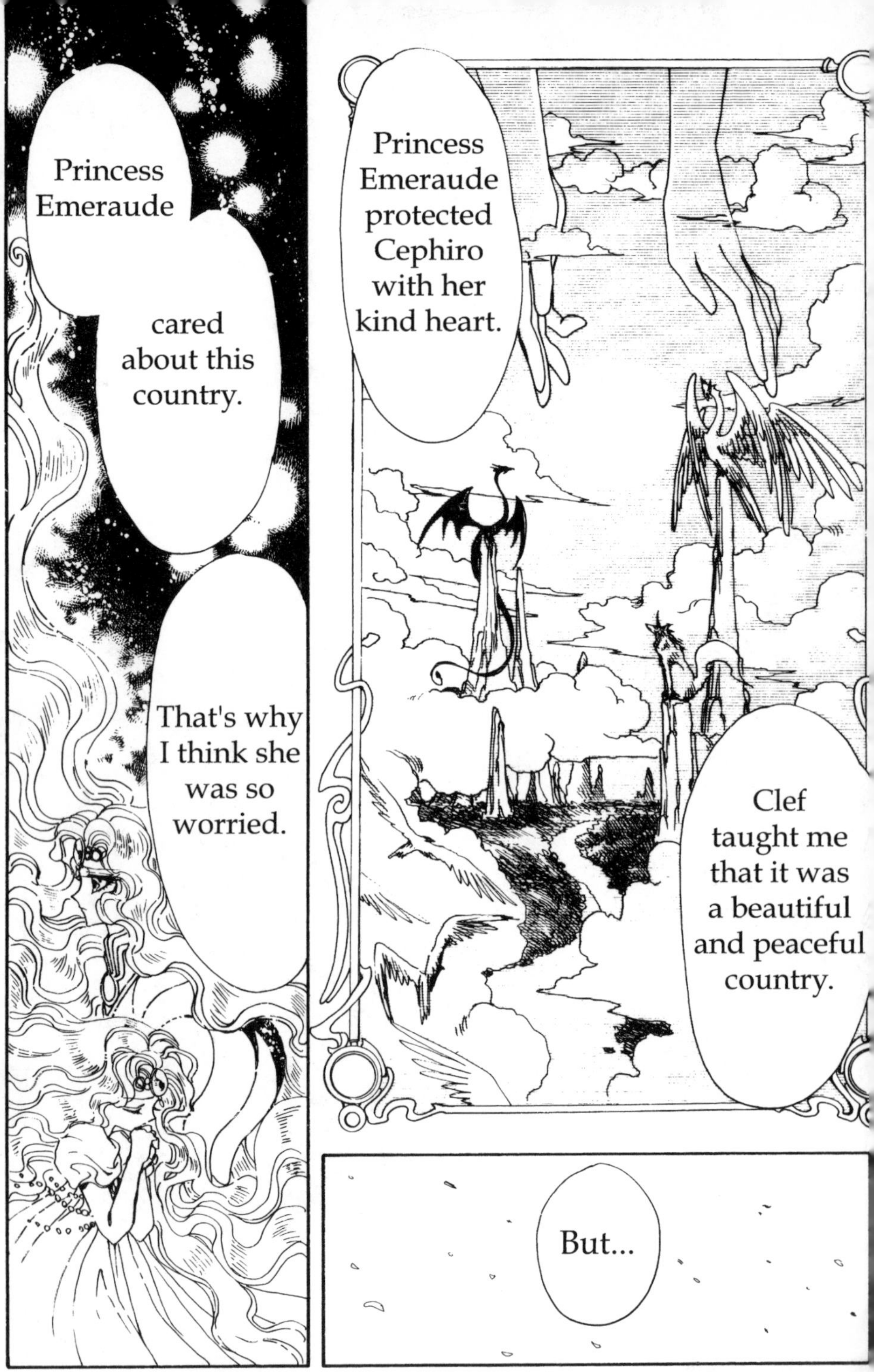
Princess Emeraude
cared about this country.
That's why I think she was so worried.
Princess Emeraude protected Cephiro with her kind heart.
Clef taught me that it was a beautiful and peaceful country.
But...

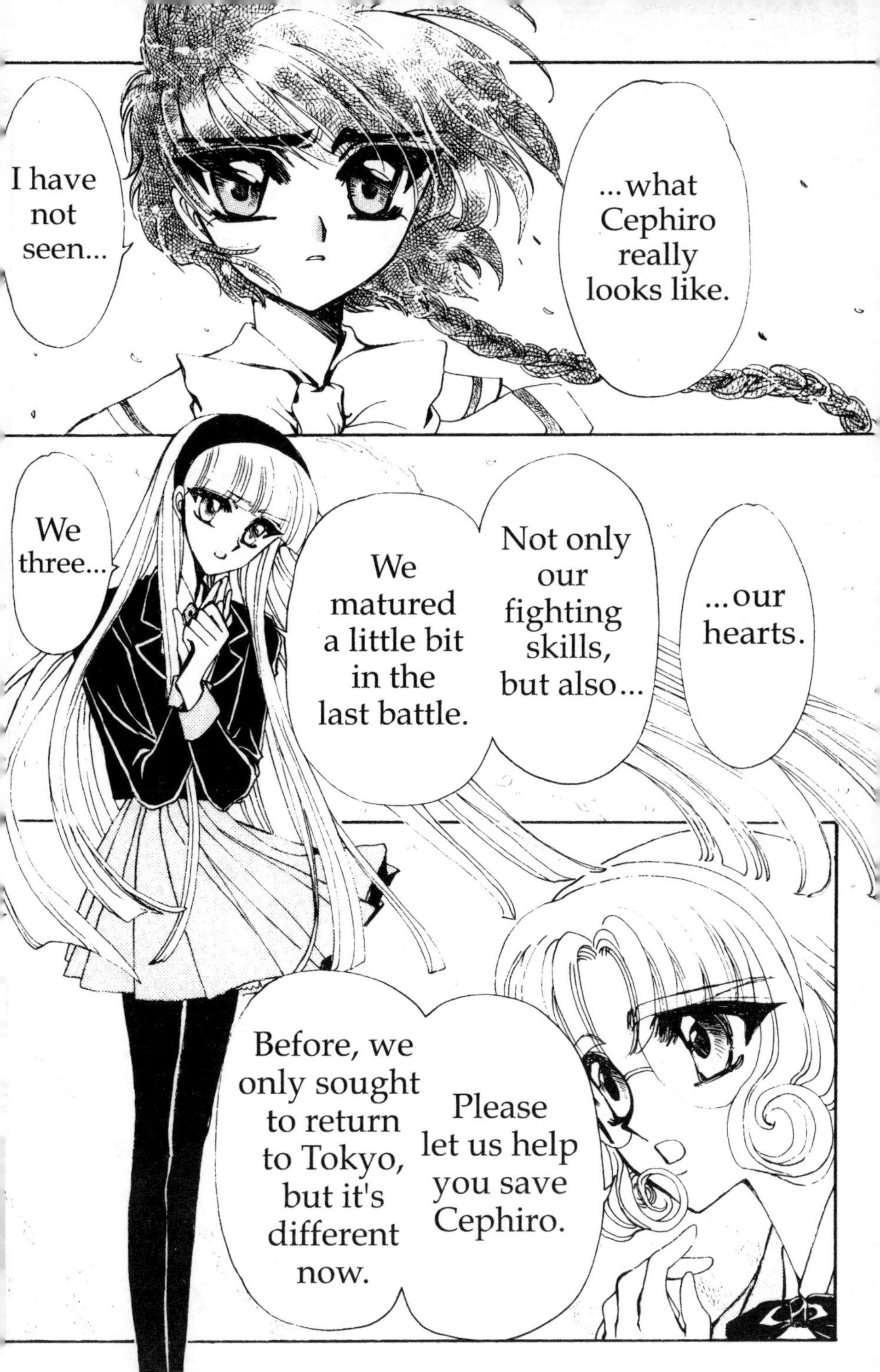
I have not seen...
...what Cephiro really looks like.
We three...
We matured a little bit in the last battle.
Not only our fighting skills, but also...
...our hearts.
Before, we only sought to return to Tokyo, but it's different now.
Please let us help you save Cephiro.

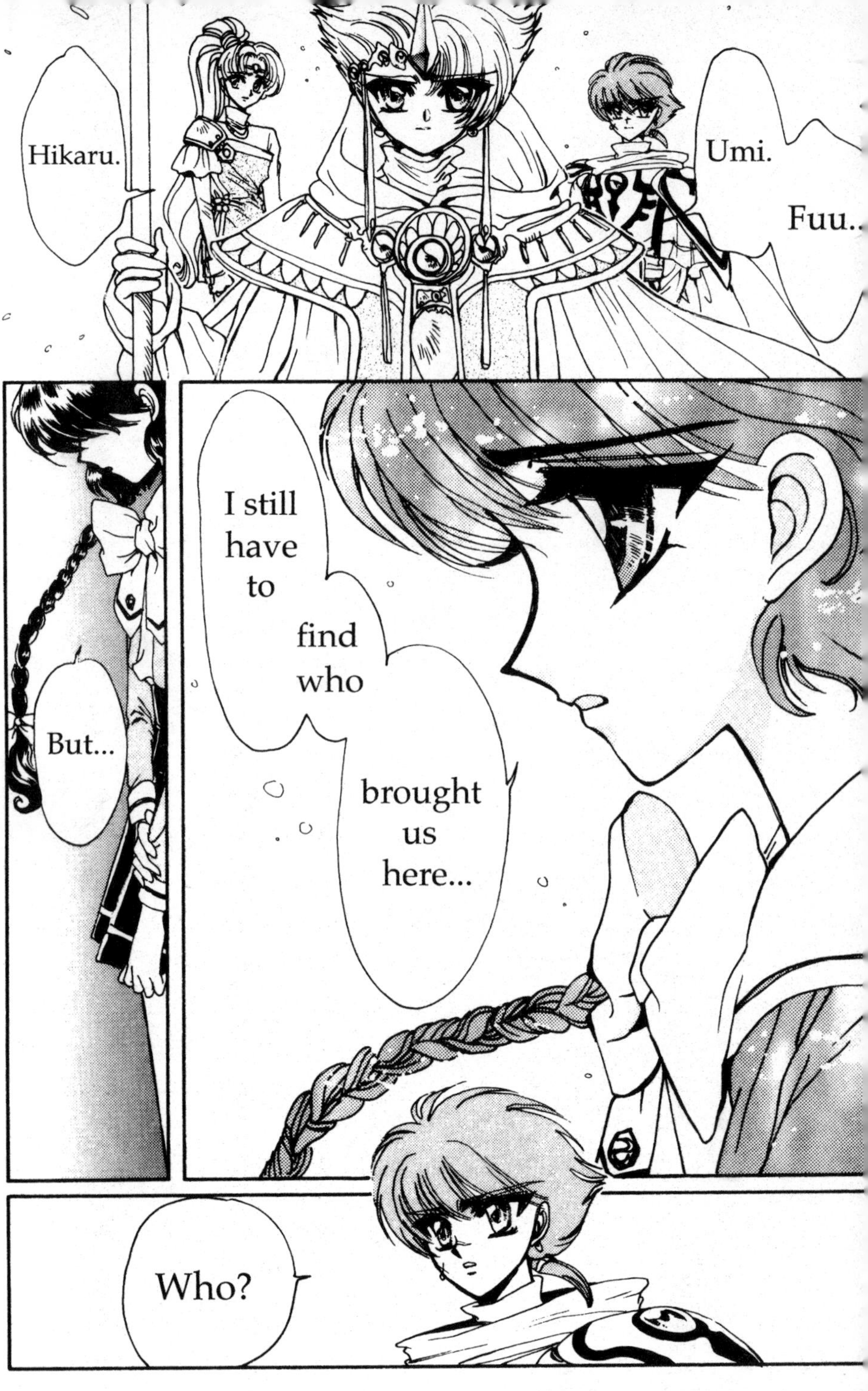
Umi.
Fuu...
Hikaru.
I still have to find who brought us here...
But...
Who?

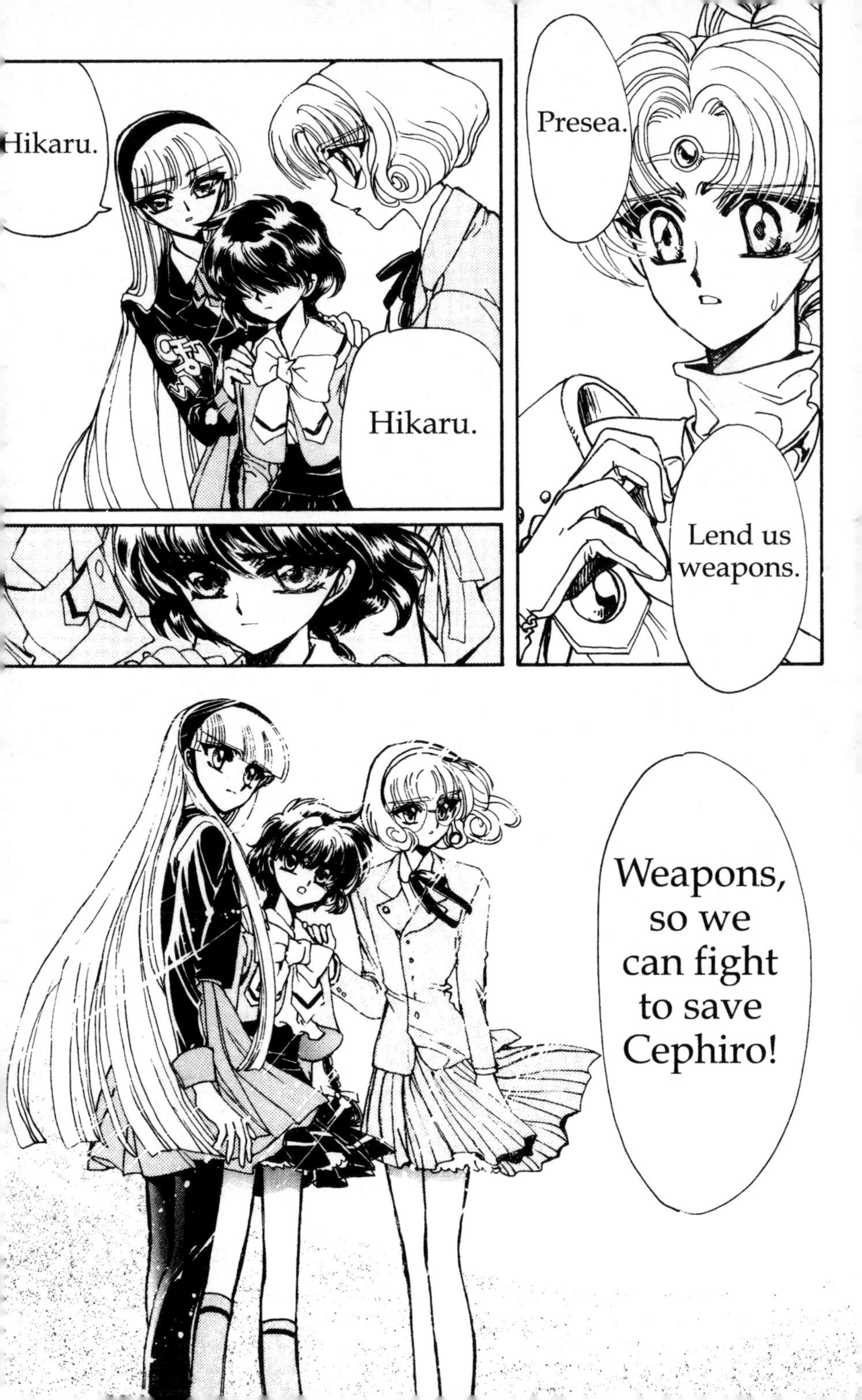
Presea.
Lend us weapons.
Hikaru.
Hikaru.
Weapons, so we can fight to save Cephiro!

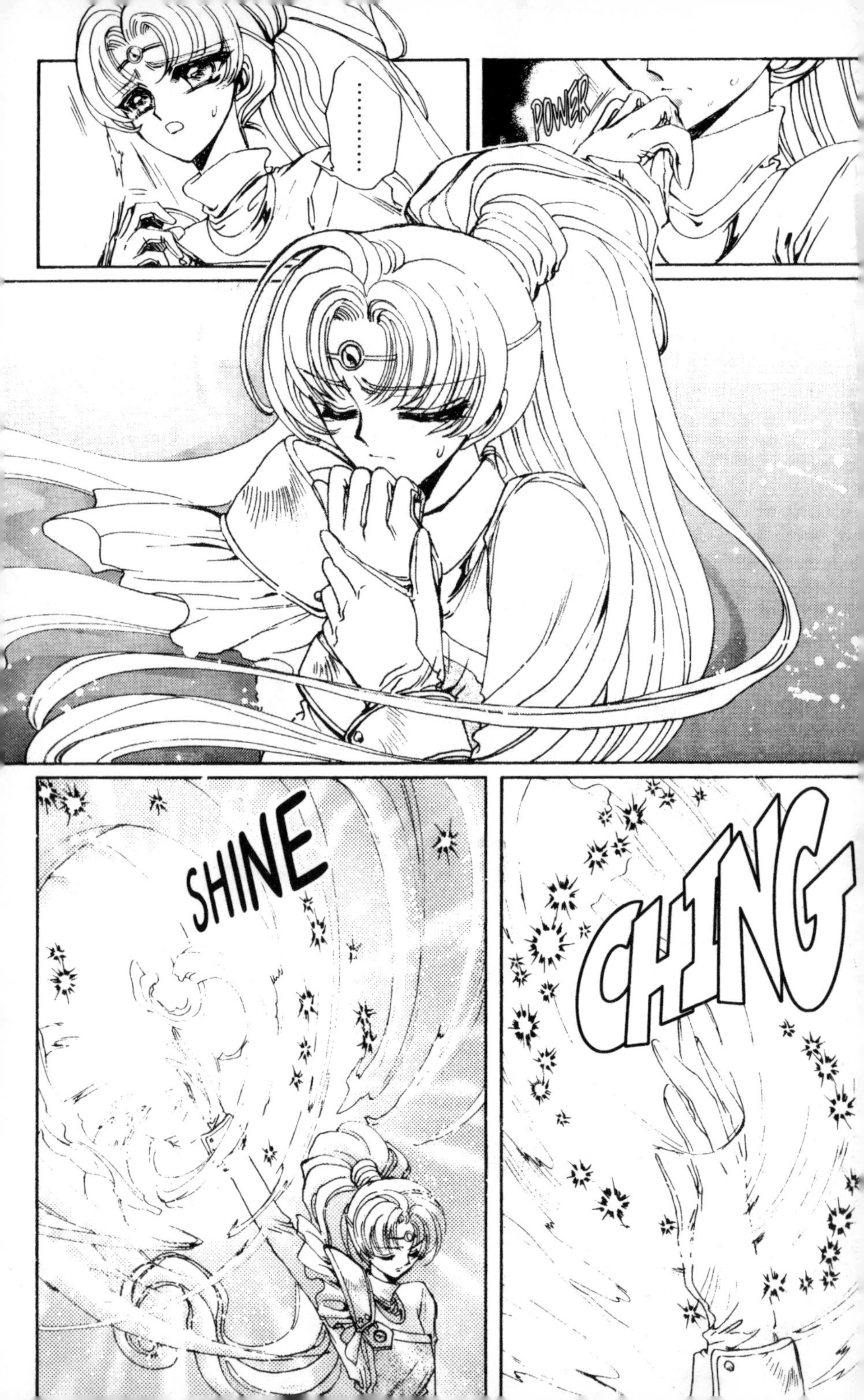
POWER
......
SHINE
CHING

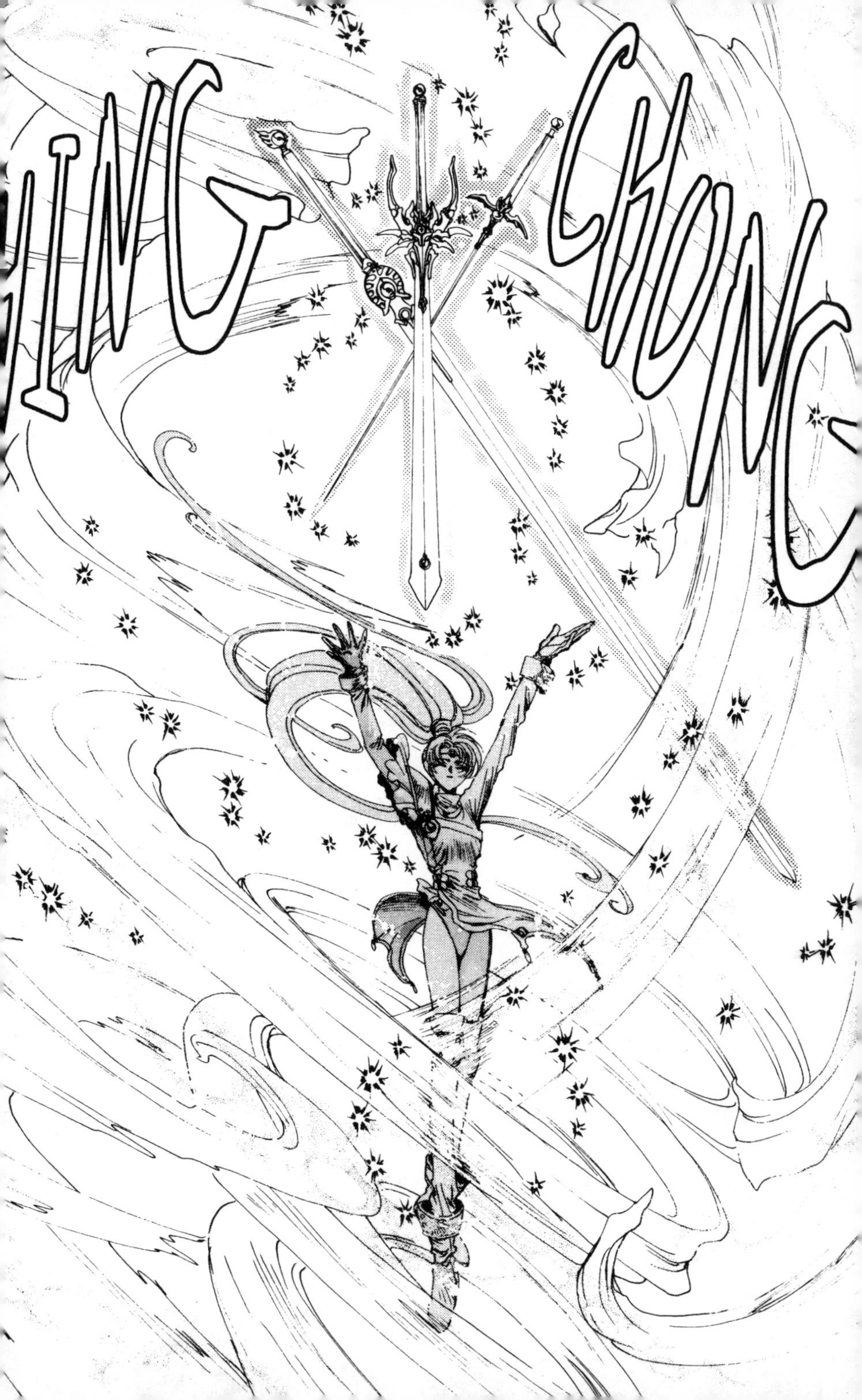

HING
CHUNG

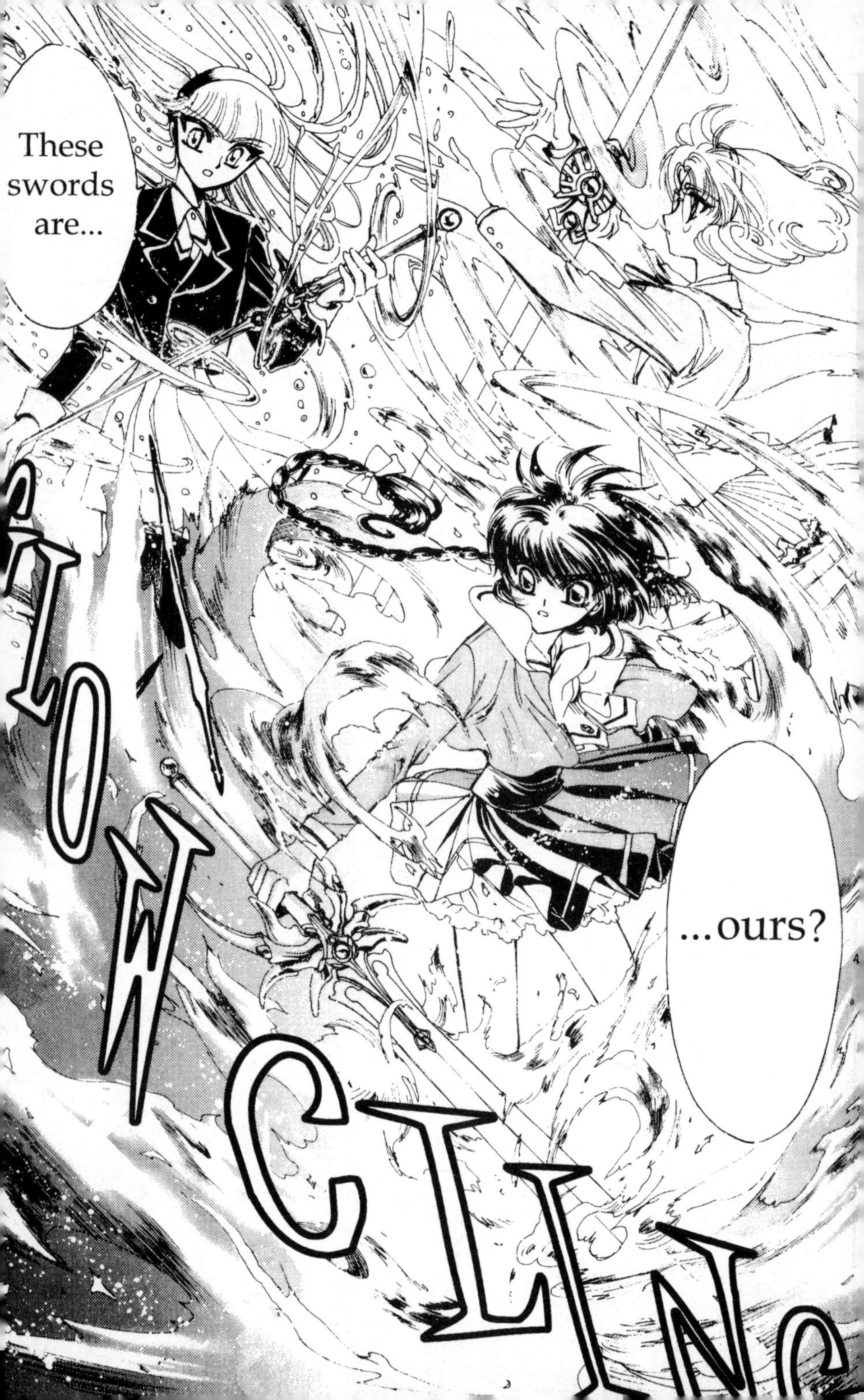
These swords are...
FLOW
...ours?
CLING

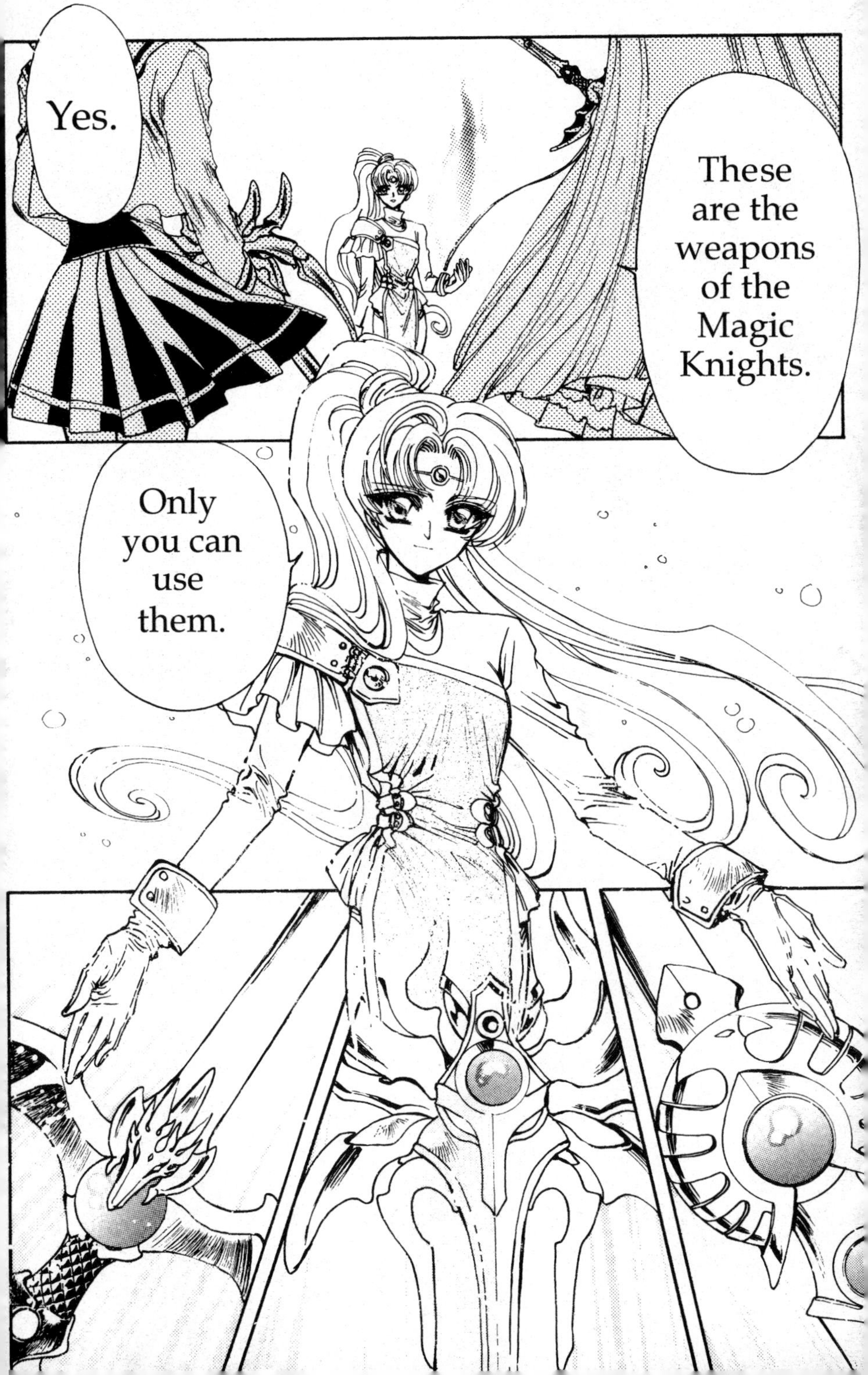
These are the weapons of the Magic Knights.
Yes.
Only you can use them.

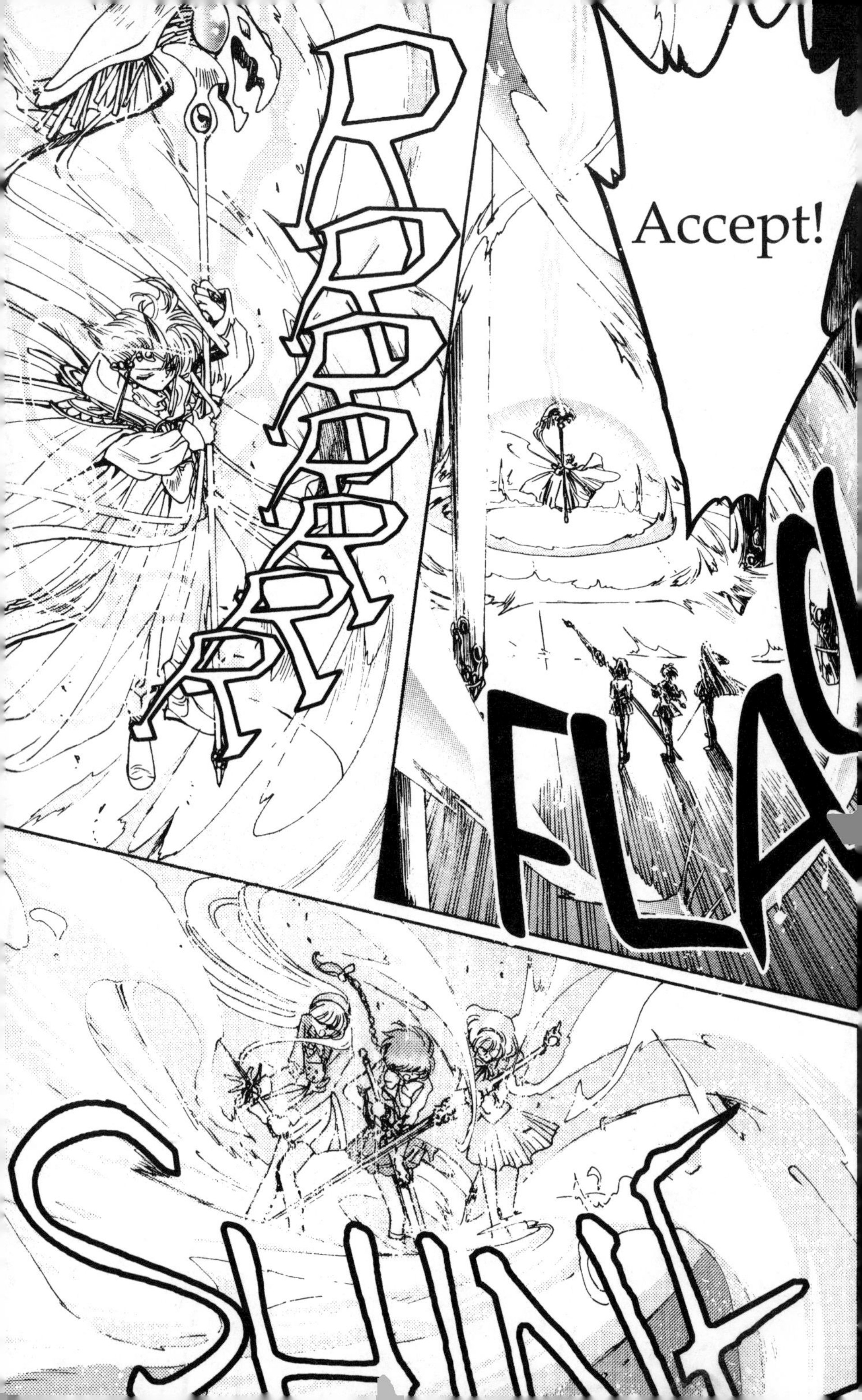
Accept!
FLA
SHIN

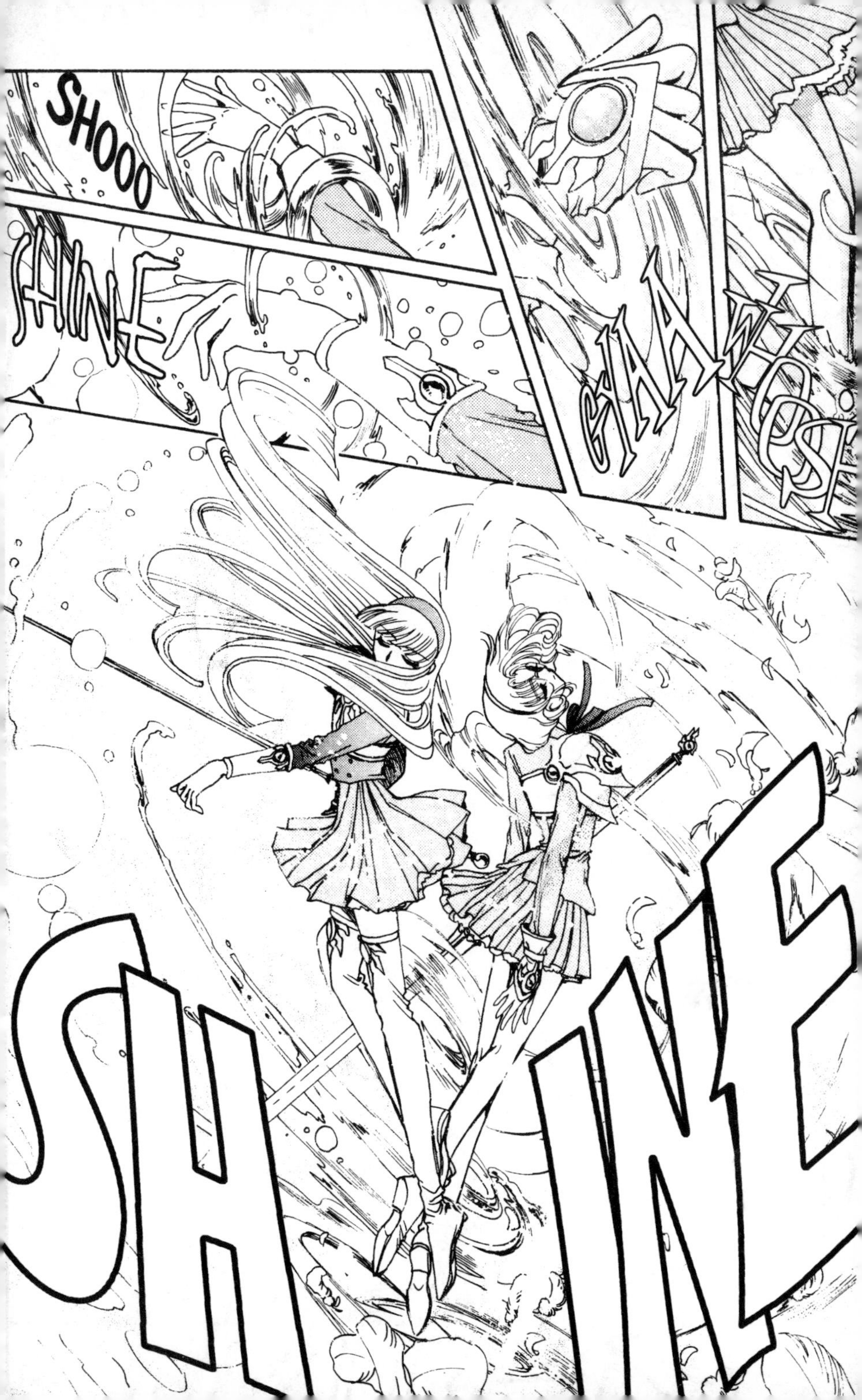
GAA
WHOOS
SHOOO
SHINE
SHINE

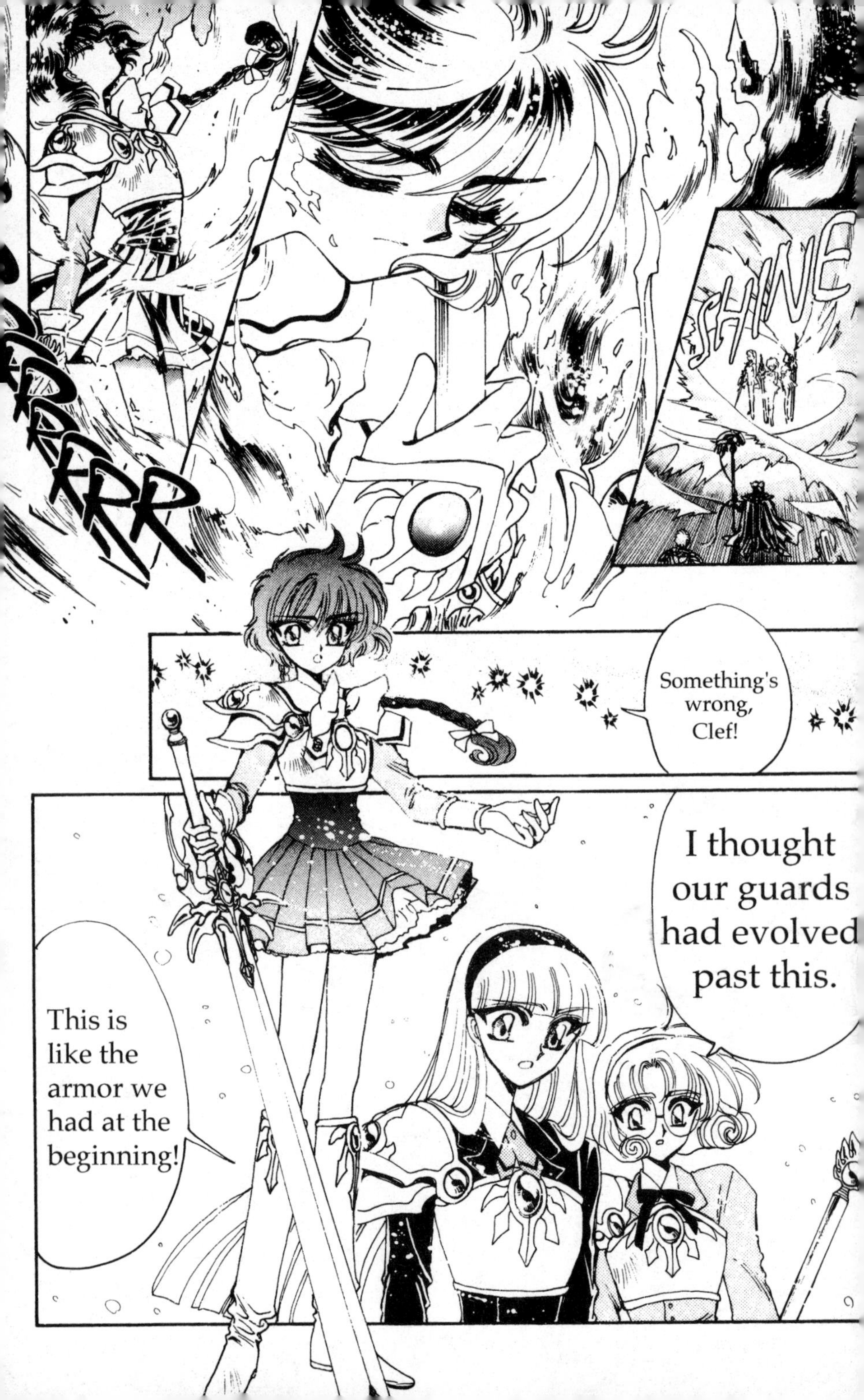
SHINE
RRRRRR
Something's wrong, Clef!
I thought our guards had evolved past this.
This is like the armor we had at the beginning!

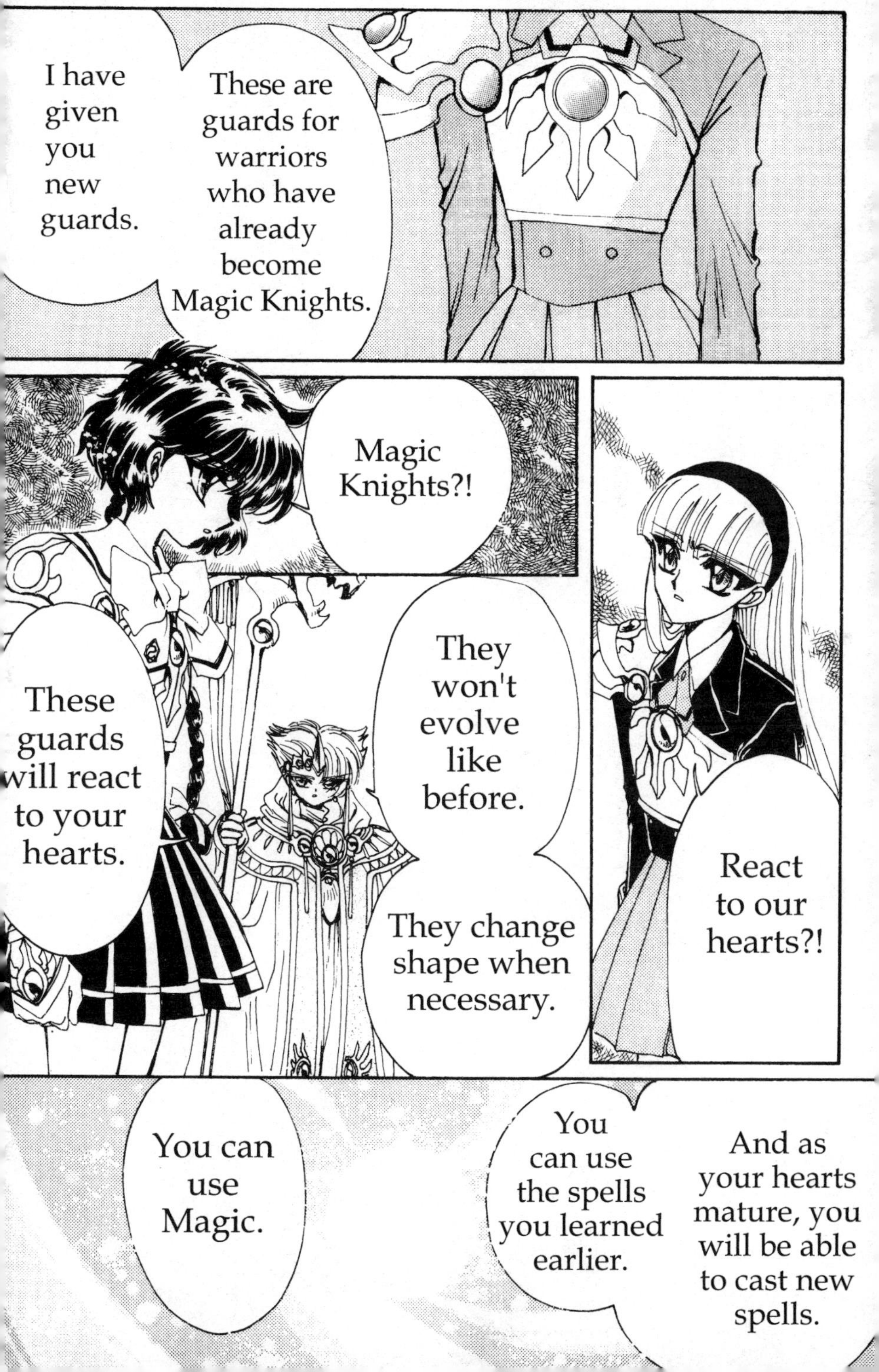

I have given you new guards.
These are guards for warriors who have already become Magic Knights.
Magic Knights?!
These guards will react to your hearts.
They won't evolve like before.
They change shape when necessary.
React to our hearts?!
You can use Magic.
You can use the spells you learned earlier.
And as your hearts mature, you will be able to cast new spells.

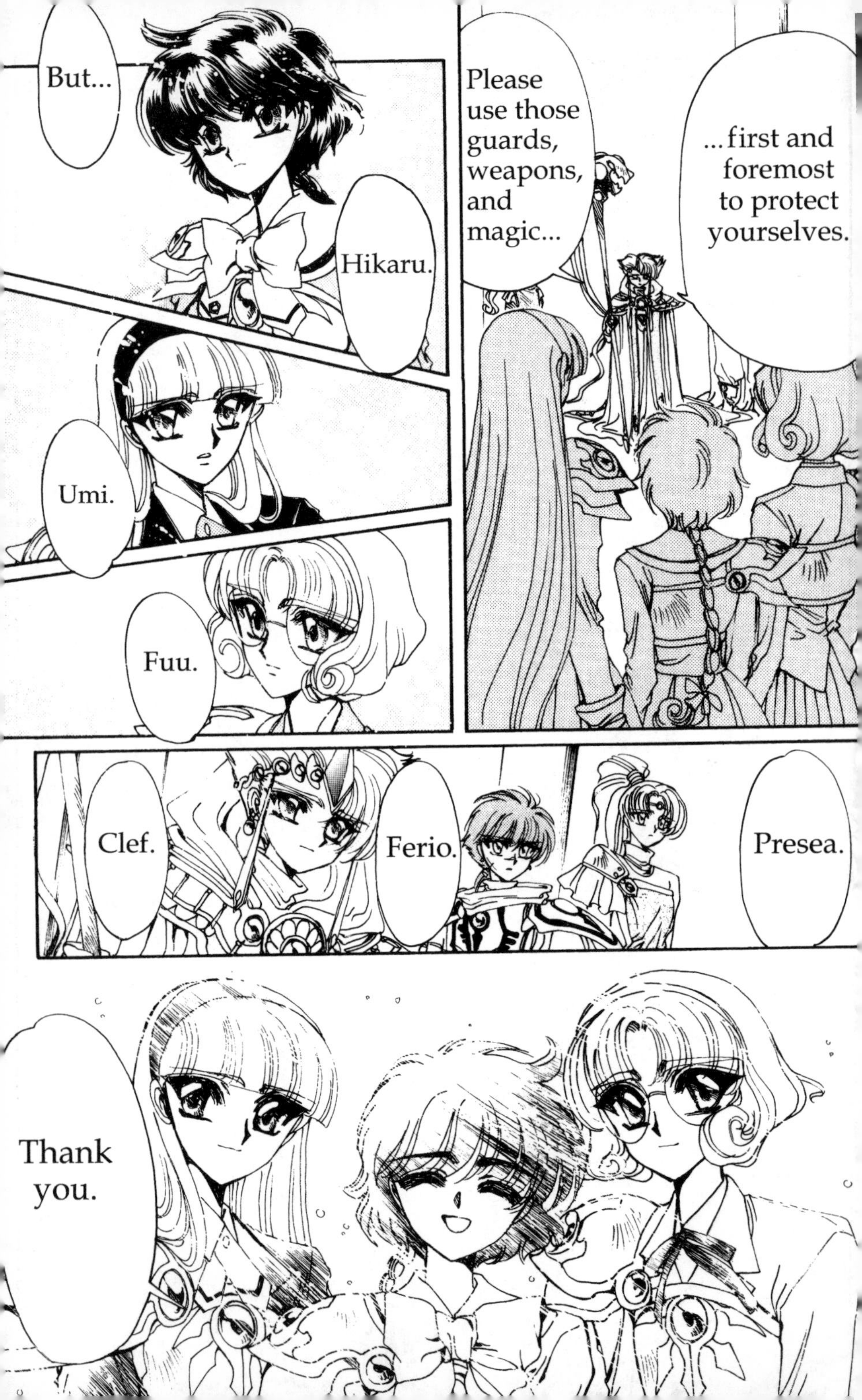
But...
Hikaru.
Umi.
Fuu.
Please use those guards, weapons, and magic...
...first and foremost to protect yourselves.
Clef.
Ferio.
Presea.
Thank you.

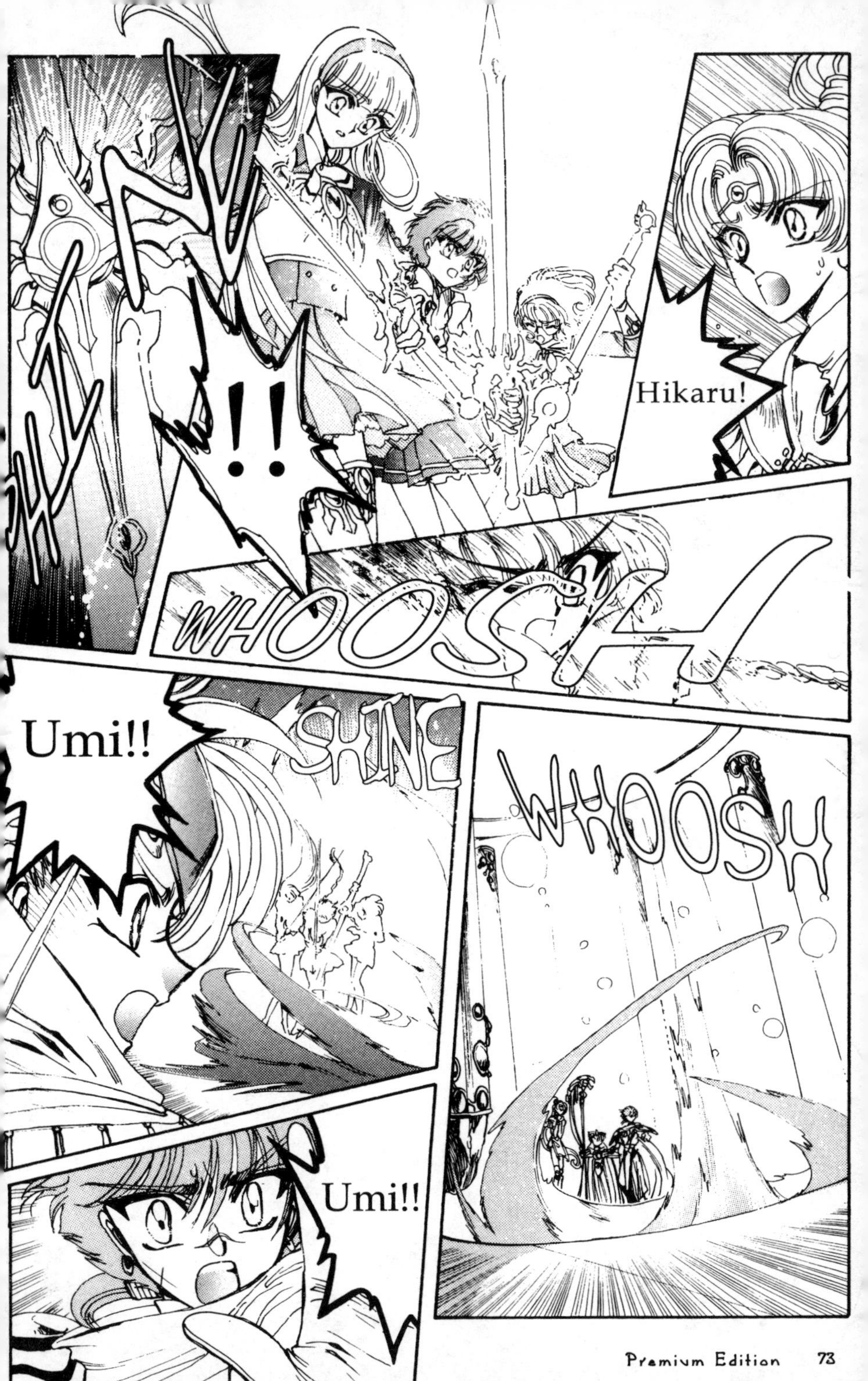
Hikaru!
!!
WHOOSH
WHOOSH
Umi!!
SHINE
Umi!!

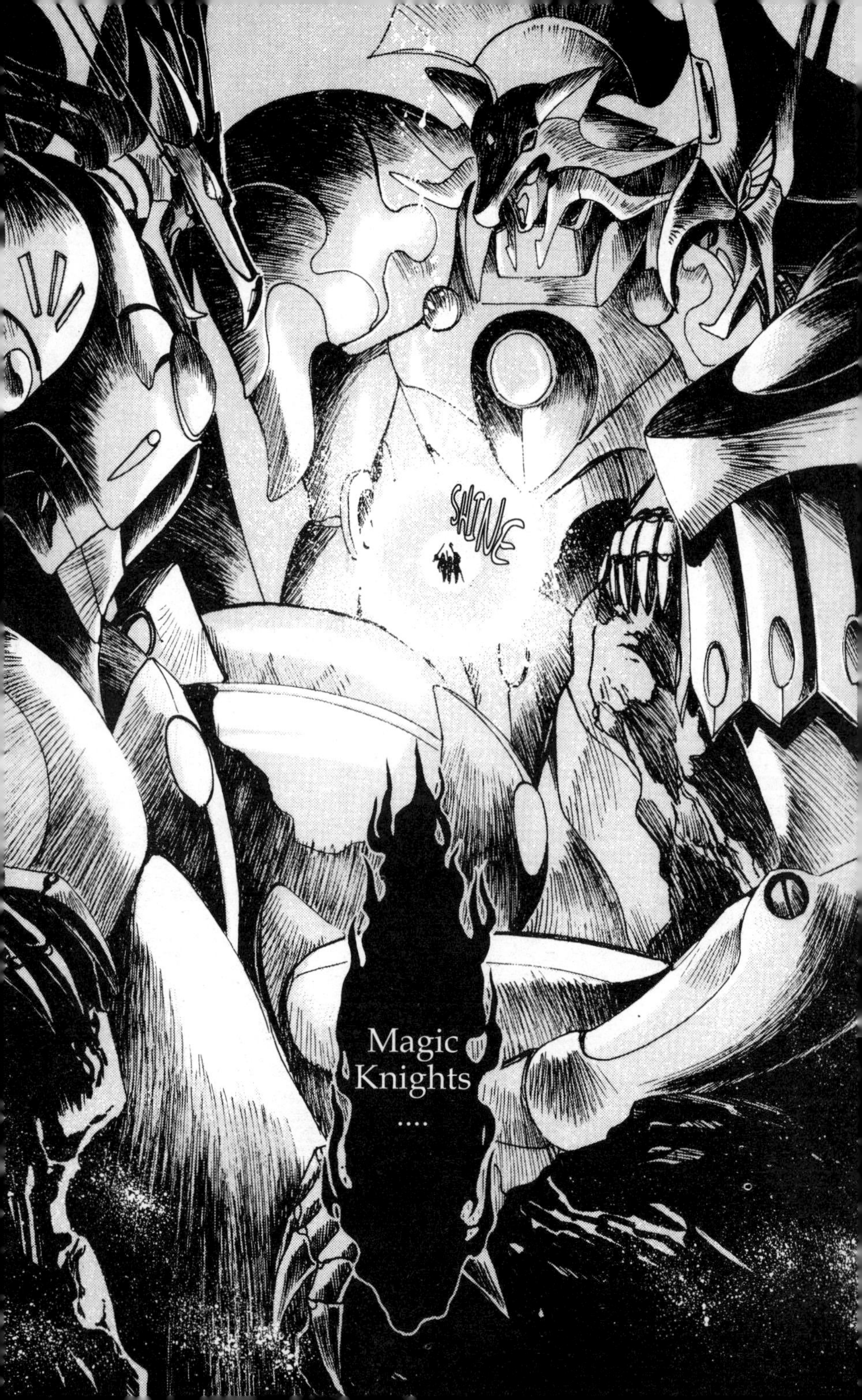
SHINE
Magic Knights
....

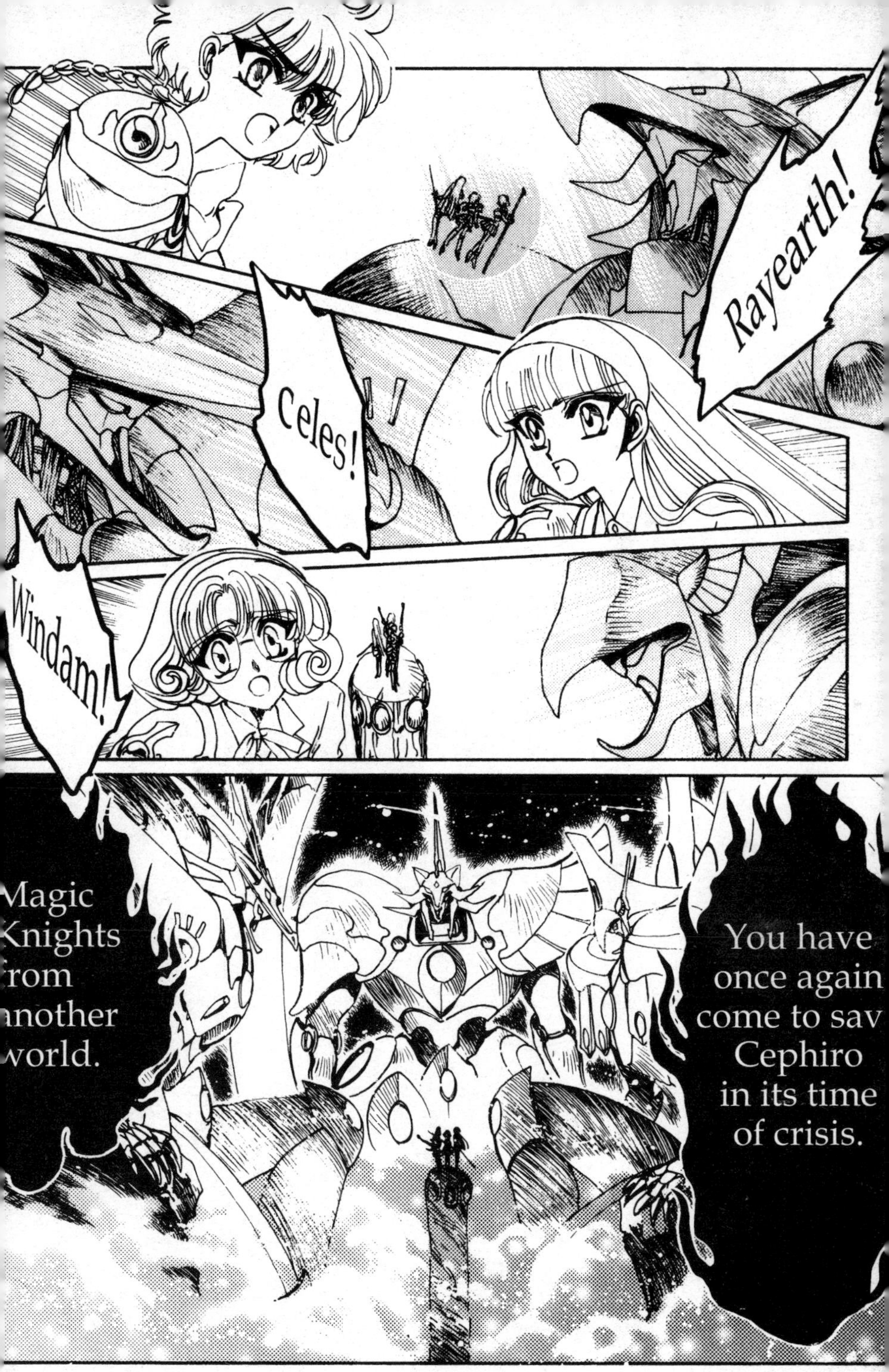
Rayearth!
Celes!
Windam!
You have once again come to sav Cephiro in its time of crisis.
Magic Knights rom nother world.

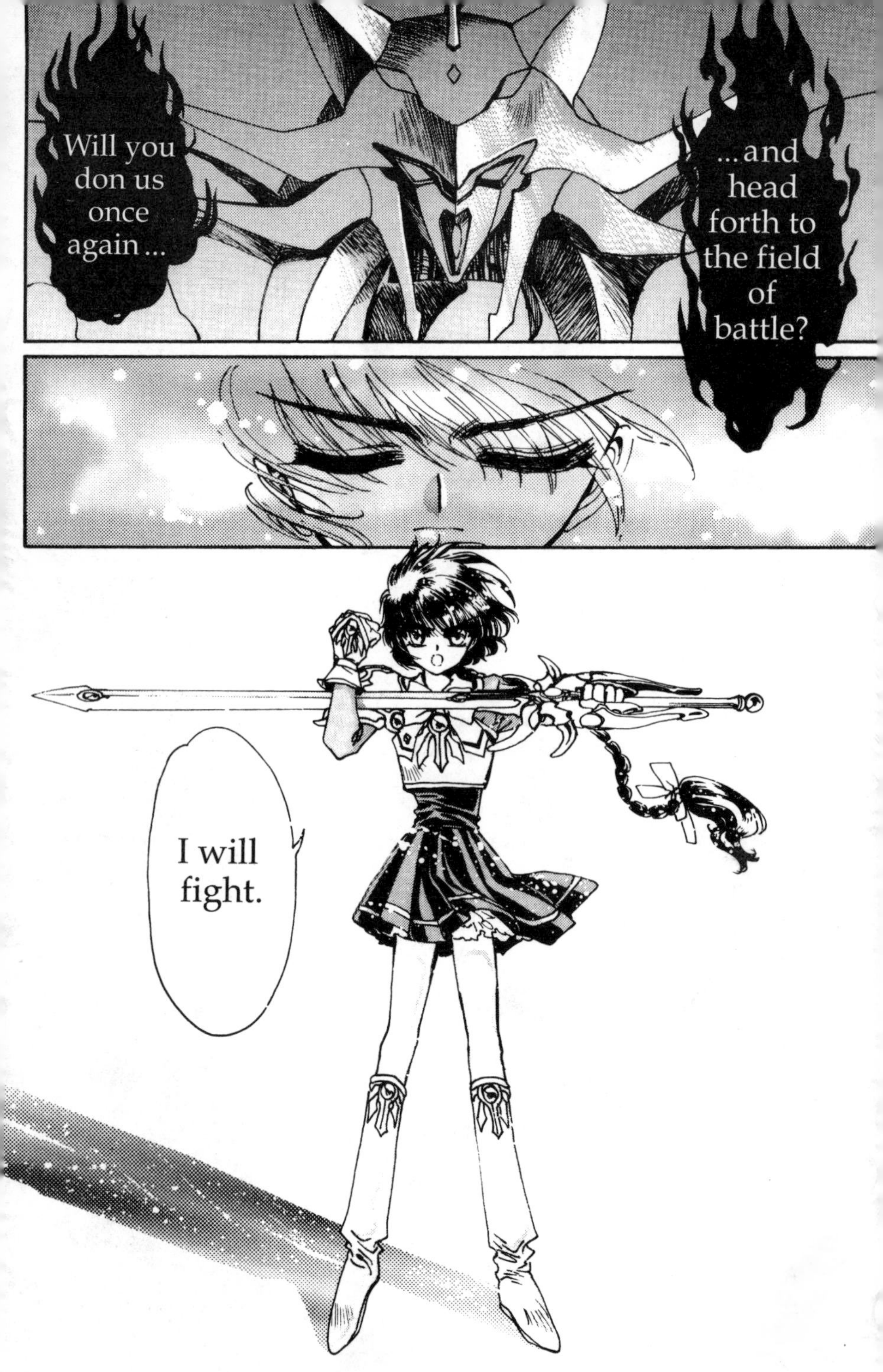
Will you don us once again ...
... and head forth to the field of battle?
I will fight.

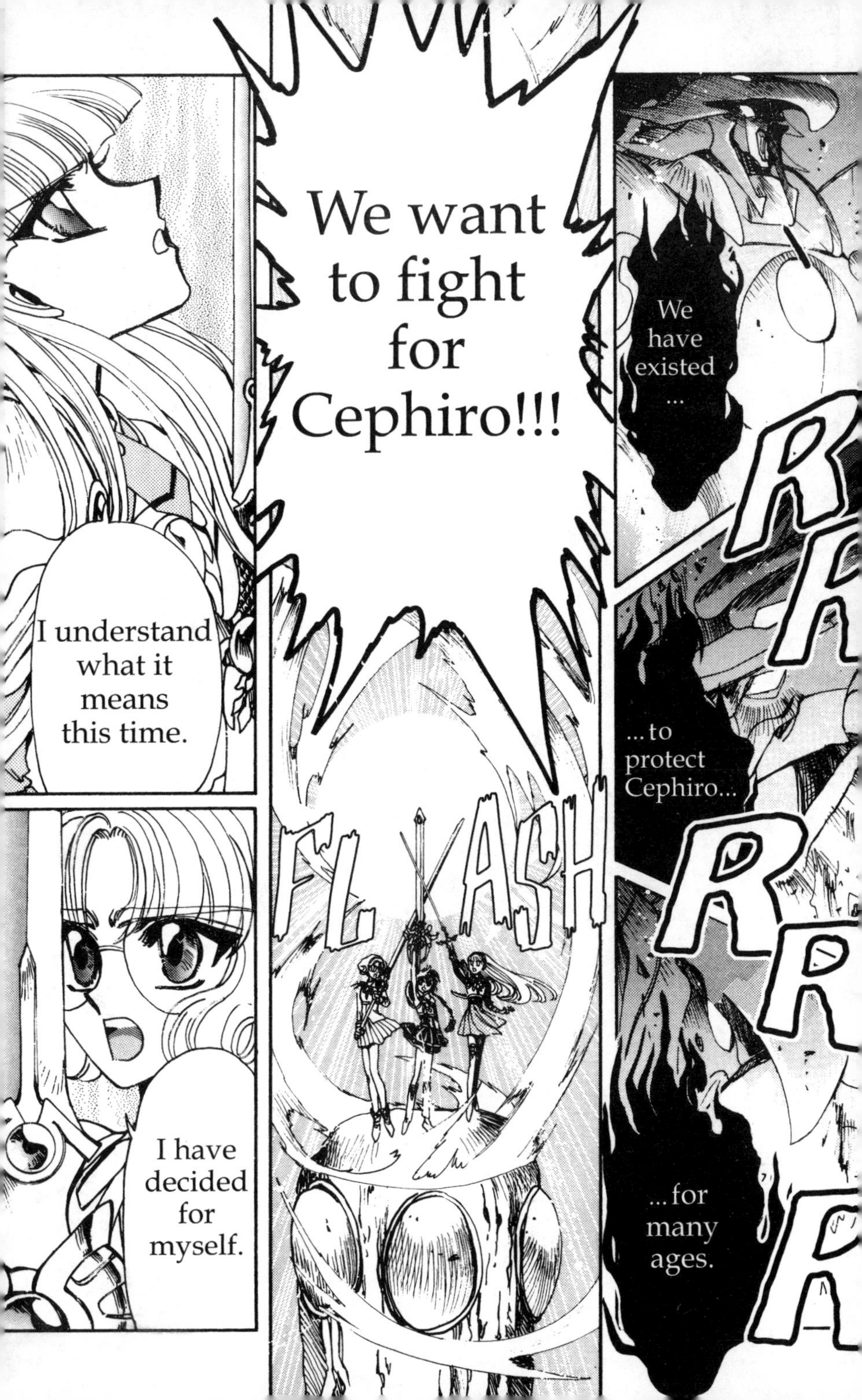

We have existed ...
... to protect Cephiro...
... for many ages.
RRRR
We want to fight for Cephiro!!!
FLASH
I understand what it means this time.
I have decided for myself.

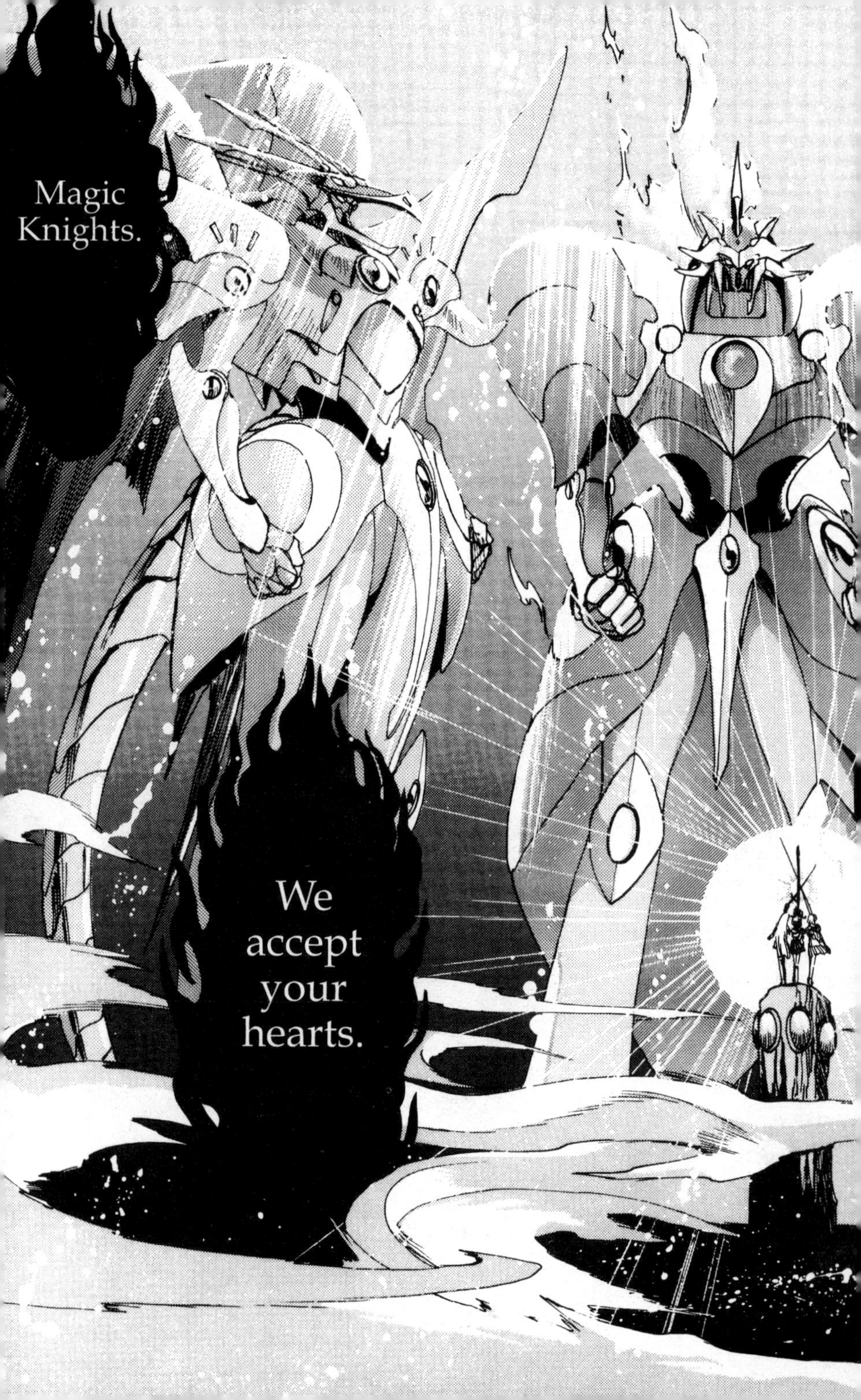
Magic Knights.
We accept your hearts.

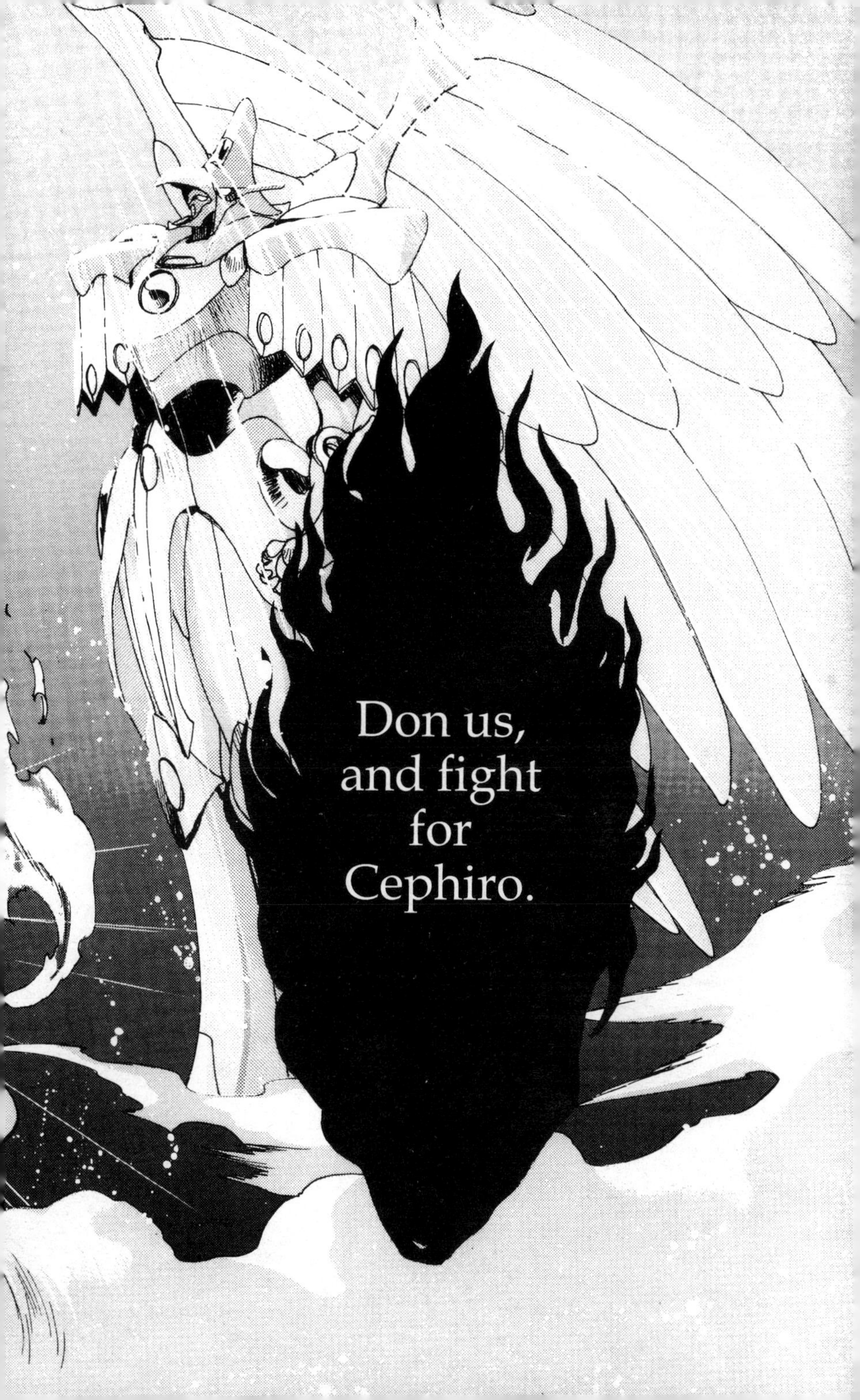
Don us,
and fight
for
Cephiro.

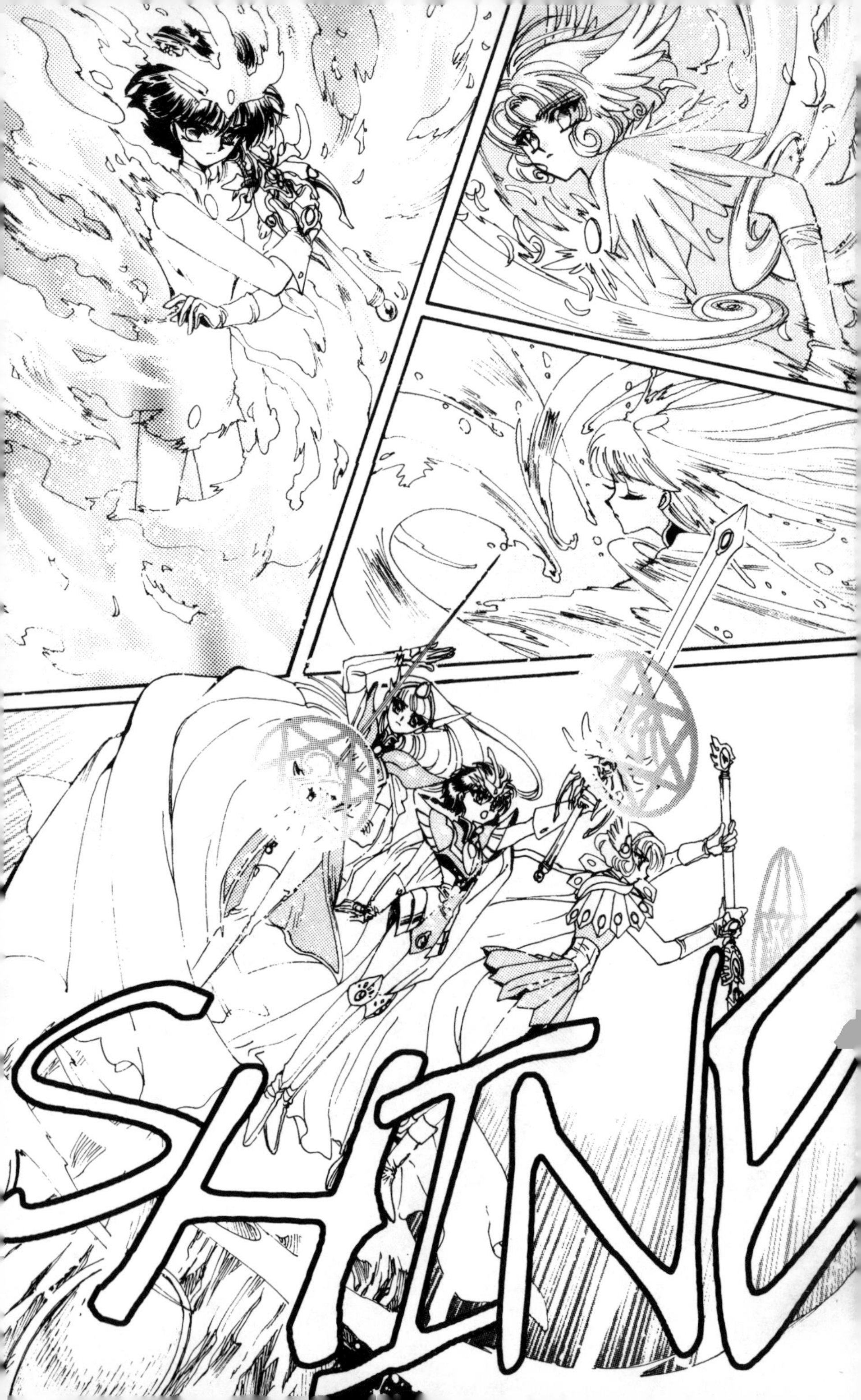
SHIN

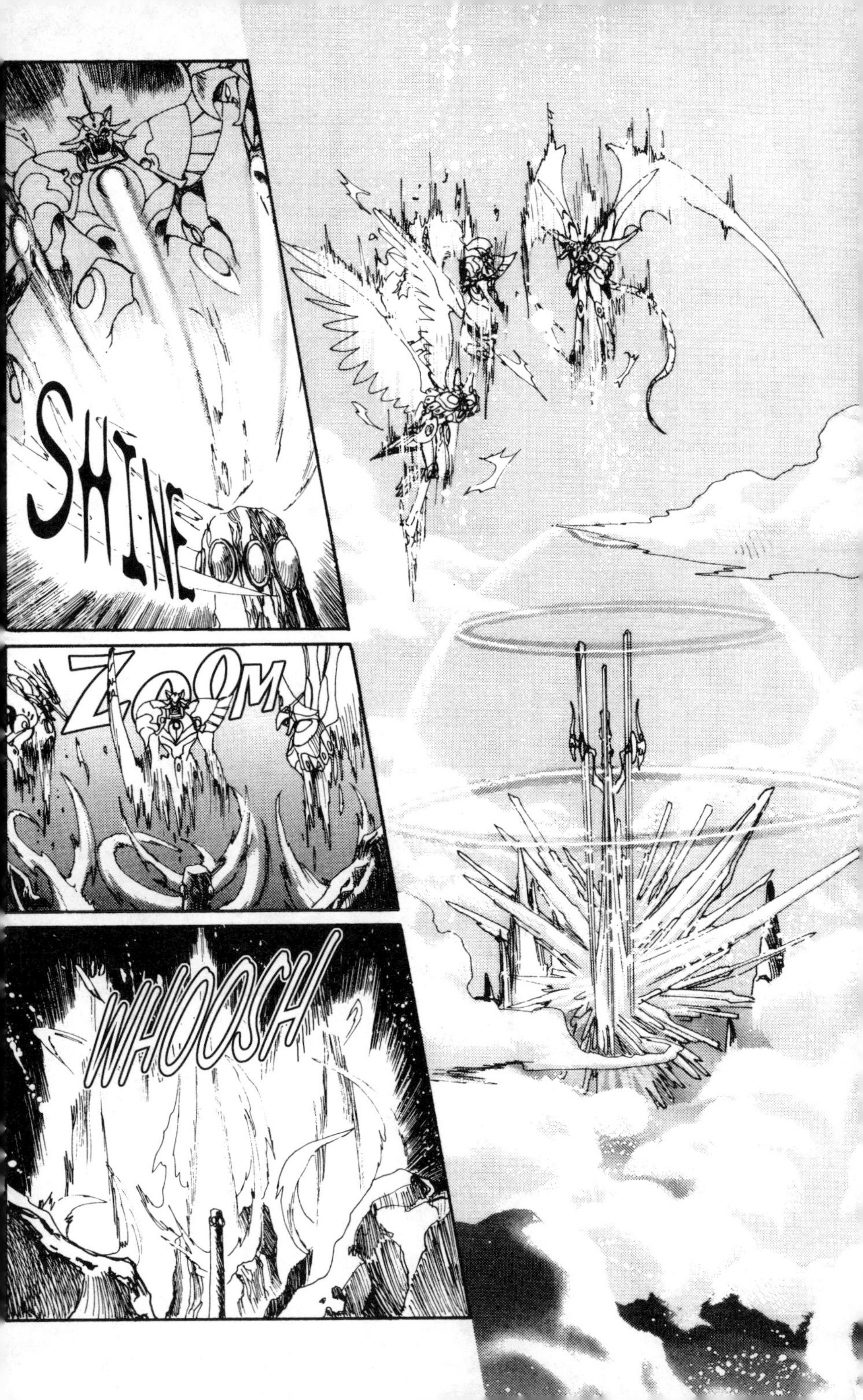

SHINE
ZOOM
WHOOSH

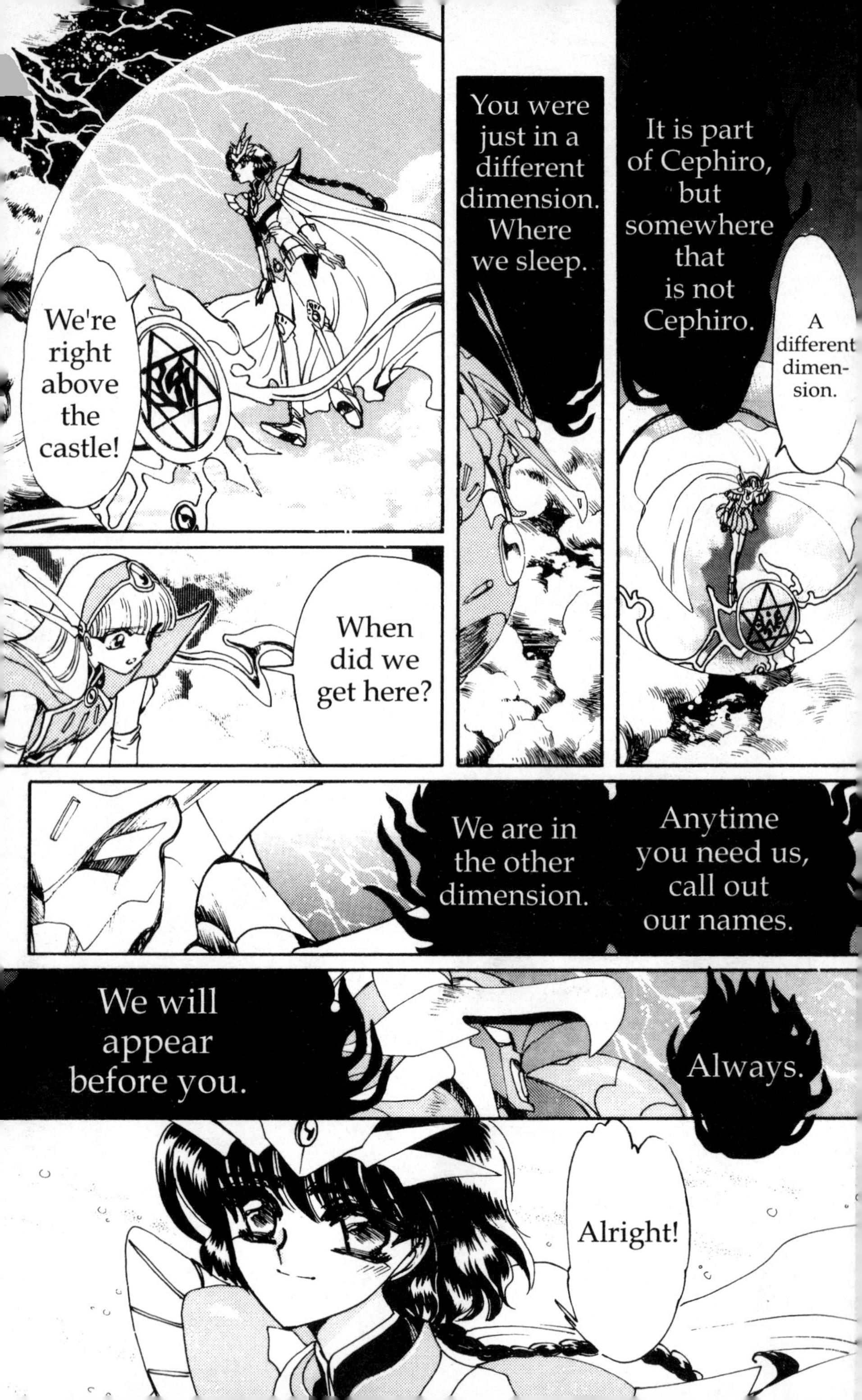
We're right above the castle!
When did we get here?
You were just in a different dimension. Where we sleep.
It is part of Cephiro, but somewhere that is not Cephiro.
A different dimension.
We are in the other dimension.
Anytime you need us, call out our names.
We will appear before you.
Always.
Alright!

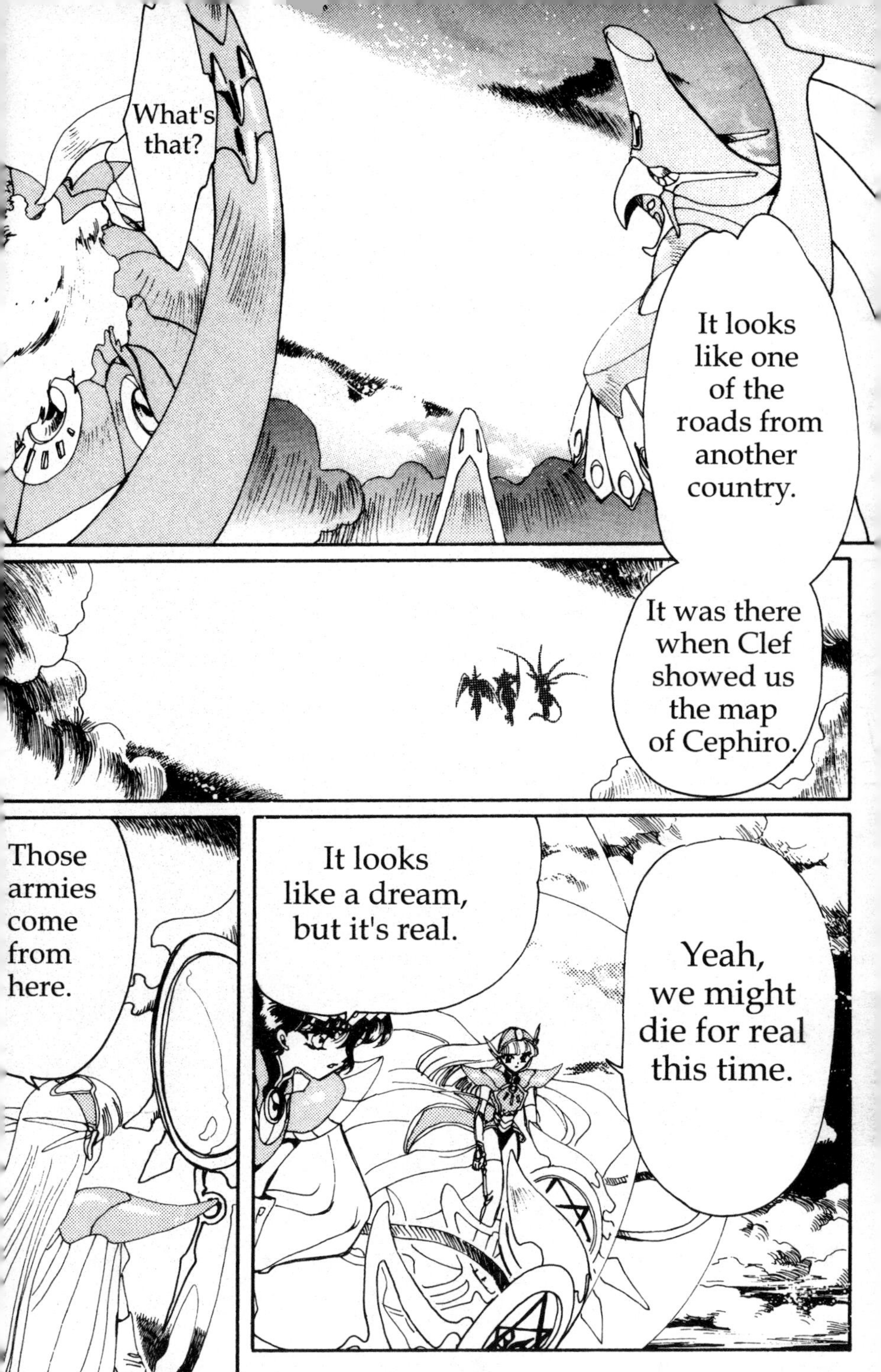
What's that?
It looks like one of the roads from another country.
It was there when Clef showed us the map of Cephiro.
Those armies come from here.
It looks like a dream, but it's real.
Yeah, we might die for real this time.

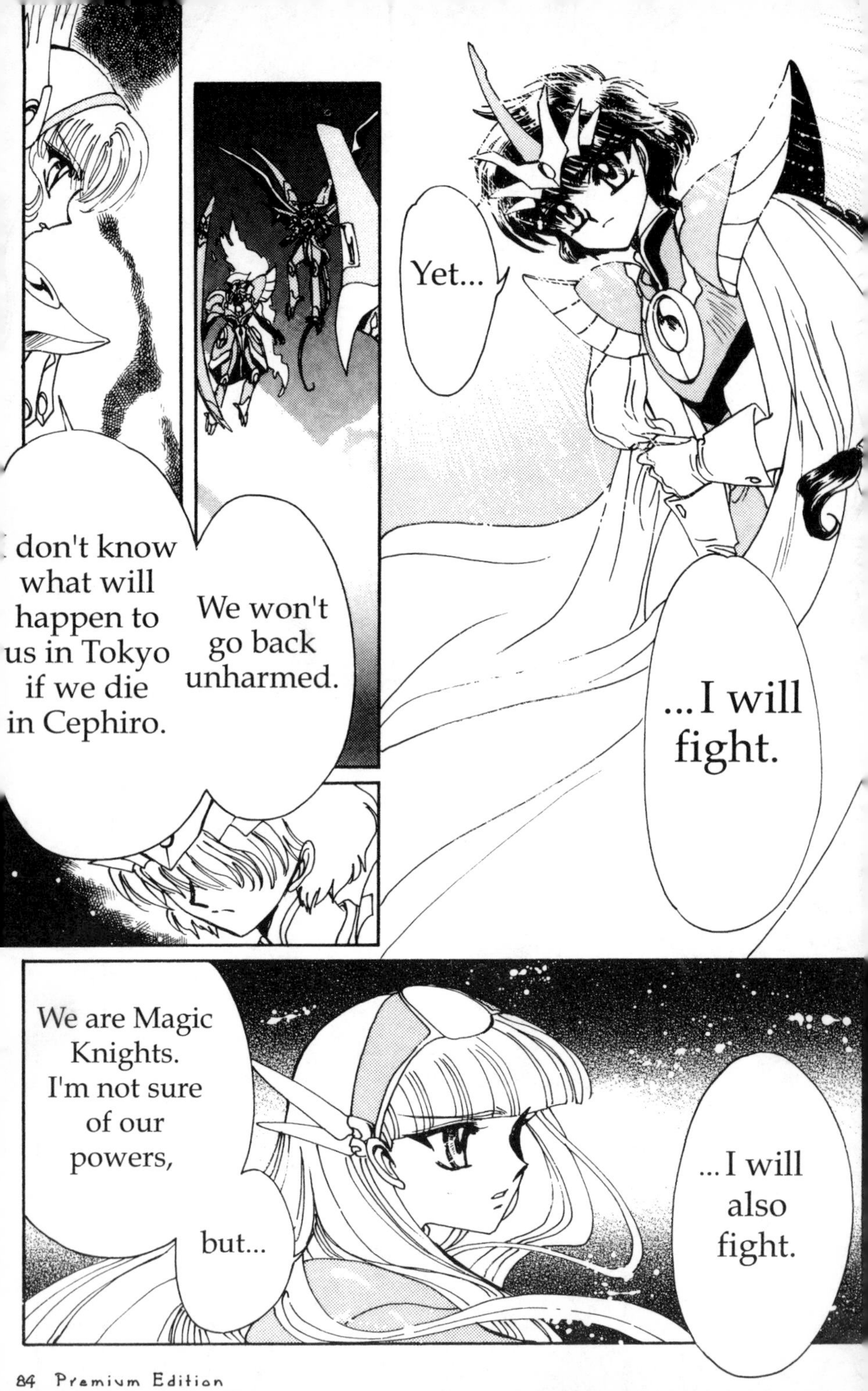
don't know what will happen to us in Tokyo if we die in Cephiro.
We won't go back unharmed.
Yet...
...I will fight.
We are Magic Knights. I'm not sure of our powers,
but...
...I will also fight.

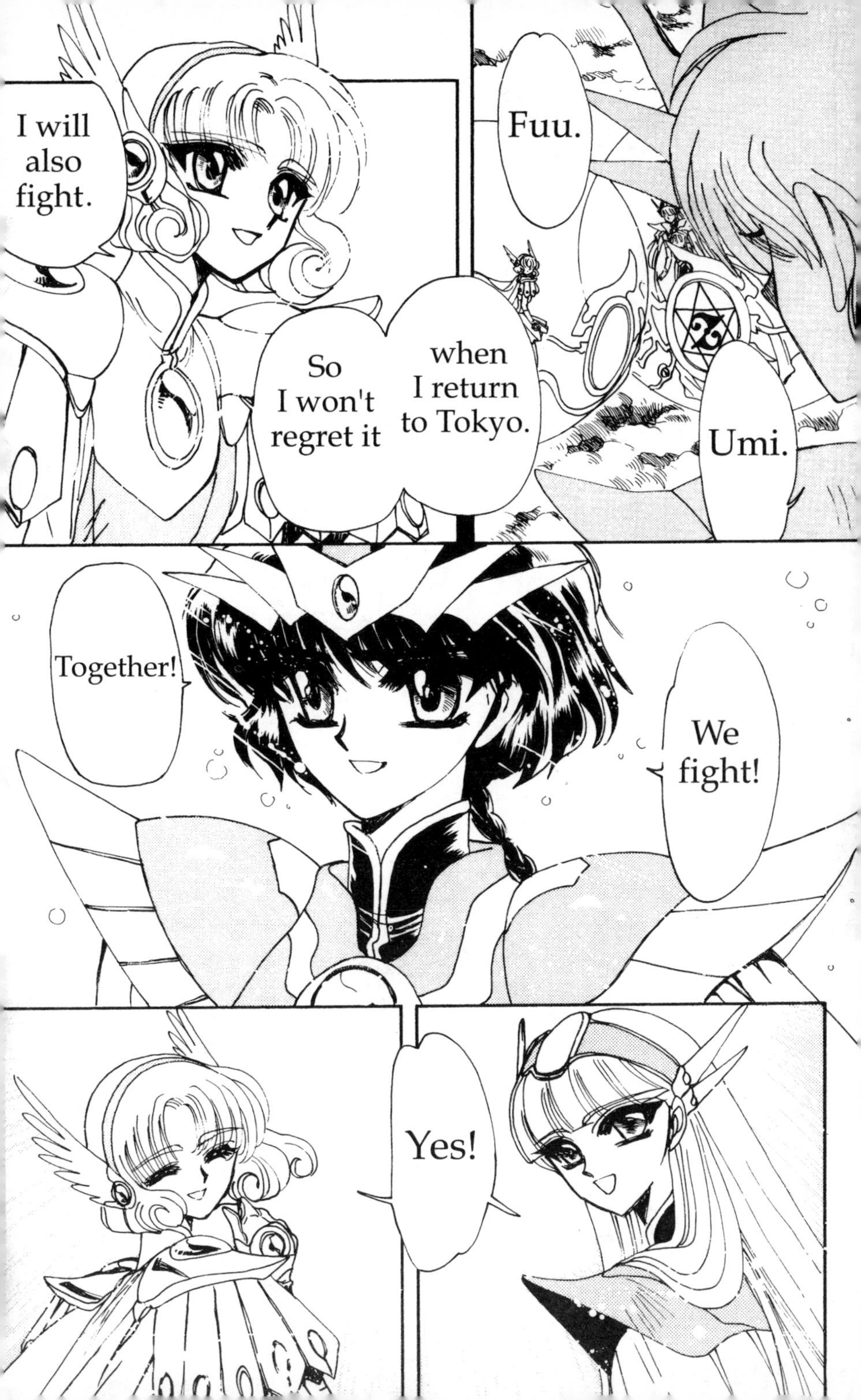
I will also fight.
So I won't regret it
when I return to Tokyo.
Fuu.
Umi.
Together!
We fight!
Yes!

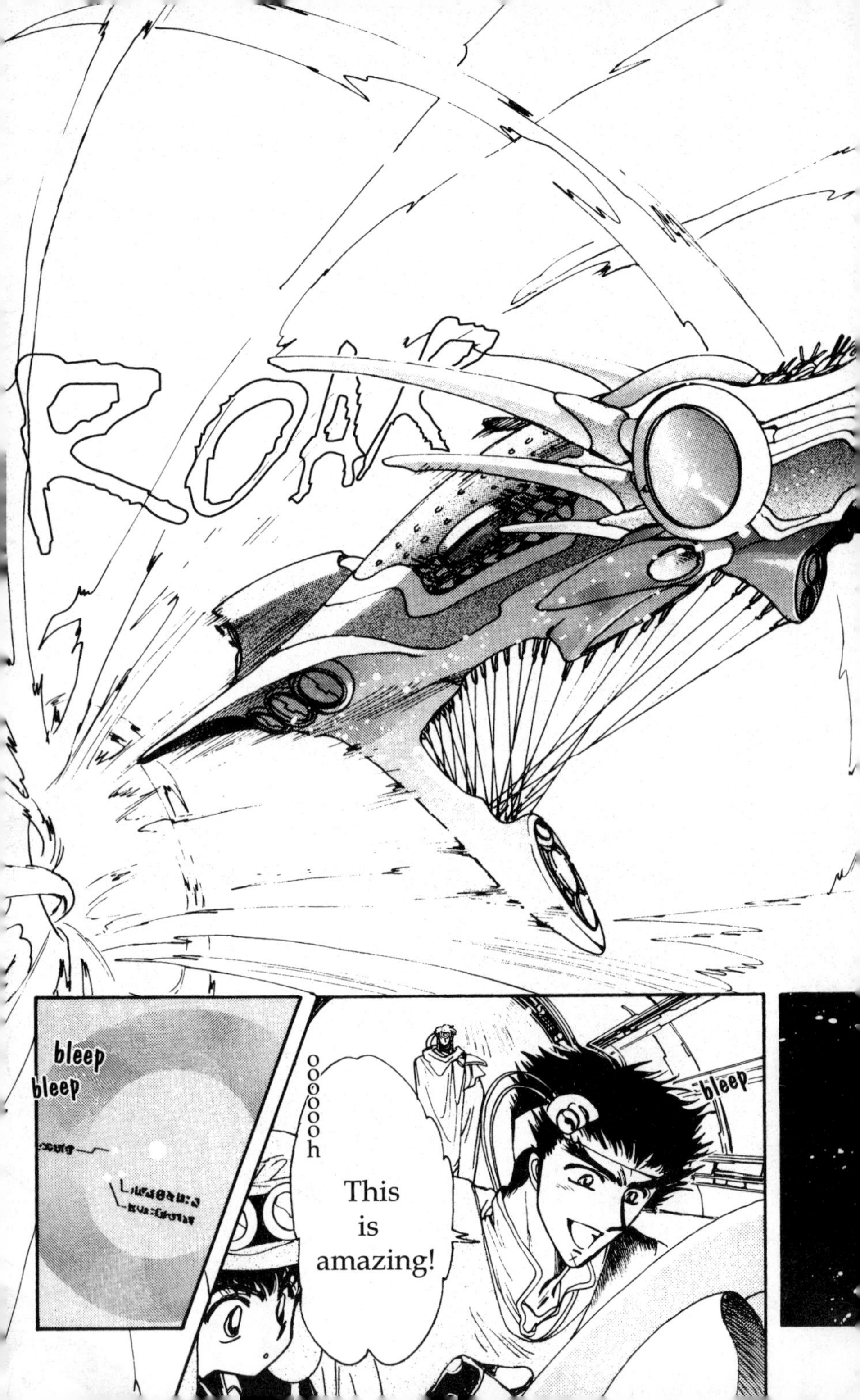
ROAR
bleep
bleep
bleep
Oooooooh
This is amazing!

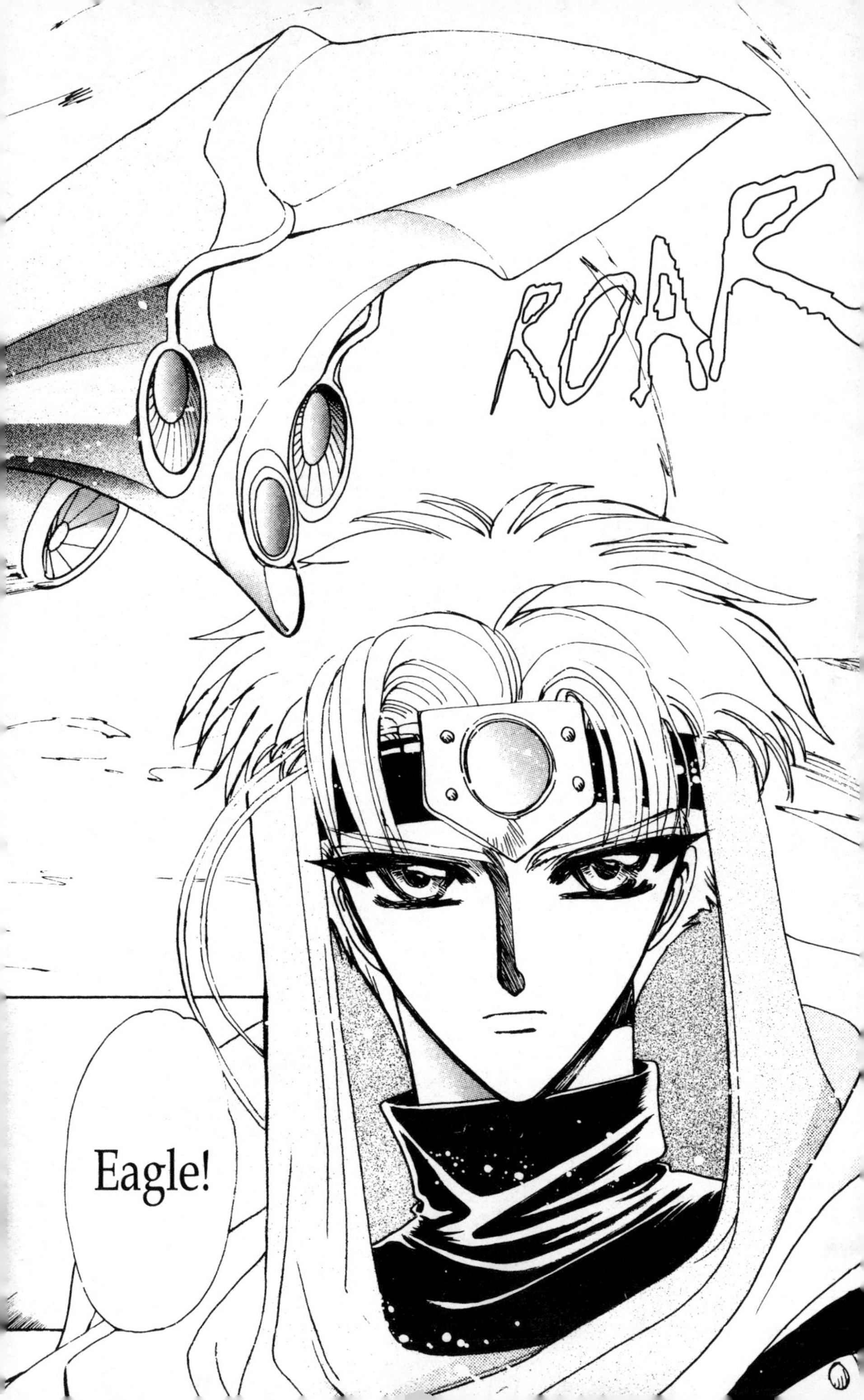
ROAR
Eagle!

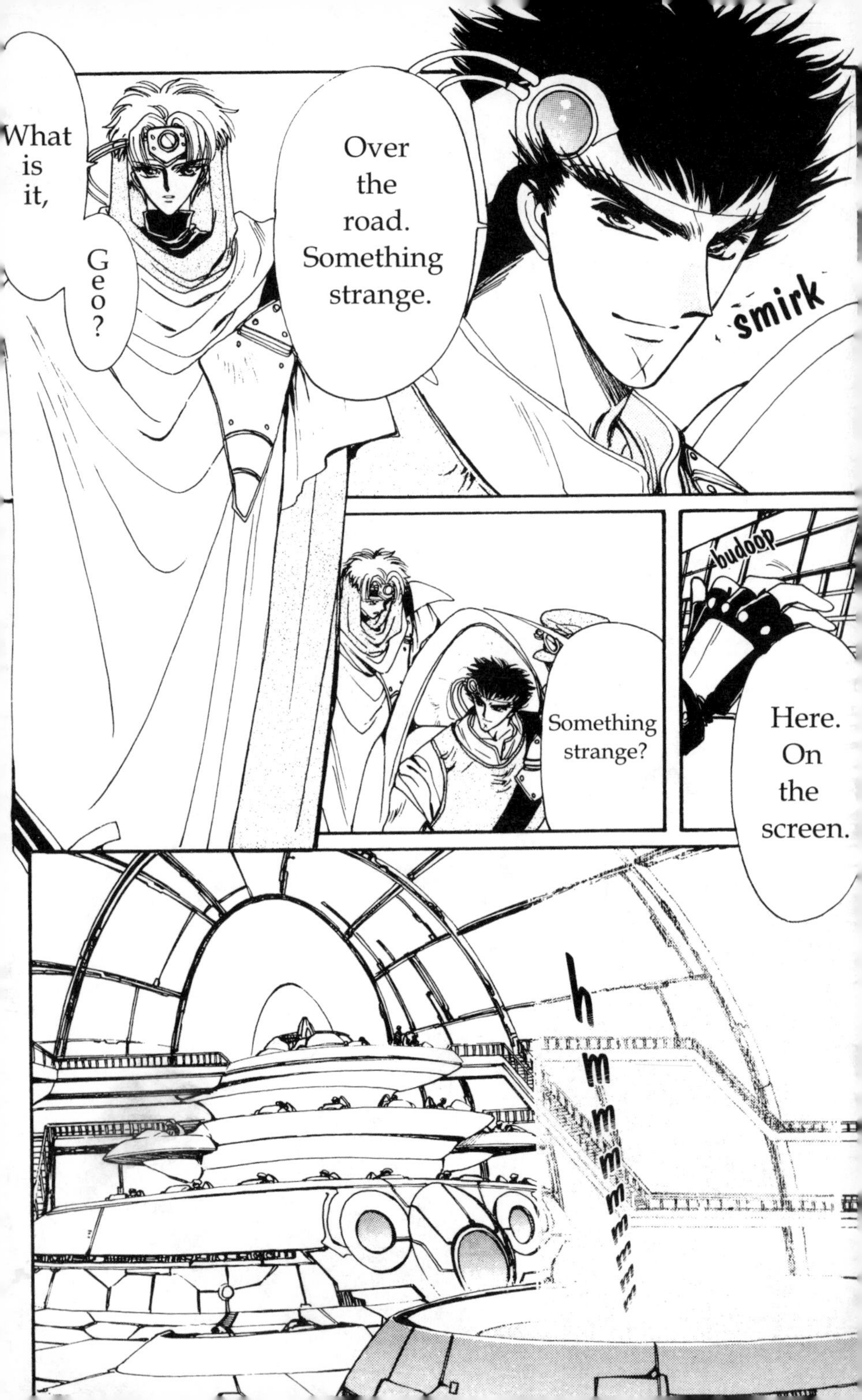
What is it, Geo?
Over the road. Something strange.
smirk
budoop
Something strange?
Here. On the screen.
hmmmmmmmm

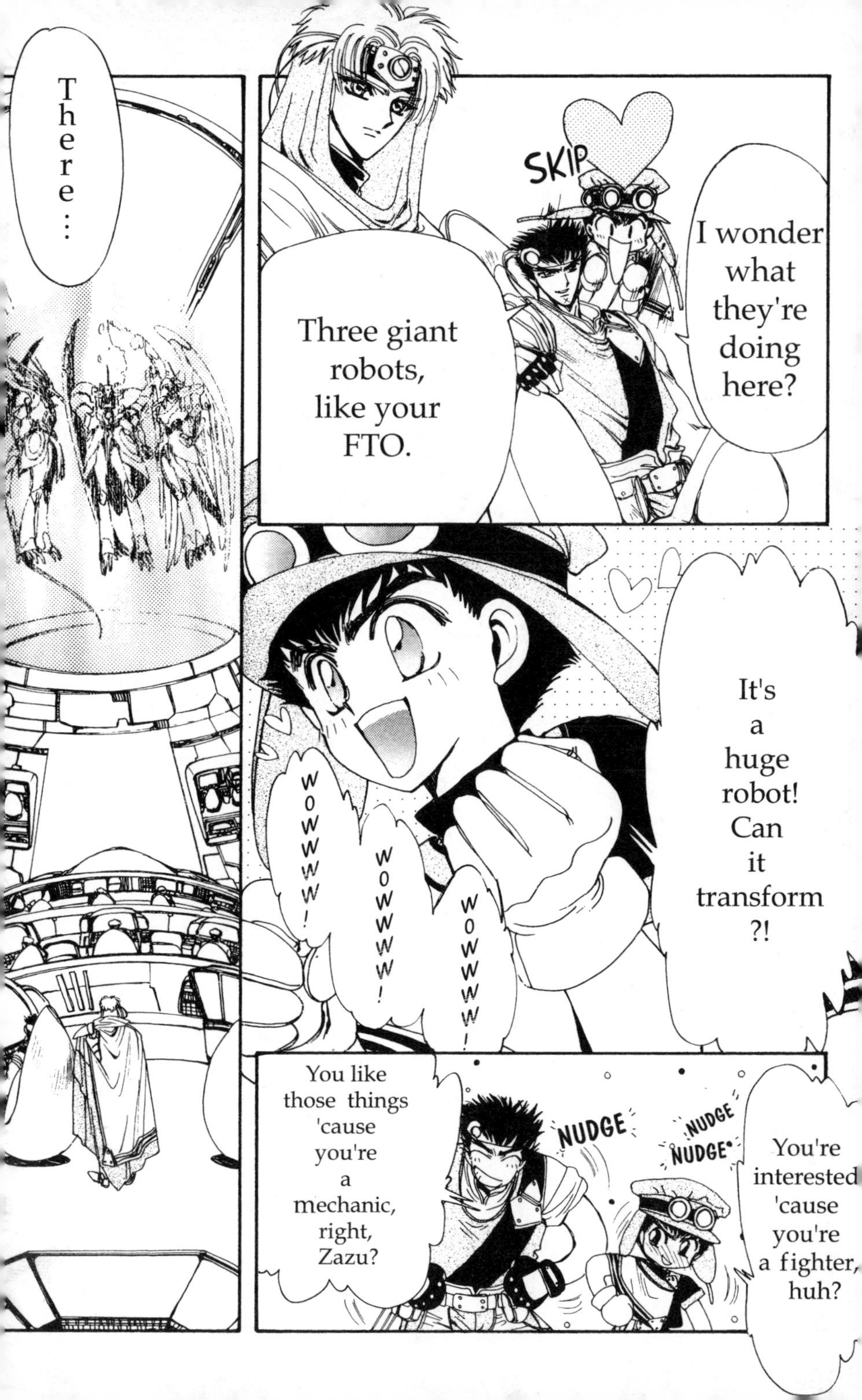

There...
Three giant robots, like your FTO.
SKIP
I wonder what they're doing here?
It's a huge robot! Can it transform?!
WOWWWWW!
WOWWWW!
WOWWWWW!
NUDGE
NUDGE NUDGE
You're interested 'cause you're a fighter, huh?
You like those things 'cause you're a mechanic, right, Zazu?

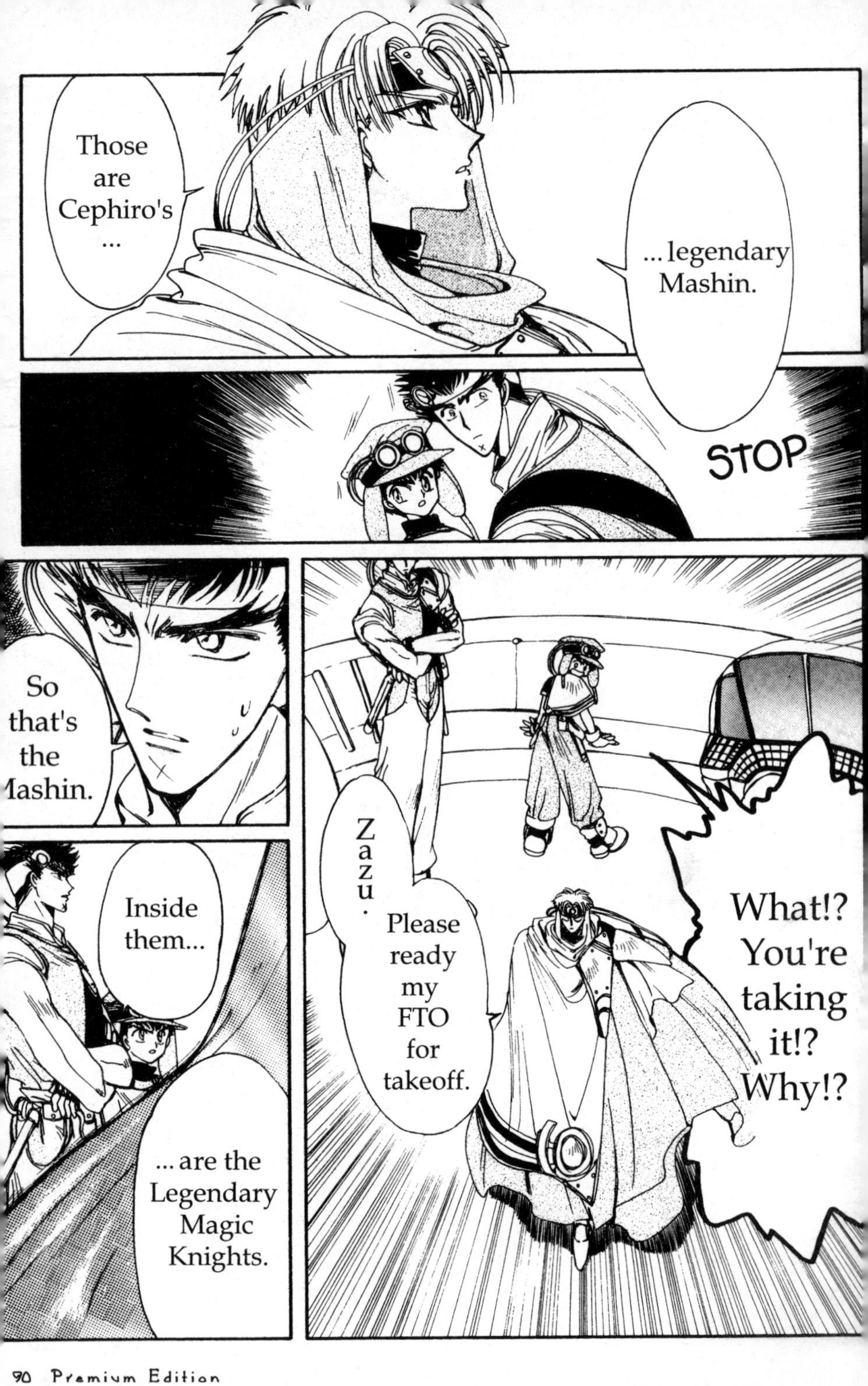

Those are Cephiro's ...
... legendary Mashin.
STOP
So that's the Mashin.
Inside them...
... are the Legendary Magic Knights.
Zazu.
Please ready my FTO for takeoff.
What!? You're taking it!? Why!?

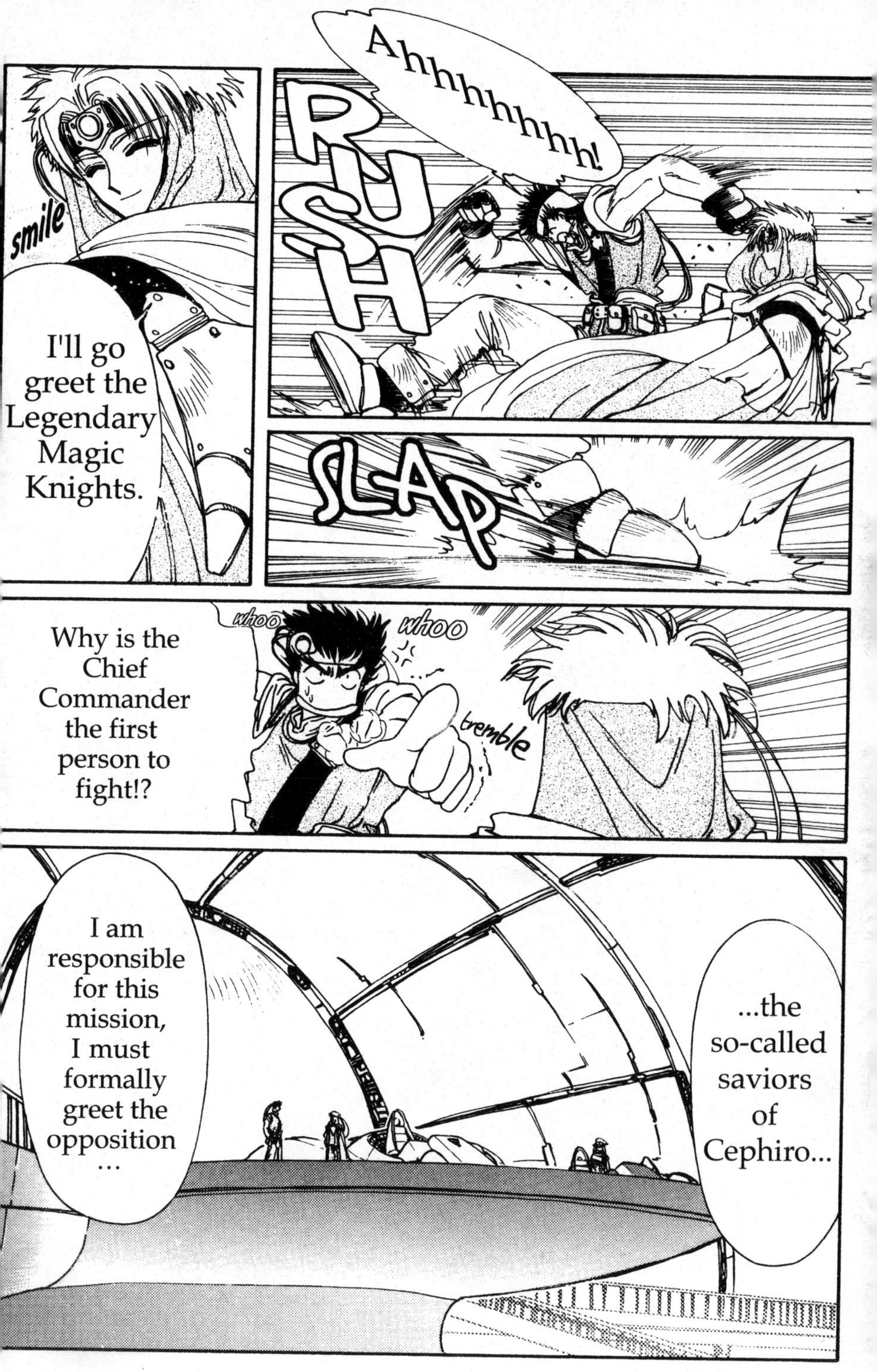
smile
I'll go greet the Legendary Magic Knights.
Ahhhhhhhh!
RUSH
SLAP
Why is the Chief Commander the first person to fight!?
whoo
whoo
tremble
I am responsible for this mission, I must formally greet the opposition ...
...the so-called saviors of Cephiro...

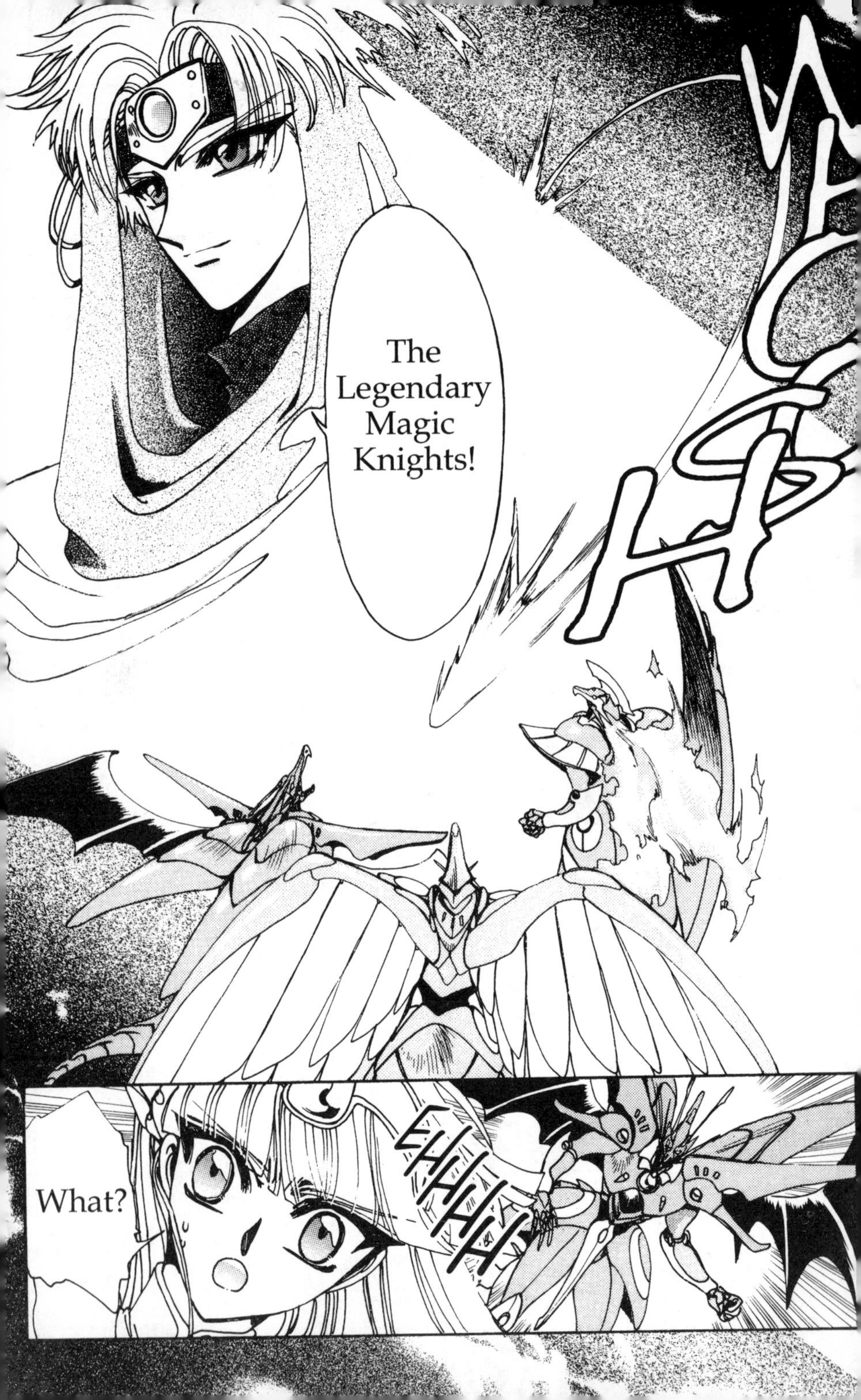
The Legendary Magic Knights!
What?

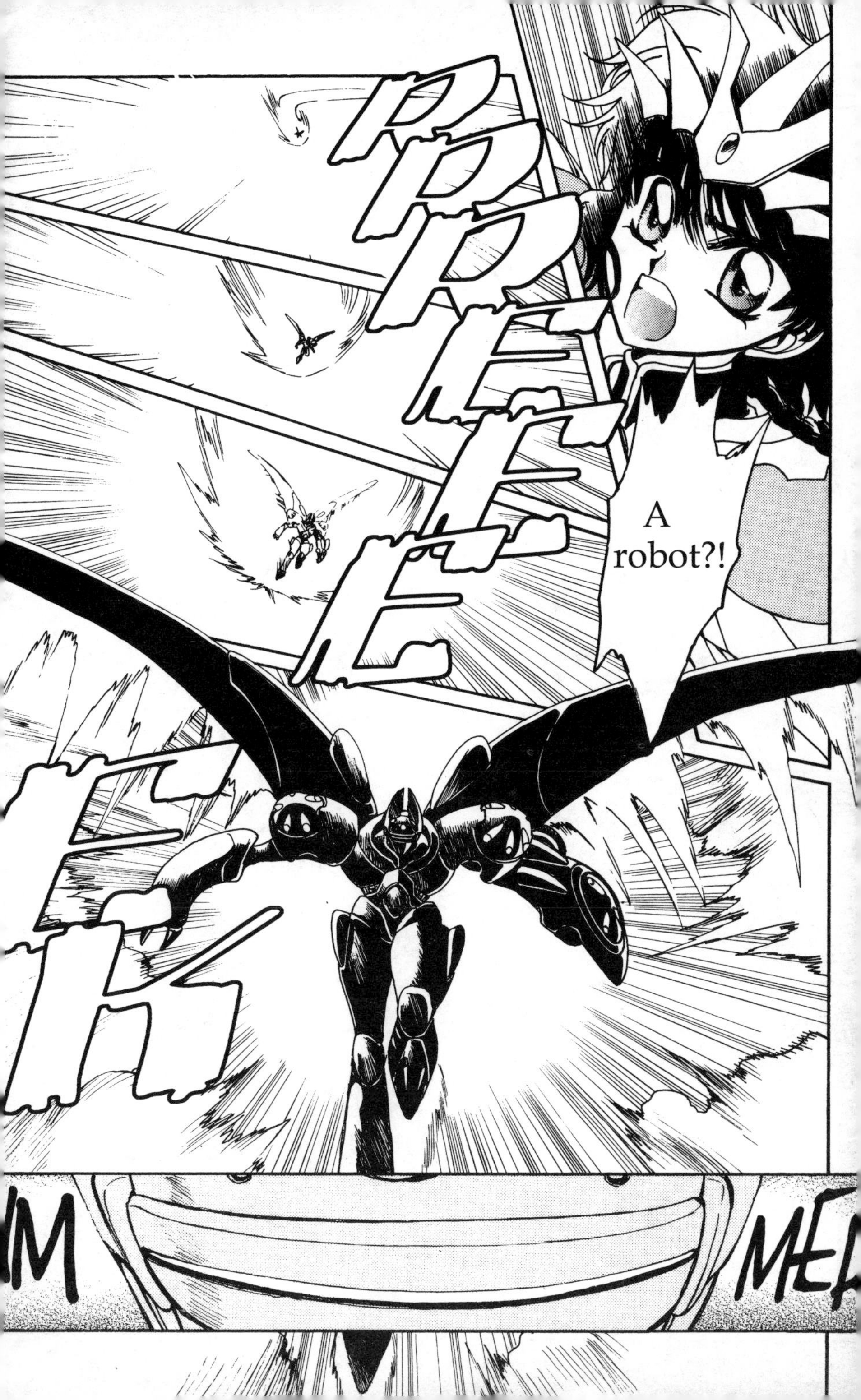
A robot?!

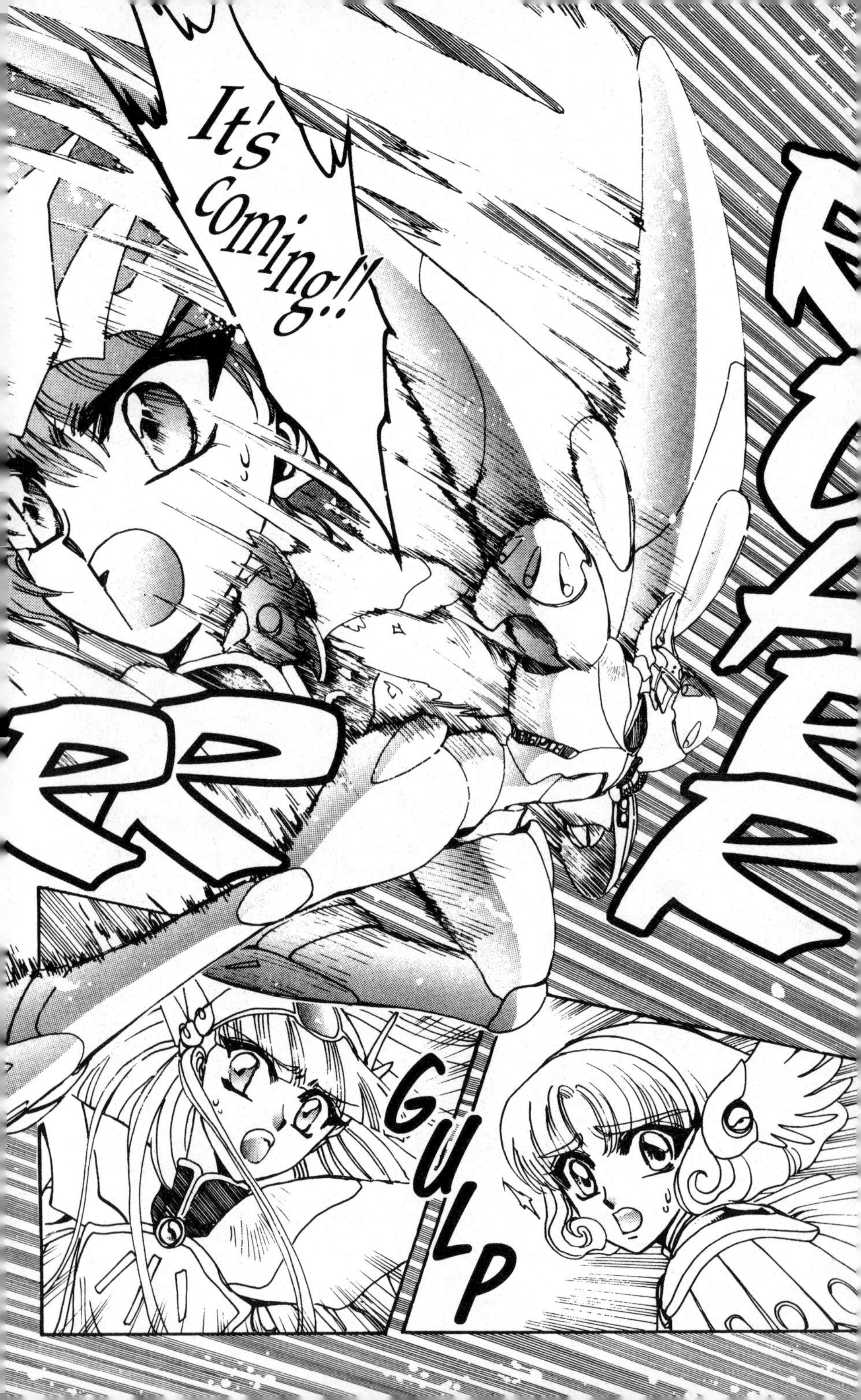
It's coming!!
GULP

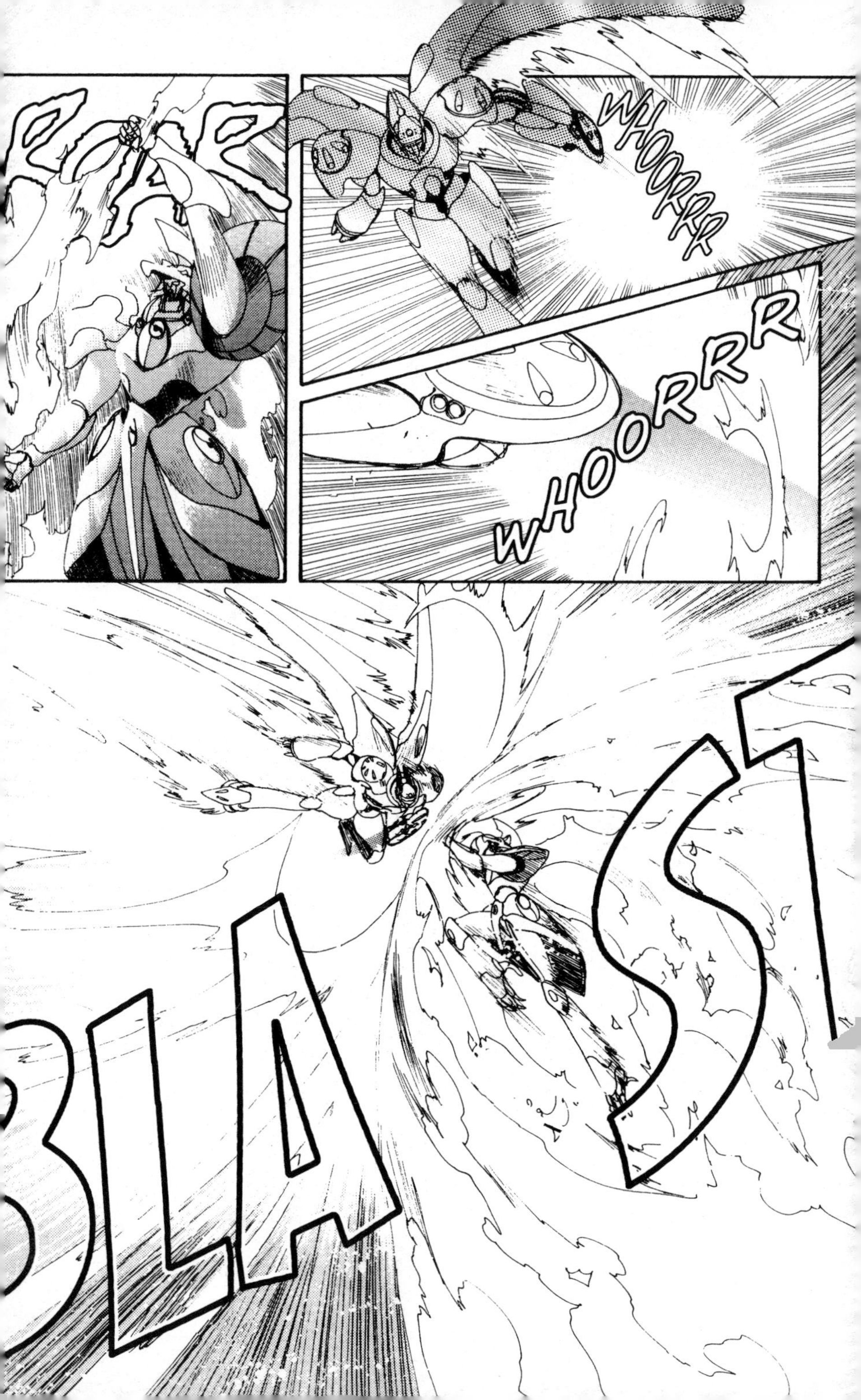
WHOORRR
WHOORRR
BLAST

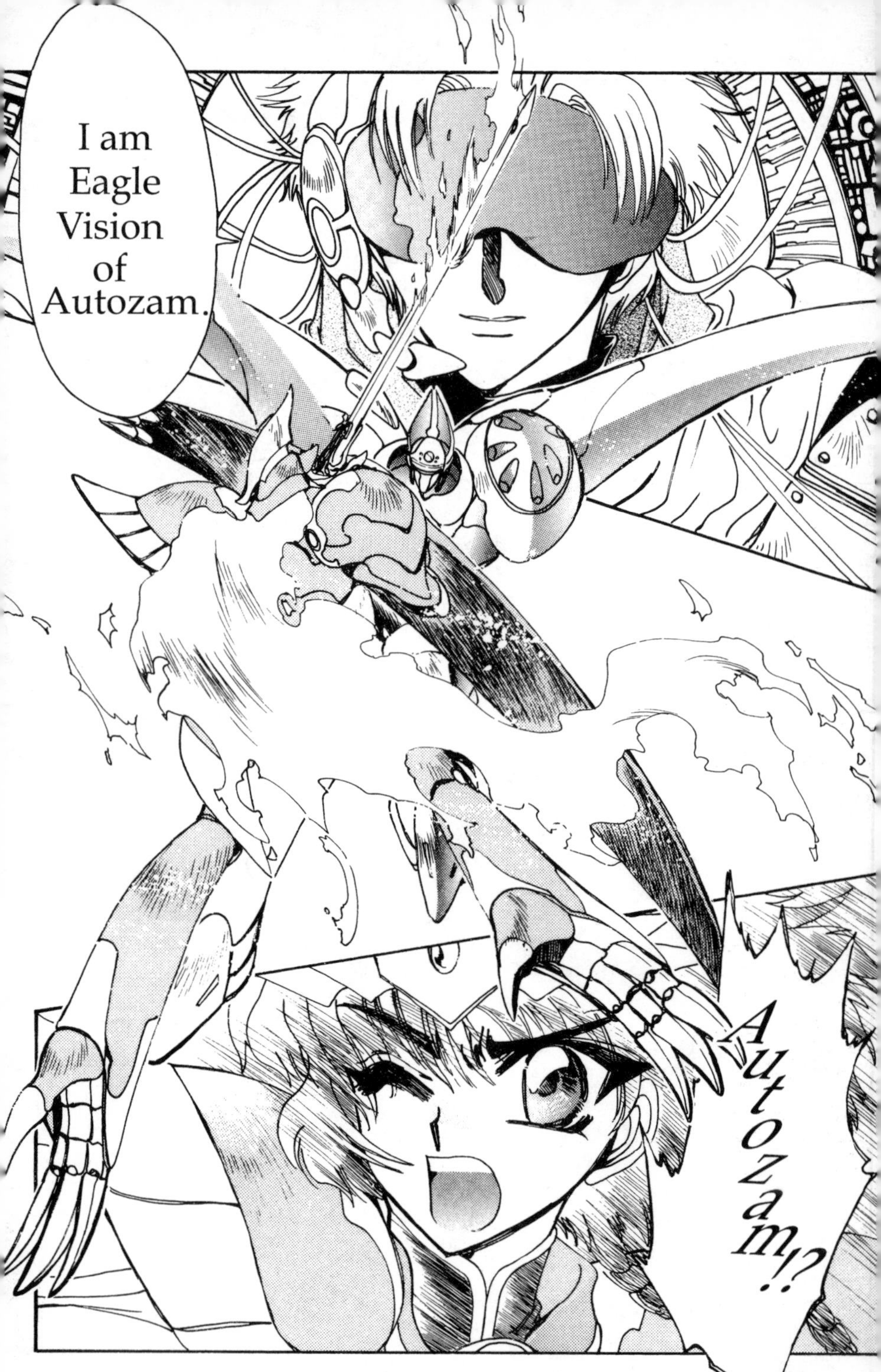
I am Eagle Vision of Autozam.
Autozam!?

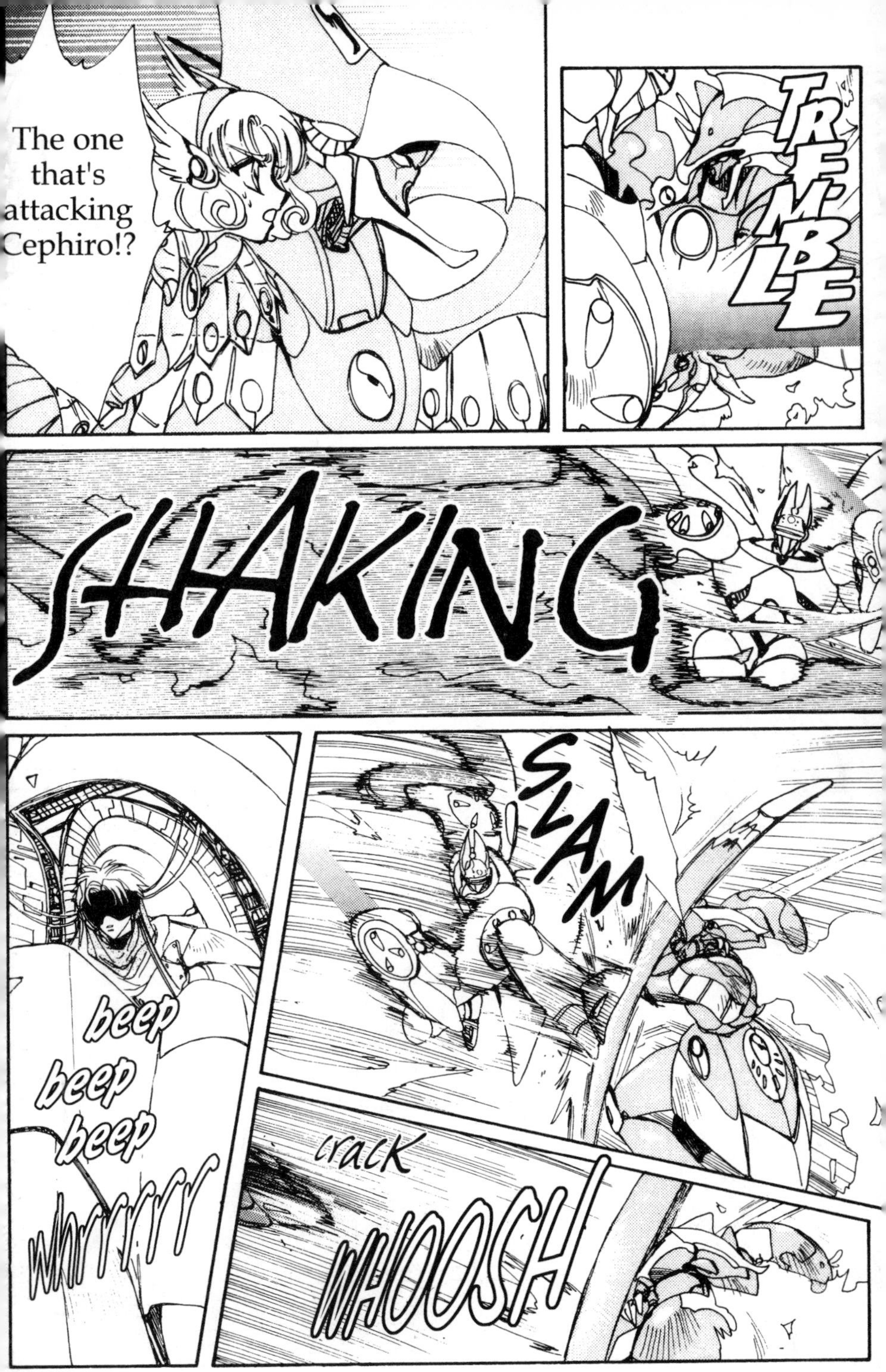
The one that's attacking Cephiro!?
TREMBLE
SHAKING
beep beep beep
whrrrrrrr
SLAM
crack
WHOOSH

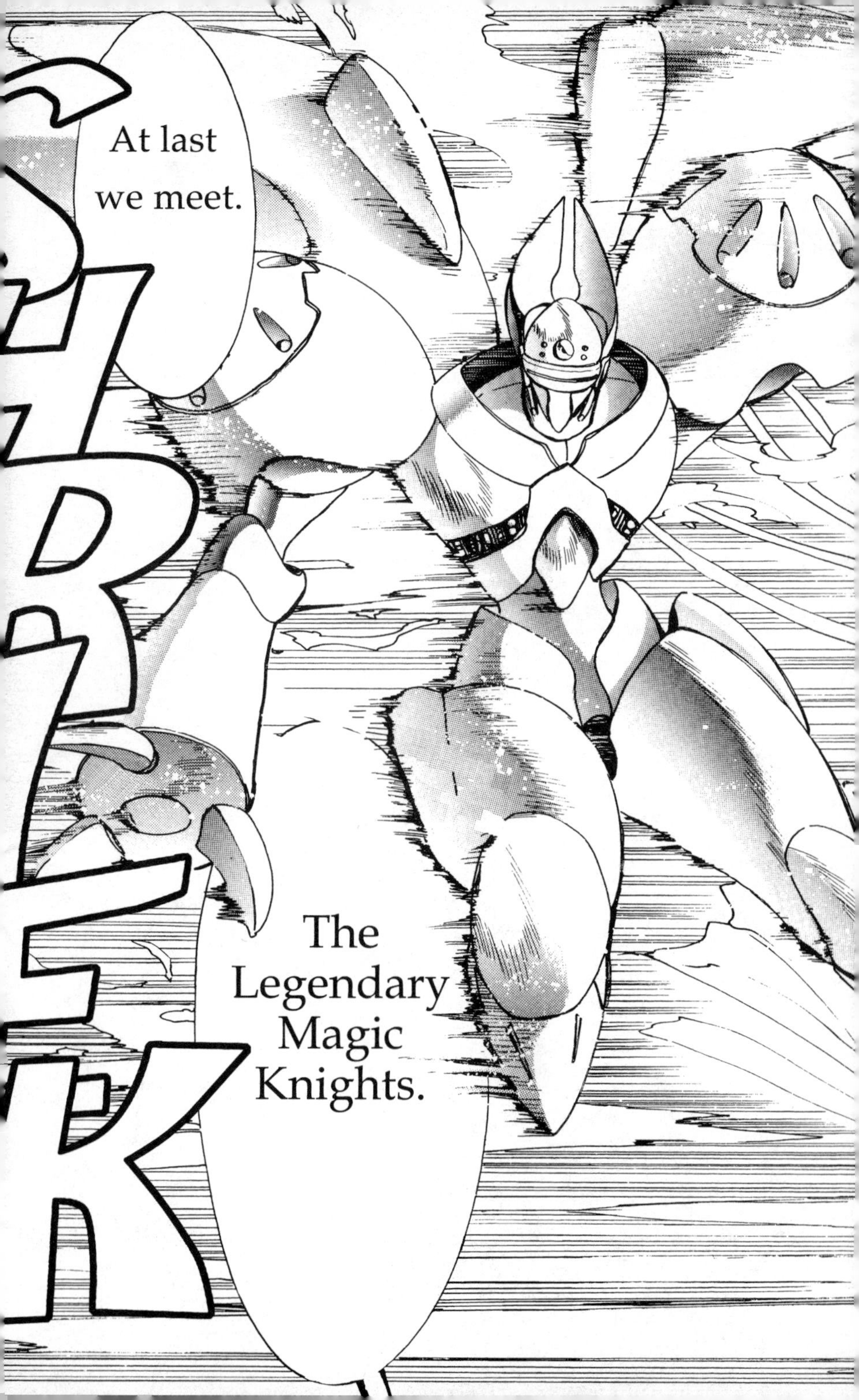
At last we meet.
The Legendary Magic Knights.

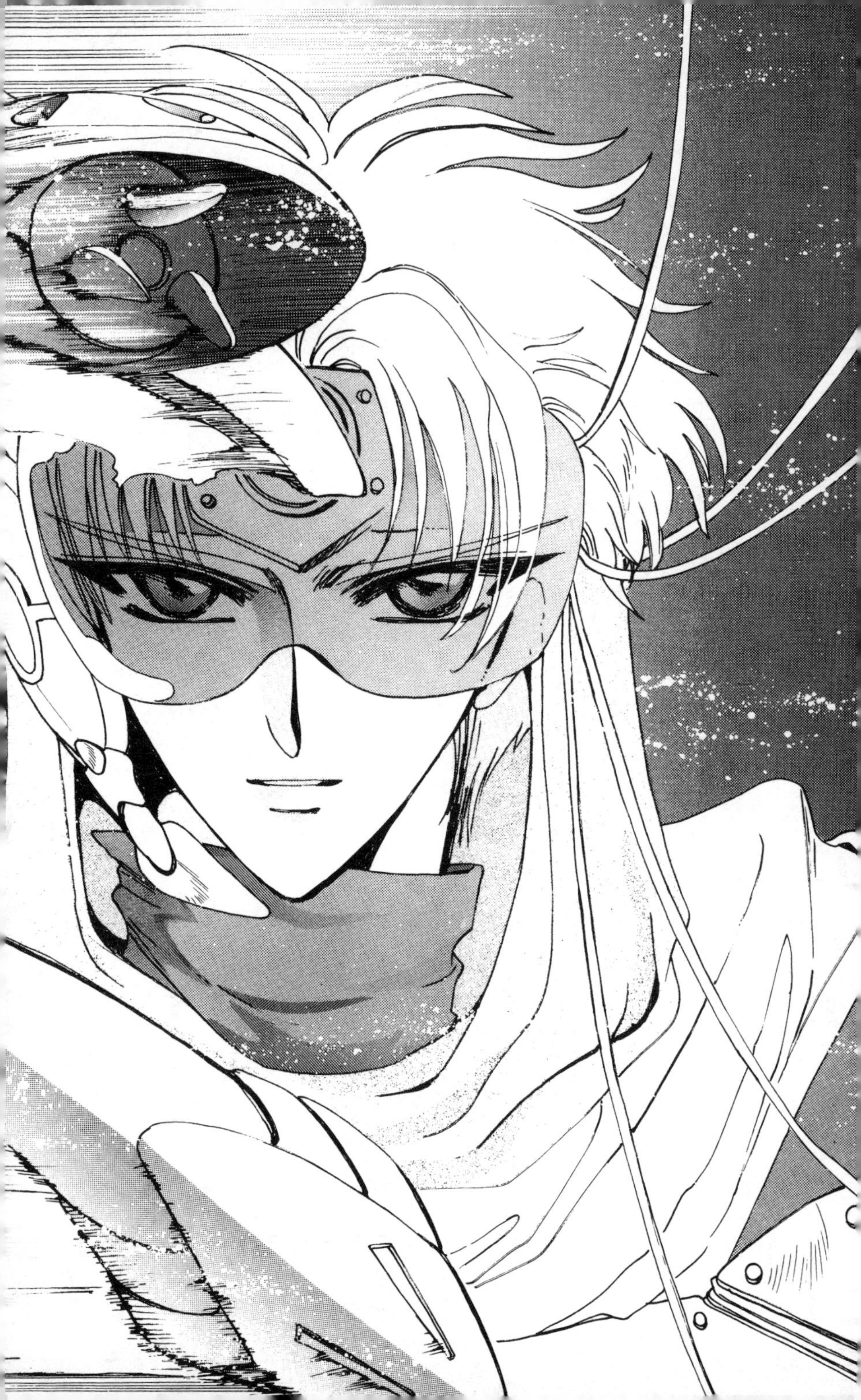

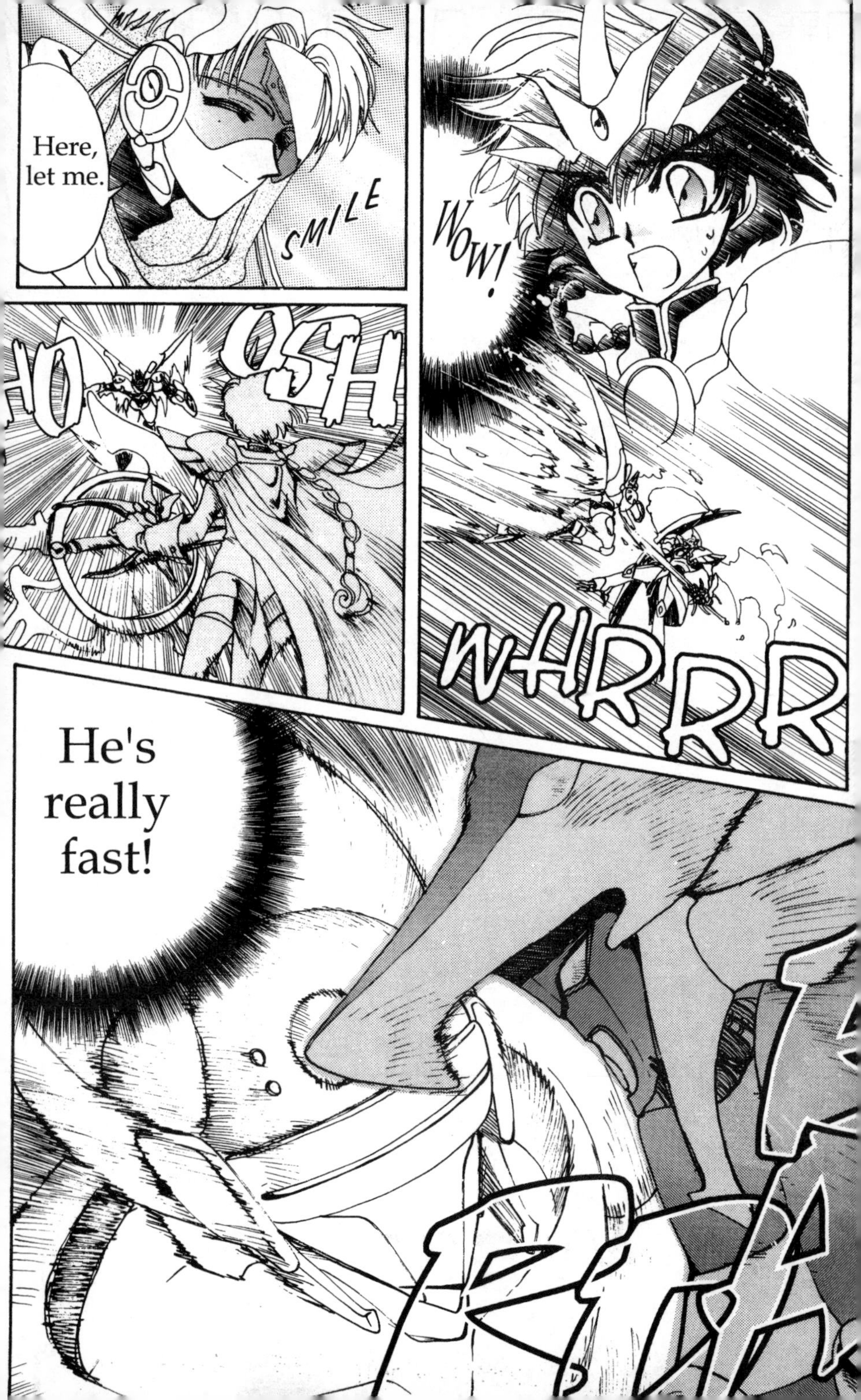
WOW!
Here, let me.
SMILE
WHOOSH
WHRRR
He's really fast!

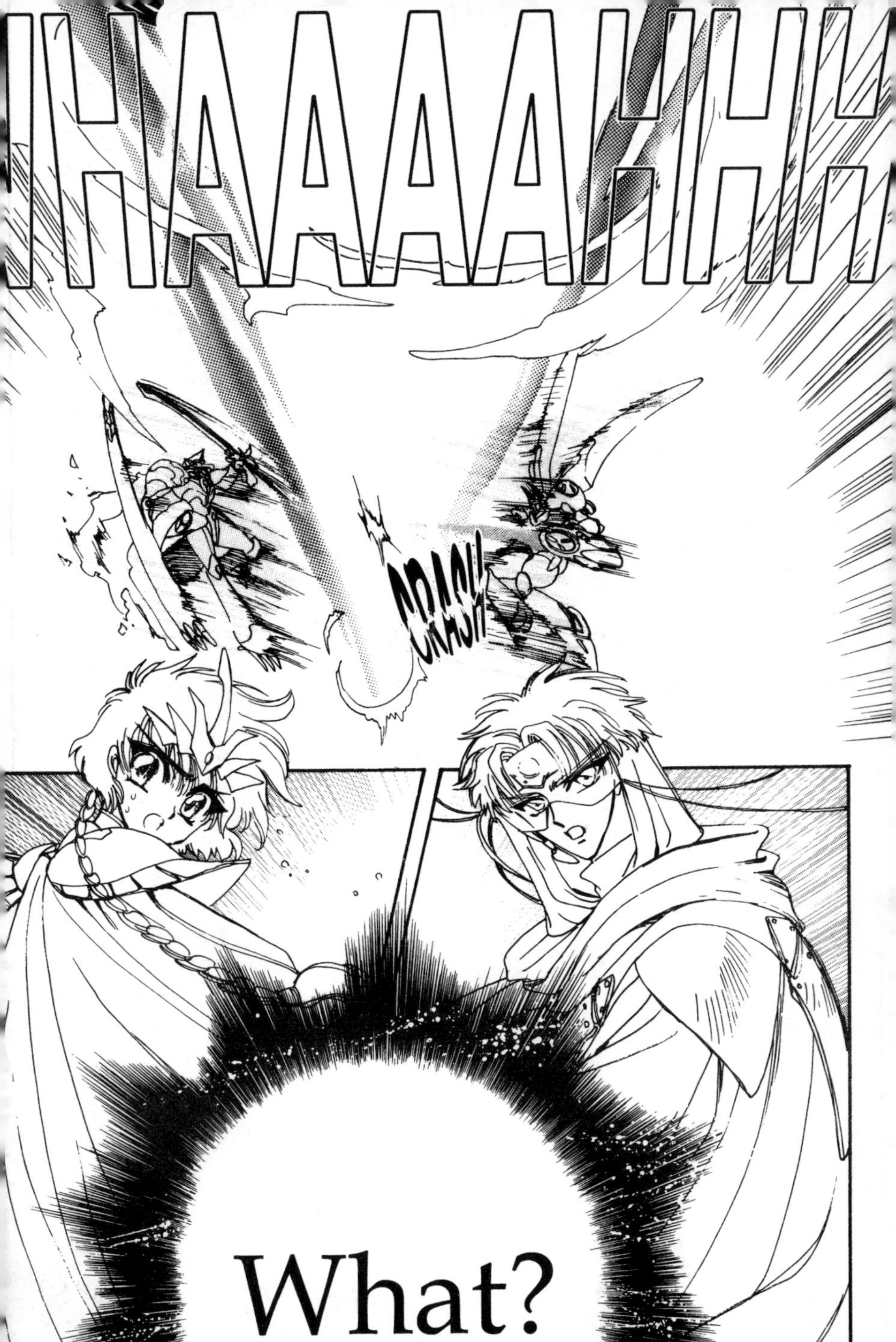
HAAAAHHH
CRASH
What?

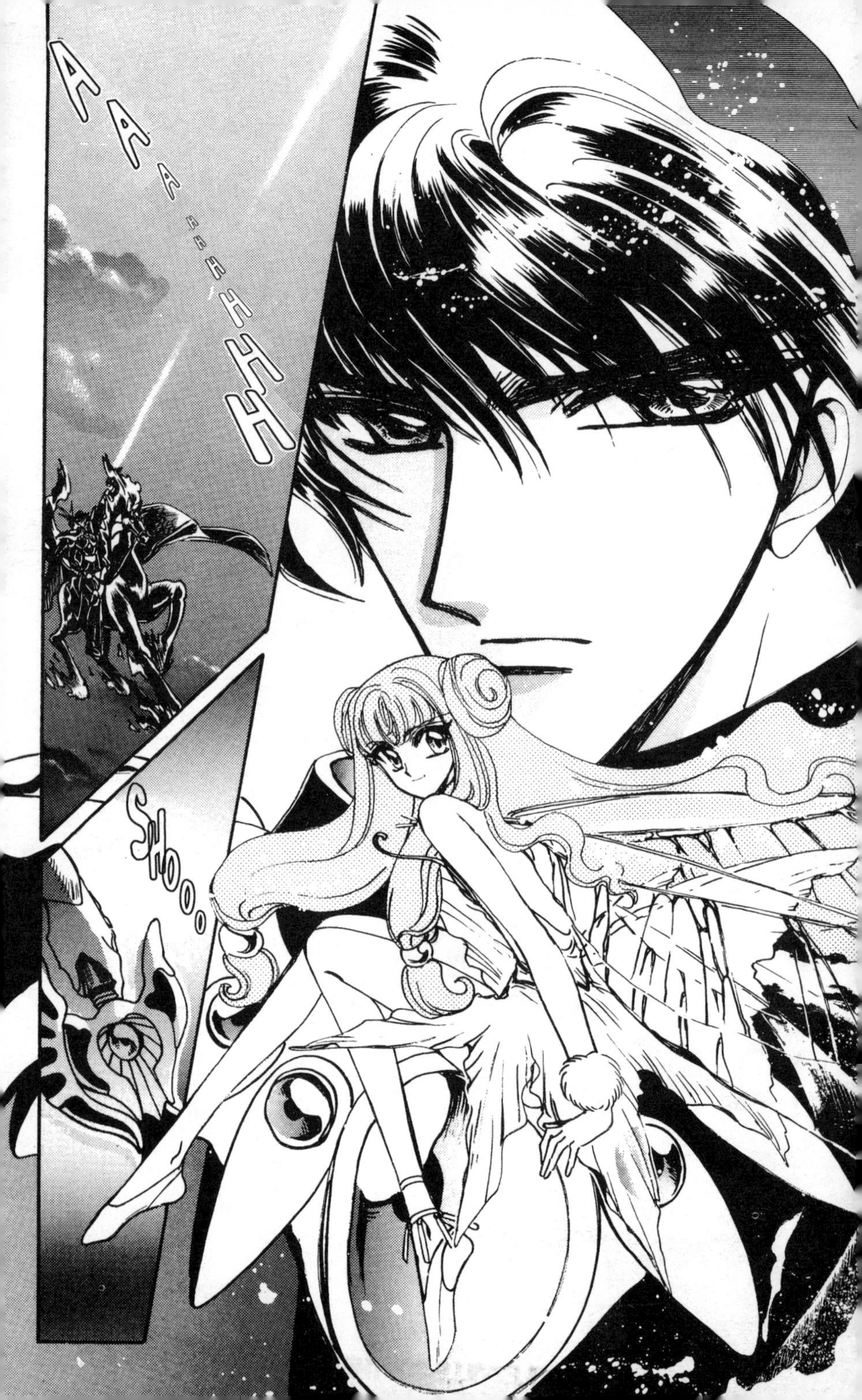
AAAHHHHHH
SHOOOO

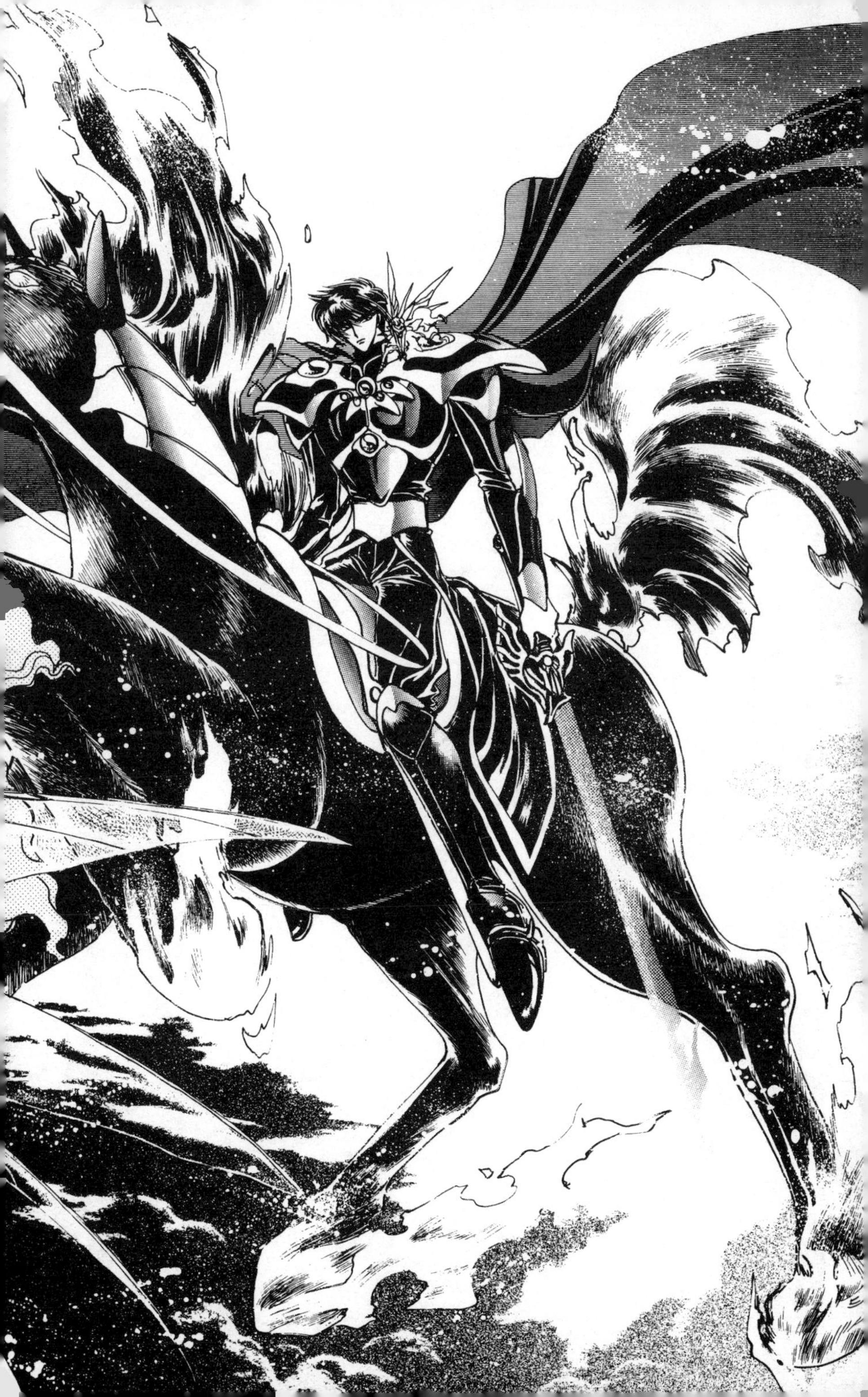

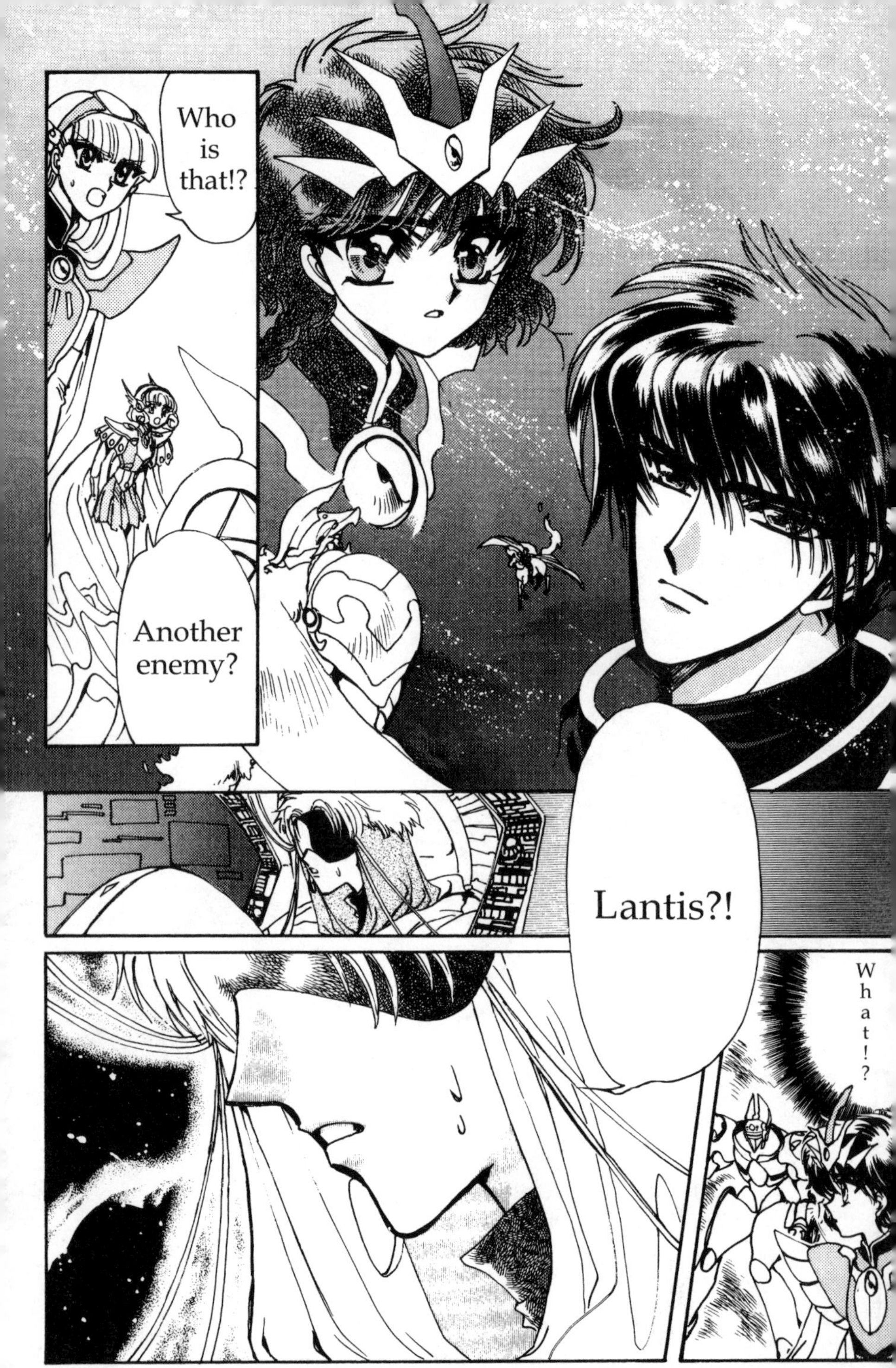
Who is that!?
Another enemy?
Lantis?!
What!?

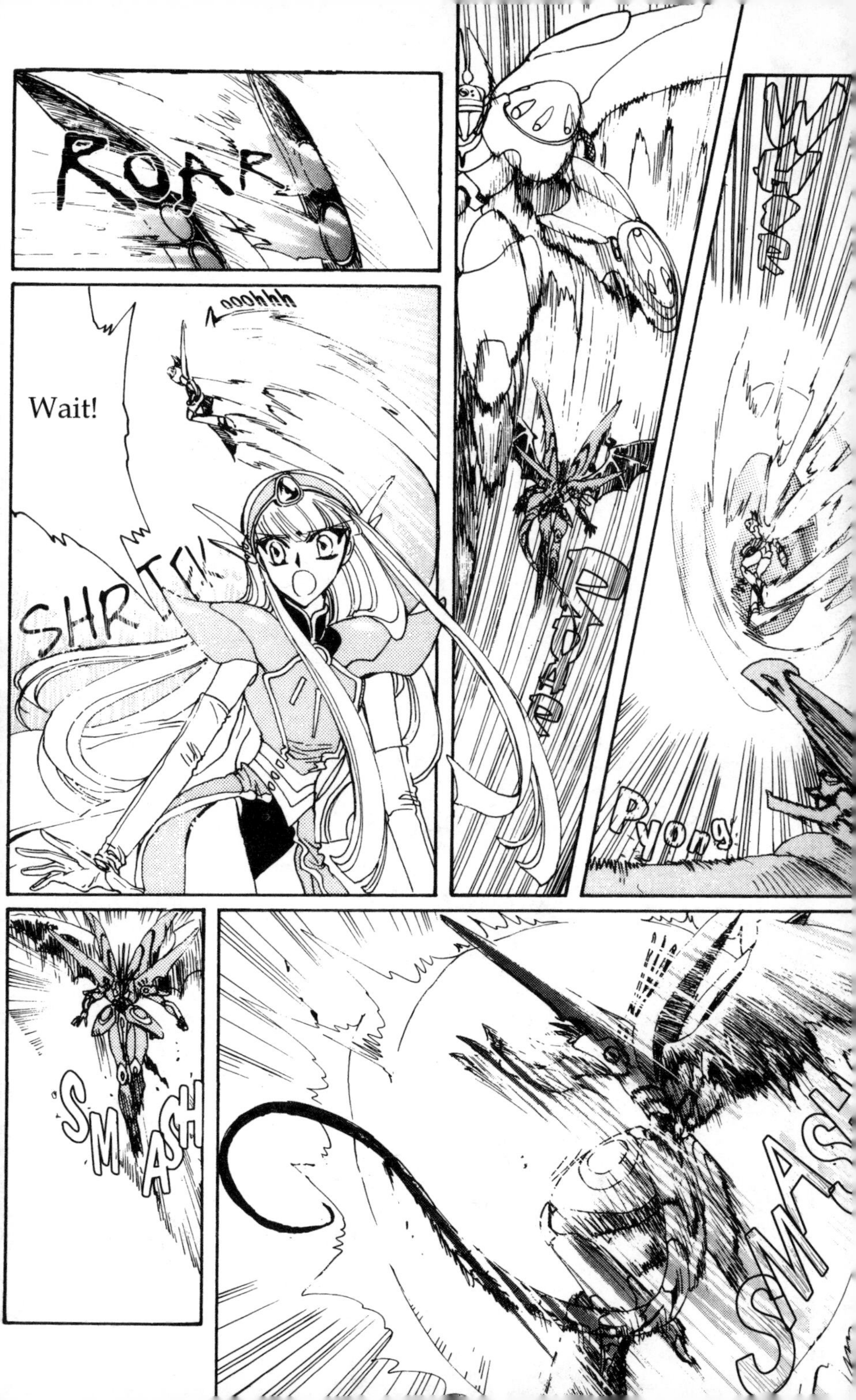
ROAR
ooohhh
Wait!
Pyong
SMASH
SMASH

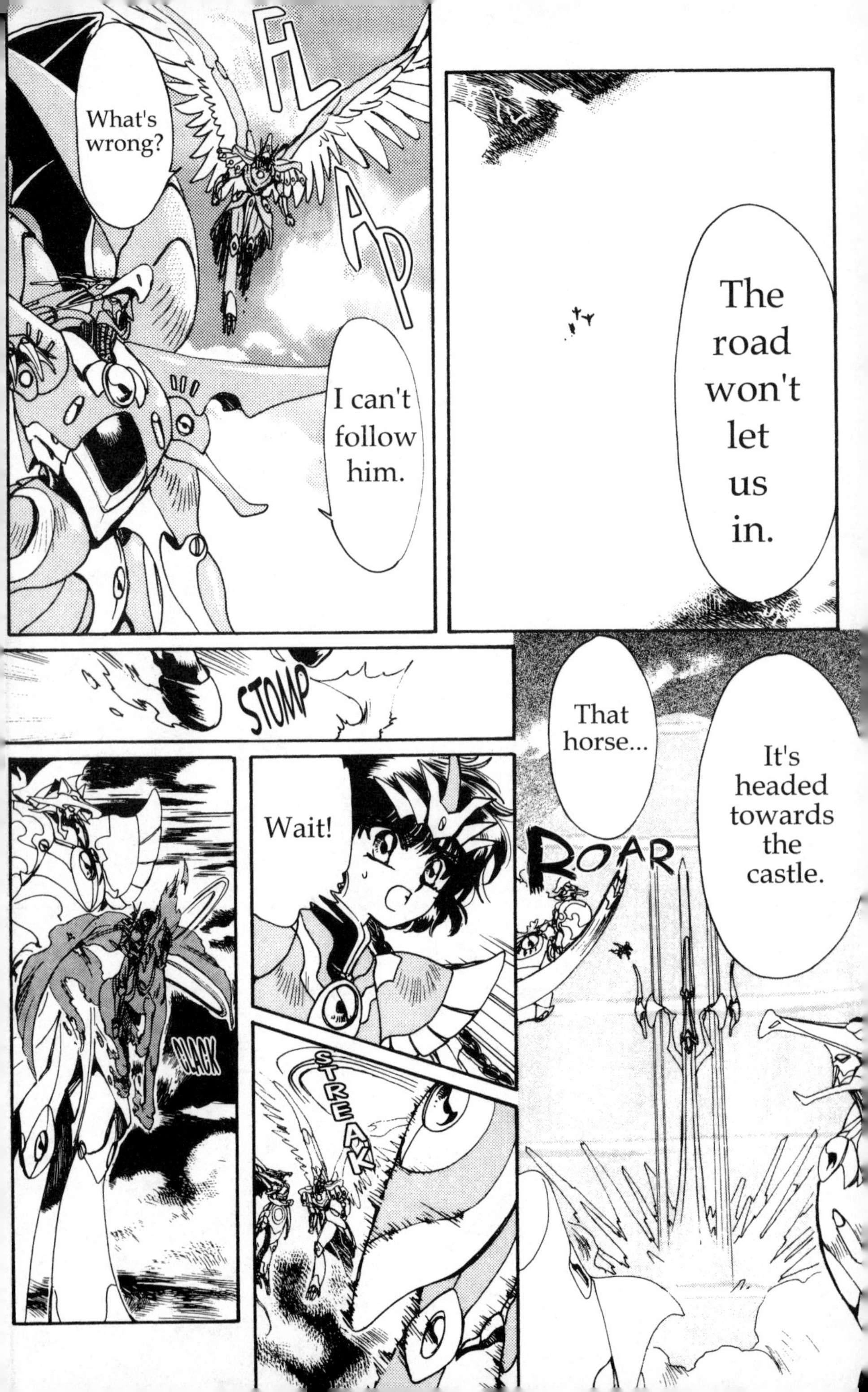
What's wrong?
FLAP
I can't follow him.
The road won't let us in.
STOMP
BLACK
Wait!
STREAK
That horse...
It's headed towards the castle.
ROAR

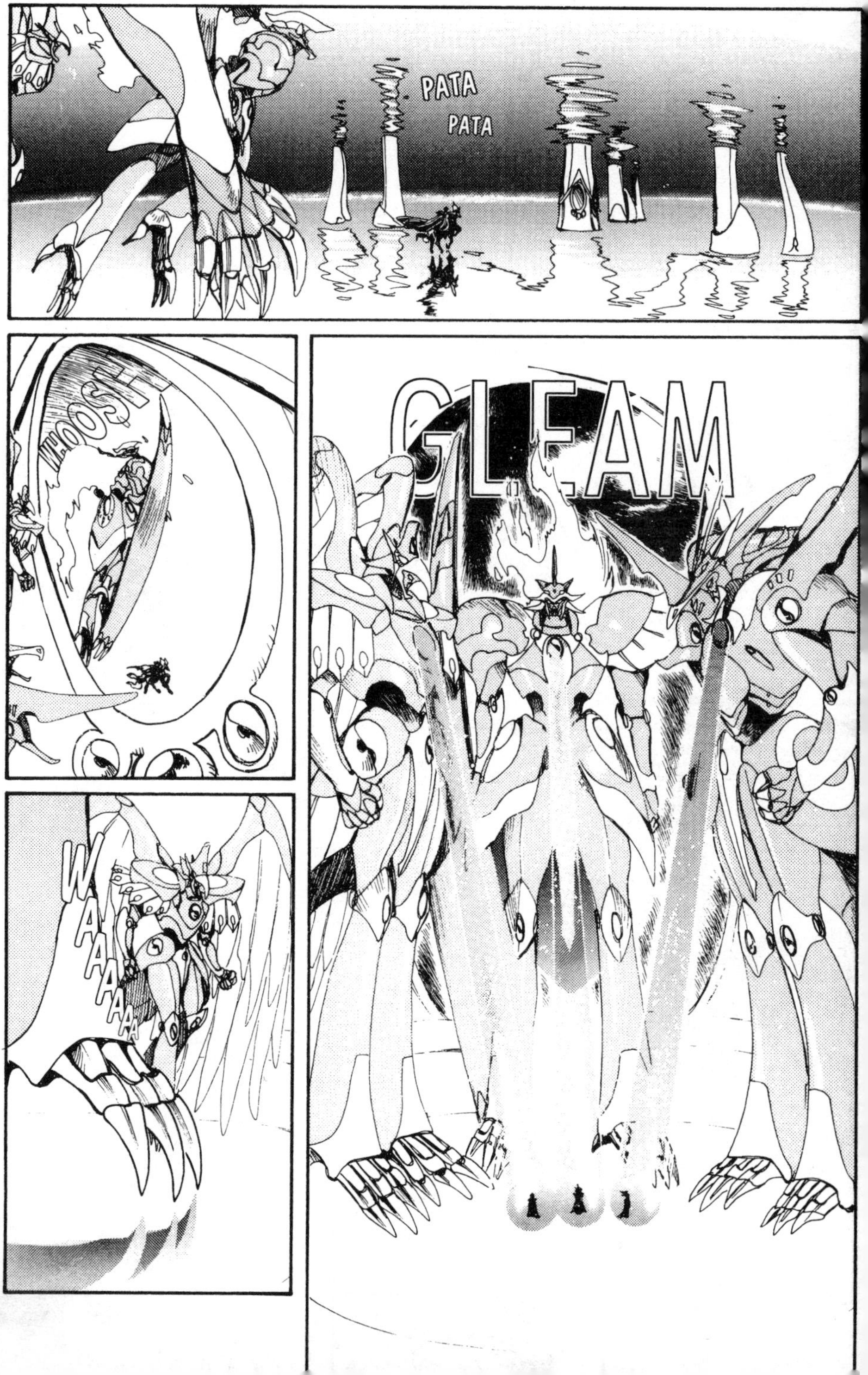
PATA
PATA
WHOOSH
GLEAM
WAAAAAA

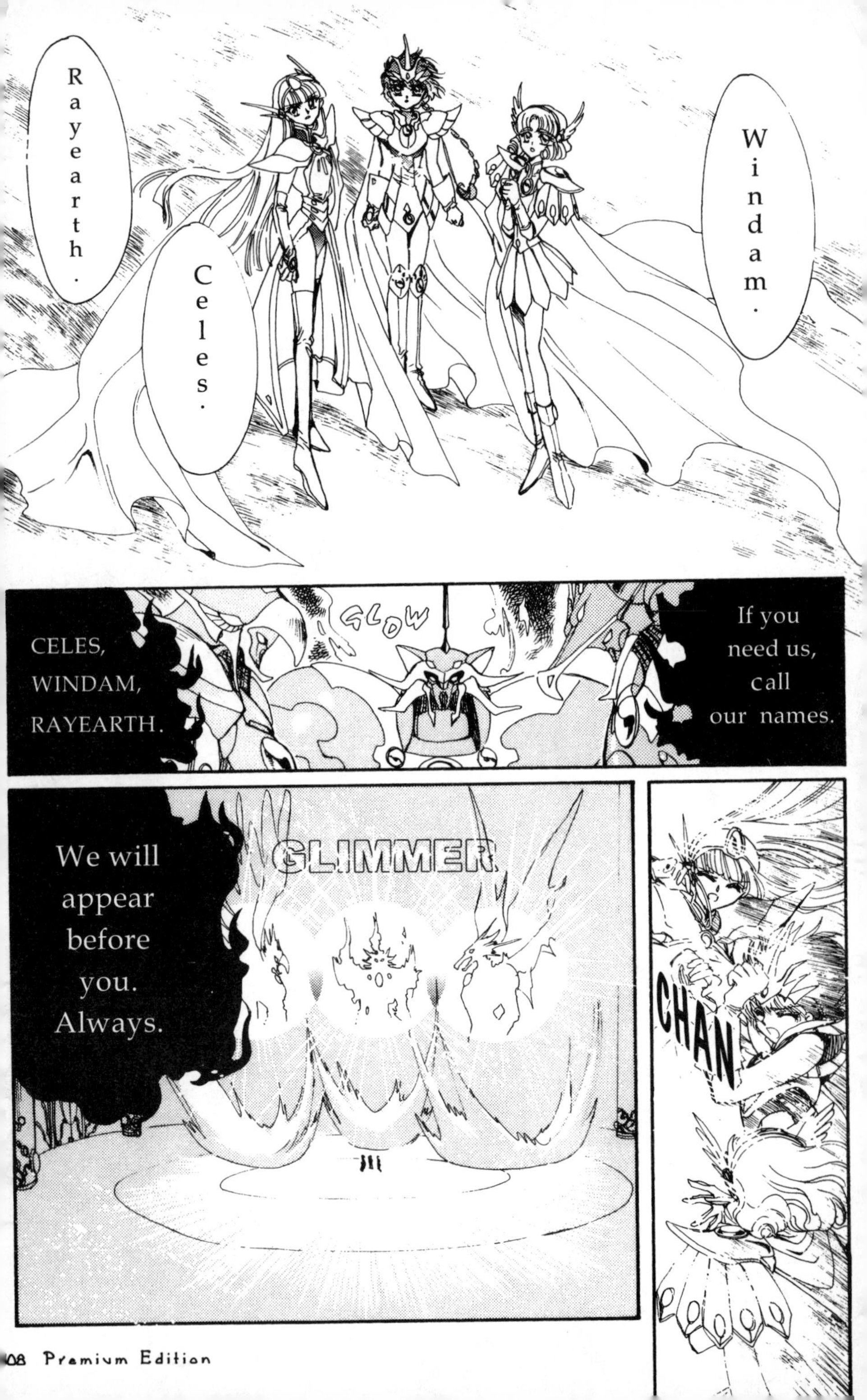

Windam.
Rayearth.
Celes.
If you need us, call our names.
GLOW
CELES, WINDAM, RAYEARTH.
CHAN
GLIMMER
We will appear before you. Always.

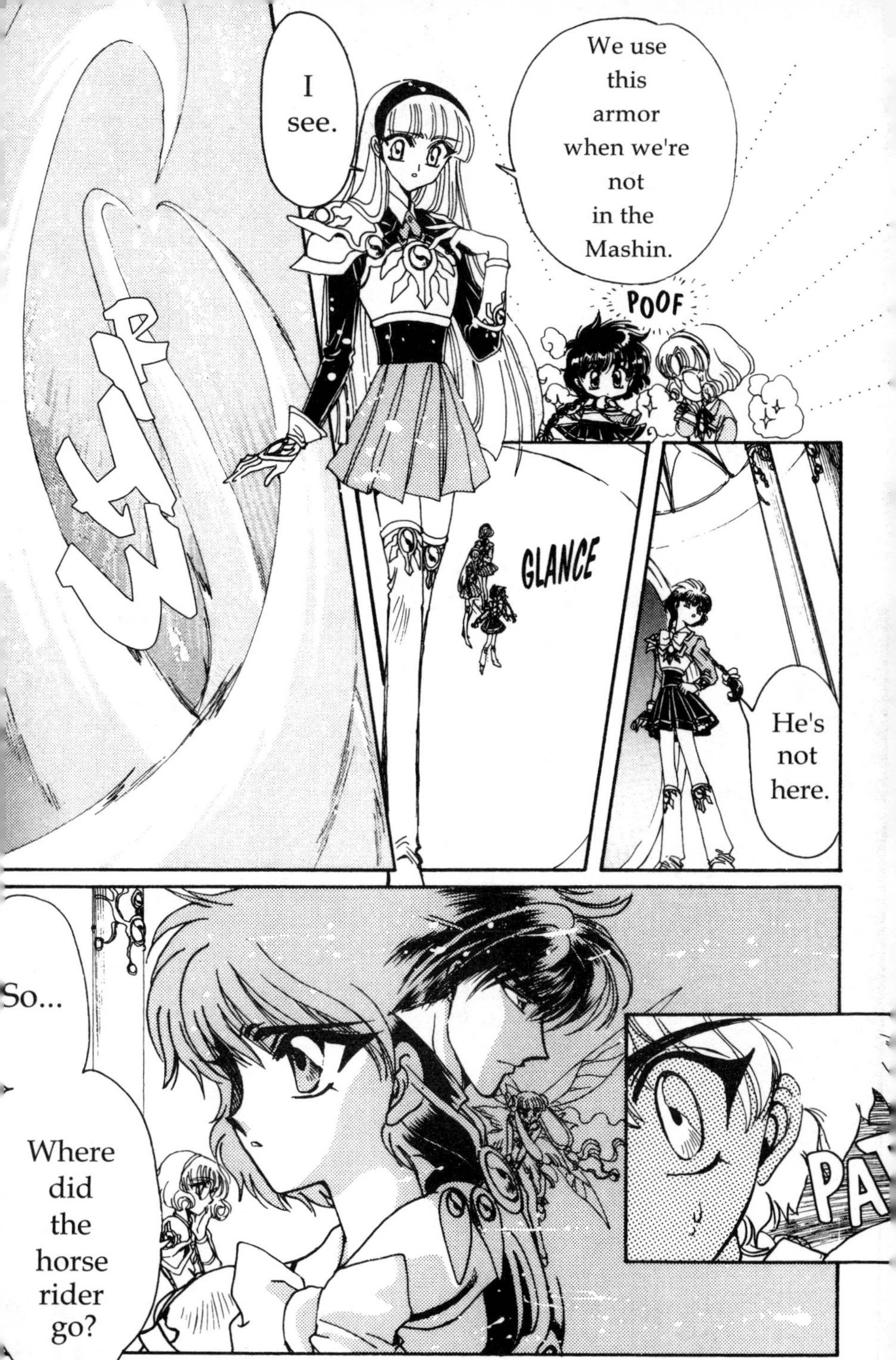
We use this armor when we're not in the Mashin.
I see.
POOF
GLANCE
He's not here.
PAT
So...
Where did the horse rider go?

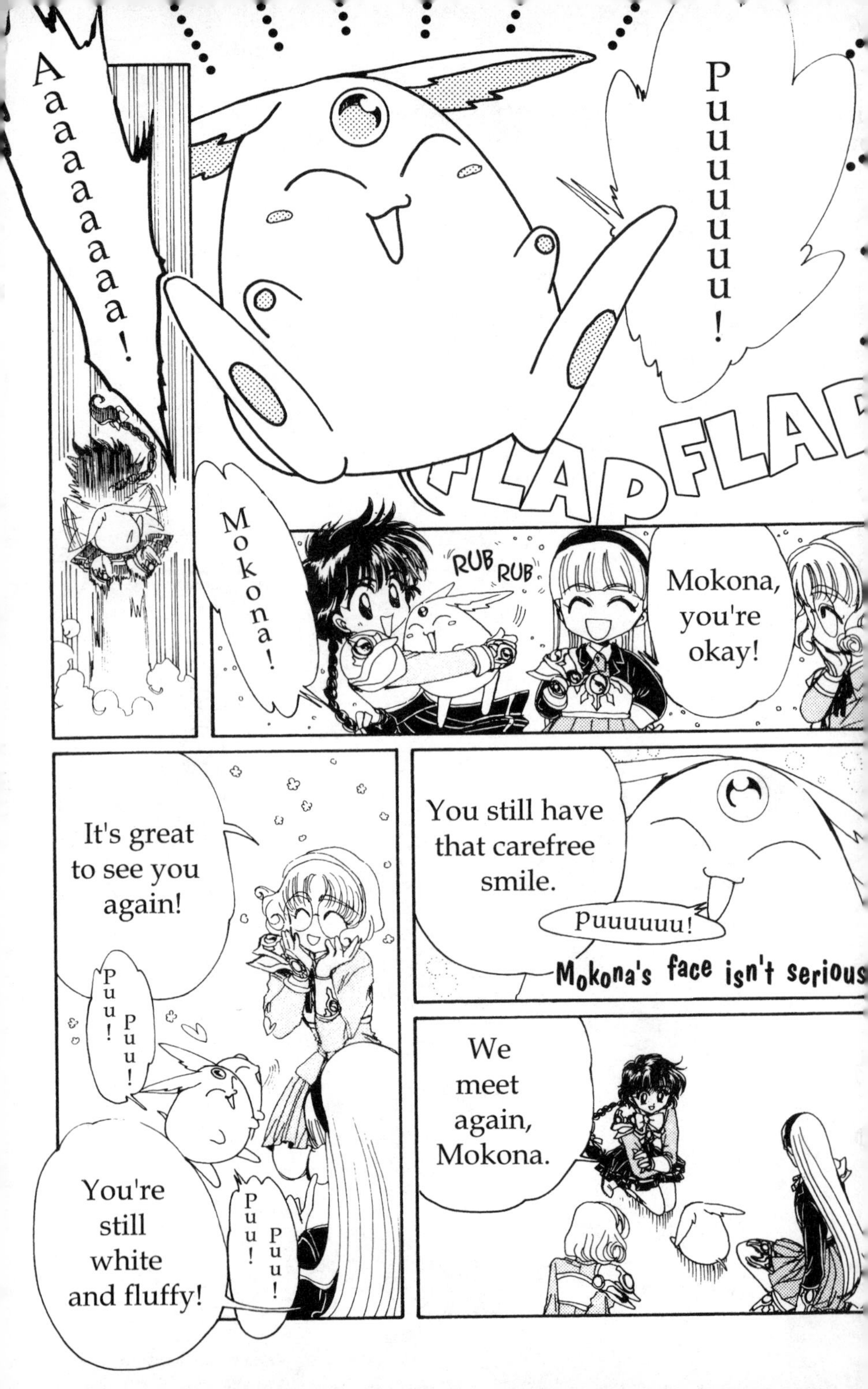

Puuuuuuuu!
FLAP FLAP
Aaaaaaaaaaa!
Mokona, you're okay!
RUB RUB
Mokona!
You still have that carefree smile.
Puuuuuu!
Mokona's face isn't serious
We meet again, Mokona.
It's great to see you again!
Puu! Puu!
You're still white and fluffy!
Puu! Puu!

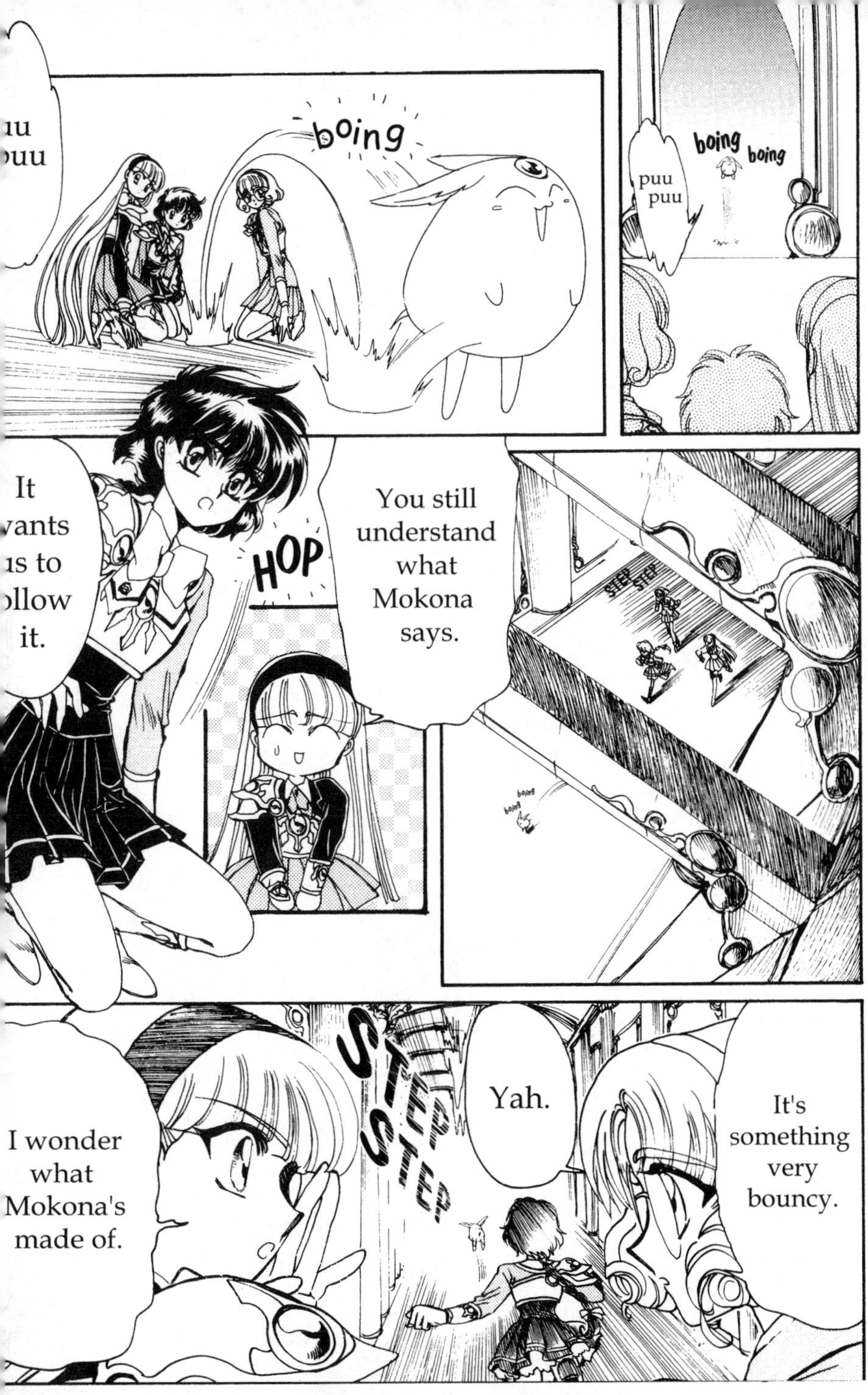
boing boing
puu puu
boing
STEP STEP
boing boing
You still understand what Mokona says.
HOP
It ants s to llow it.
It's something very bouncy.
Yah.
STEP STEP STEP
I wonder what Mokona's made of.

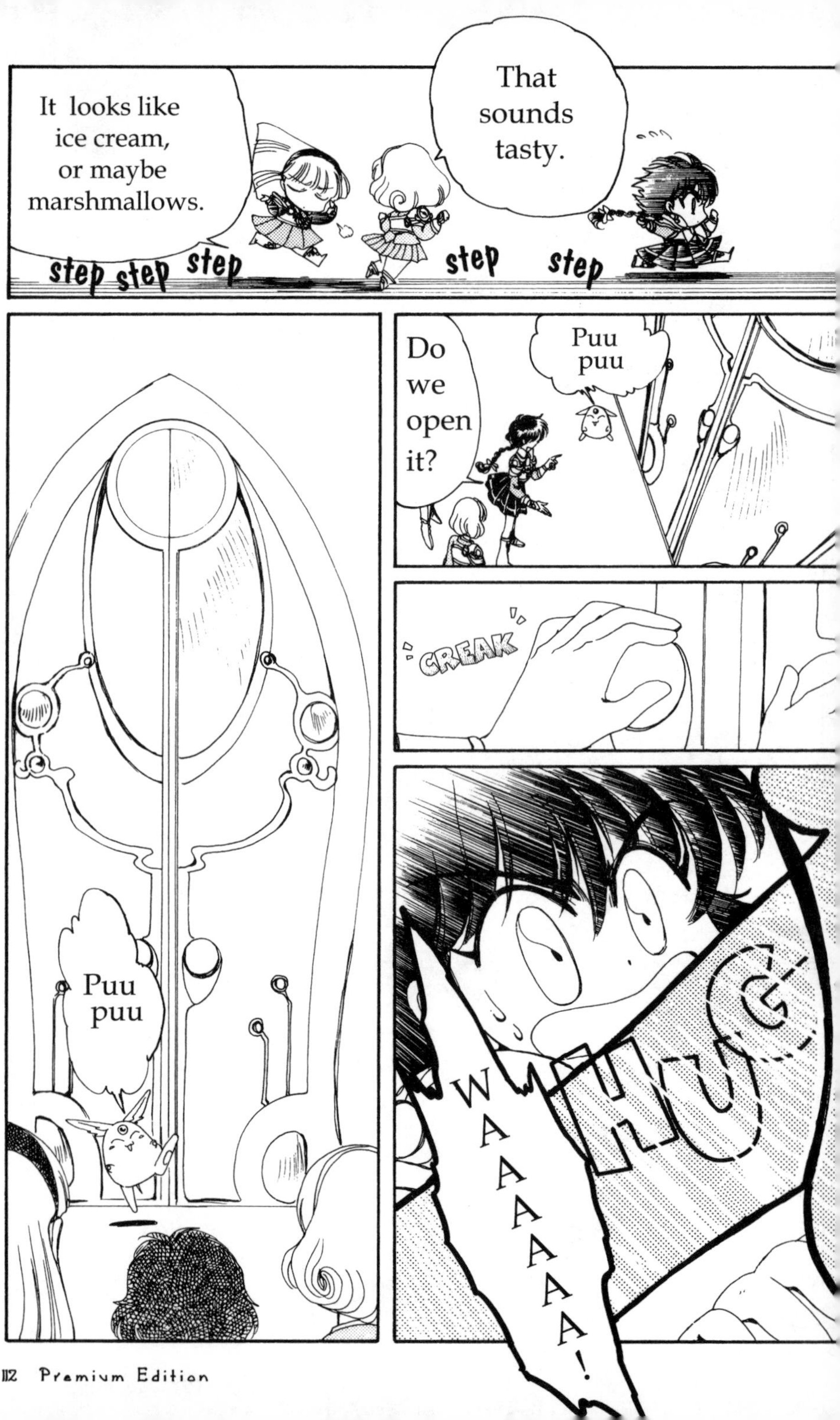

It looks like ice cream, or maybe marshmallows.
That sounds tasty.
step step step
step
step
Puu puu
Do we open it?
Puu puu
CREAK
WAAAAAAA!
HUG

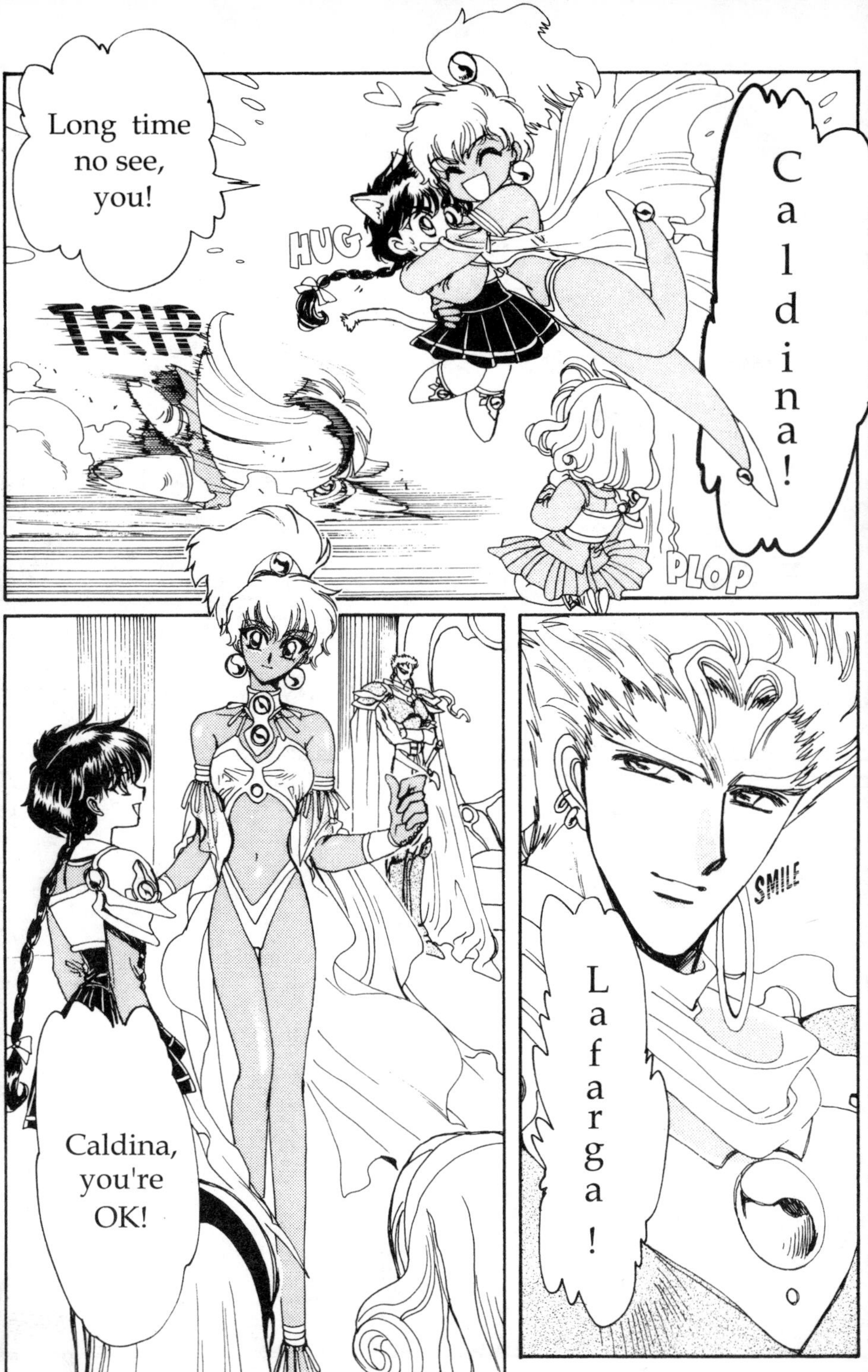
Long time no see, you!
HUG
TRIP
Caldina!
PLOP
Caldina, you're OK!
Lafarga!
SMILE

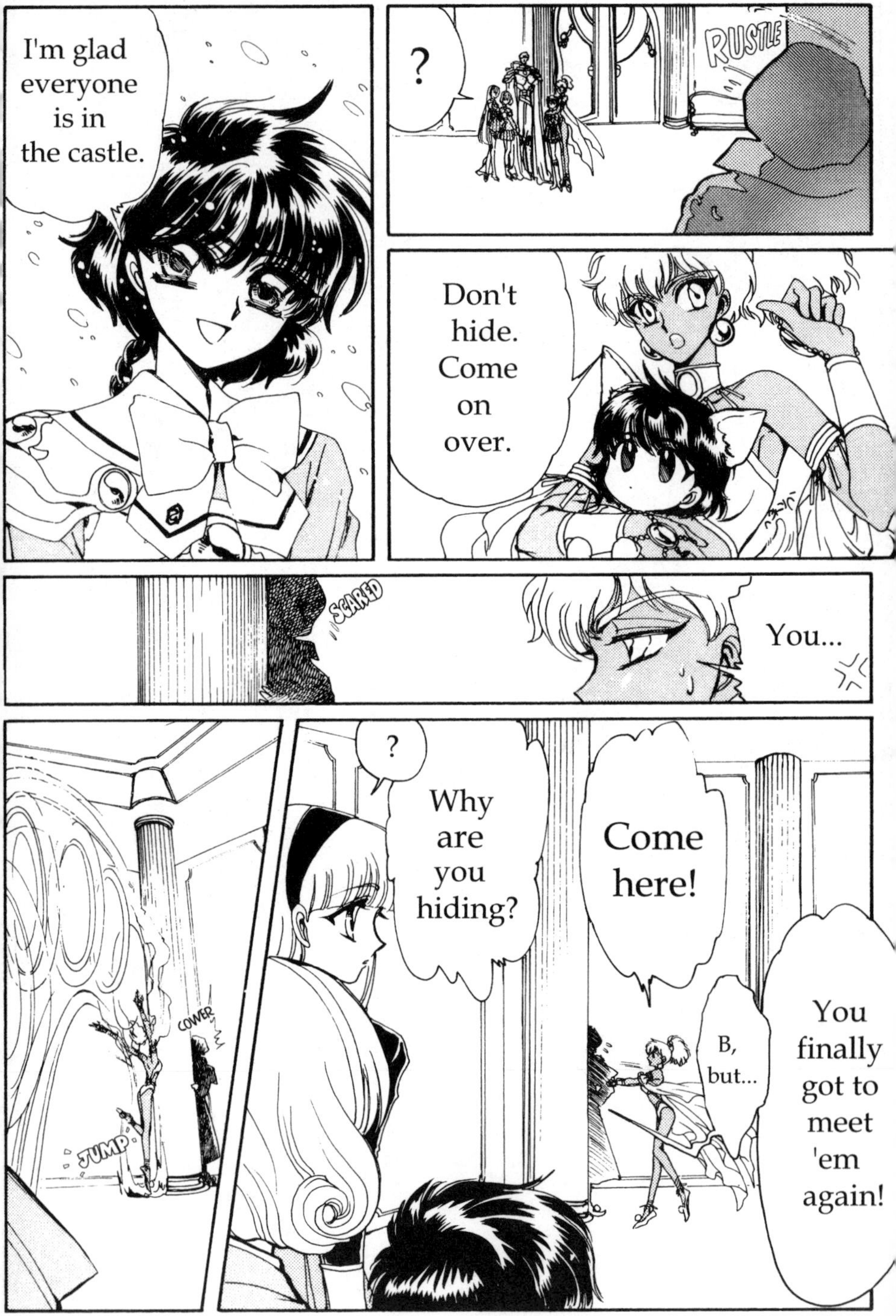
I'm glad everyone is in the castle.
?
RUSTLE
Don't hide. Come on over.
SCARED
You...
COWER
JUMP
?
Why are you hiding?
Come here!
B, but...
You finally got to meet 'em again!

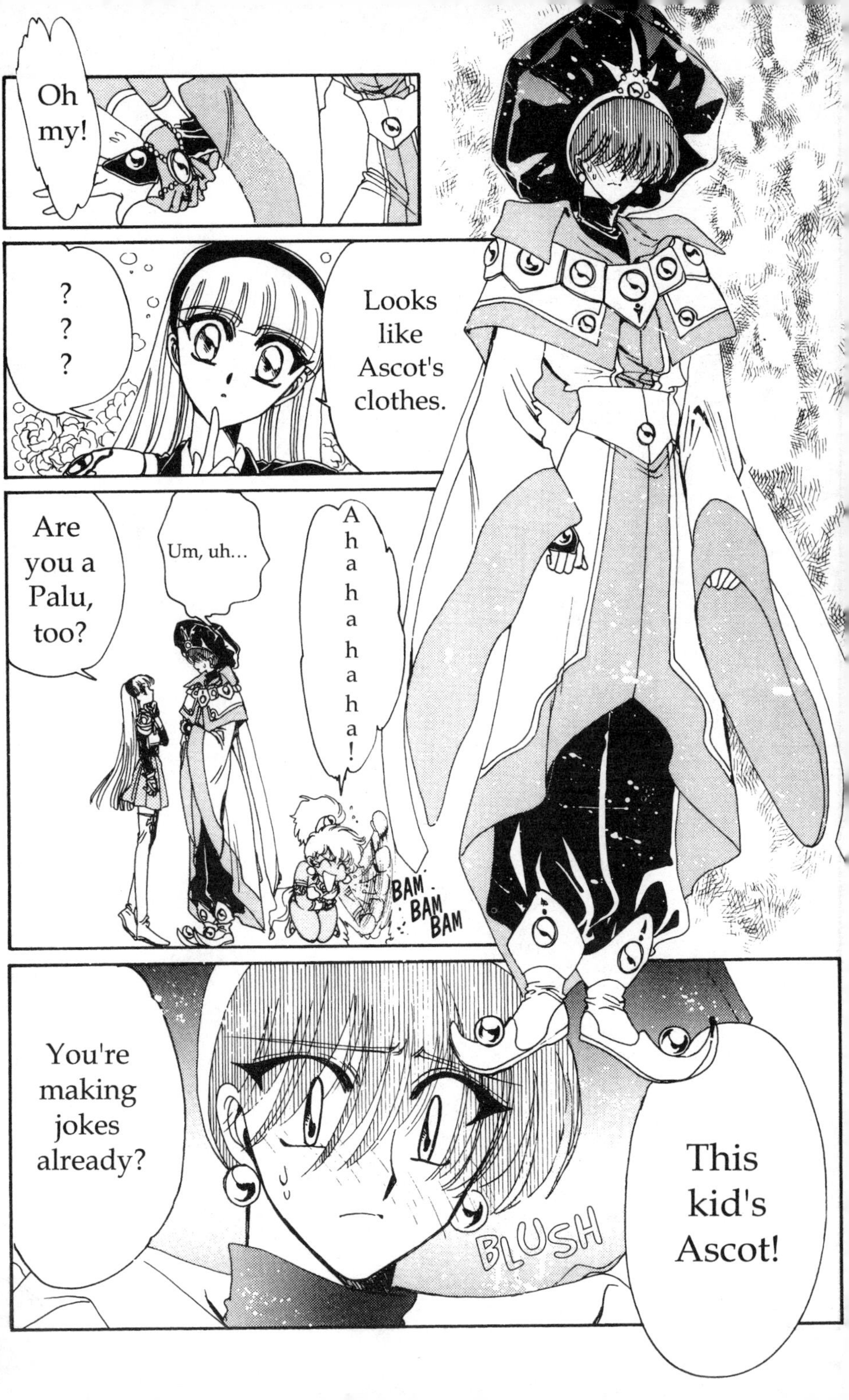
Oh my!
???
Looks like Ascot's clothes.
Are you a Palu, too?
Um, uh...
Ahahahahaha!
BAM BAM BAM
You're making jokes already?
BLUSH
This kid's Ascot!

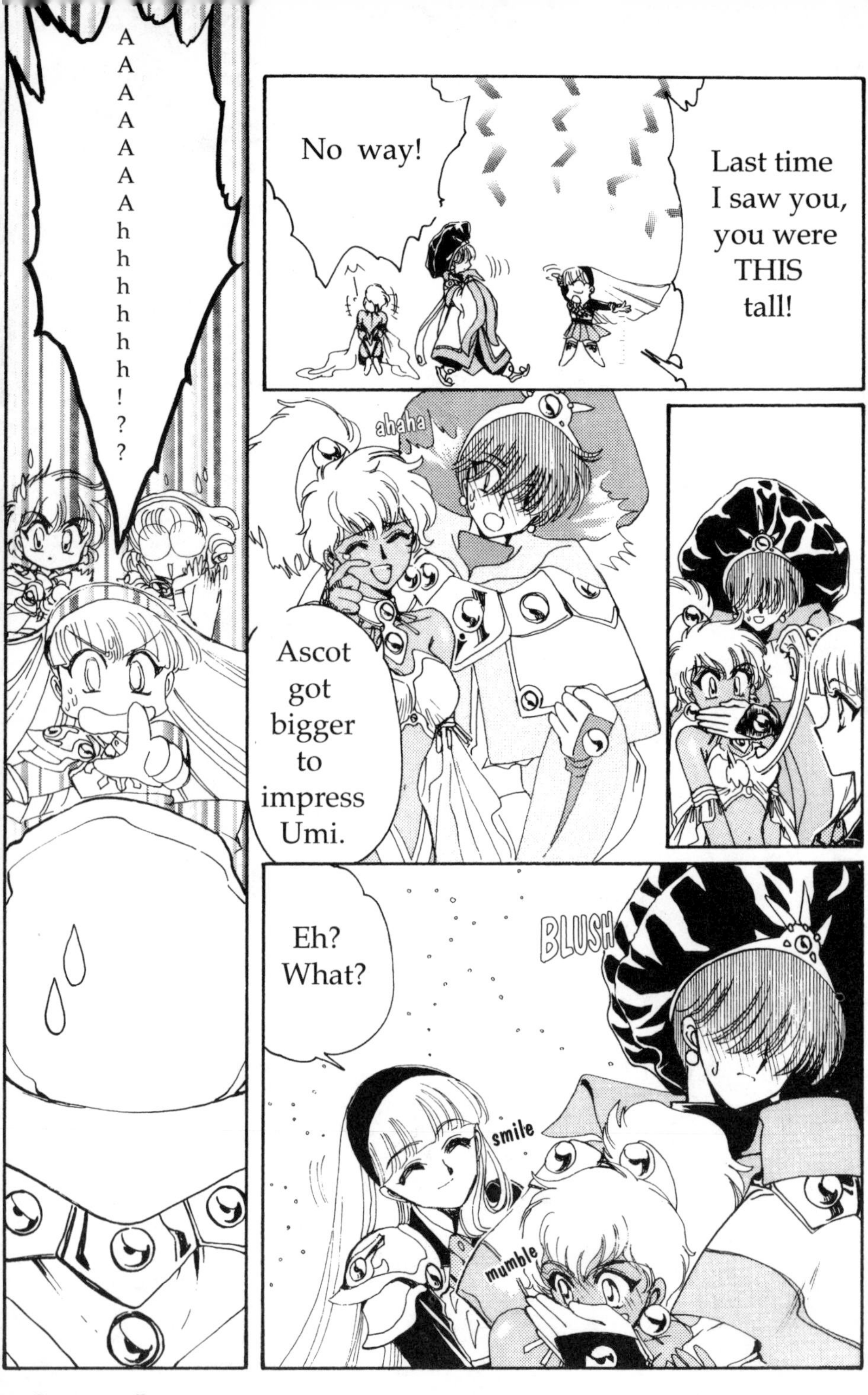
AAAAAAAAhhhhhh!??
No way!
Last time I saw you, you were THIS tall!
ahaha
Ascot got bigger to impress Umi.
Eh? What?
BLUSH
smile
mumble

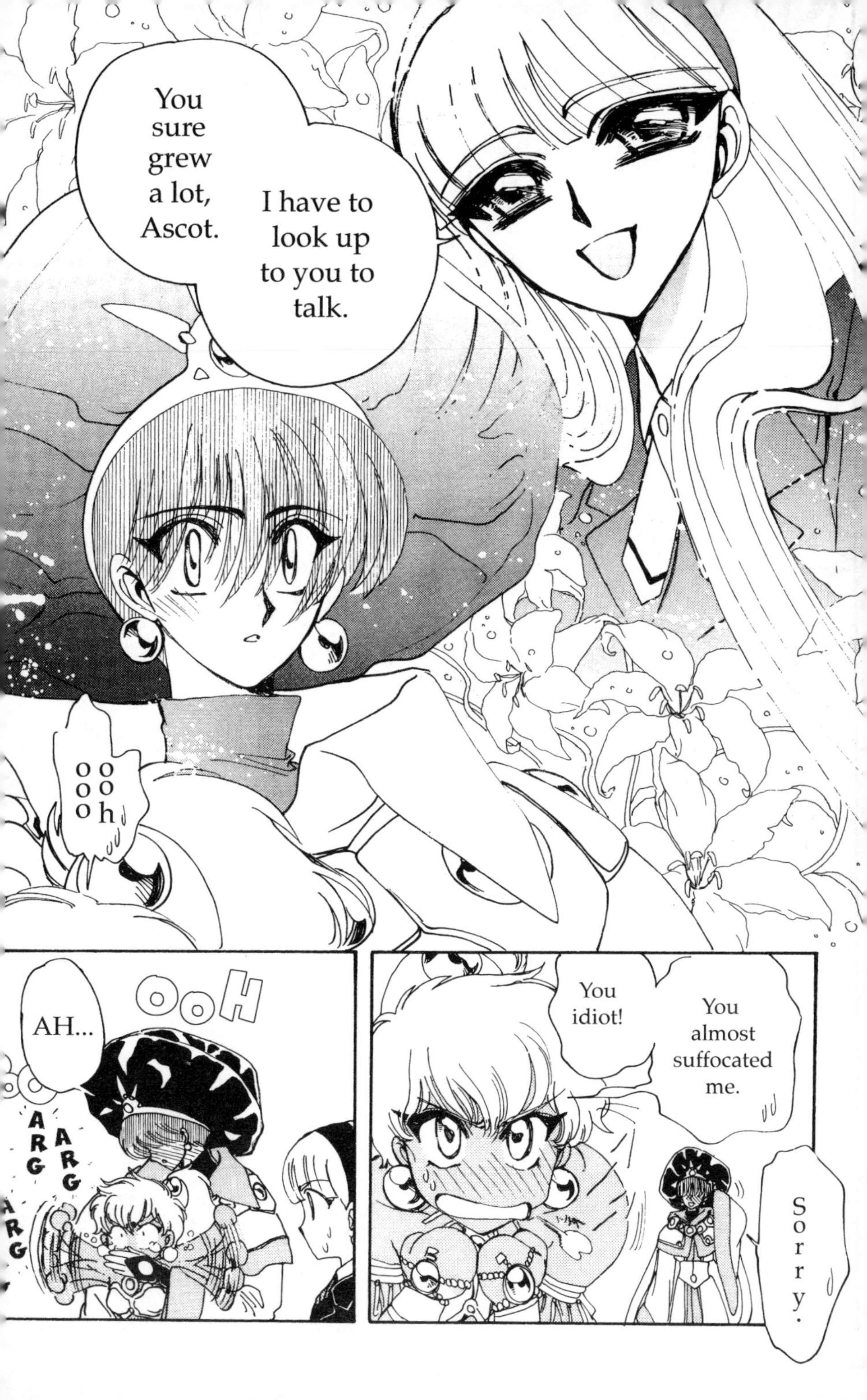
You sure grew a lot, Ascot.
I have to look up to you to talk.
ooooooh
AH...
OOH
ARG ARG ARG
You idiot!
You almost suffocated me.
Sorry.

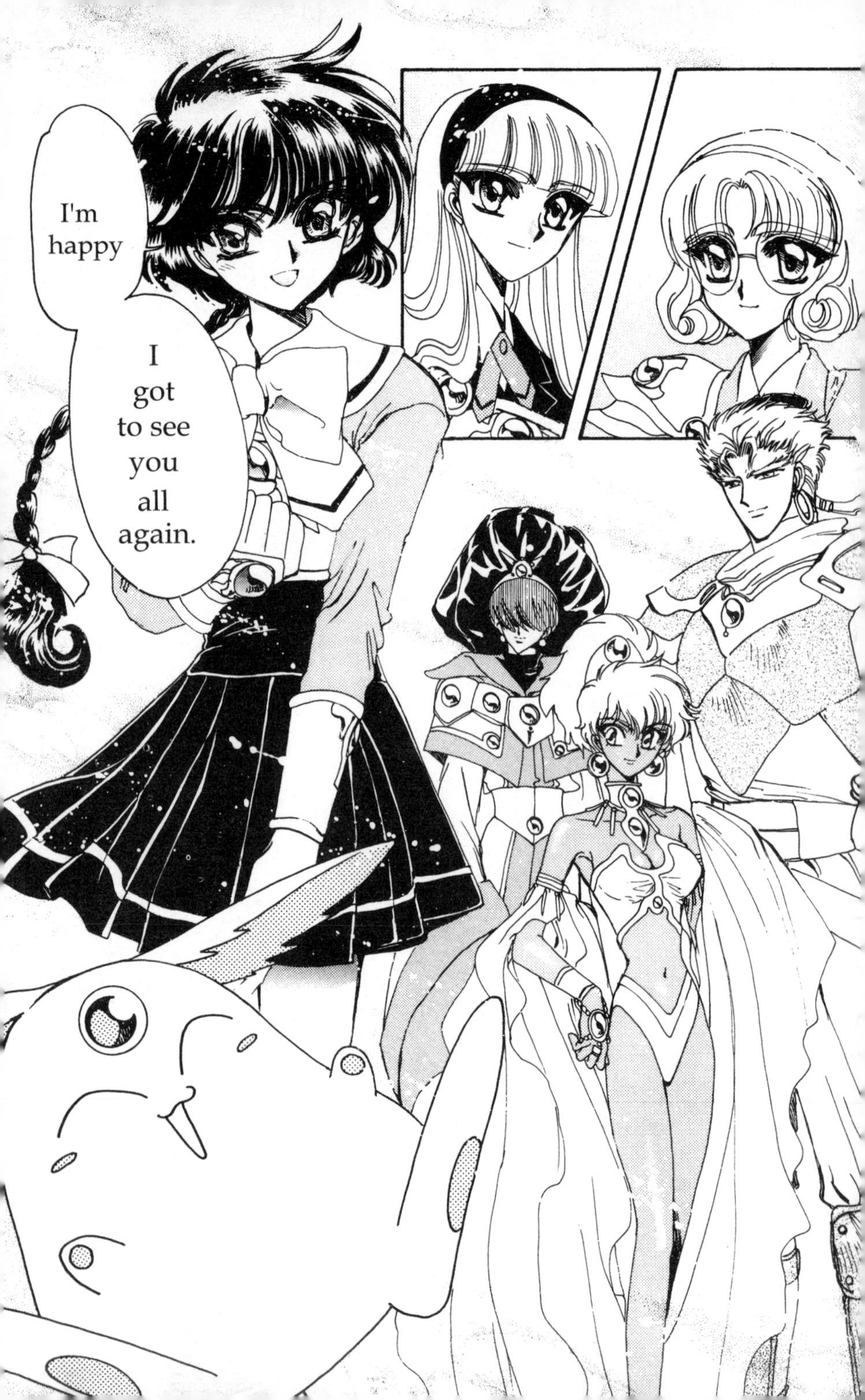
I'm happy
I got to see you all again.

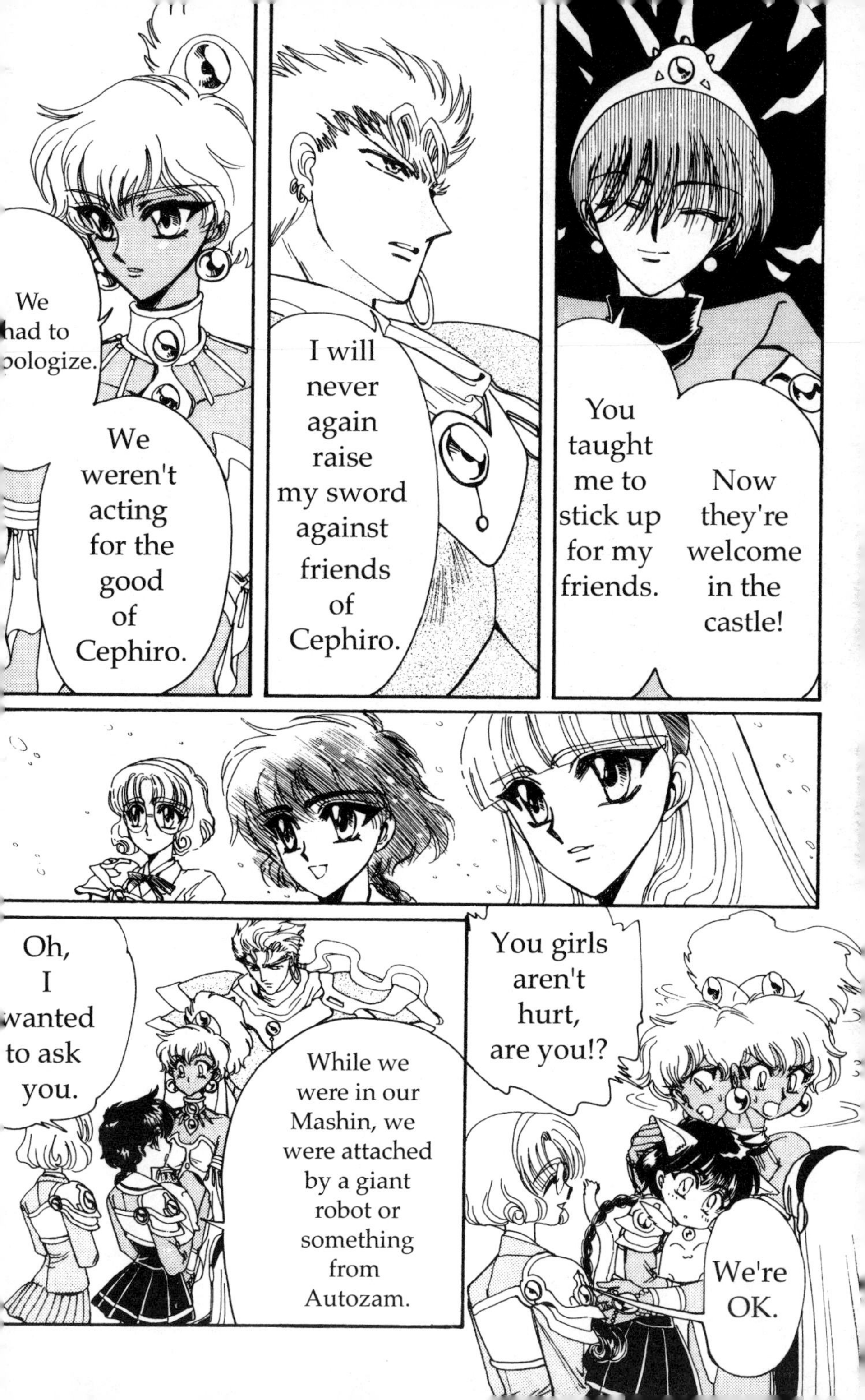
We had to apologize.
We weren't acting for the good of Cephiro.
I will never again raise my sword against friends of Cephiro.
You taught me to stick up for my friends.
Now they're welcome in the castle!
Oh, I wanted to ask you.
While we were in our Mashin, we were attached by a giant robot or something from Autozam.
You girls aren't hurt, are you!?
We're OK.

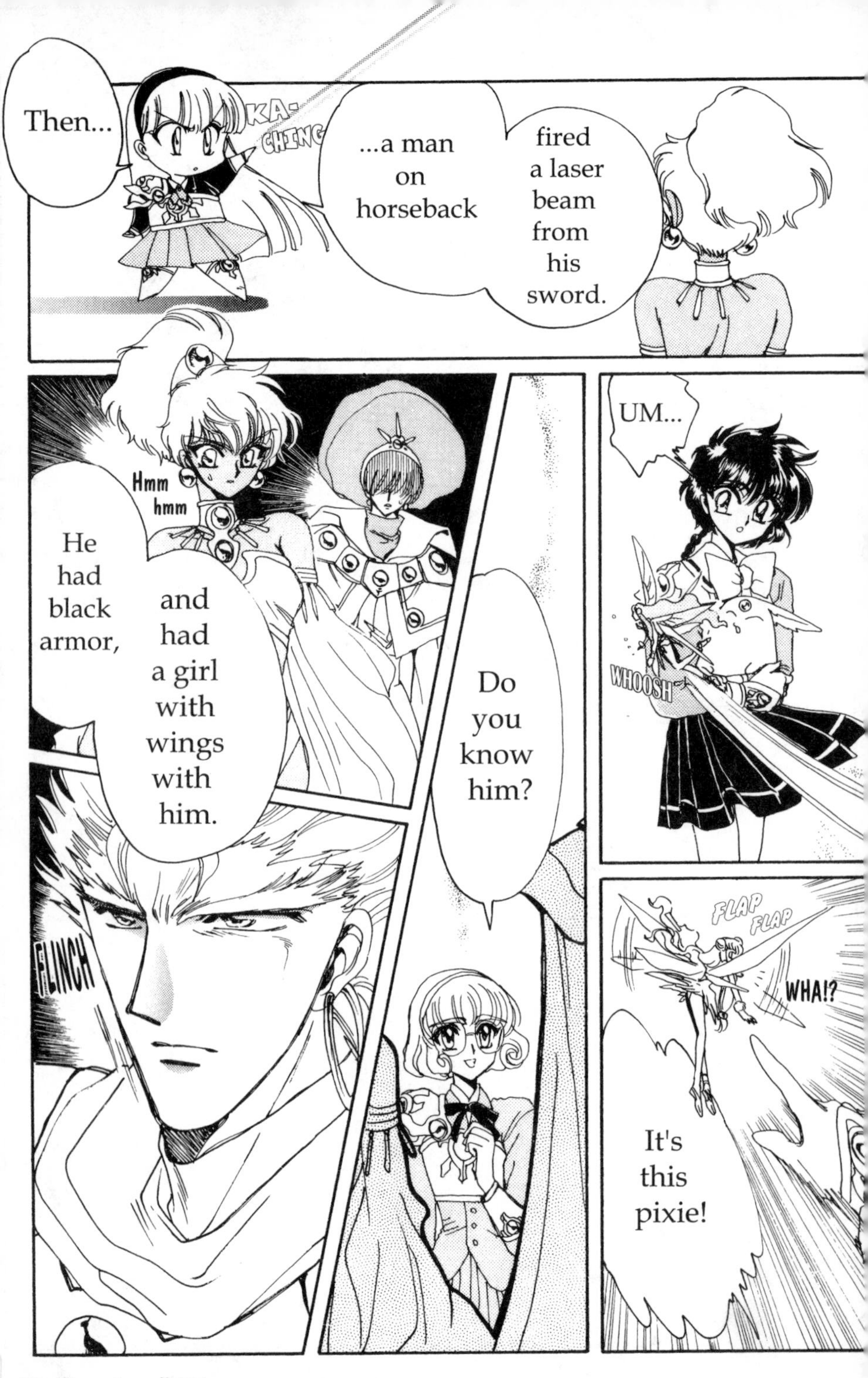
Then...
KA-CHING
...a man on horseback
fired a laser beam from his sword.
Hmm hmm
He had black armor,
and had a girl with wings with him.
FLINCH
Do you know him?
UM...
WHOOSH
FLAP FLAP
WHA!?
It's this pixie!

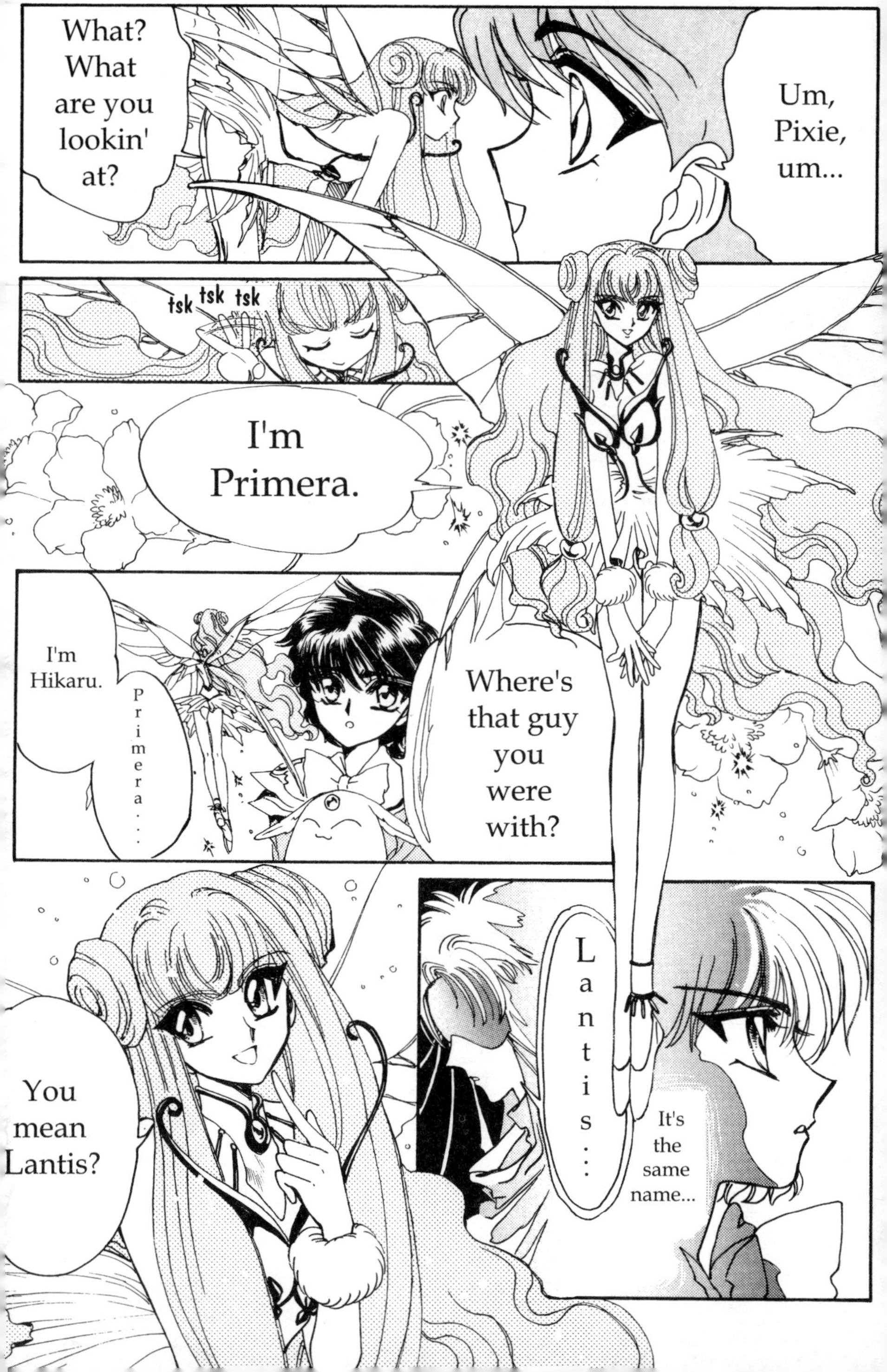
Um, Pixie, um...
What? What are you lookin' at?
tsk tsk tsk
I'm Primera.
Primera...
I'm Hikaru.
Where's that guy you were with?
You mean Lantis?
Lantis...
It's the same name...

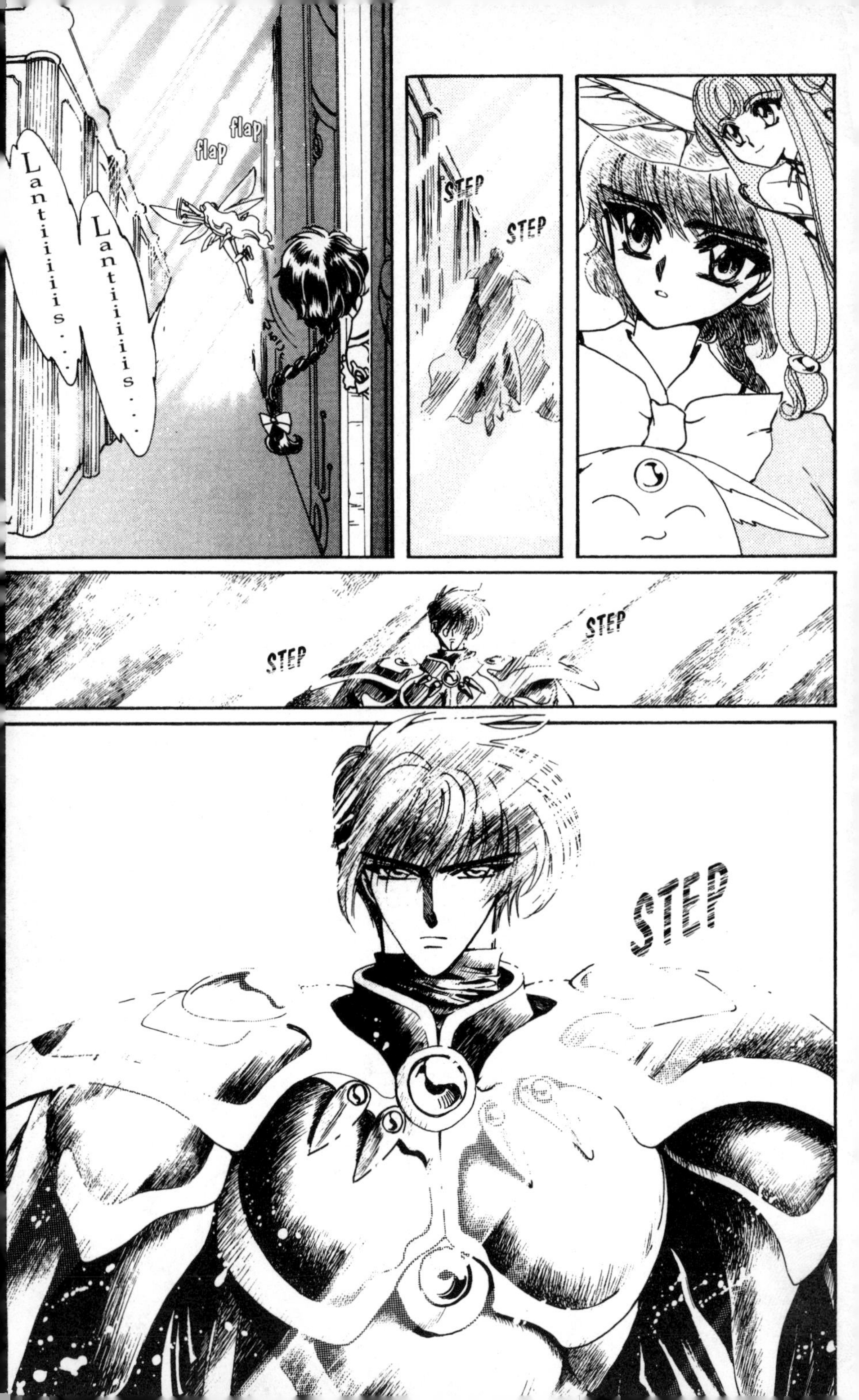

STEP
STEP
flap
flap
Lantiiiiis...
Lantiiiiis...
STEP
STEP
STEP

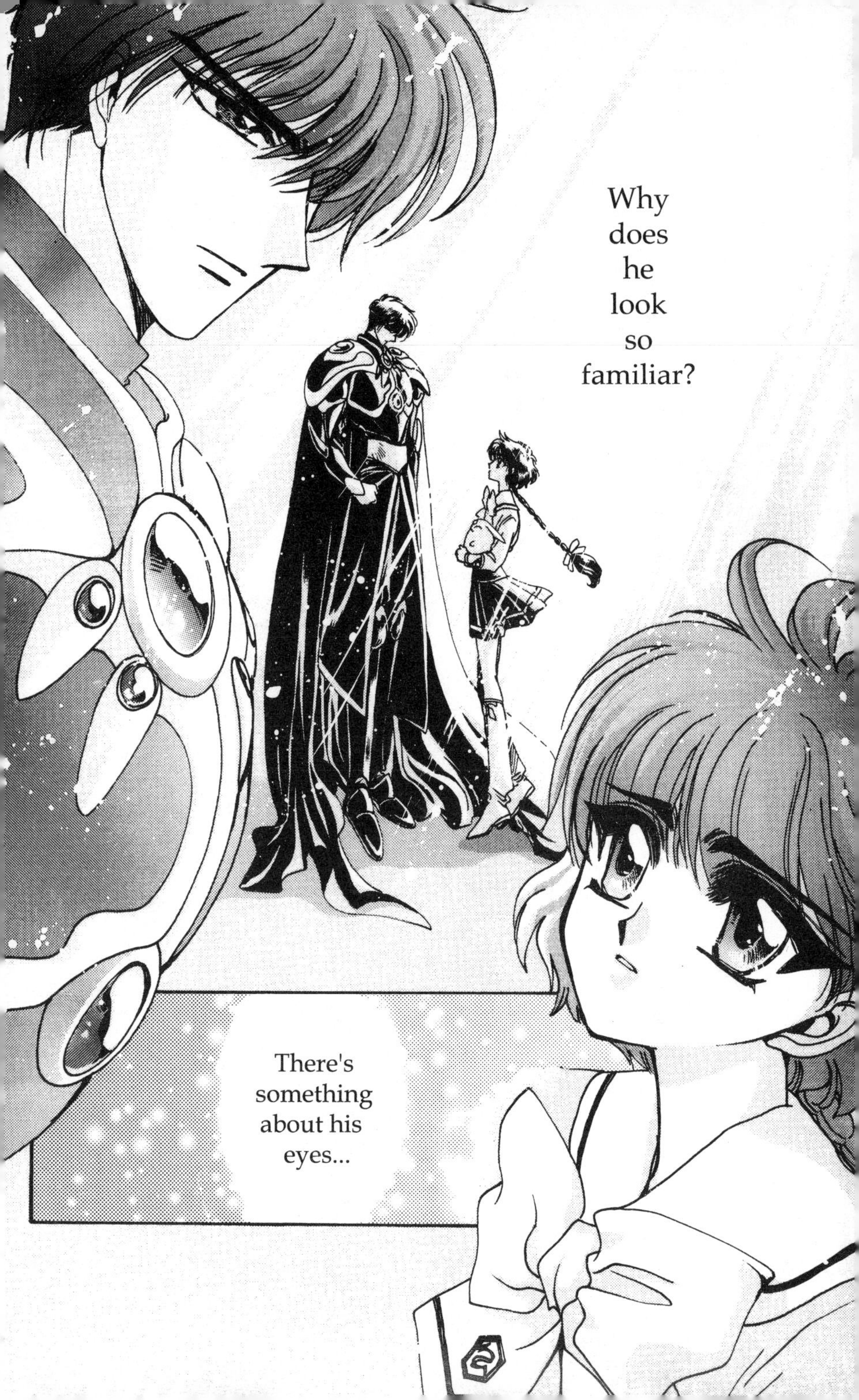
Why does he look so familiar?
There's something about his eyes...

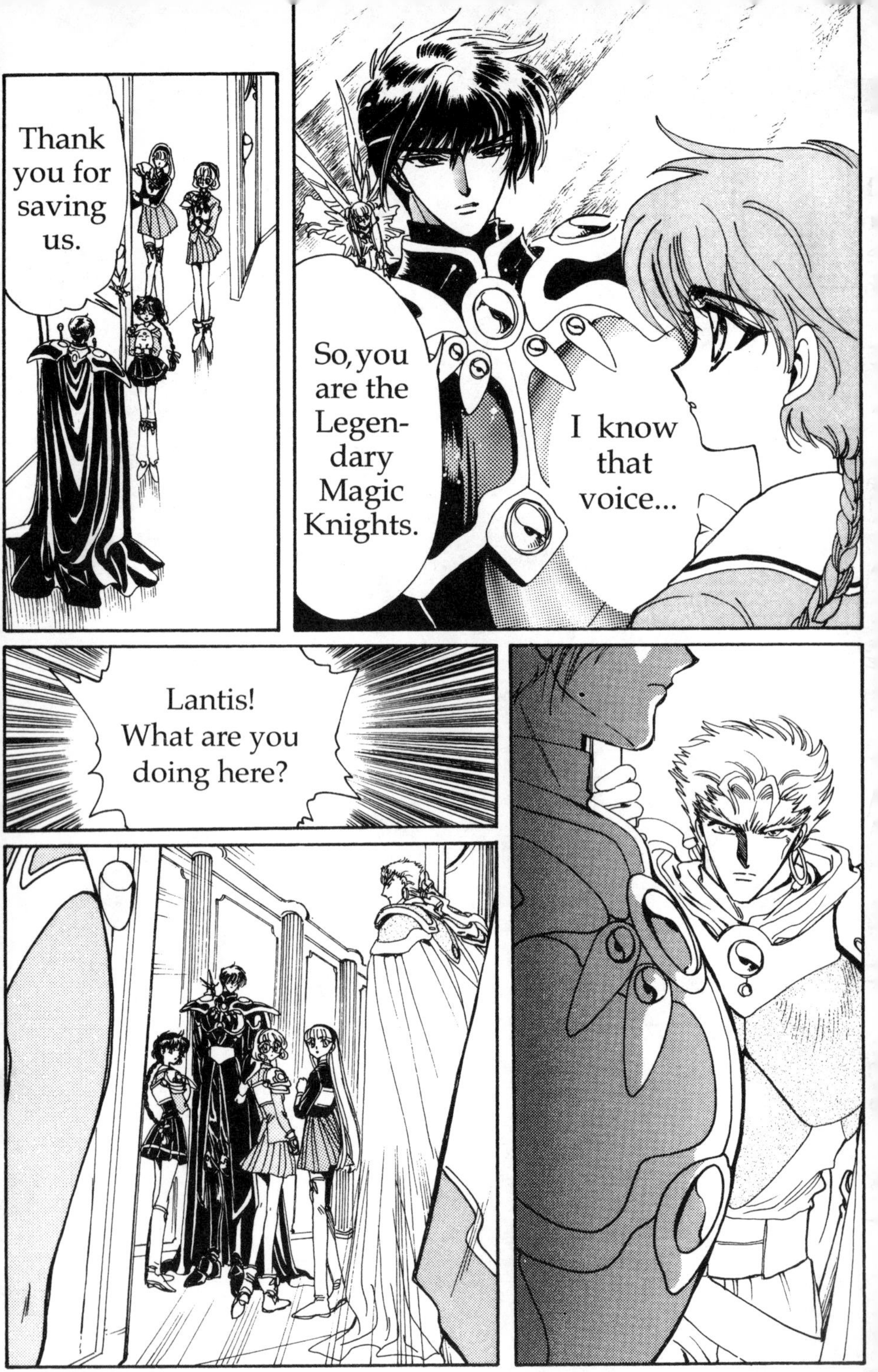
Thank you for saving us.
So, you are the Legendary Magic Knights.
I know that voice...
Lantis! What are you doing here?

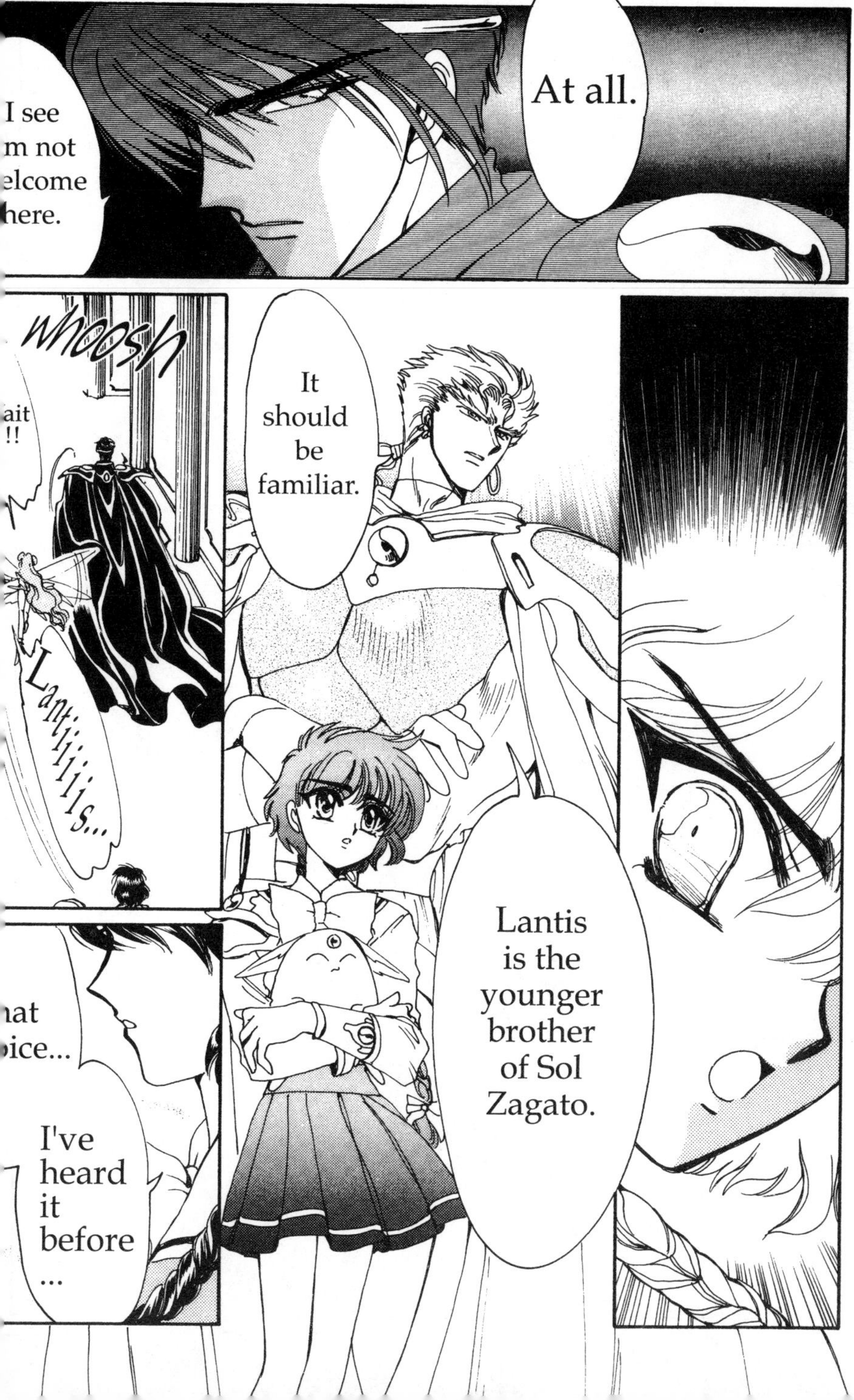
I see
m not
elcome
here.
At all.
whoosh
ait
!!
Lantiiiiiis...
hat
oice...
I've heard it before ...
It should be familiar.
Lantis is the younger brother of Sol Zagato.

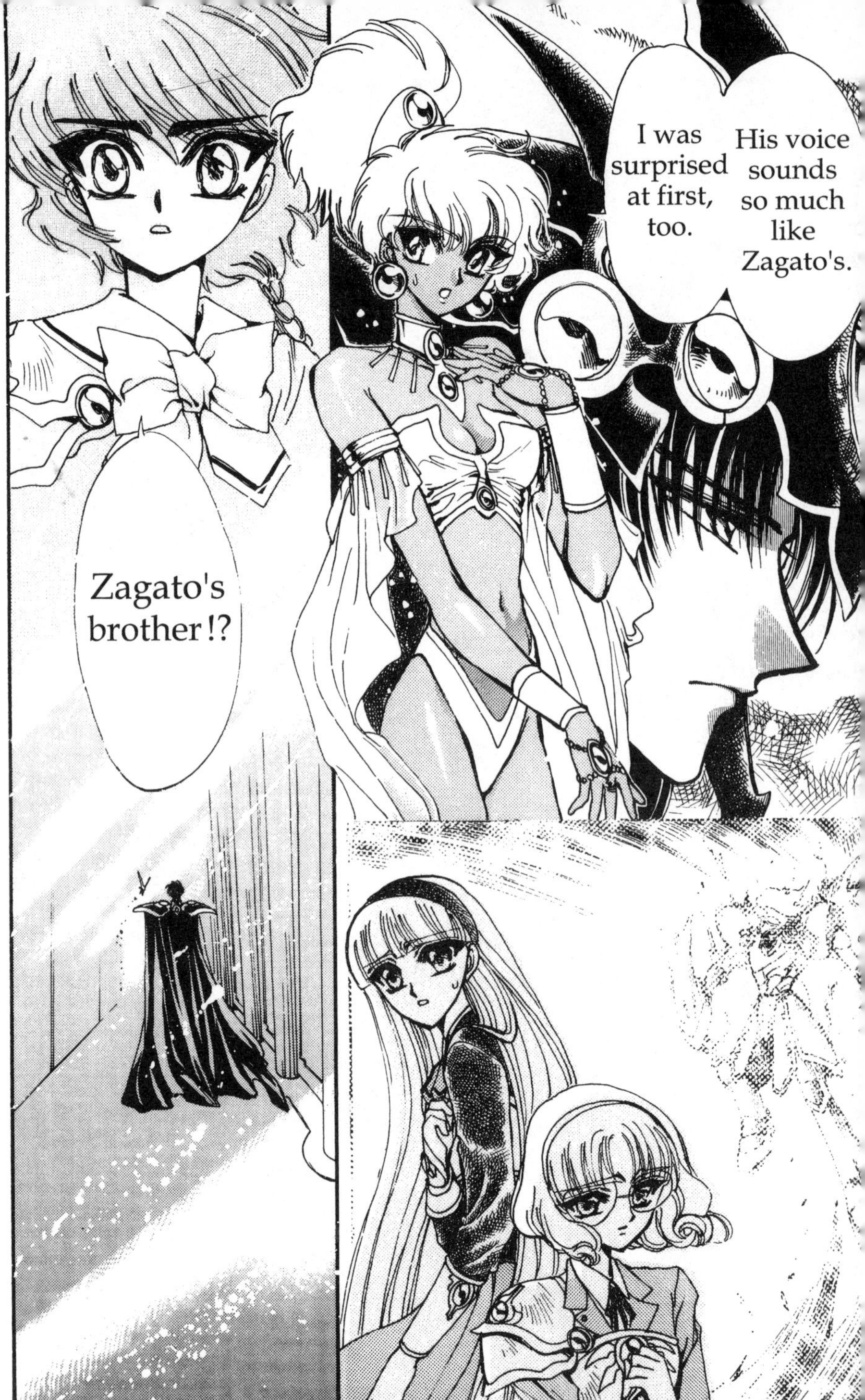
His voice sounds so much like Zagato's.
I was surprised at first, too.
Zagato's brother!?

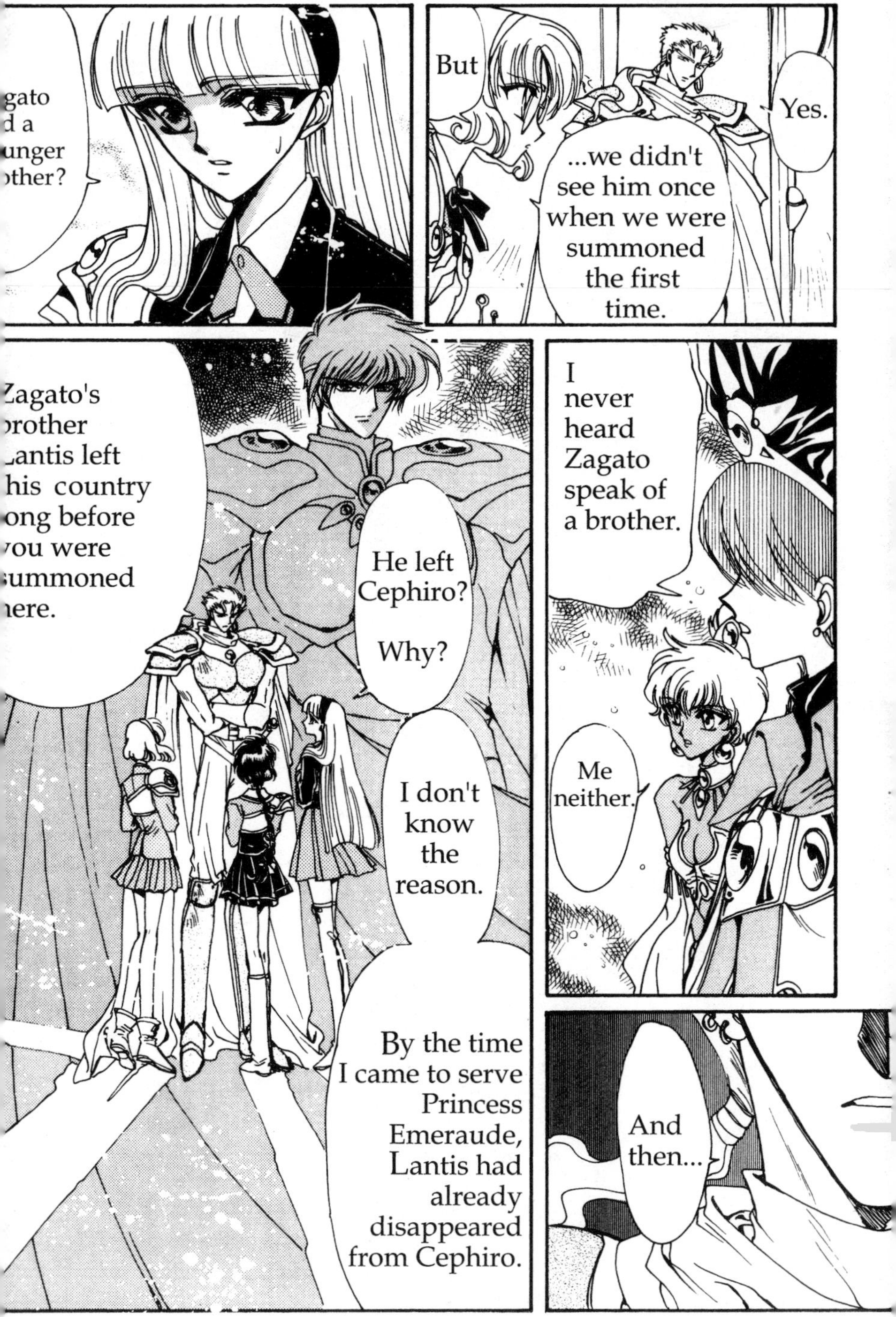
gato d a unger other?
Yes.
But
...we didn't see him once when we were summoned the first time.
Zagato's brother Lantis left his country ong before you were summoned here.
He left Cephiro?
Why?
I don't know the reason.
By the time I came to serve Princess Emeraude, Lantis had already disappeared from Cephiro.
I never heard Zagato speak of a brother.
Me neither.
And then...

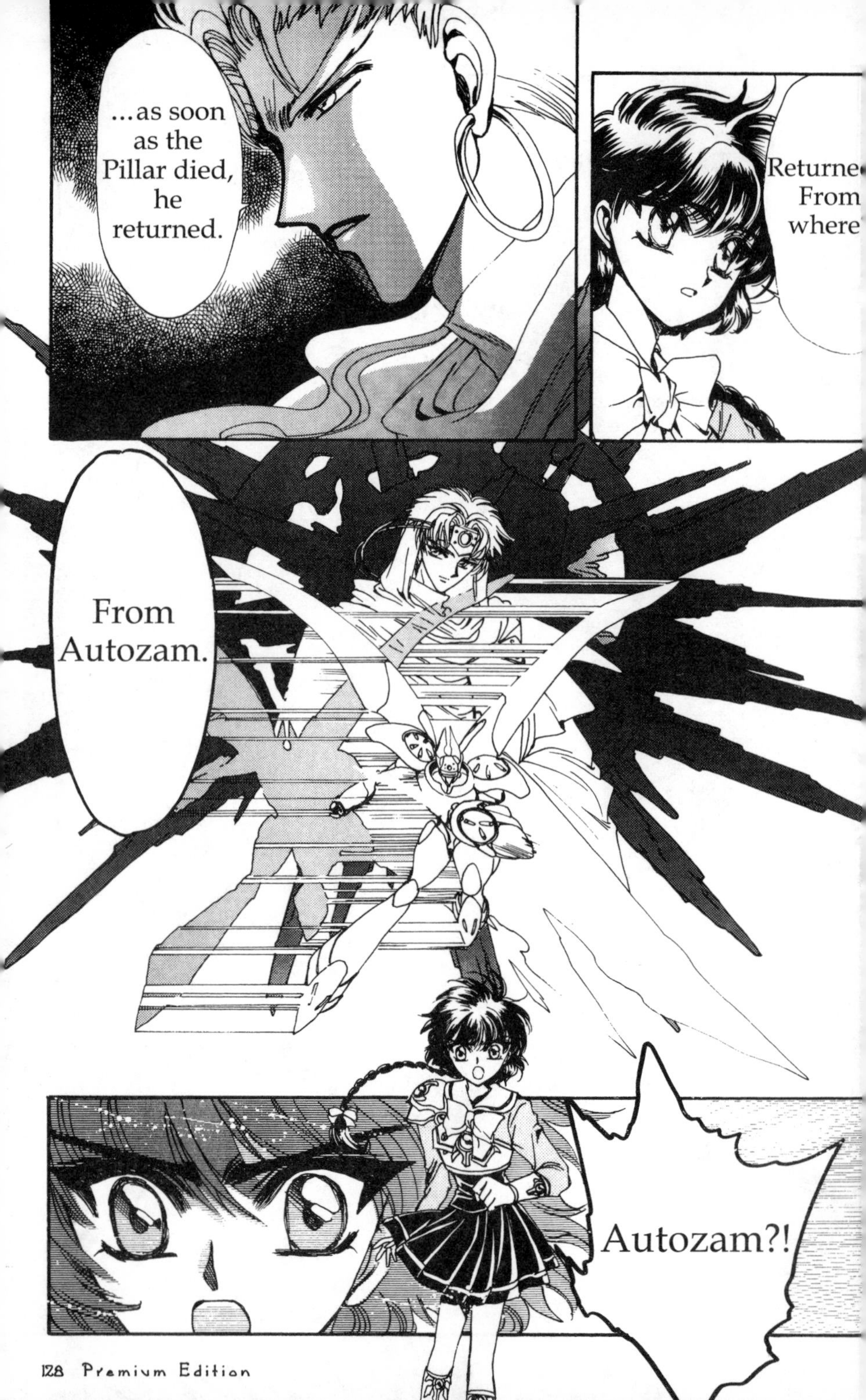
Returne
From
where
...as soon as the Pillar died, he returned.
From Autozam.
Autozam?!

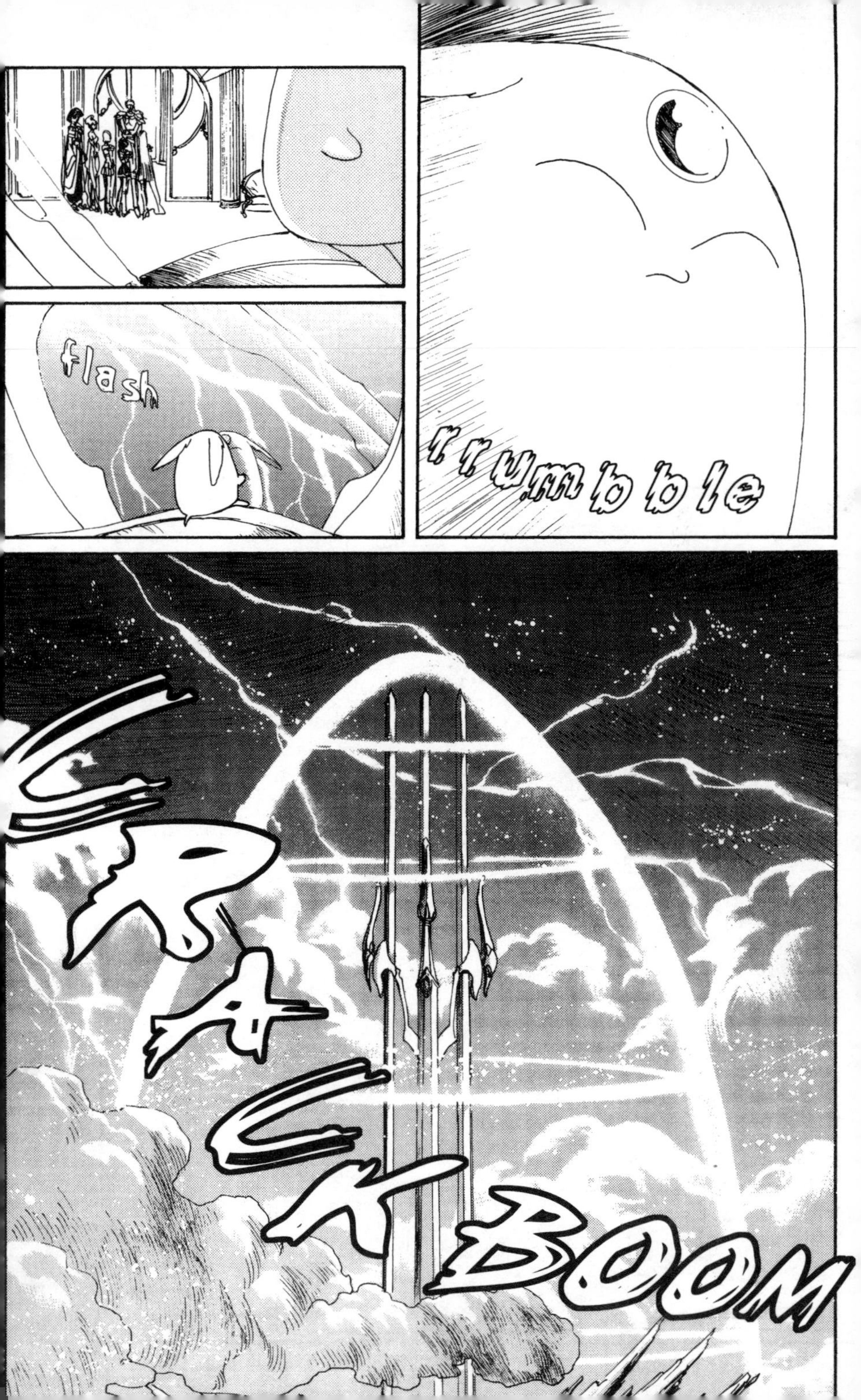
flash
rrumbble
CRACK BOOM

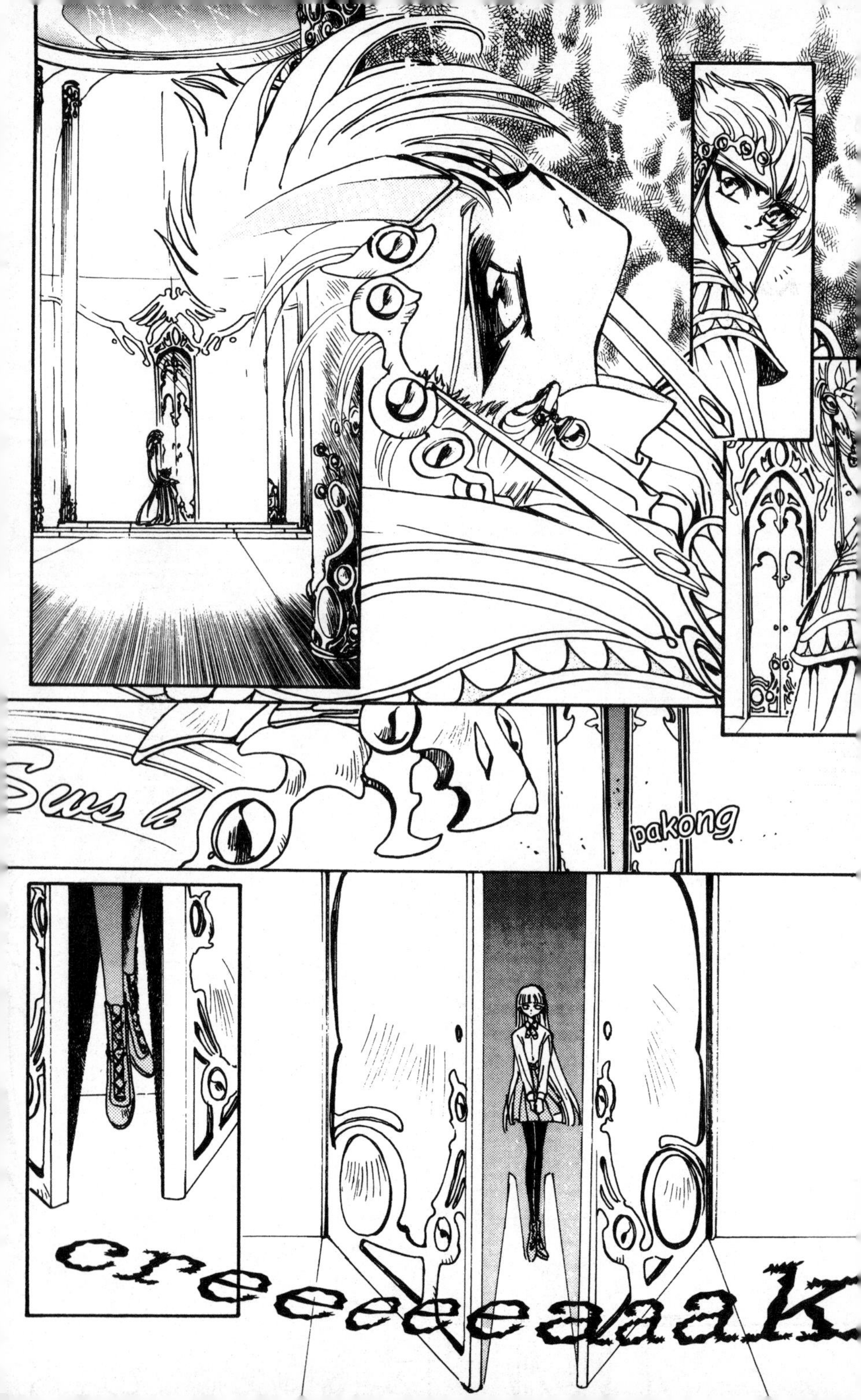
pakong
creeeeeaaaK

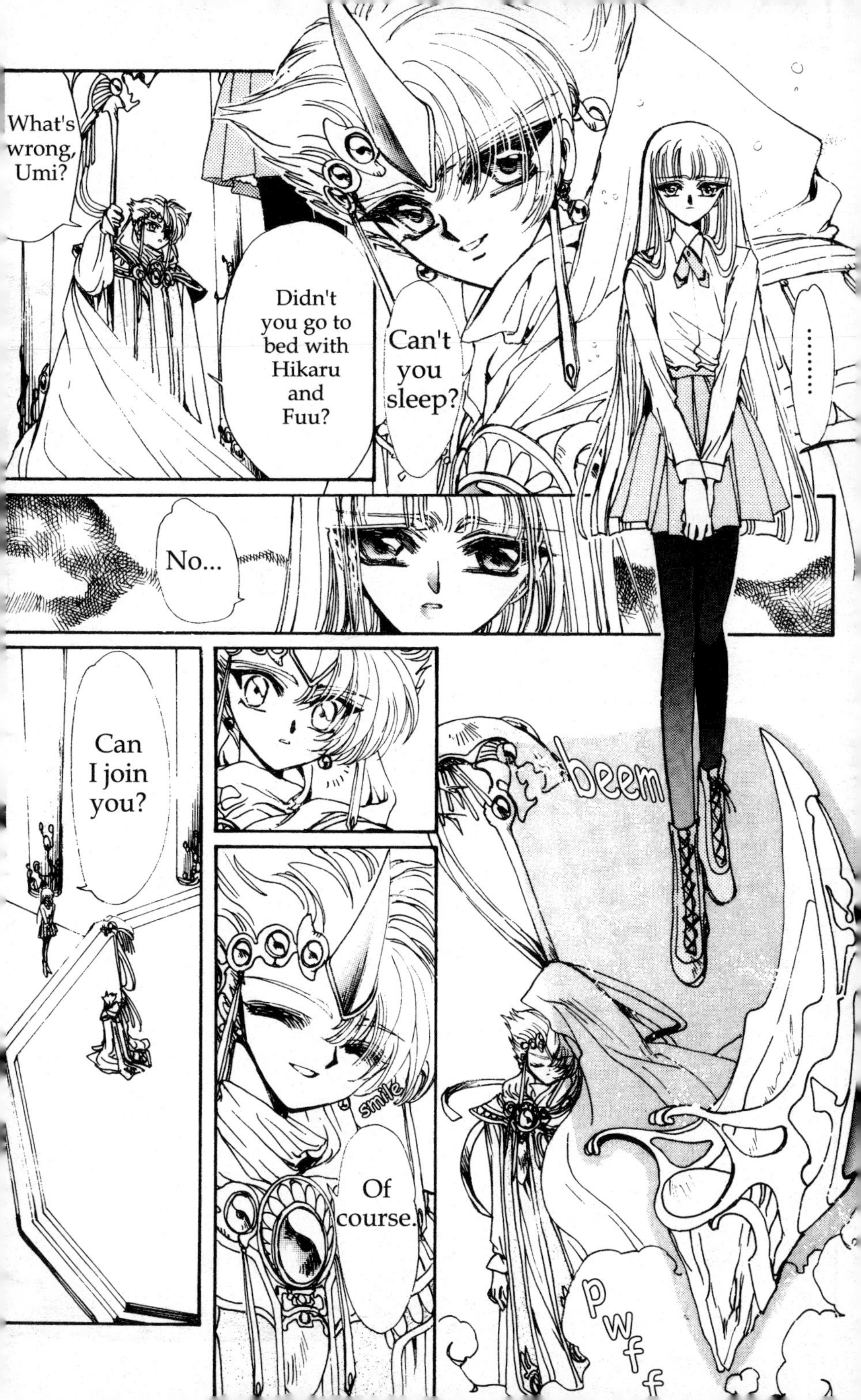
What's wrong, Umi?
Didn't you go to bed with Hikaru and Fuu?
Can't you sleep?
......
No...
Can I join you?
beem
smile
Of course.
pwff

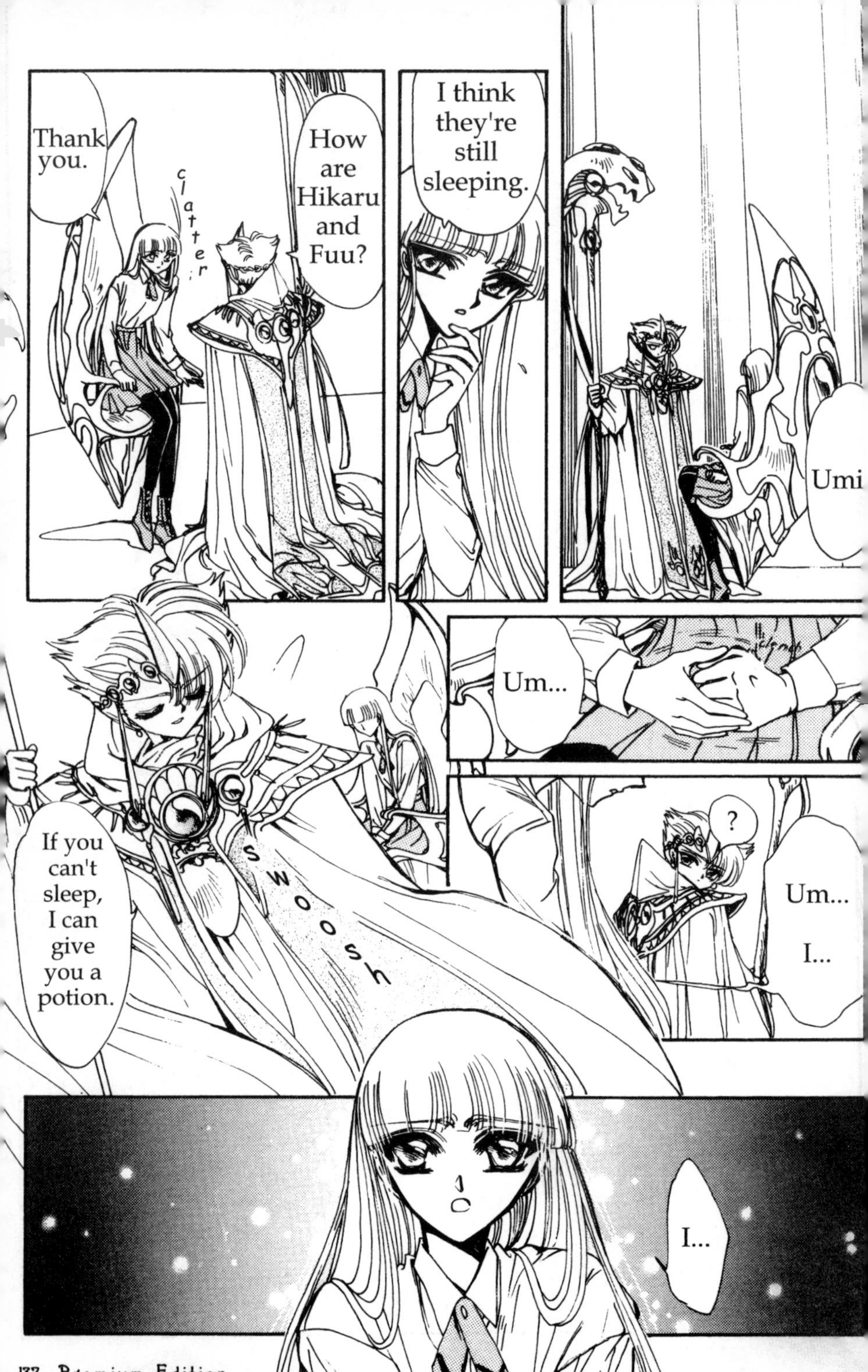
Thank you.
clatter
How are Hikaru and Fuu?
I think they're still sleeping.
Umi
If you can't sleep, I can give you a potion.
swoosh
Um...
clench
?
Um... I...
I...

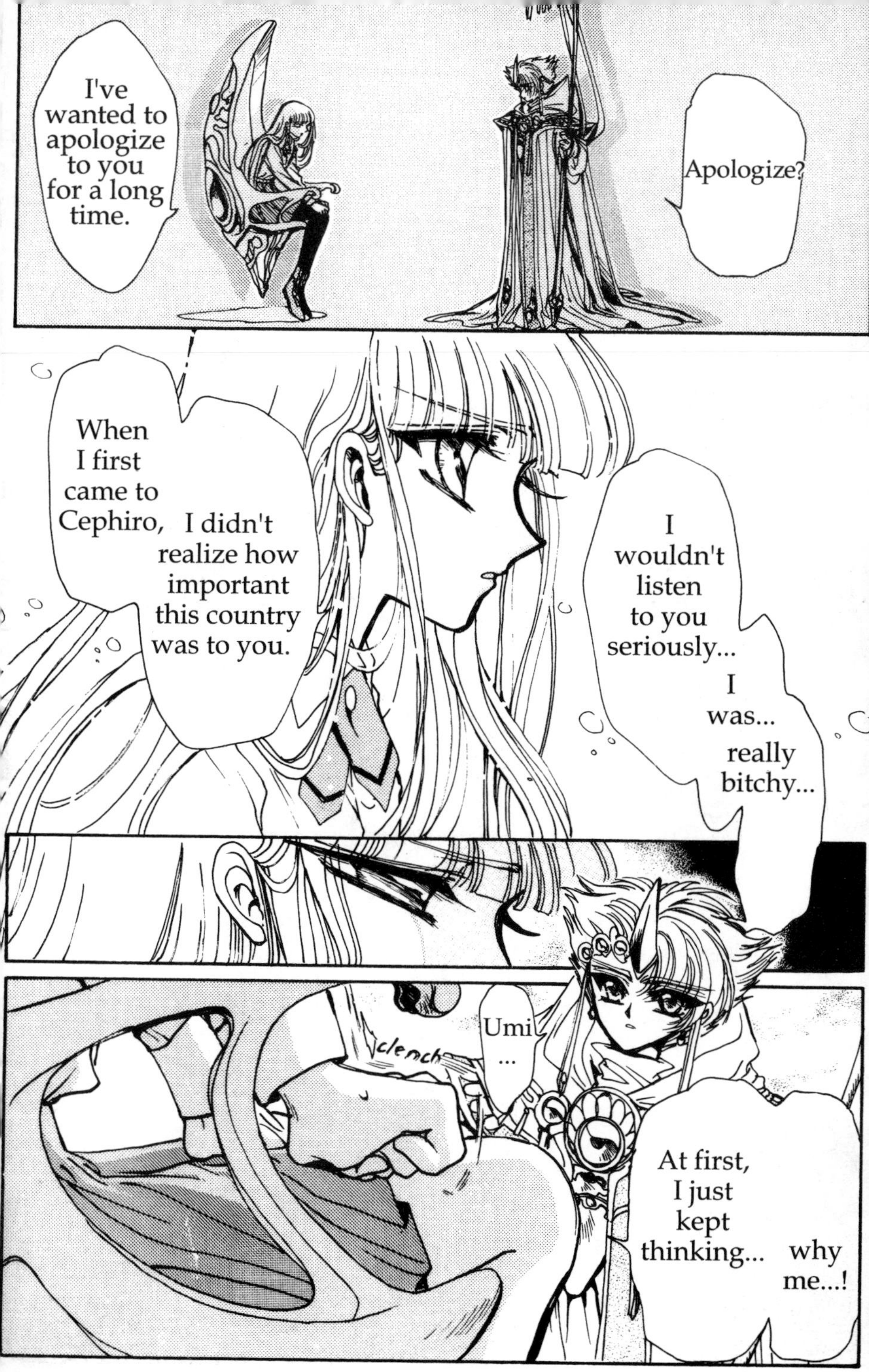
I've wanted to apologize to you for a long time.
Apologize?
When I first came to Cephiro,
I didn't realize how important this country was to you.
I wouldn't listen to you seriously...
I was... really bitchy...
clench
Umi...
At first, I just kept thinking... why me...!

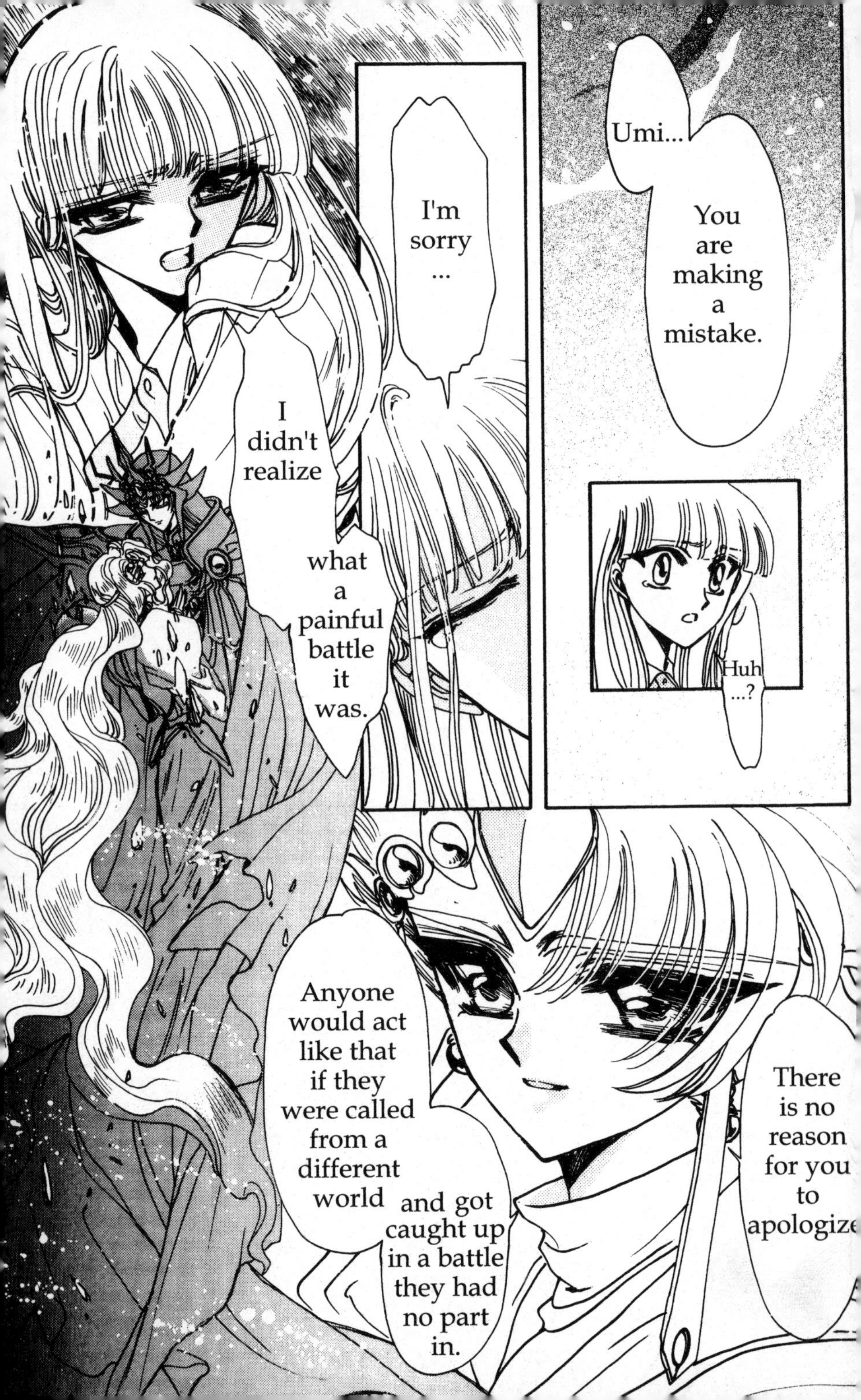
I'm sorry ...
I didn't realize
what a painful battle it was.
Umi...
You are making a mistake.
Huh ...?
There is no reason for you to apologize
Anyone would act like that if they were called from a different world
and got caught up in a battle they had no part in.

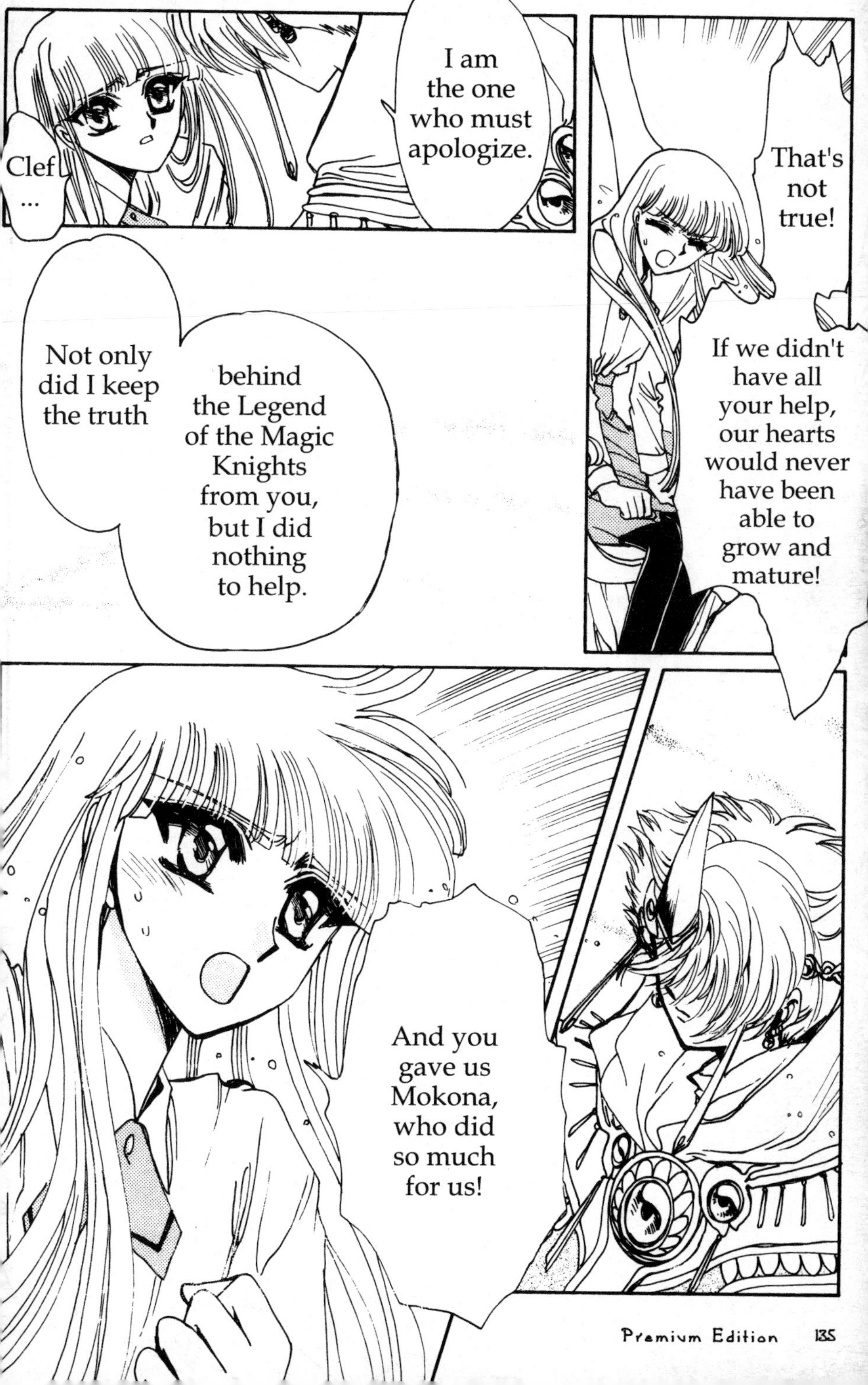
Clef ...
I am the one who must apologize.
That's not true!
If we didn't have all your help, our hearts would never have been able to grow and mature!
Not only did I keep the truth
behind the Legend of the Magic Knights from you, but I did nothing to help.
And you gave us Mokona, who did so much for us!

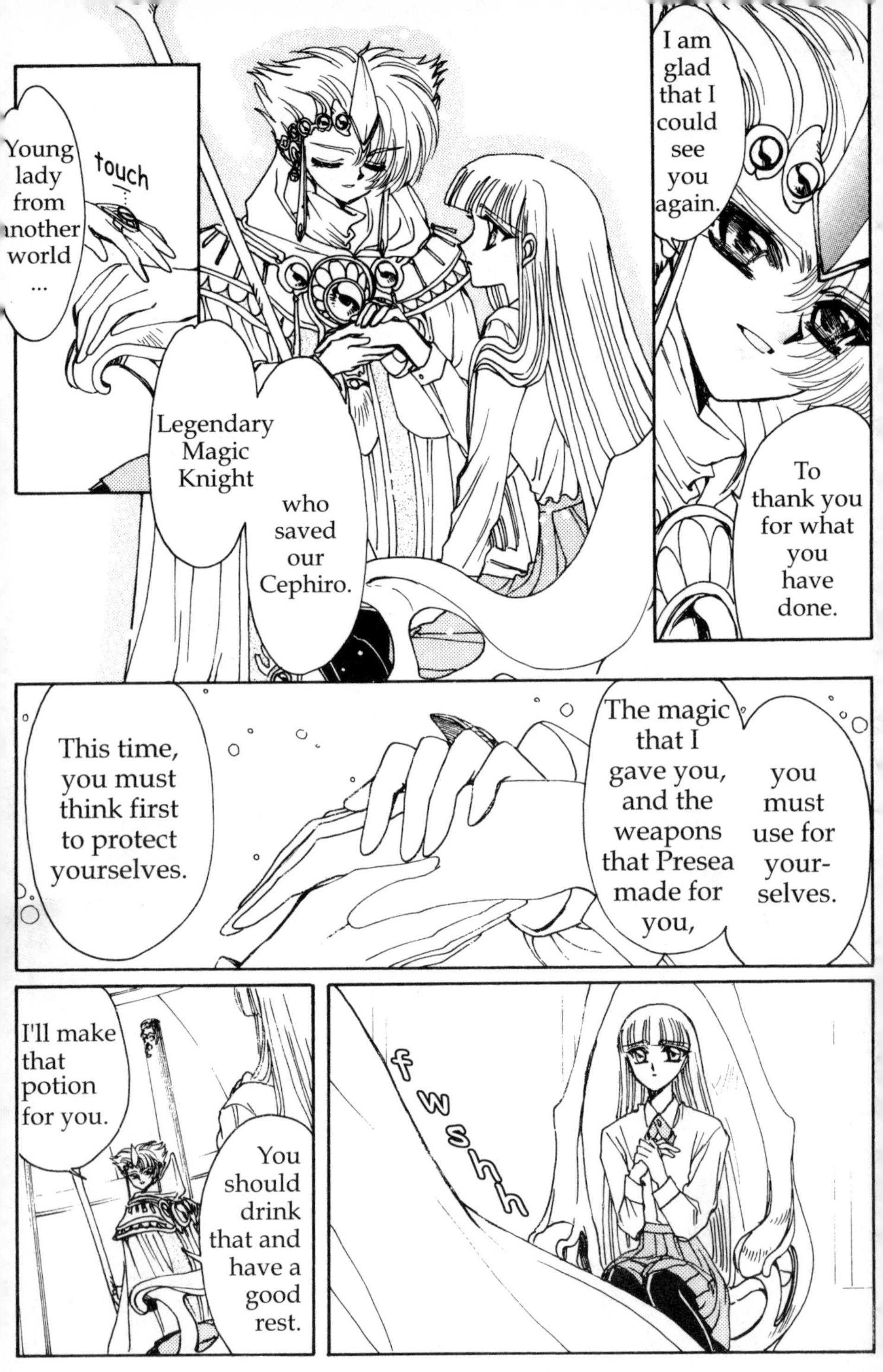
I am glad that I could see you again.
To thank you for what you have done.
Young lady from another world ...
touch
Legendary Magic Knight
who saved our Cephiro.
The magic that I gave you, and the weapons that Presea made for you,
you must use for yourselves.
This time, you must think first to protect yourselves.
fwshh
I'll make that potion for you.
You should drink that and have a good rest.

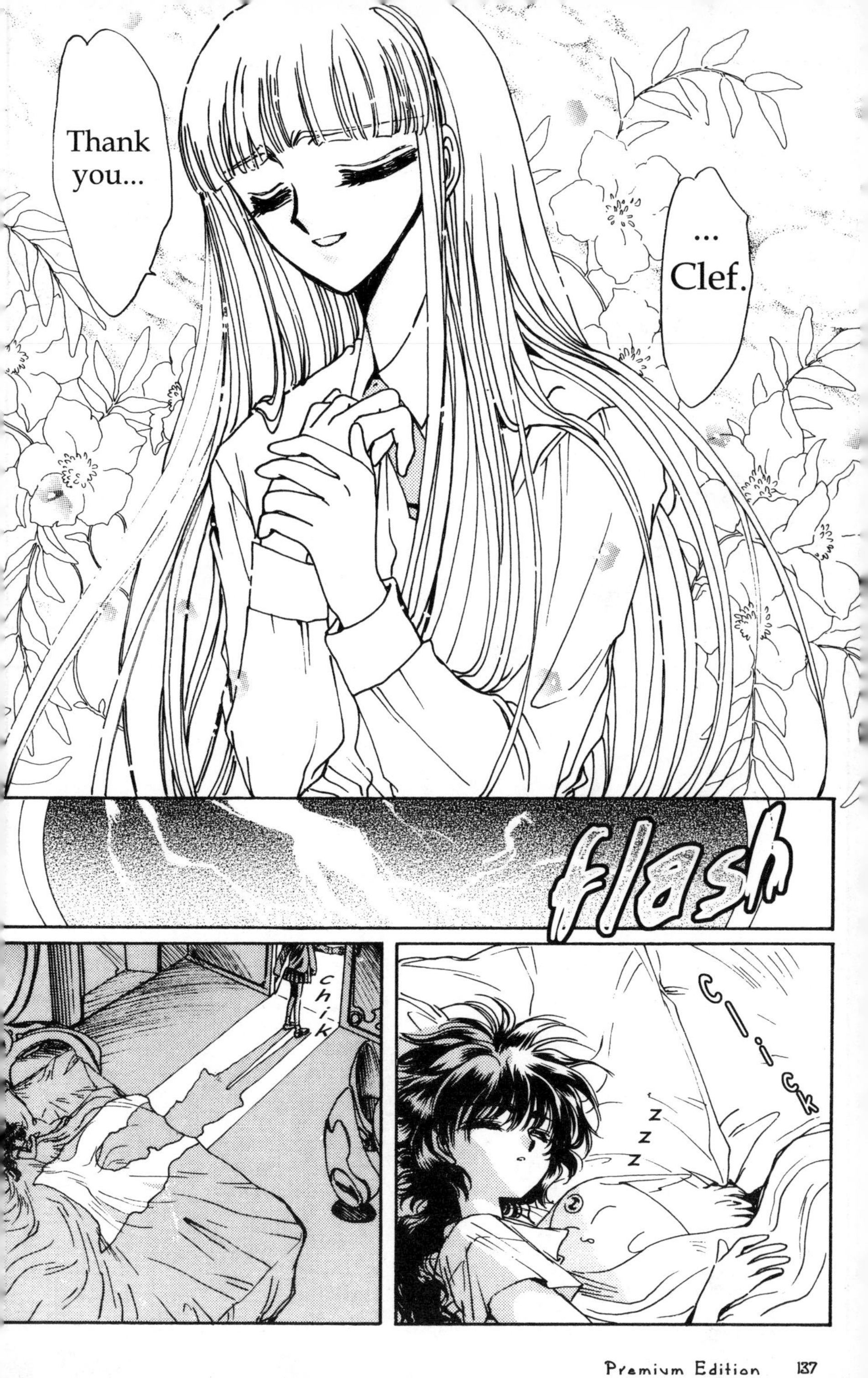
Thank you...
... Clef.
flash
Click
Z Z Z
chik

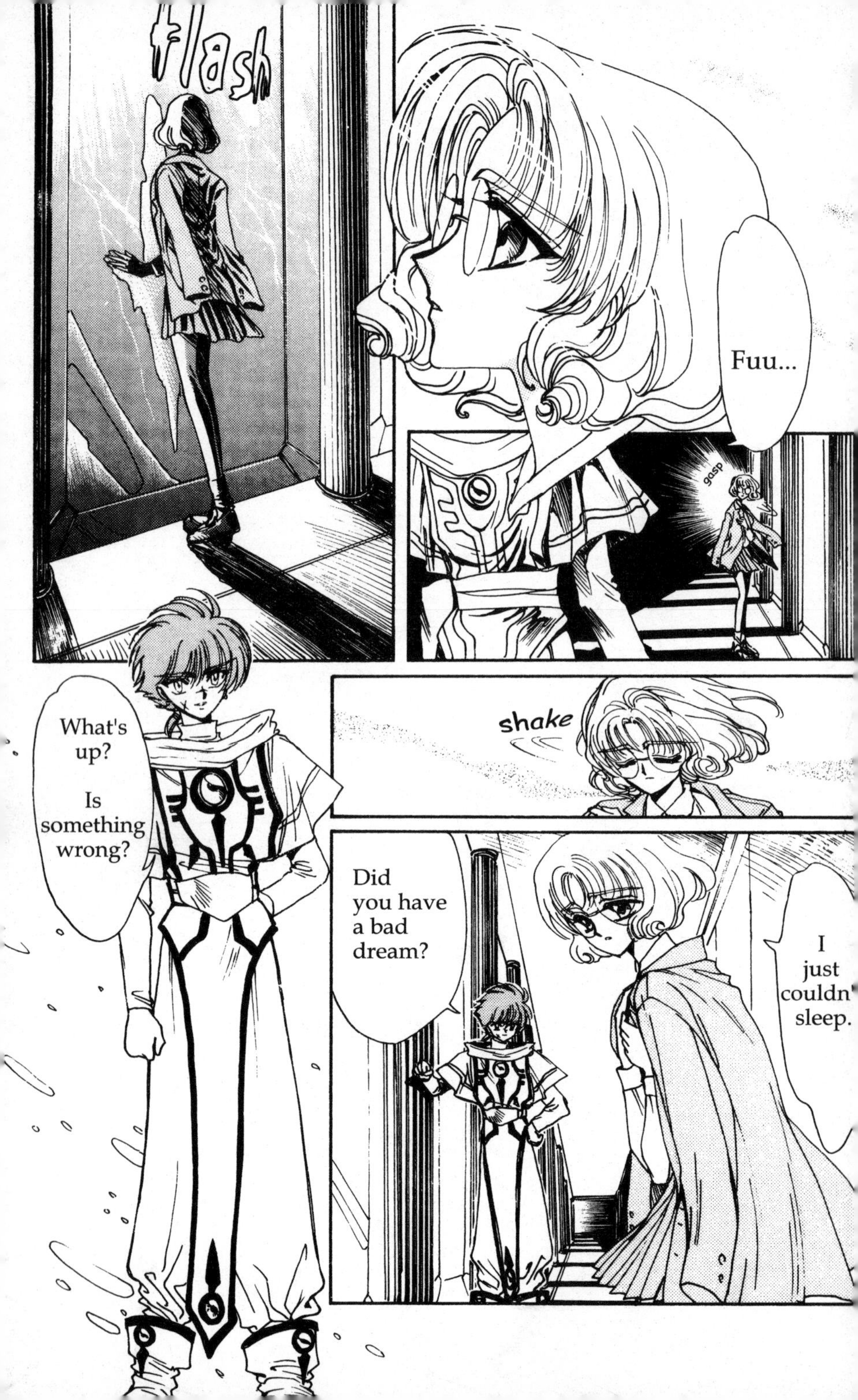
flash
Fuu...
gasp
shake
What's up?
Is something wrong?
Did you have a bad dream?
I just couldn't sleep.

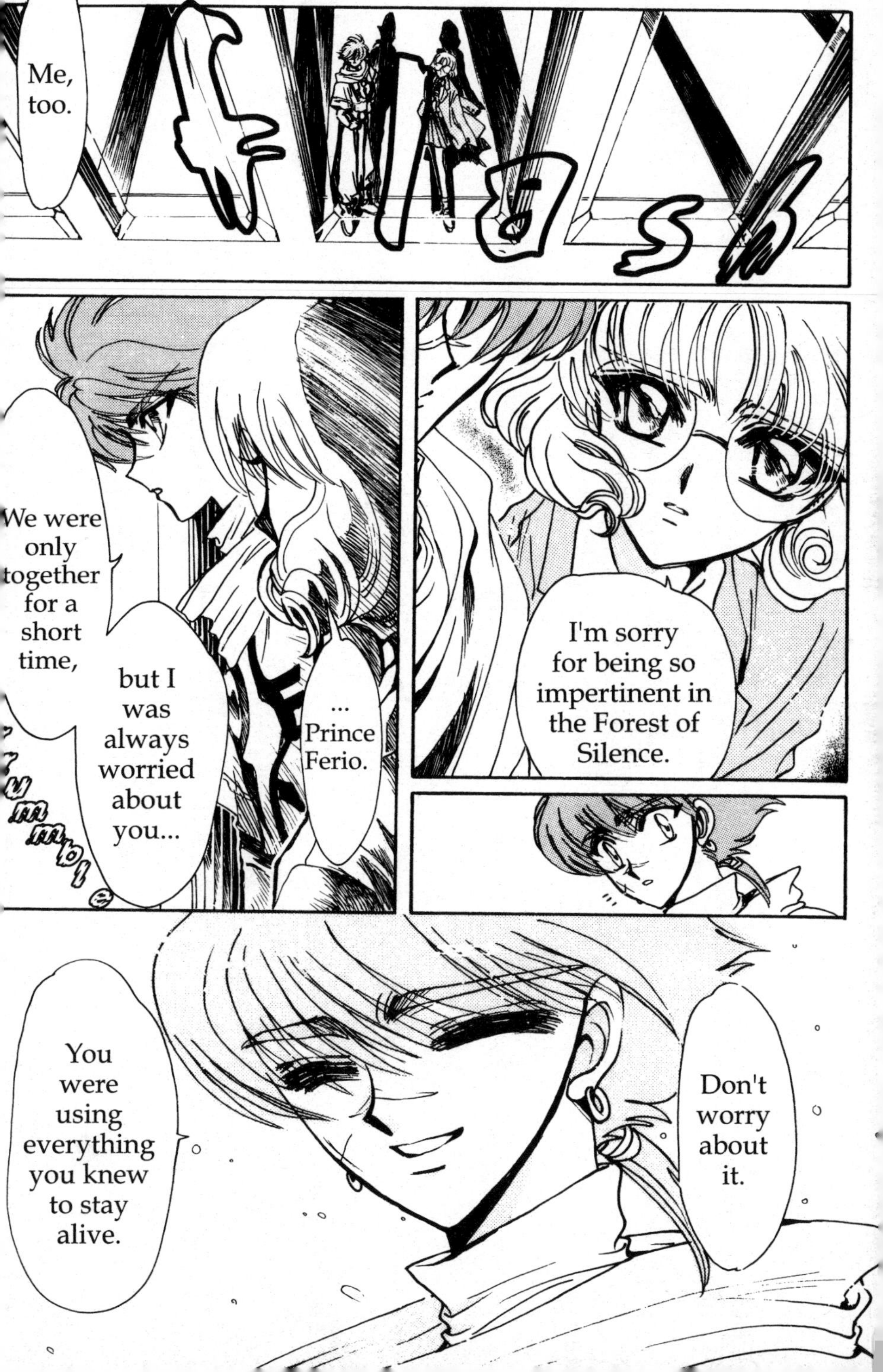
Me, too.
We were only together for a short time,
but I was always worried about you...
... Prince Ferio.
I'm sorry for being so impertinent in the Forest of Silence.
Don't worry about it.
You were using everything you knew to stay alive.

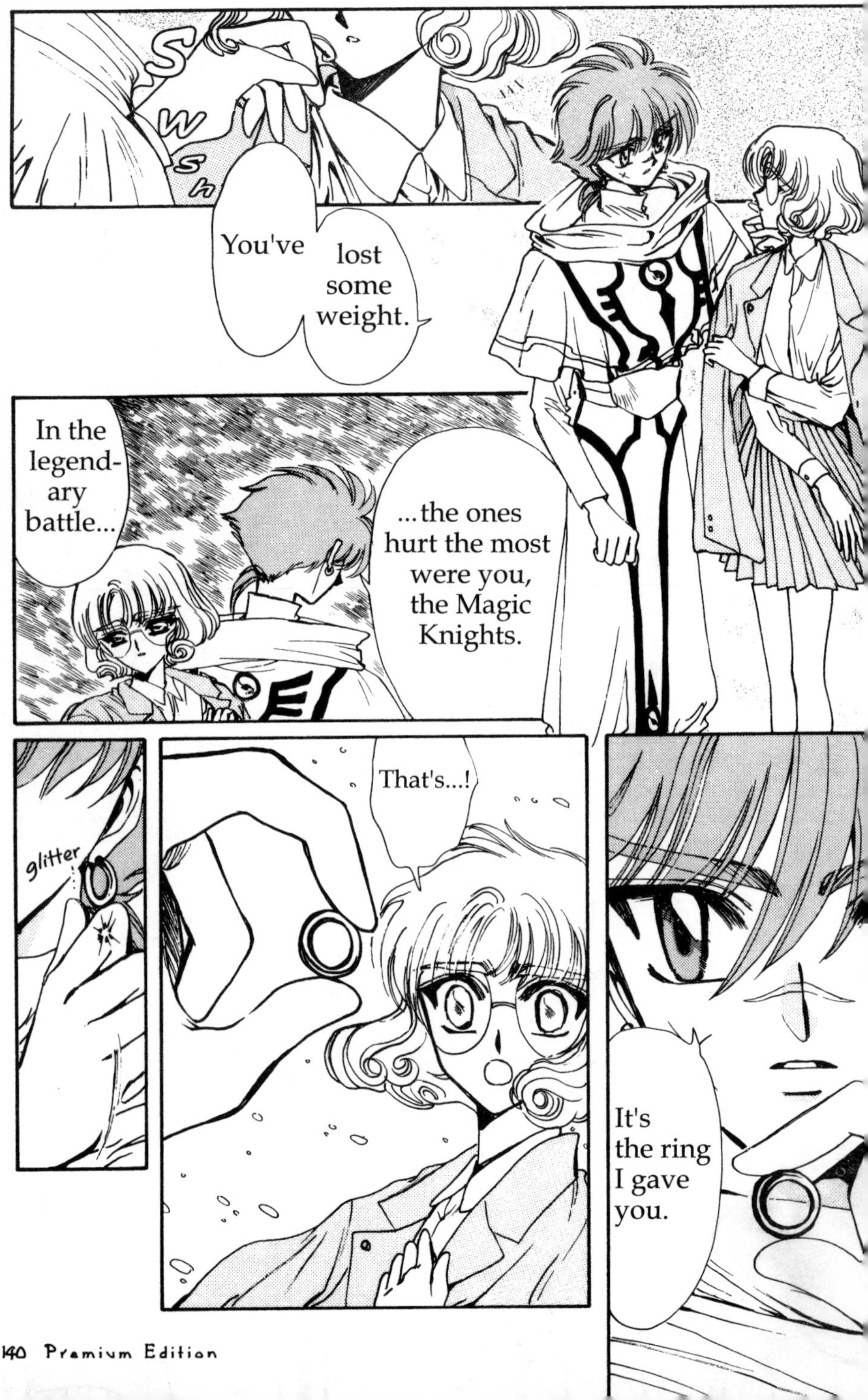
Swsh
You've lost some weight.
In the legendary battle...
...the ones hurt the most were you, the Magic Knights.
glitter
That's...!
It's the ring I gave you.

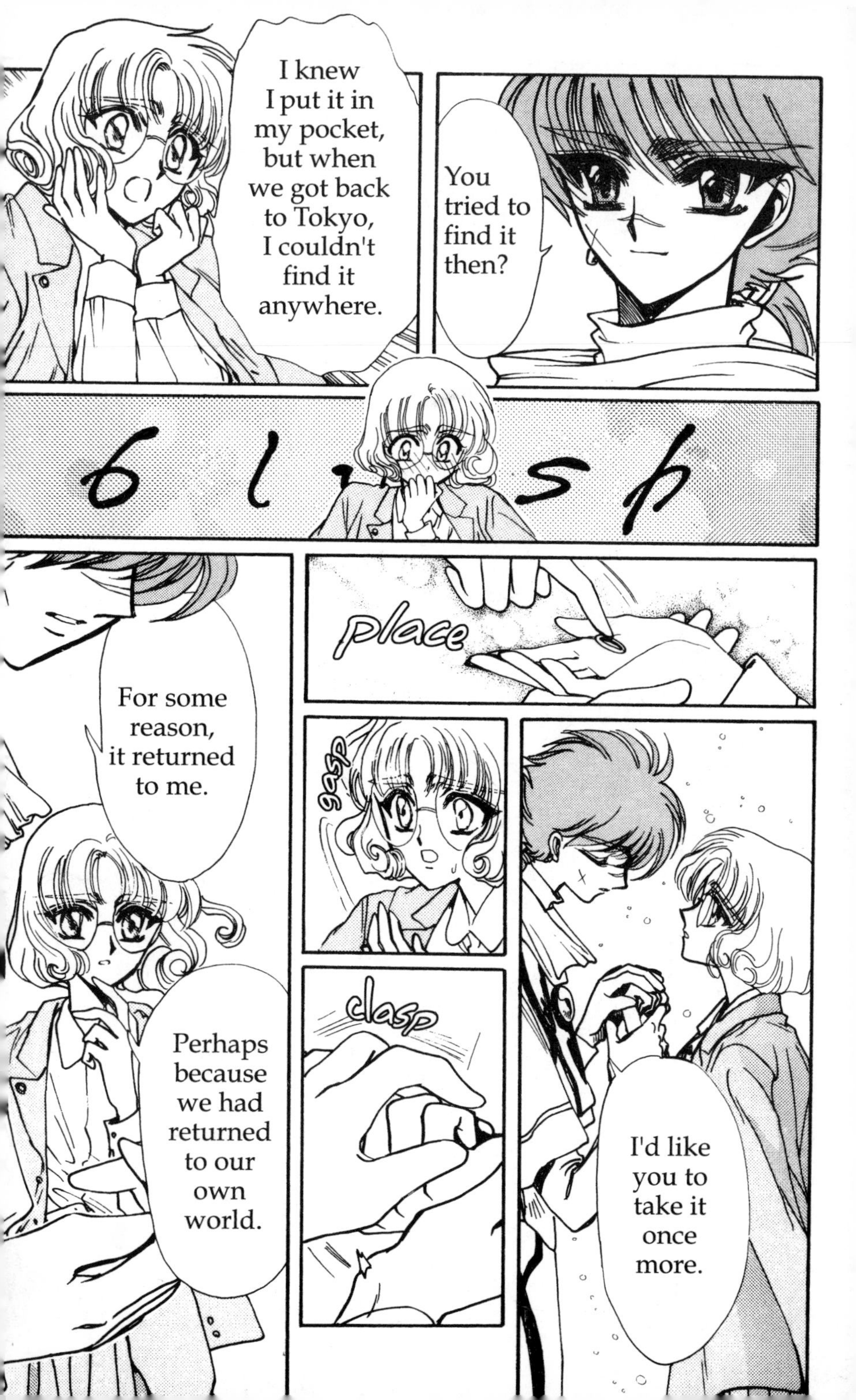
I knew I put it in my pocket, but when we got back to Tokyo, I couldn't find it anywhere.
You tried to find it then?
blush
For some reason, it returned to me.
Perhaps because we had returned to our own world.
place
gasp
clasp
I'd like you to take it once more.

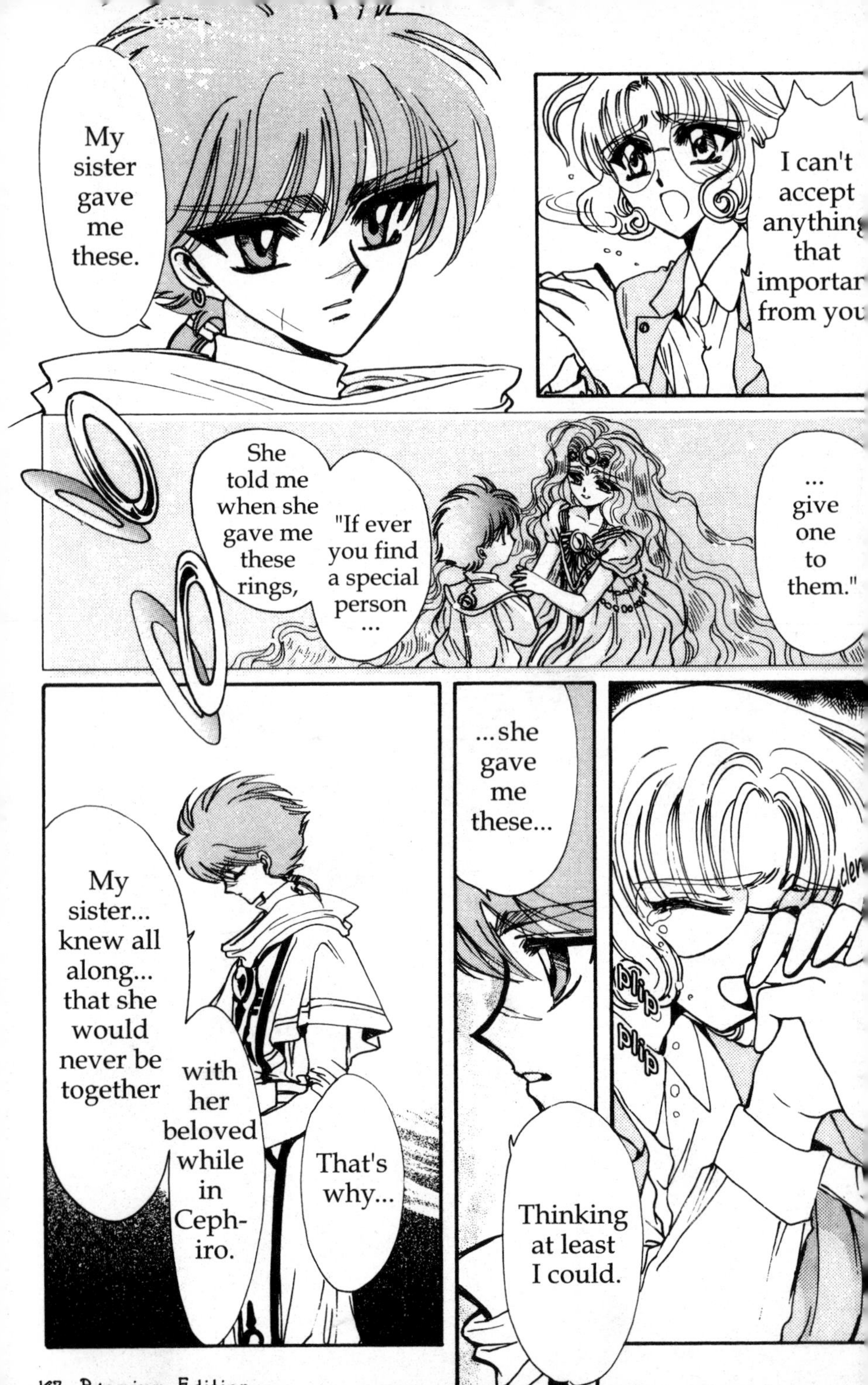
My sister gave me these.
I can't accept anythin that importar from you
She told me when she gave me these rings,
"If ever you find a special person ...
... give one to them."
My sister... knew all along... that she would never be together
with her beloved while in Ceph-iro.
That's why...
...she gave me these...
plip
plip
Thinking at least I could.

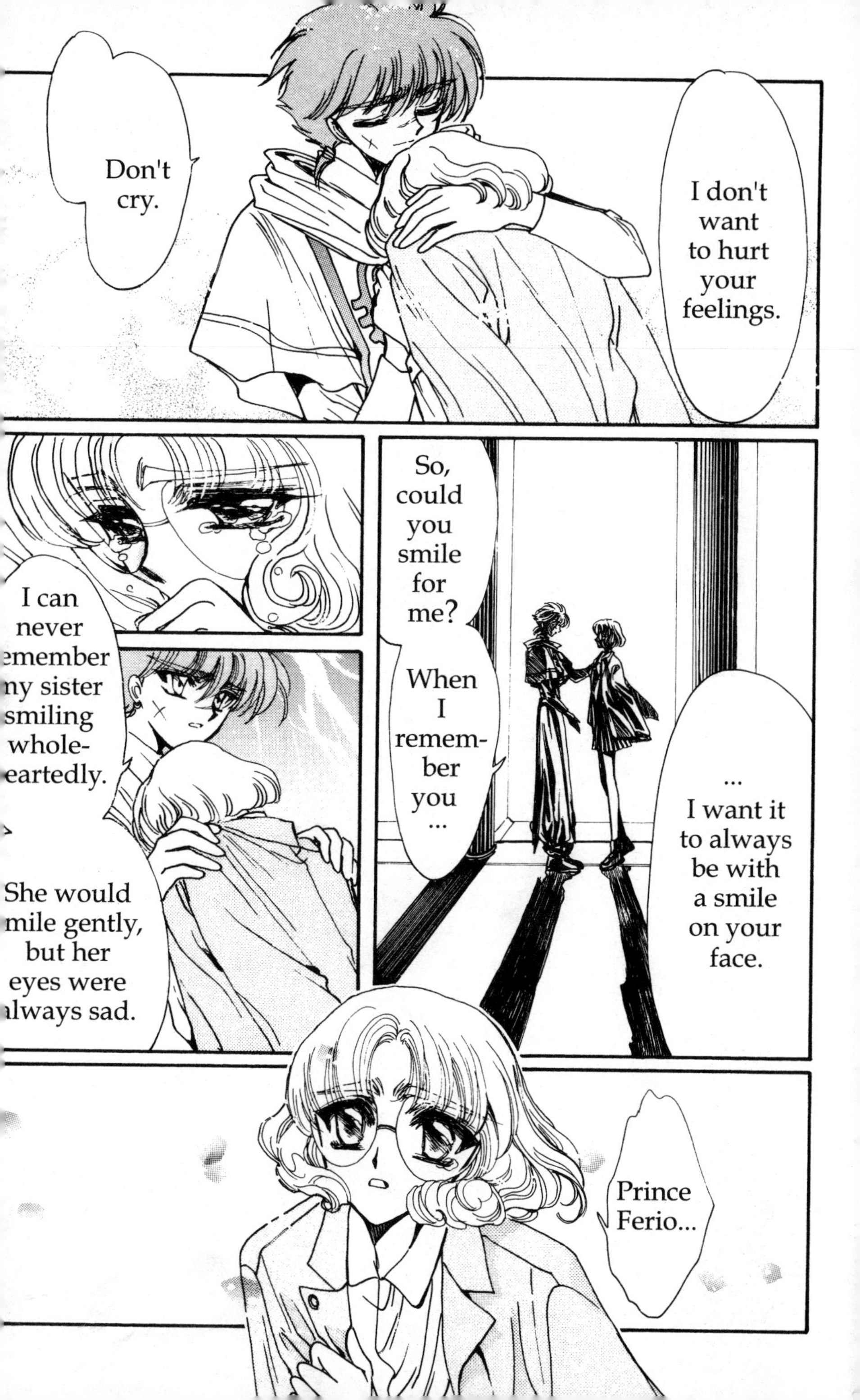
I don't want to hurt your feelings.
Don't cry.
So, could you smile for me?
When I remember you ...
... I want it to always be with a smile on your face.
I can never emember ny sister smiling whole- eartedly.
She would mile gently, but her eyes were lways sad.
Prince Ferio...

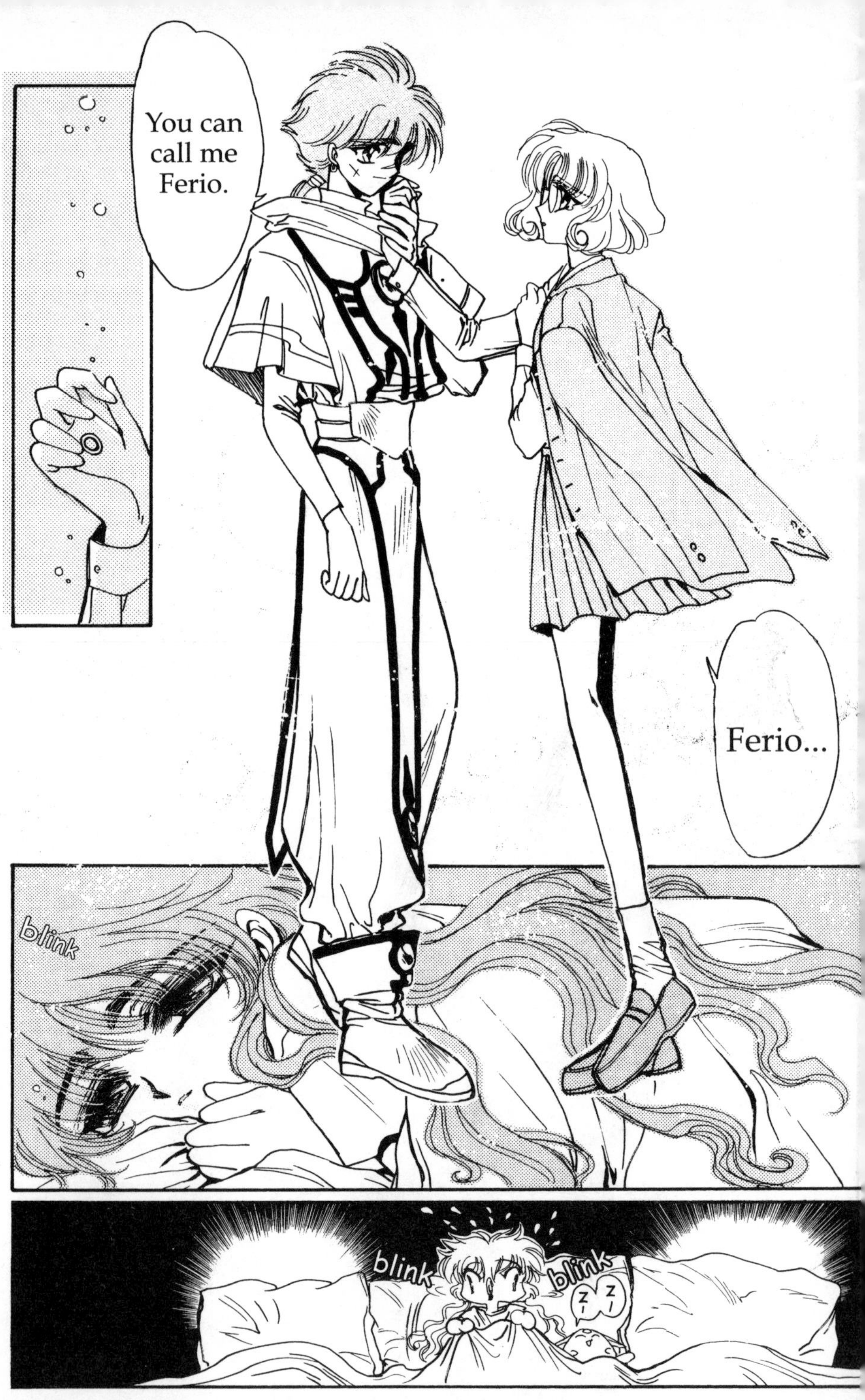
You can call me Ferio.
Ferio...
blink
blink
blink
Z Z

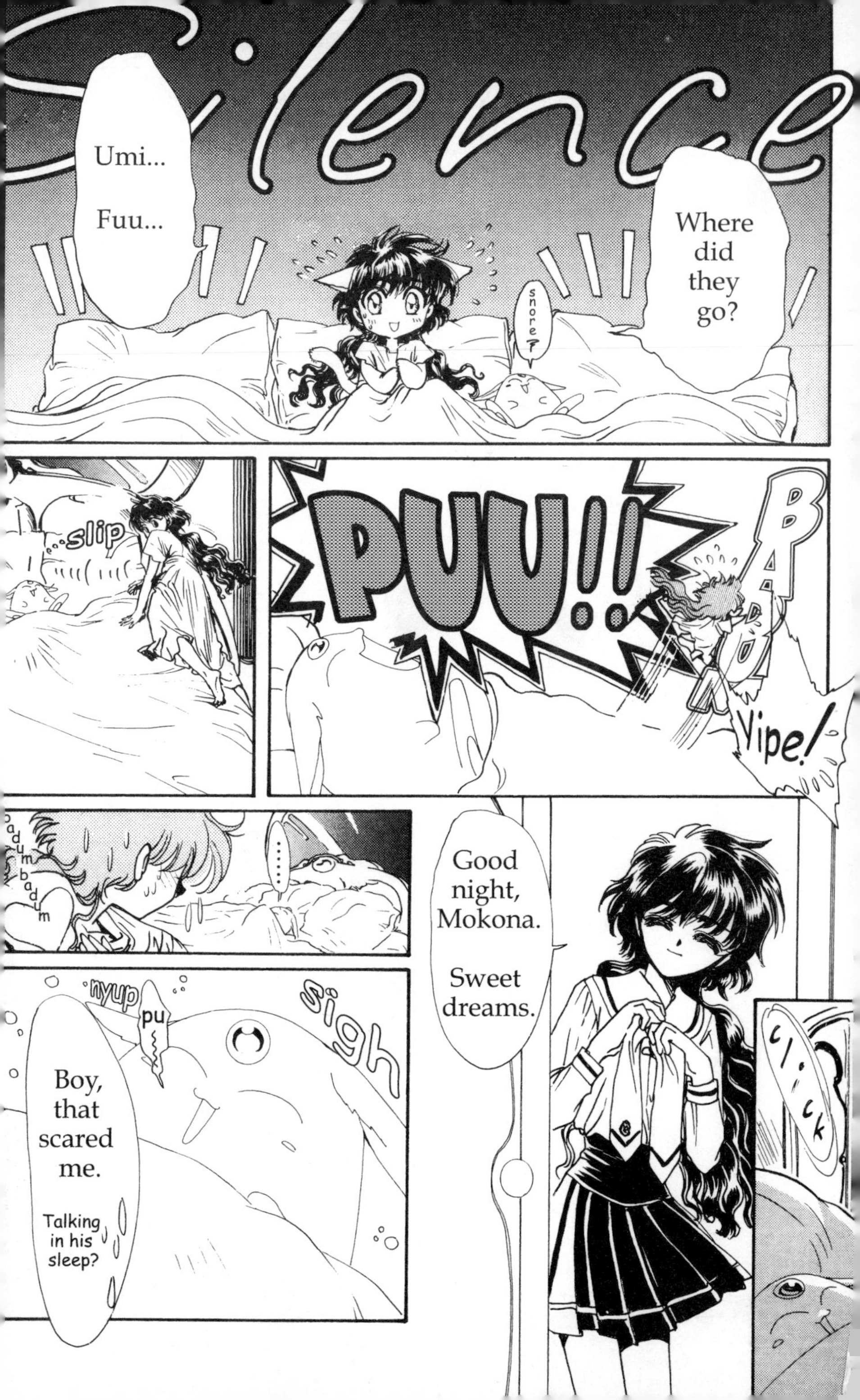
Silence
Umi...
Fuu...
snore
Where did they go?
slip
PUU!!
BADA
Yipe!
badum badum
.....
Good night, Mokona.
Sweet dreams.
nyup
pu
sigh
Boy, that scared me.
Talking in his sleep?
click

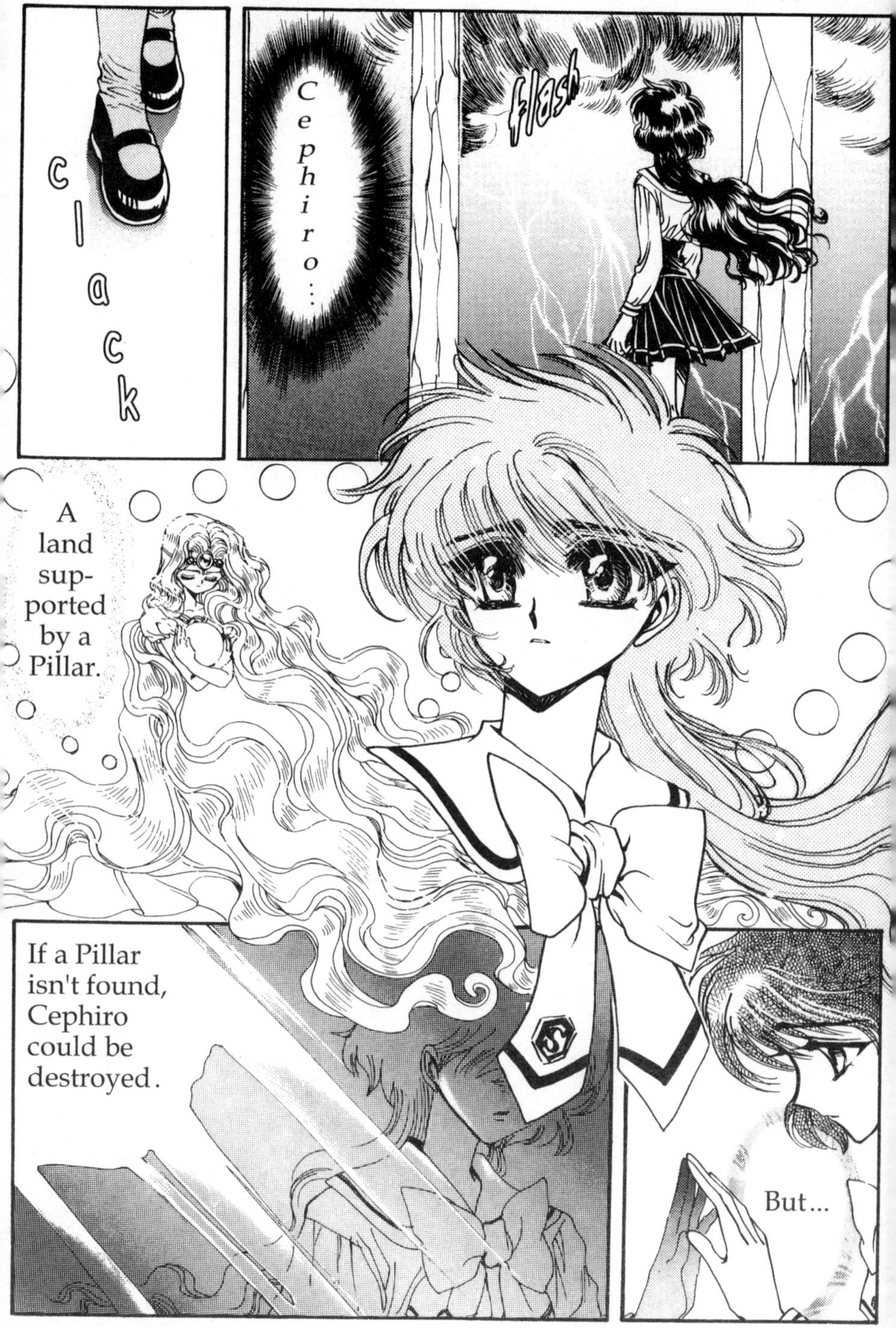
clack
Cephiro...
flash
A land sup-ported by a Pillar.
If a Pillar isn't found, Cephiro could be destroyed.
But...

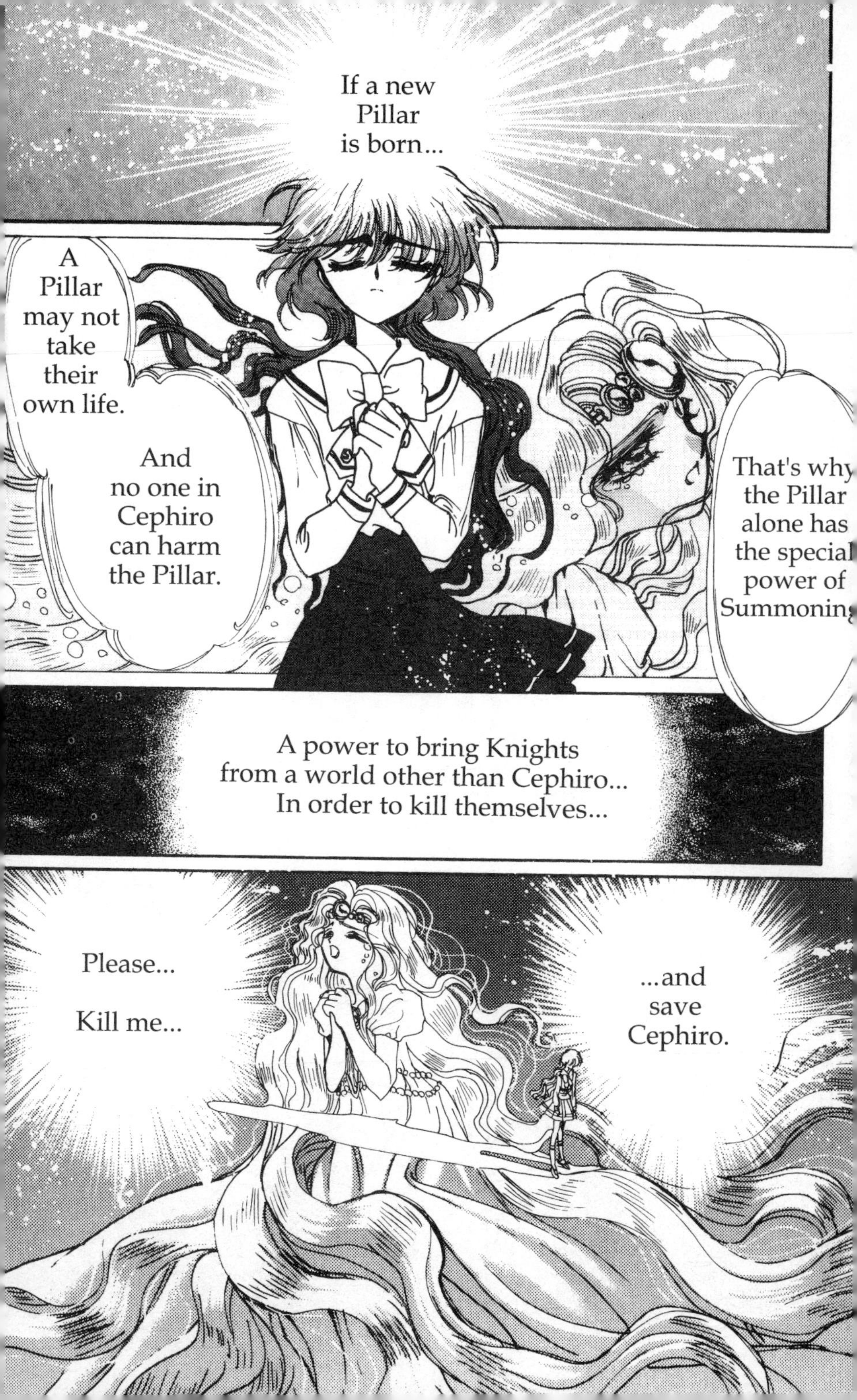
If a new Pillar is born...
A Pillar may not take their own life.
That's why the Pillar alone has the special power of Summoning
And no one in Cephiro can harm the Pillar.
A power to bring Knights from a world other than Cephiro... In order to kill themselves...
...and save Cephiro.
Please...
Kill me...

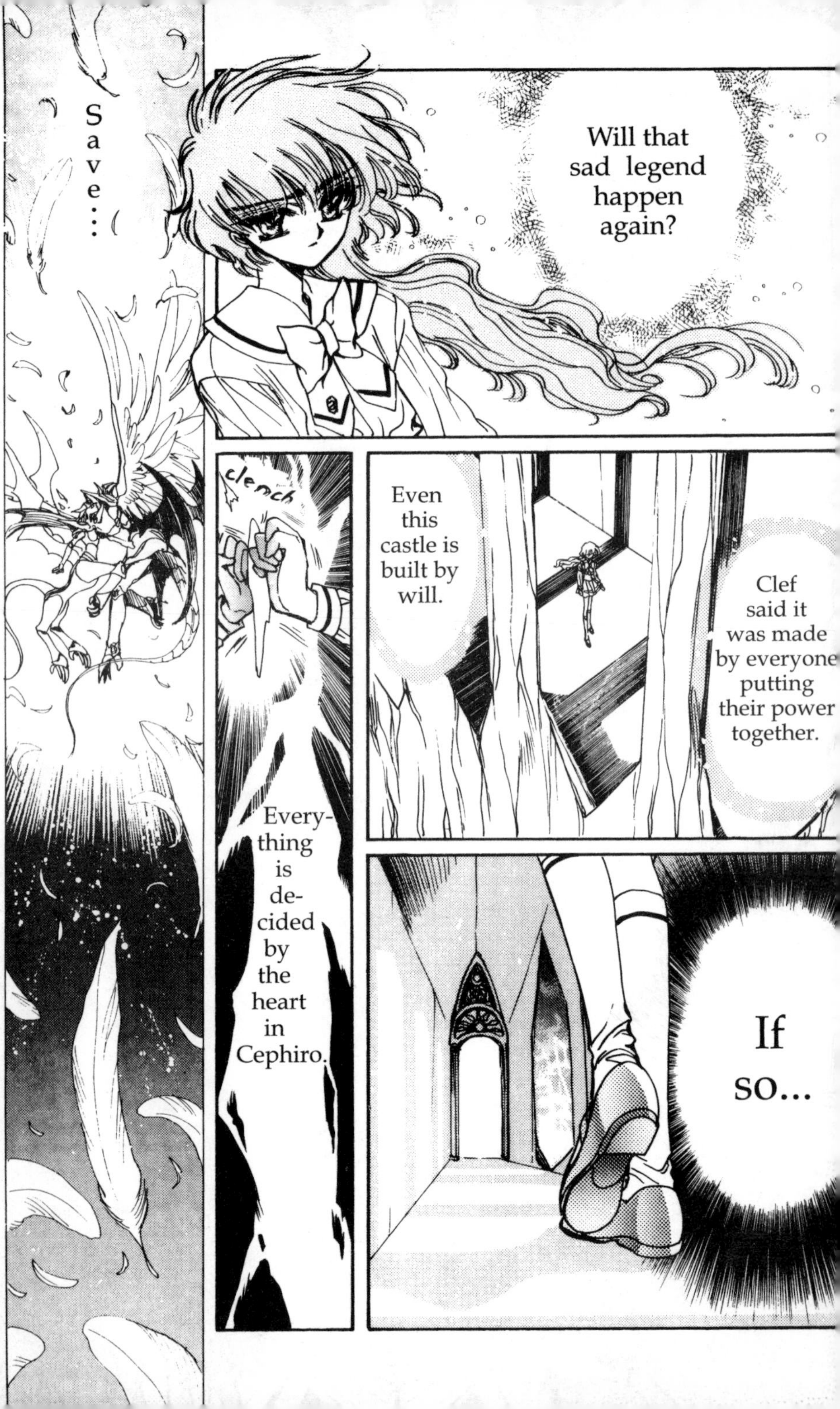

Will that sad legend happen again?
Clef said it was made by everyone putting their power together.
Even this castle is built by will.
clench
Everything is decided by the heart in Cephiro.
If so...
Save...

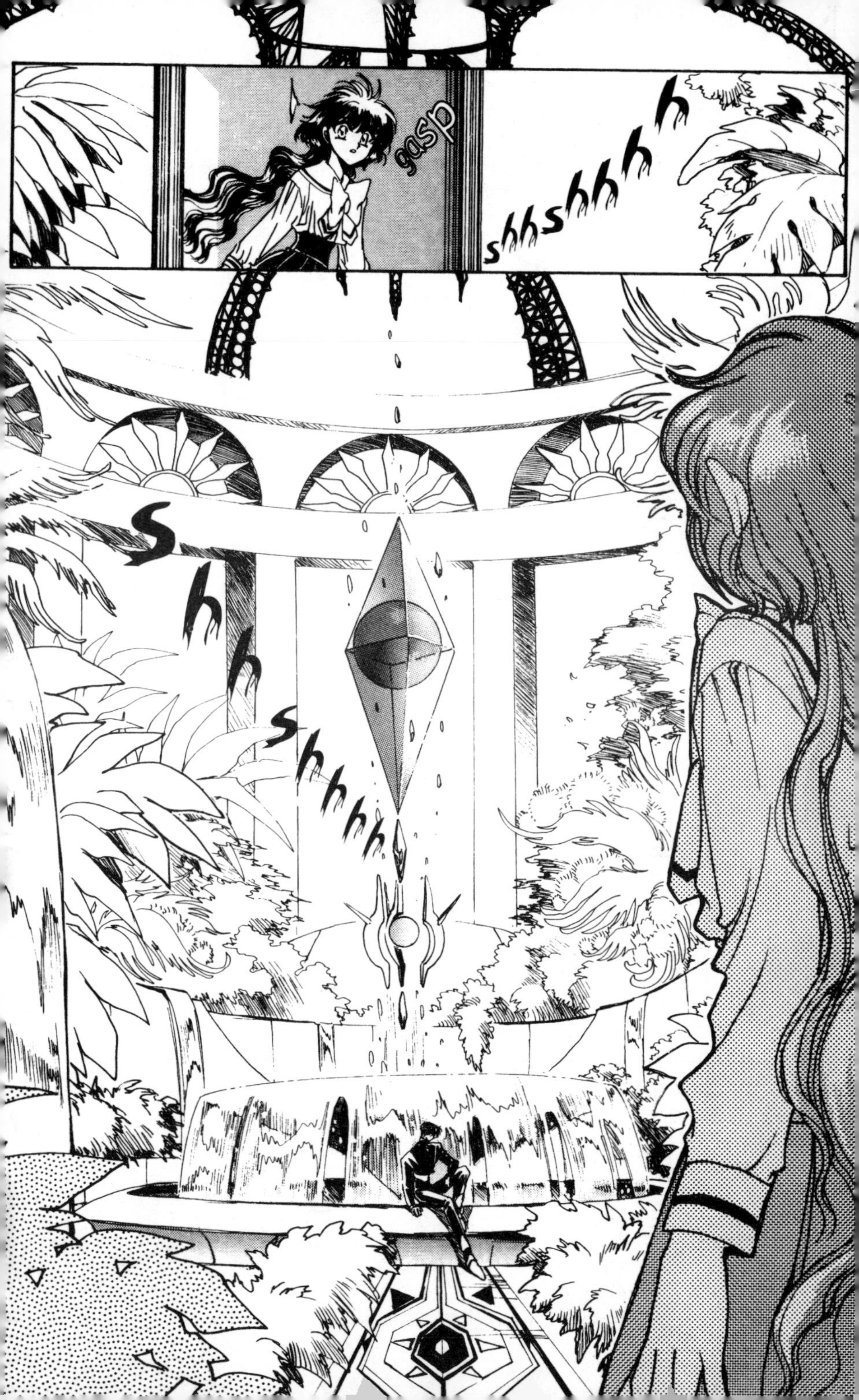
gasp
shhshhhhh
Shhshhhhh

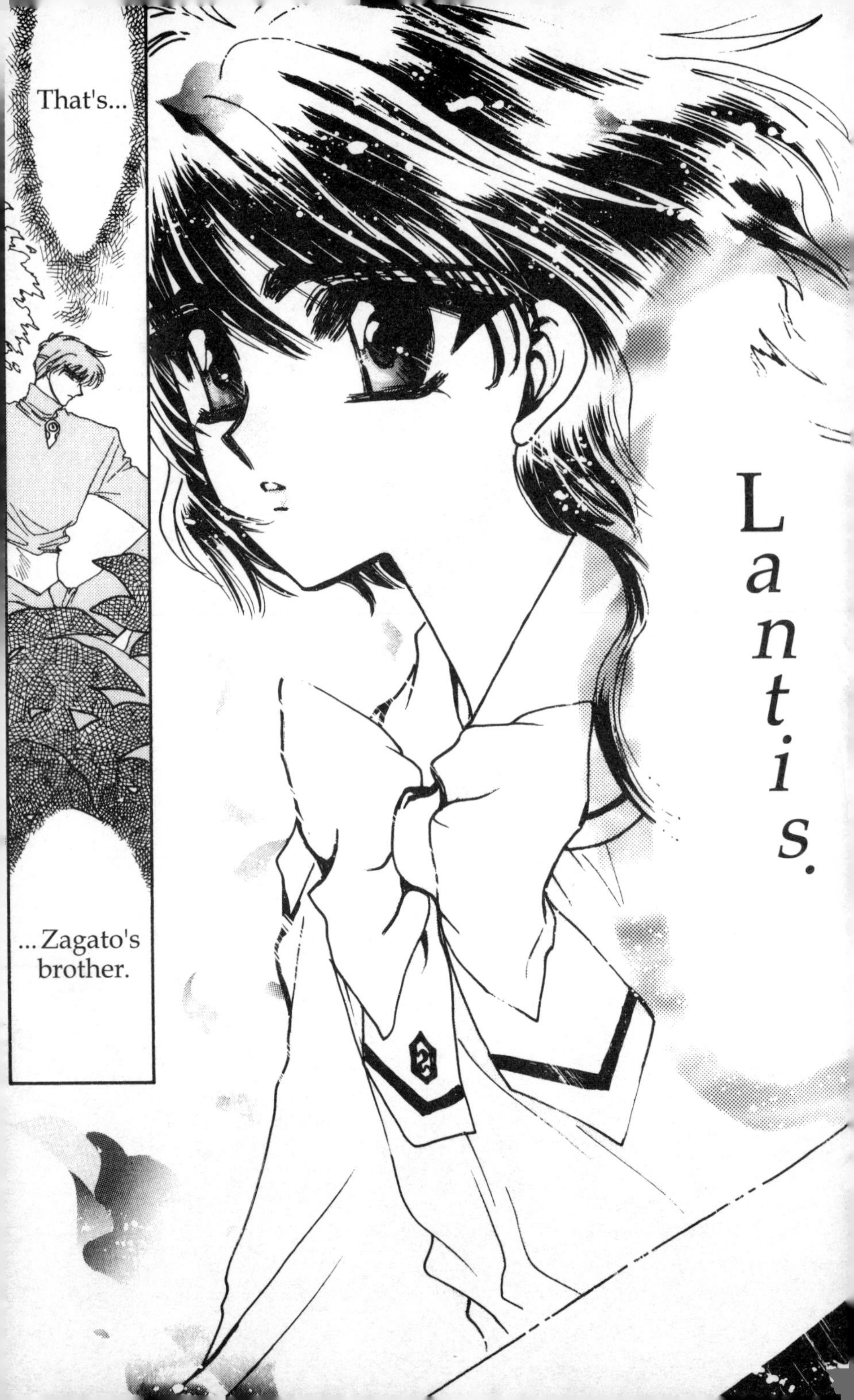

That's...
...Zagato's brother.
Lantis.

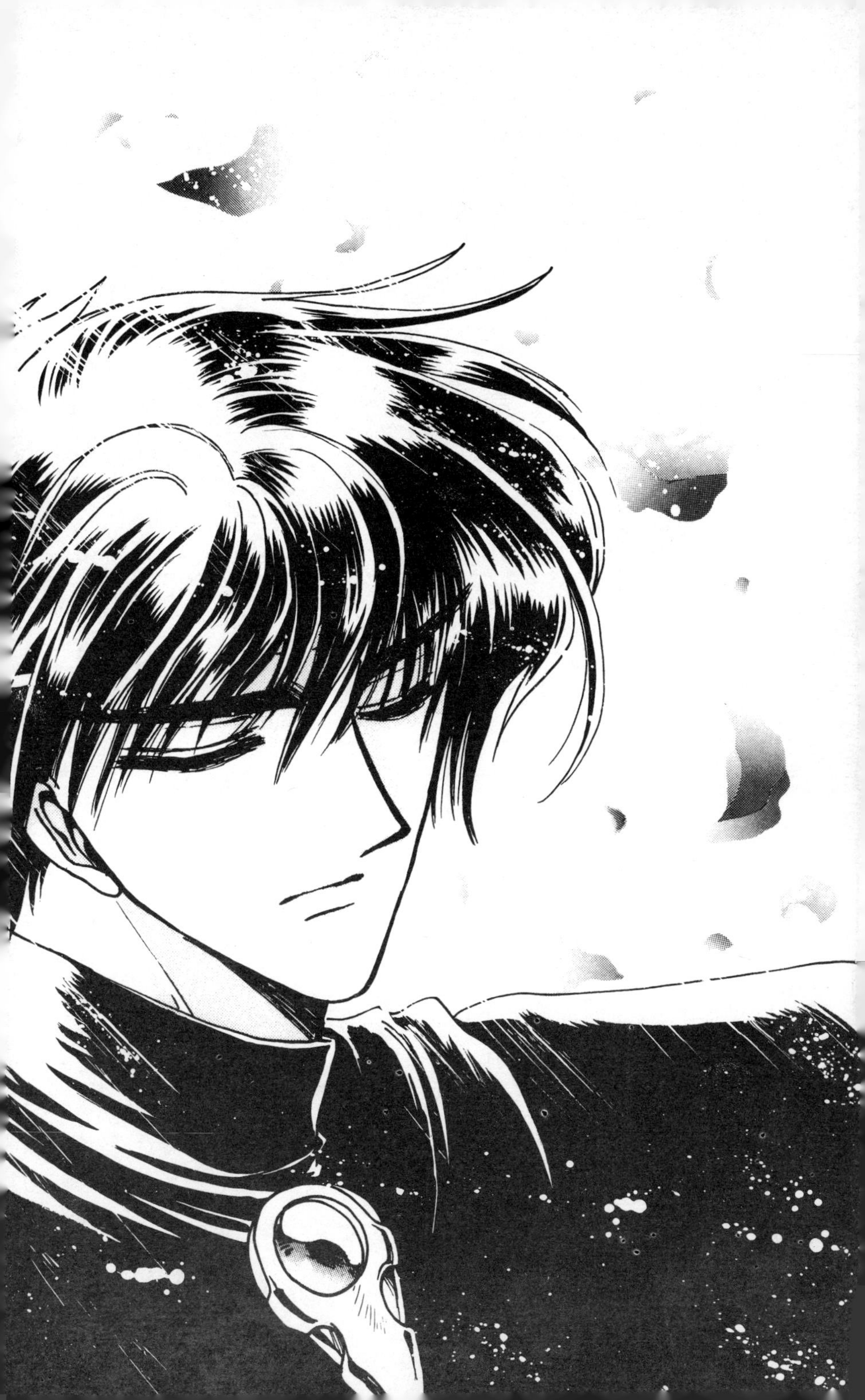

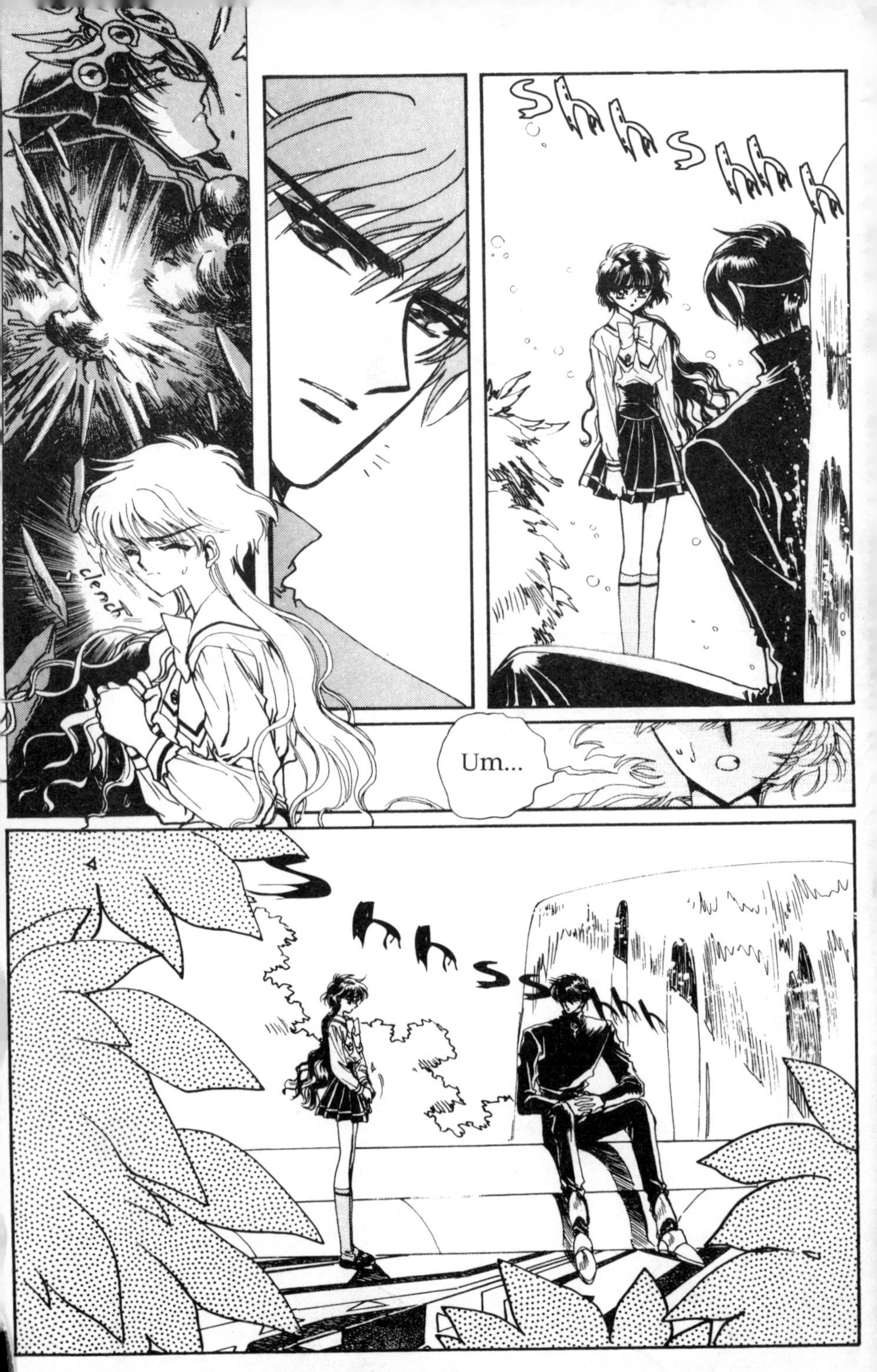
Shhhshhhk
clench
Um...
Shhsshhh

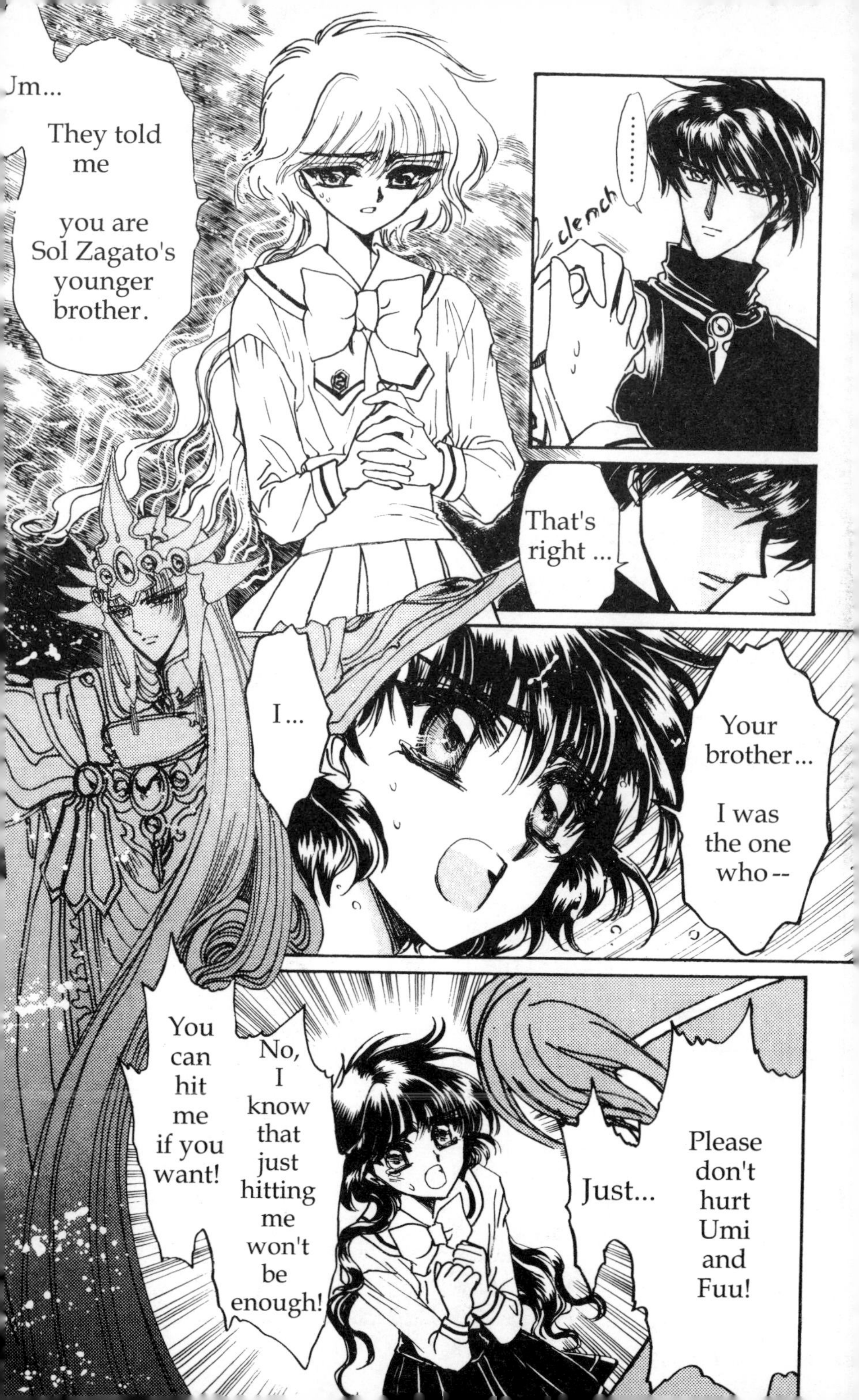
Um...
They told me
you are Sol Zagato's younger brother.
......
clench
That's right ...
Your brother...
I was the one who --
I...
Please don't hurt Umi and Fuu!
Just...
No, I know that just hitting me won't be enough!
You can hit me if you want!

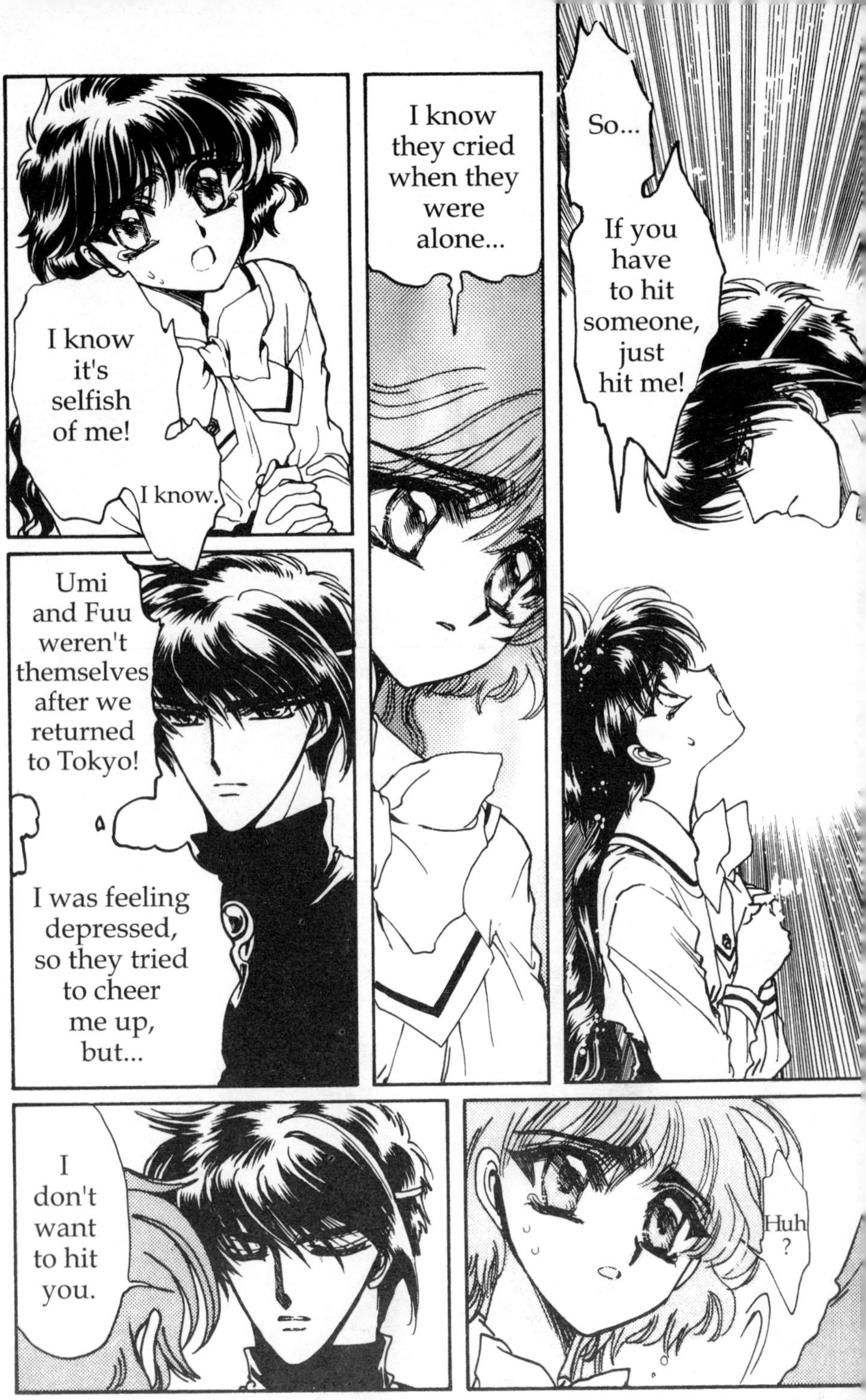

I know it's selfish of me!
I know.
Umi and Fuu weren't themselves after we returned to Tokyo!
I was feeling depressed, so they tried to cheer me up, but...
I know they cried when they were alone...
So...
If you have to hit someone, just hit me!
I don't want to hit you.
Huh?

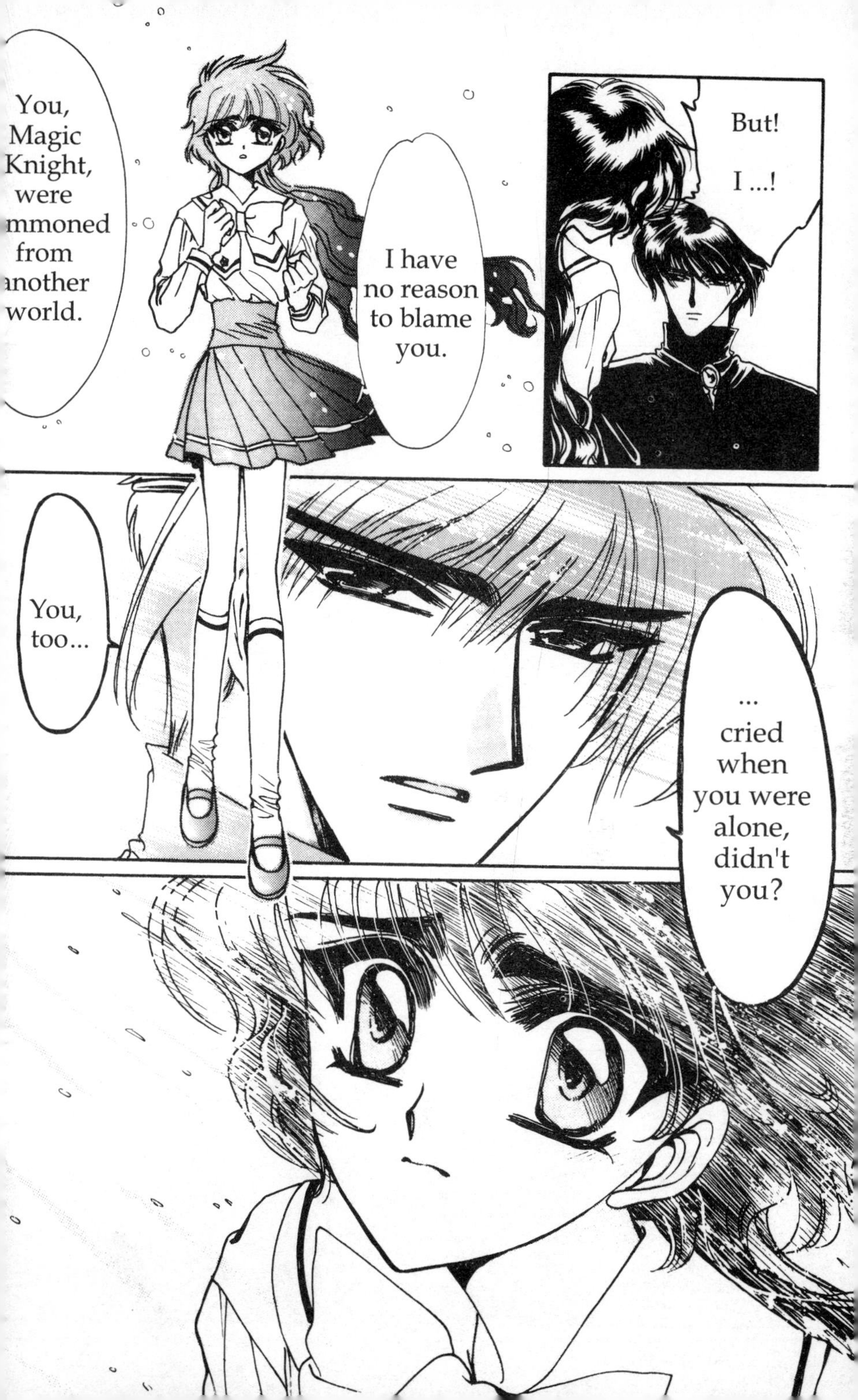
But!
I ...!
I have no reason to blame you.
You, Magic Knight, were mmoned from nother world.
... cried when you were alone, didn't you?
You, too...

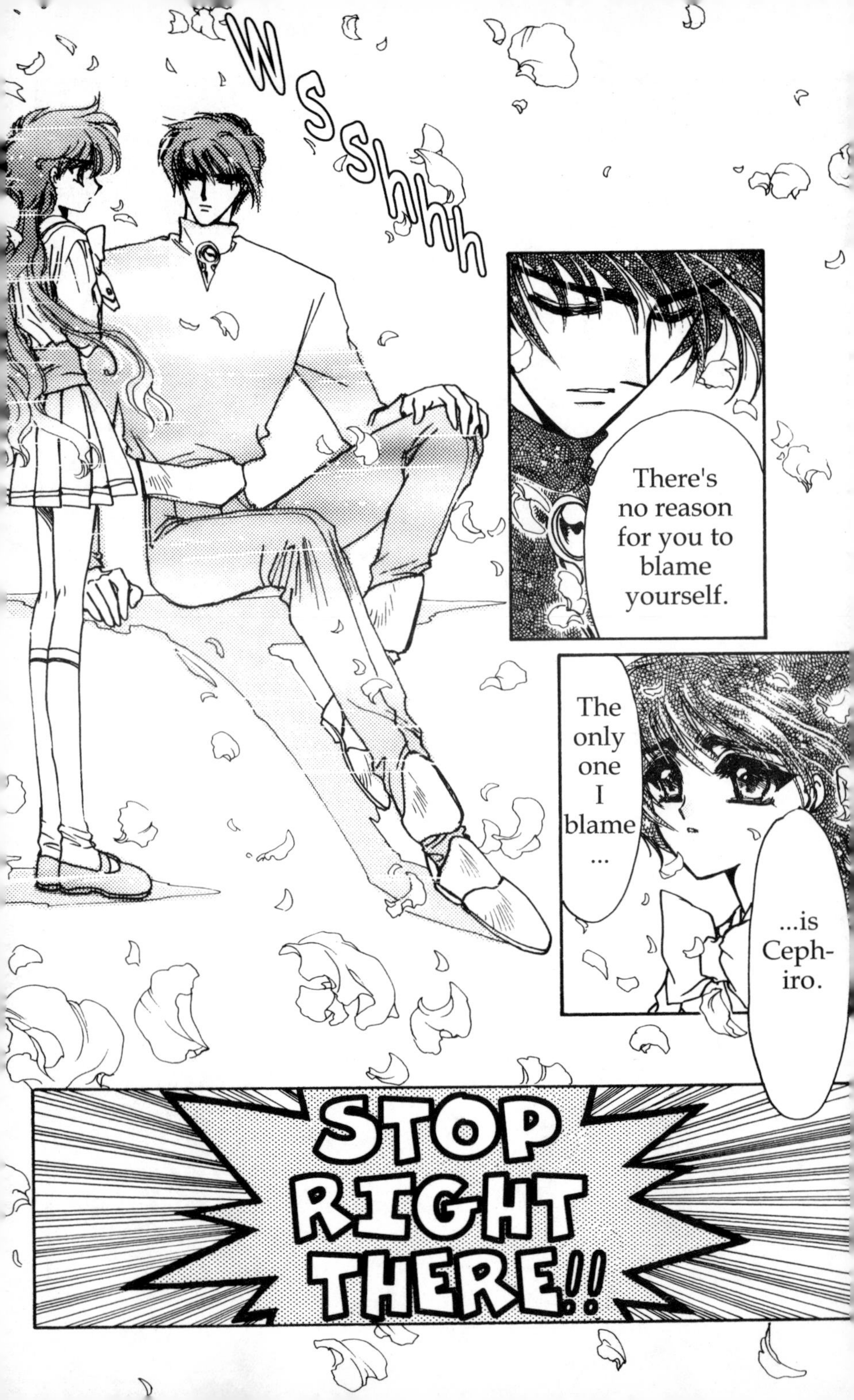
WSShhhh
There's no reason for you to blame yourself.
The only one I blame ...
...is Ceph-iro.
STOP RIGHT THERE!!

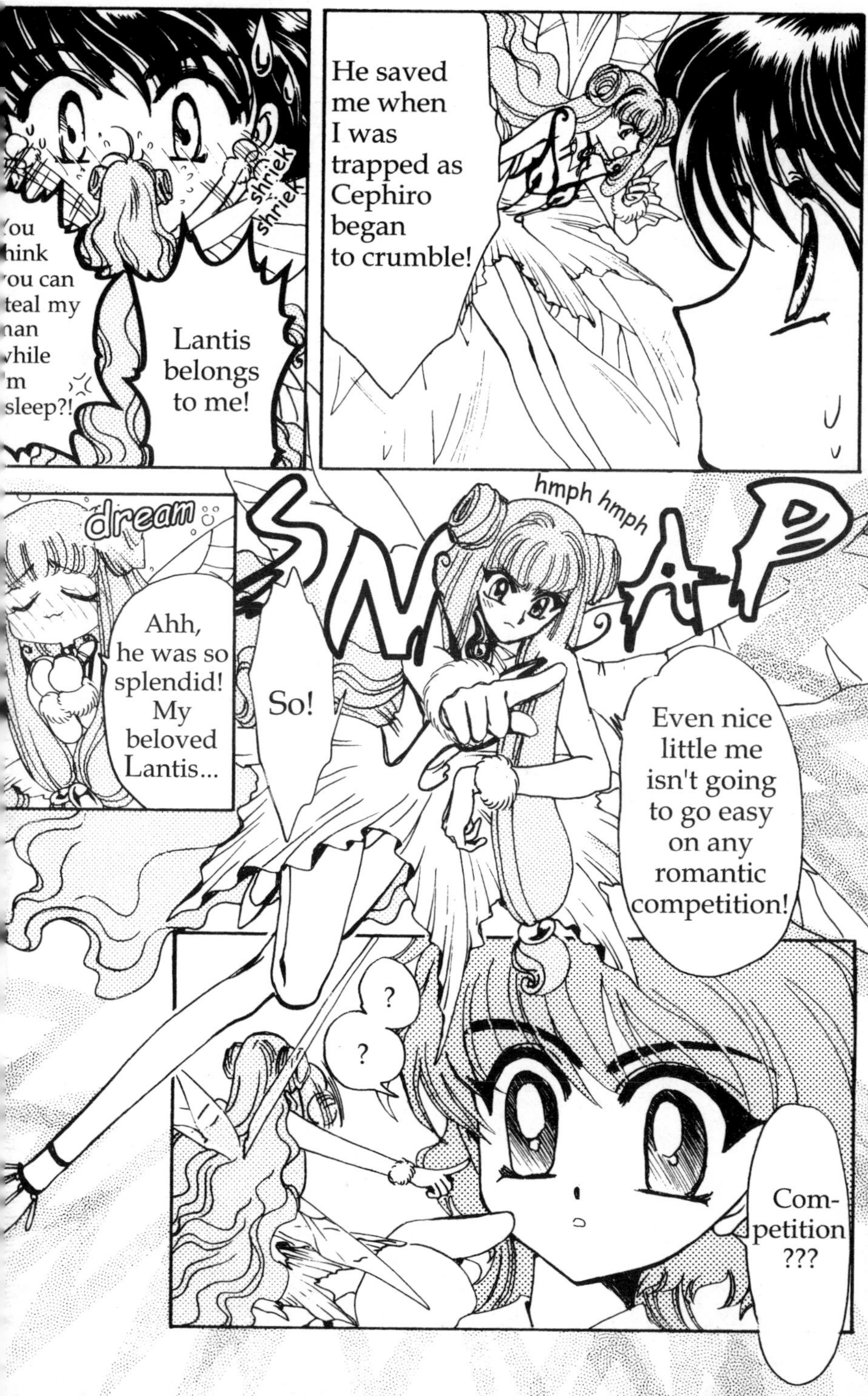

shriek shriek
ou hink ou can teal my nan vhile m sleep?!
Lantis belongs to me!
He saved me when I was trapped as Cephiro began to crumble!
dream
Ahh, he was so splendid! My beloved Lantis...
SNAP
hmph hmph
So!
Even nice little me isn't going to go easy on any romantic competition!
? ?
Com- petition ???

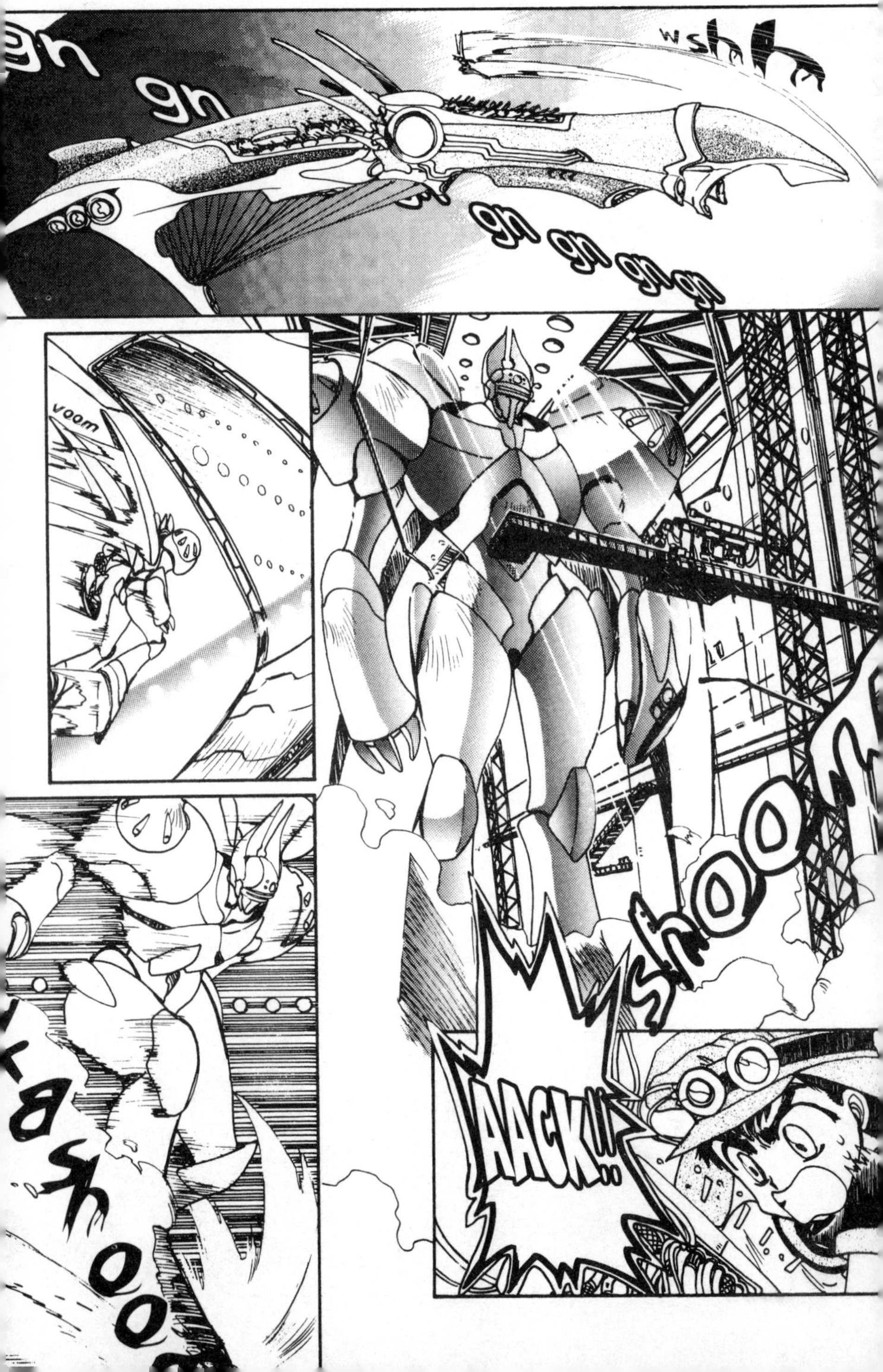
wshhh
voom
shoom
AACK!!
fwoosh

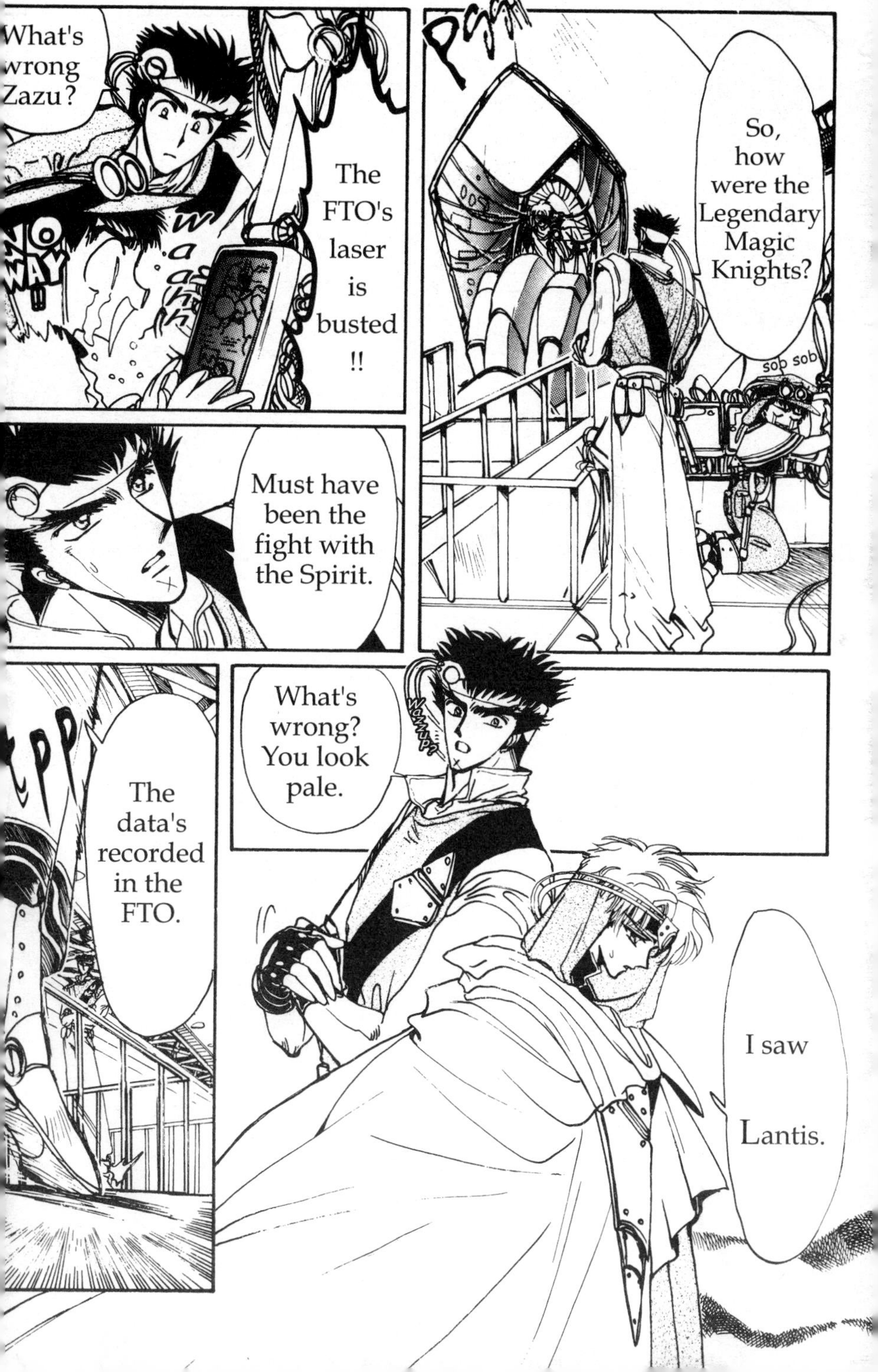

What's wrong Zazu?
NO WAY!!
waaahhh
The FTO's laser is busted!!
PSSHT
So, how were the Legendary Magic Knights?
sob sob
Must have been the fight with the Spirit.
The data's recorded in the FTO.
What's wrong? You look pale.
I saw Lantis.

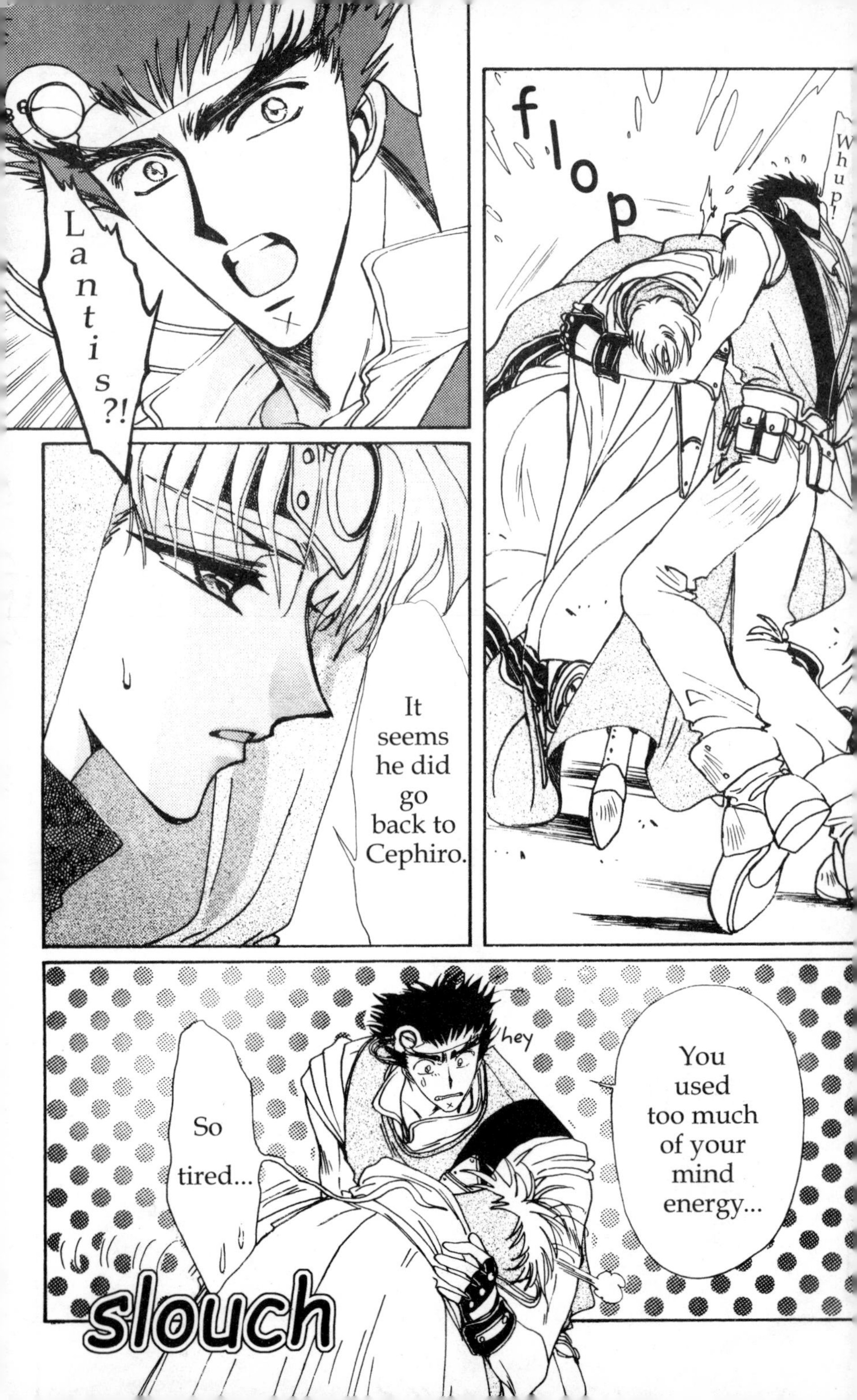

flop
Whup!
Lantis?!
It seems he did go back to Cephiro.
You used too much of your mind energy...
hey
So tired...
slouch

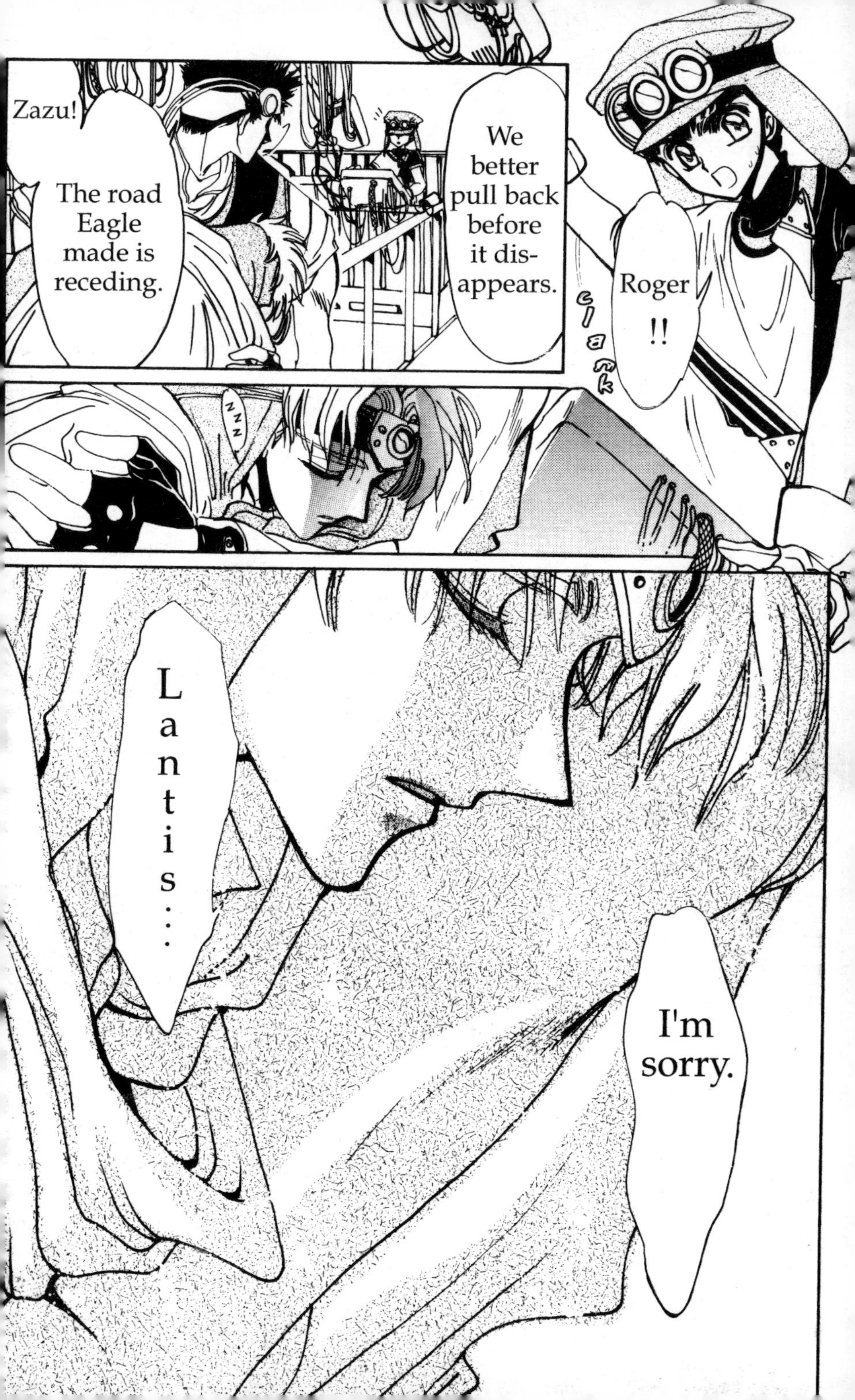
Zazu!
The road Eagle made is receding.
We better pull back before it disappears.
clank
Roger!!
Lantis...
I'm sorry.

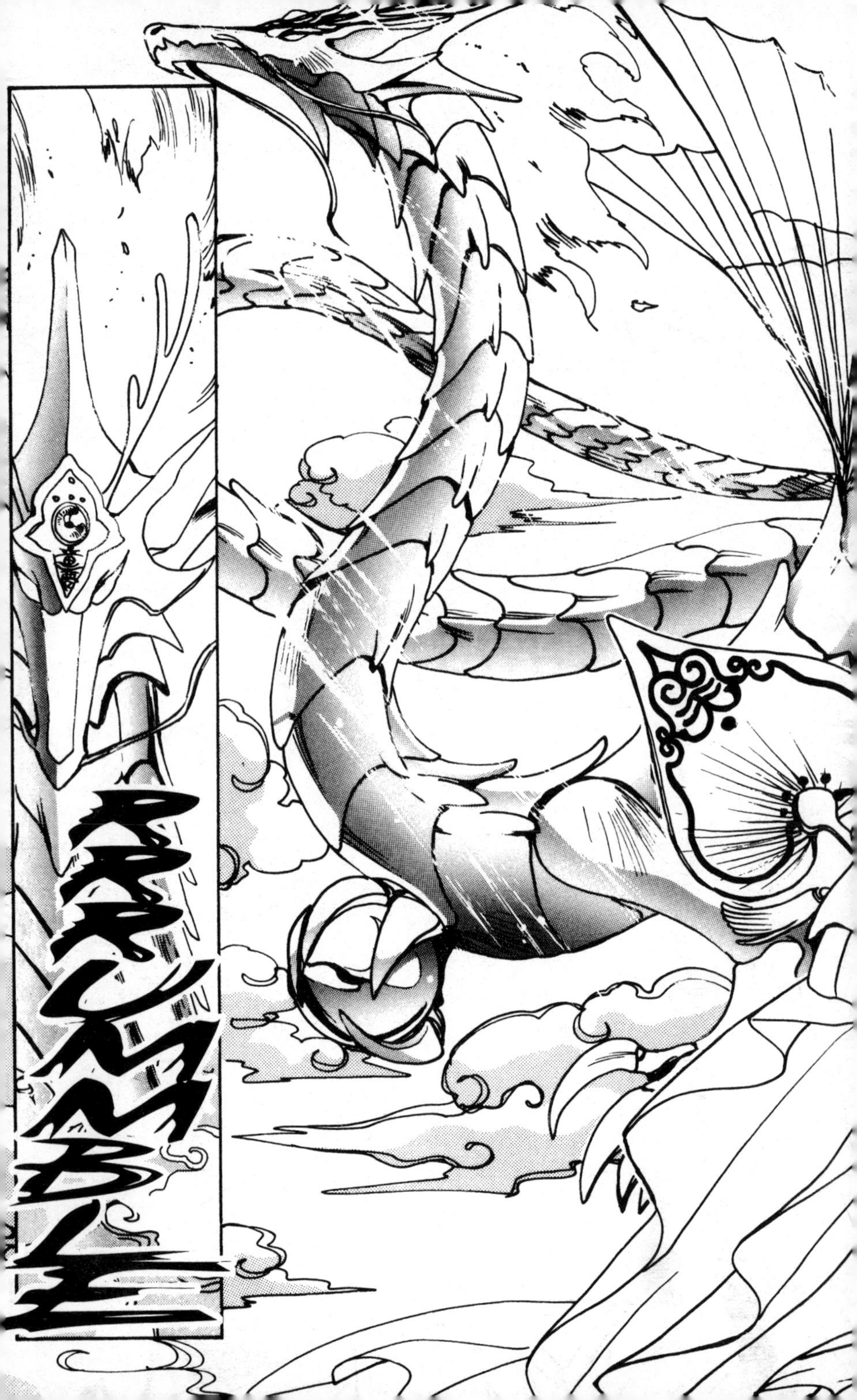
RRRUMMBLE

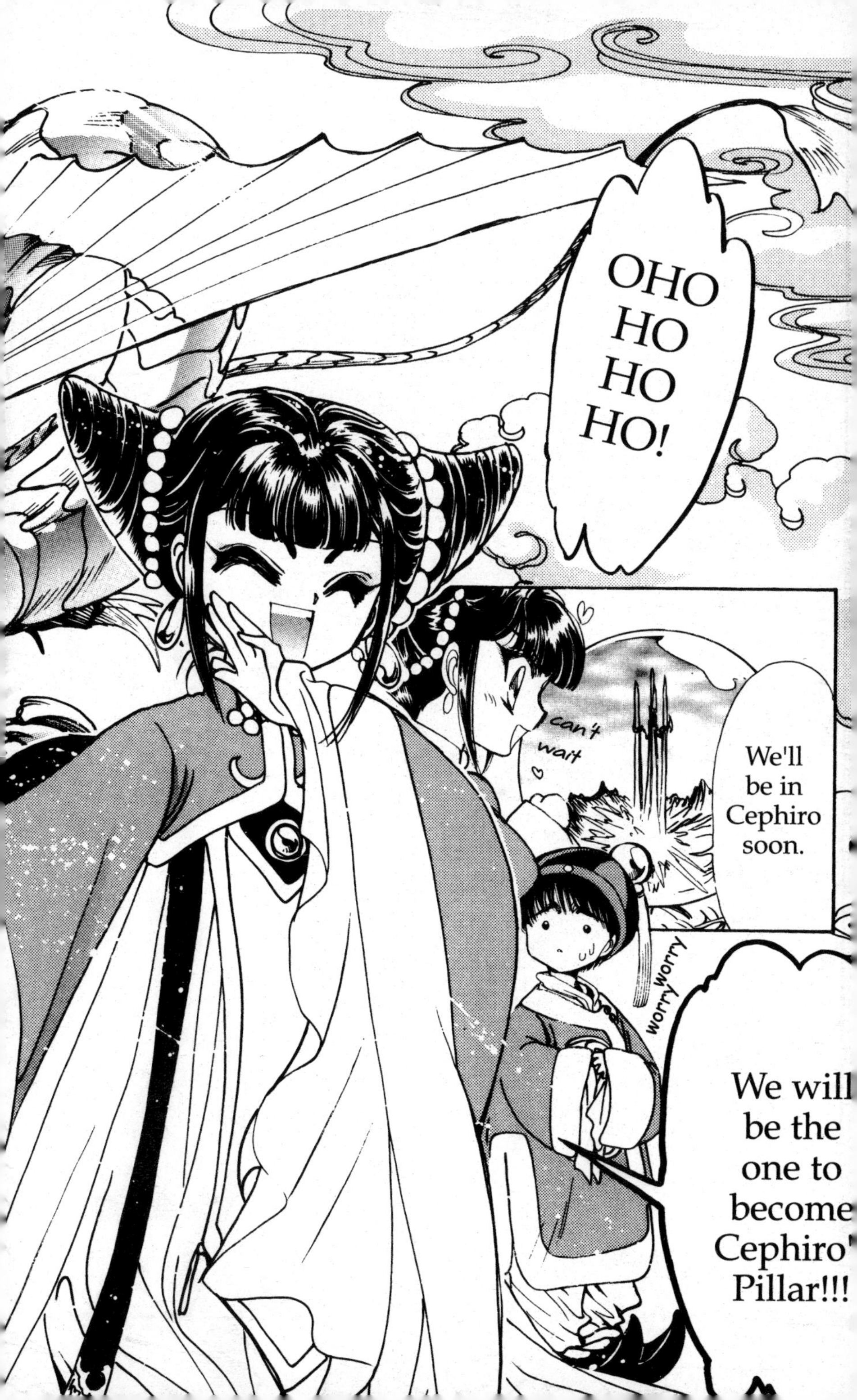
OHO HO HO HO!
We'll be in Cephiro soon.
can't wait
worry worry
We will be the one to become Cephiro' Pillar!!!

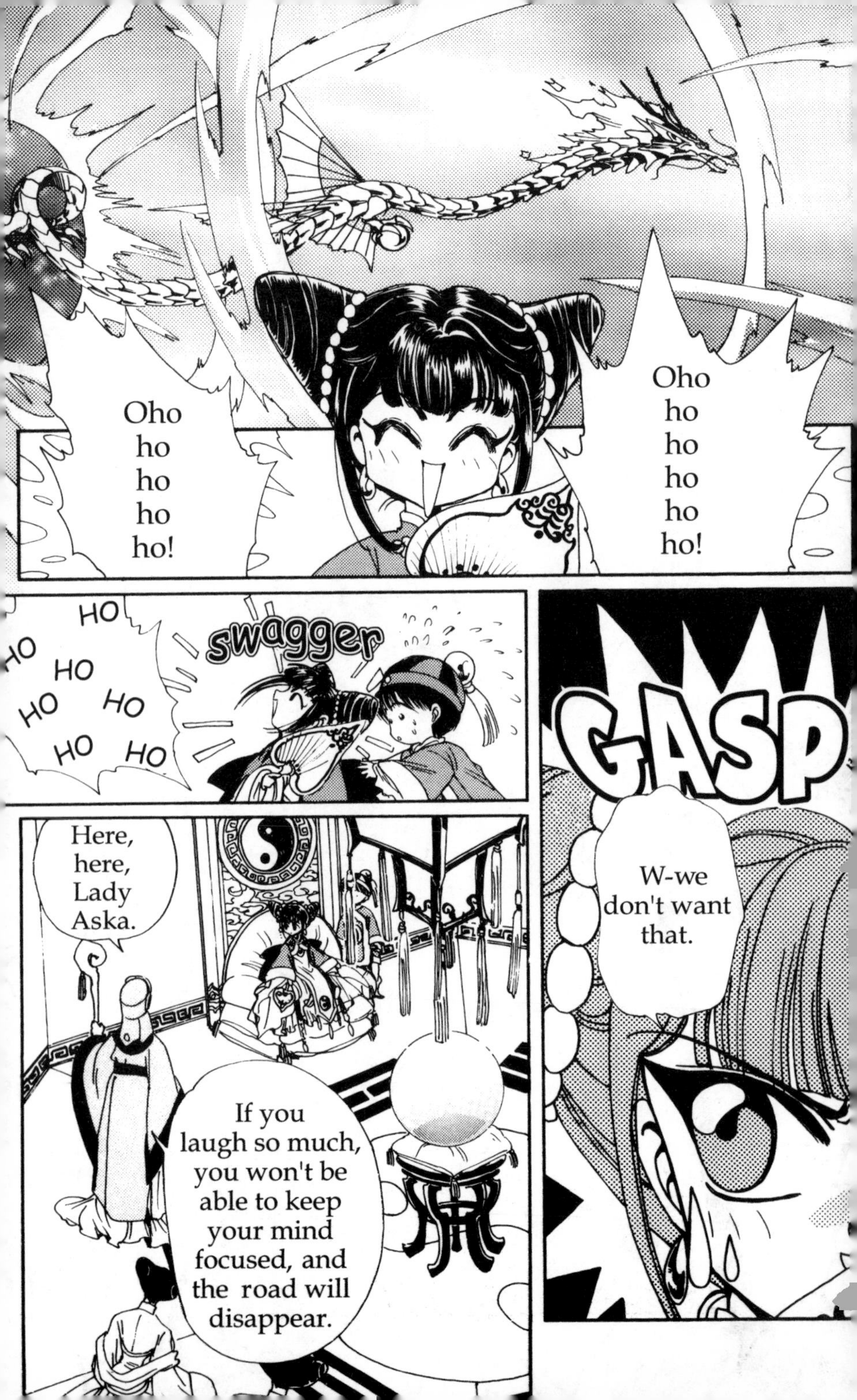

Oho ho ho ho ho!
Oho ho ho ho ho ho!
HO HO HO HO HO HO HO
swagger
Here, here, Lady Aska.
If you laugh so much, you won't be able to keep your mind focused, and the road will disappear.
GASP
W-we don't want that.

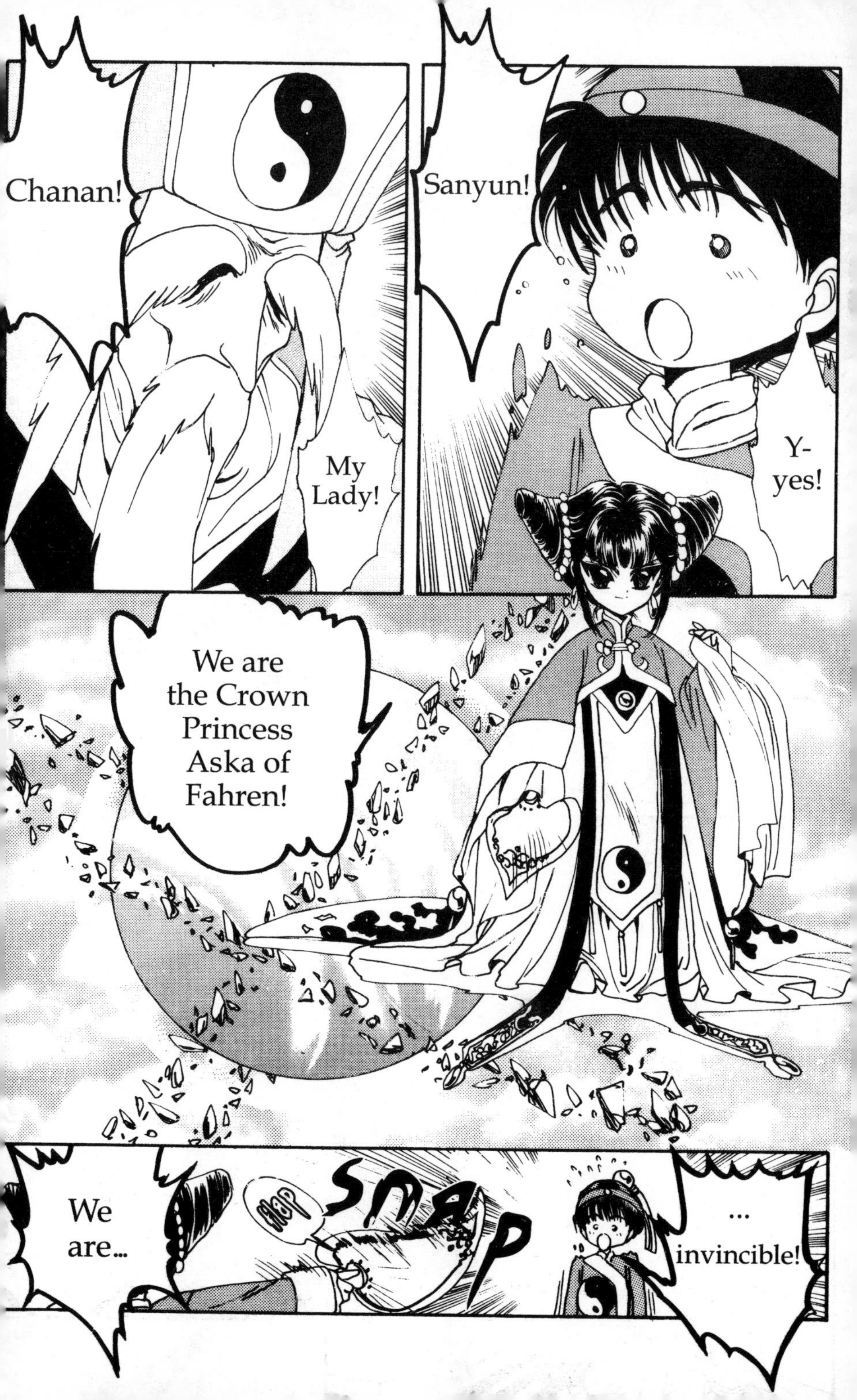

Chanan!
My Lady!
Sanyun!
Y-
yes!
We are the Crown Princess Aska of Fahren!
We are...
SNAP
...
invincible!

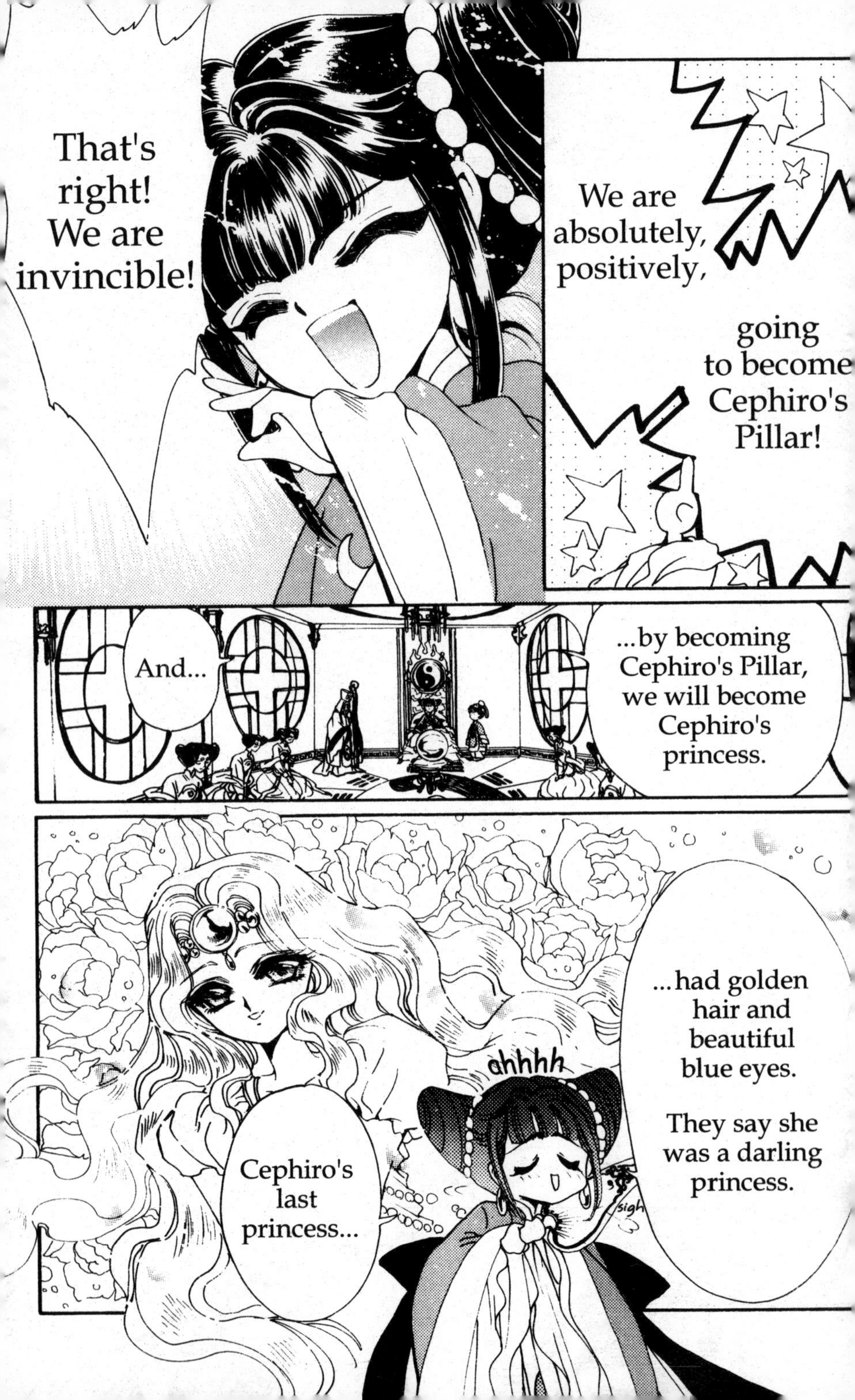
That's right! We are invincible!
We are absolutely, positively,
going to become Cephiro's Pillar!
And...
...by becoming Cephiro's Pillar, we will become Cephiro's princess.
Cephiro's last princess...
...had golden hair and beautiful blue eyes.
They say she was a darling princess.
ahhhh
sigh

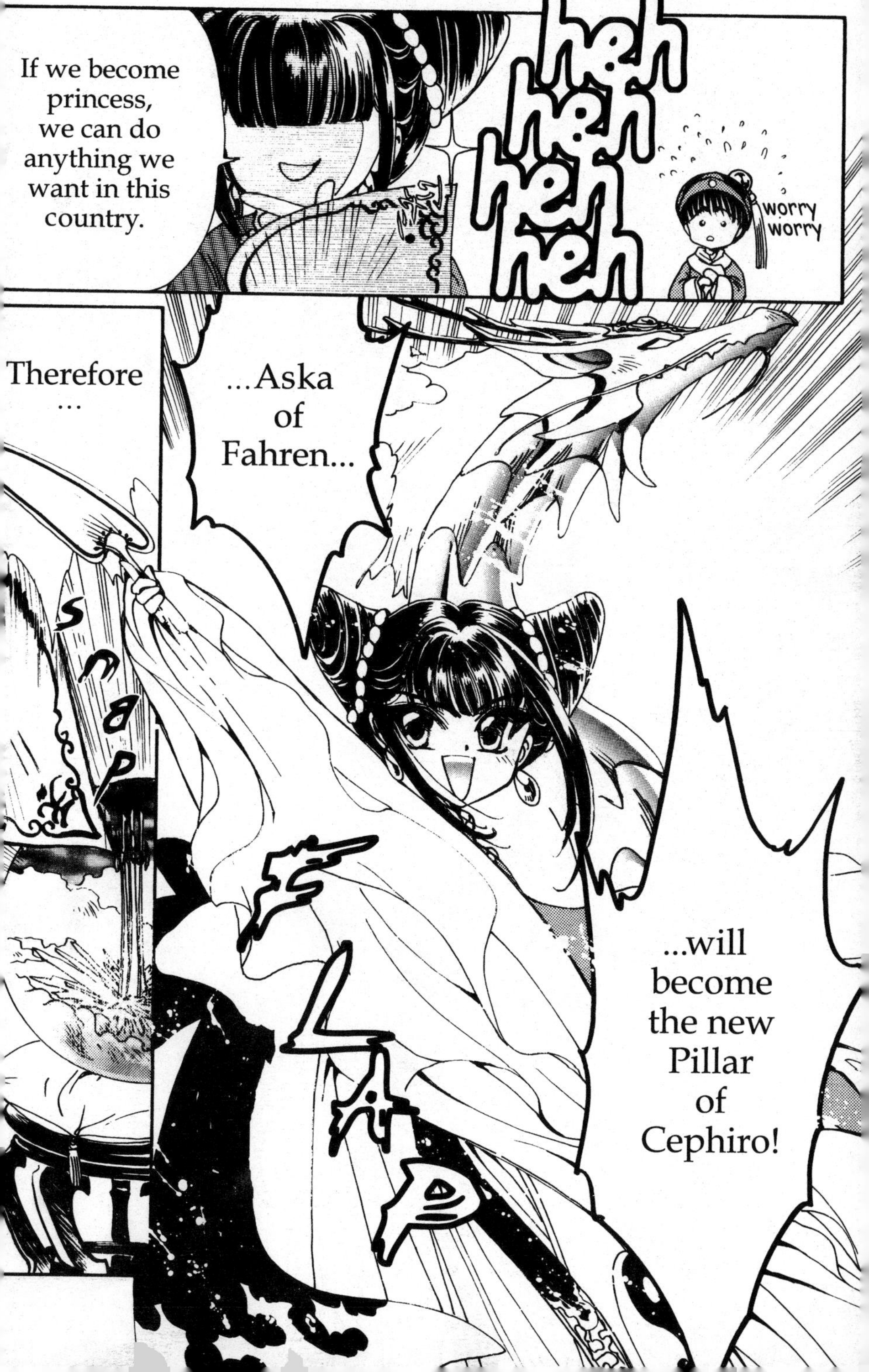
heh heh heh heh
worry worry
If we become princess, we can do anything we want in this country.
Therefore ...
...Aska of Fahren...
...will become the new Pillar of Cephiro!
snap
FLAP

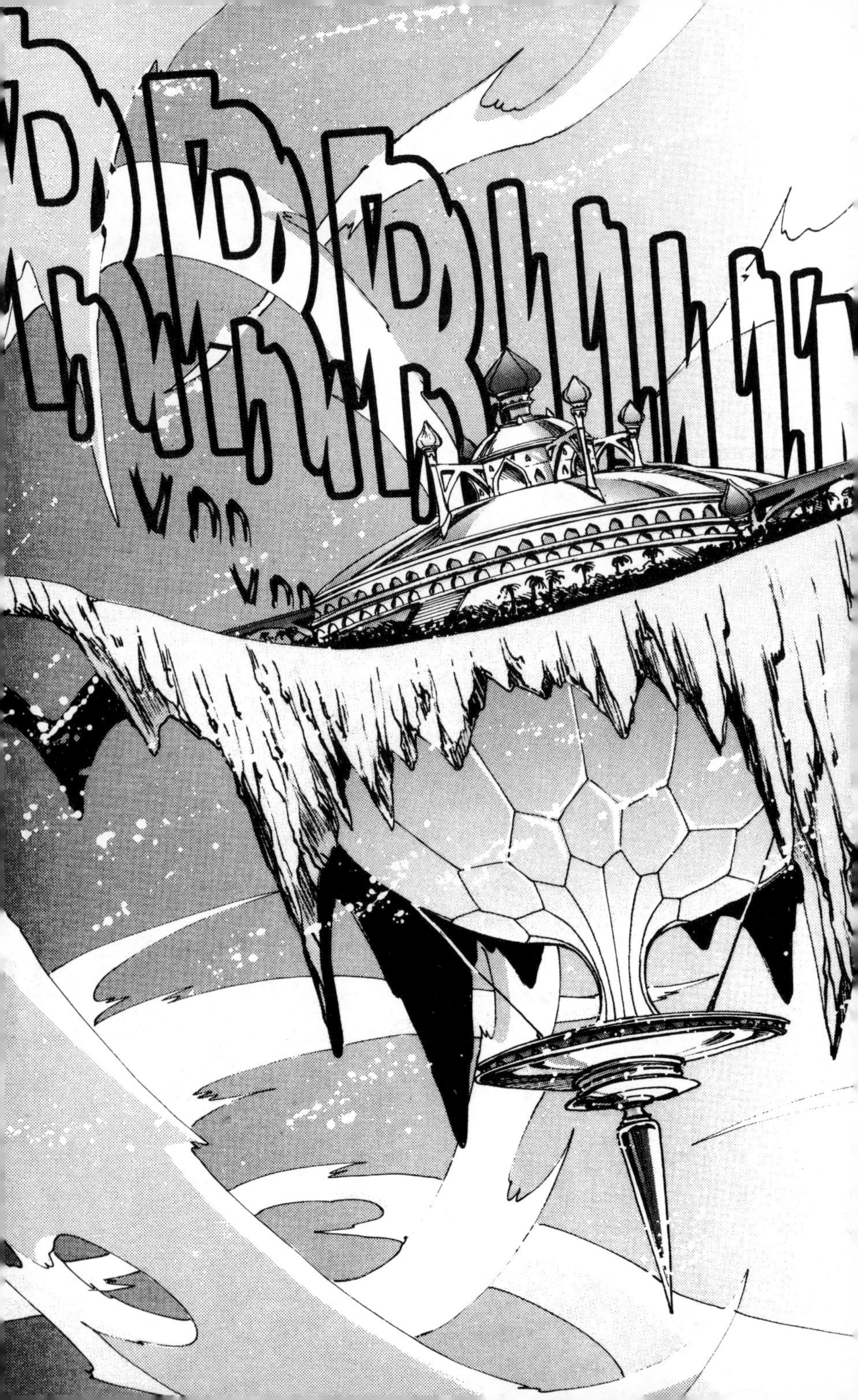

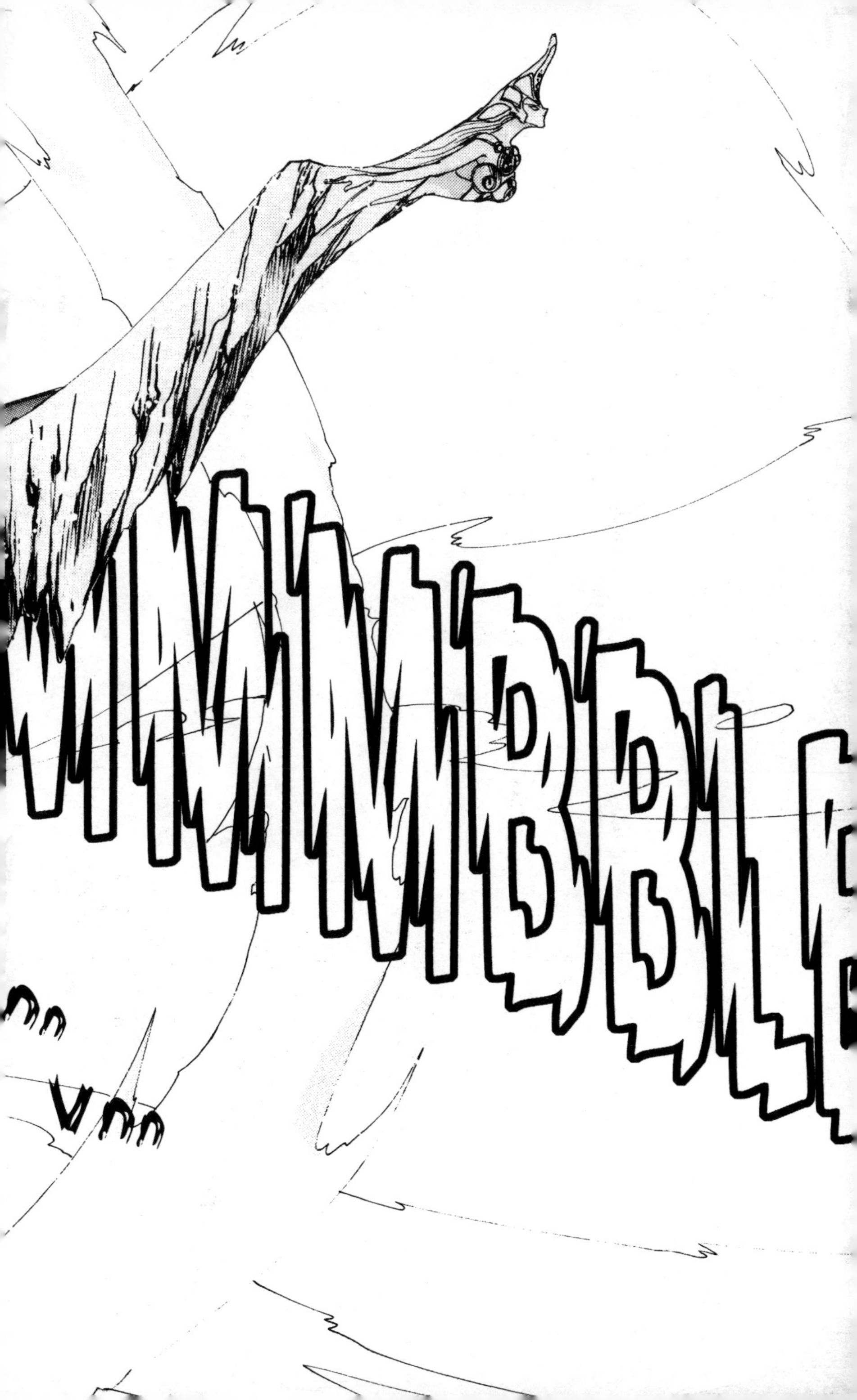
MMMBBL

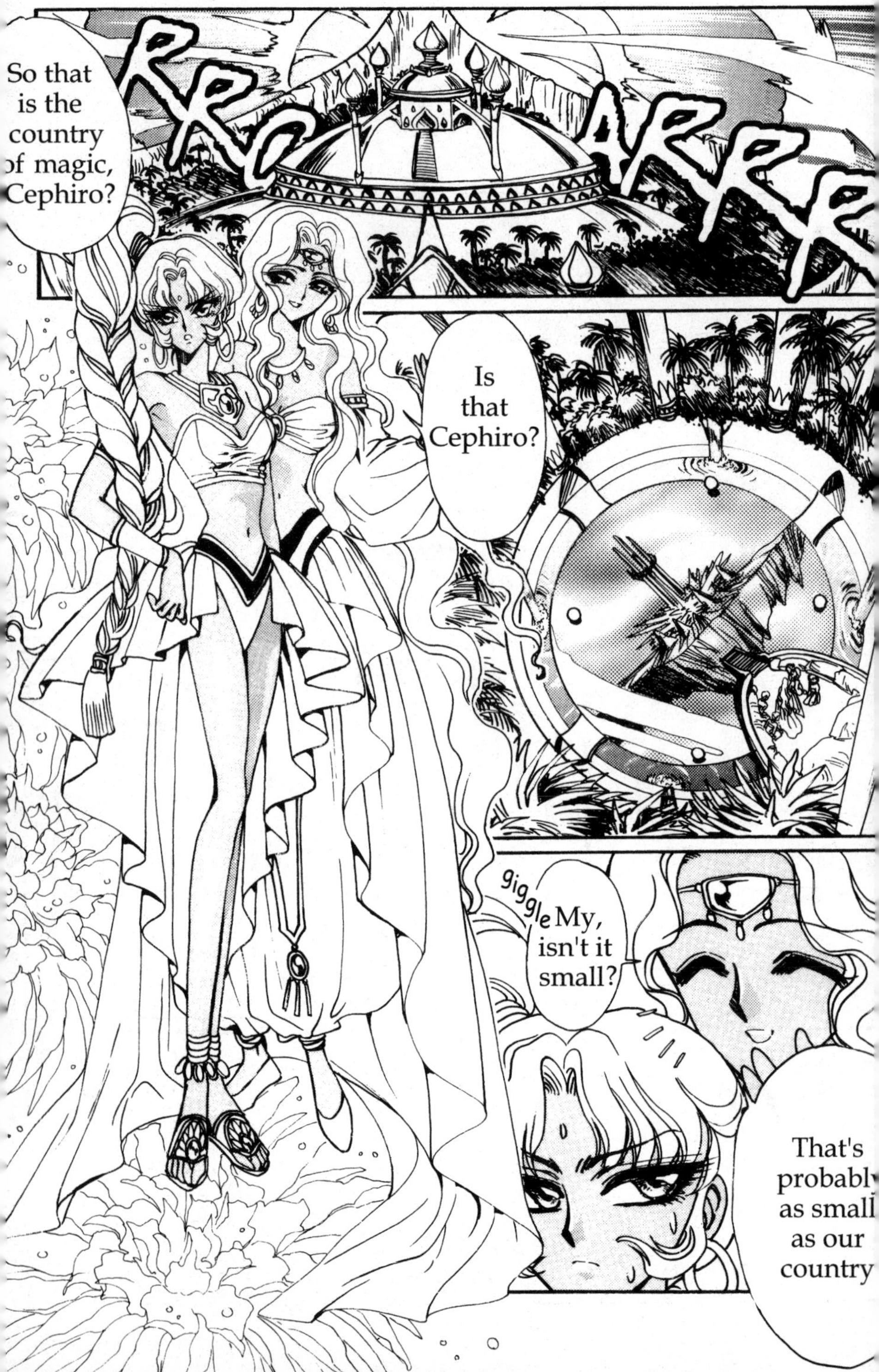

RROARRR
So that is the country of magic, Cephiro?
Is that Cephiro?
giggle
My, isn't it small?
That's probably as small as our country

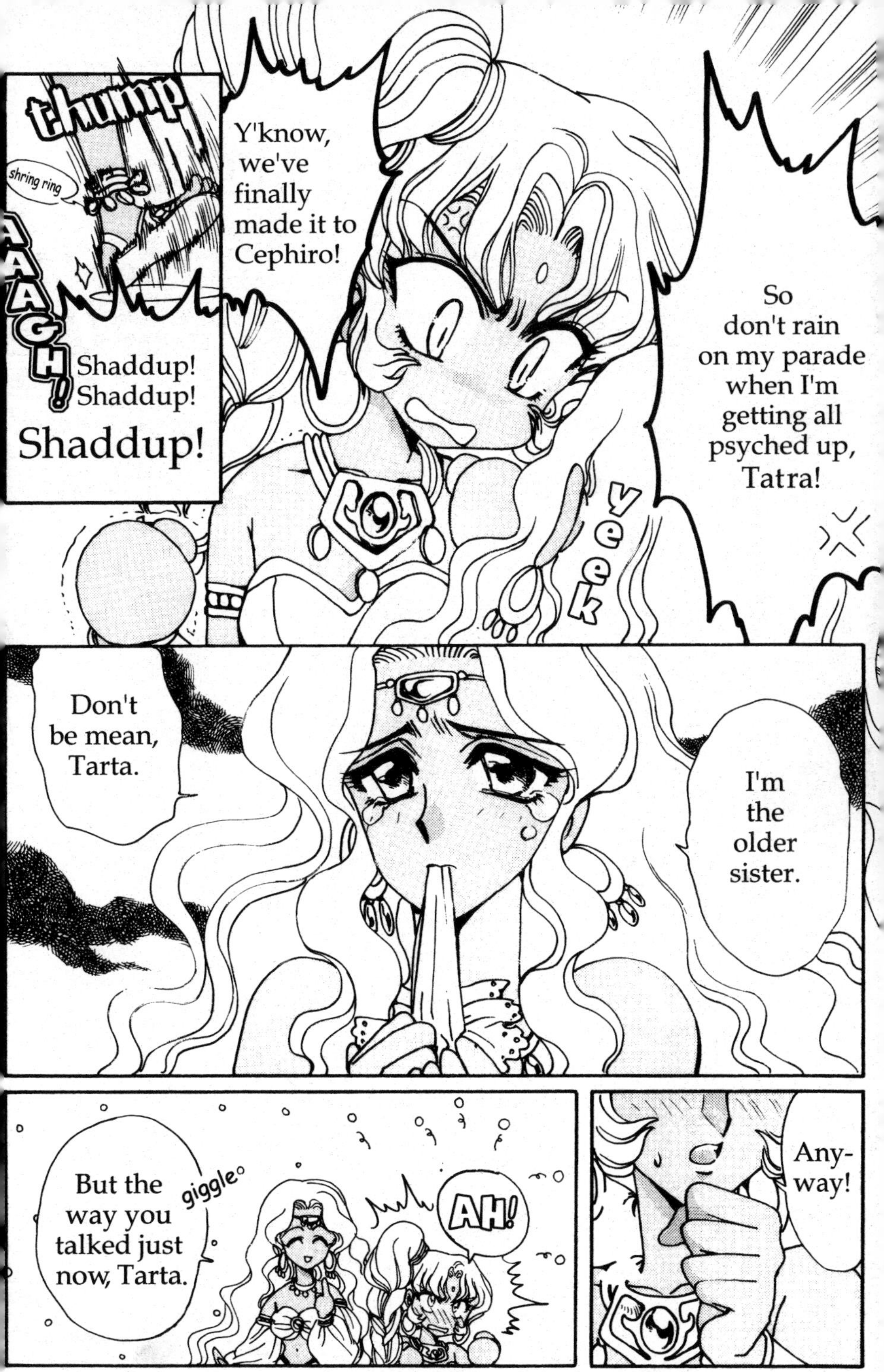

thump
shring ring
AAAGH!
Shaddup! Shaddup!
Shaddup!
Y'know, we've finally made it to Cephiro!
So don't rain on my parade when I'm getting all psyched up, Tatra!
yeek
Don't be mean, Tarta.
I'm the older sister.
But the way you talked just now, Tarta.
giggle
AH!
Any-way!

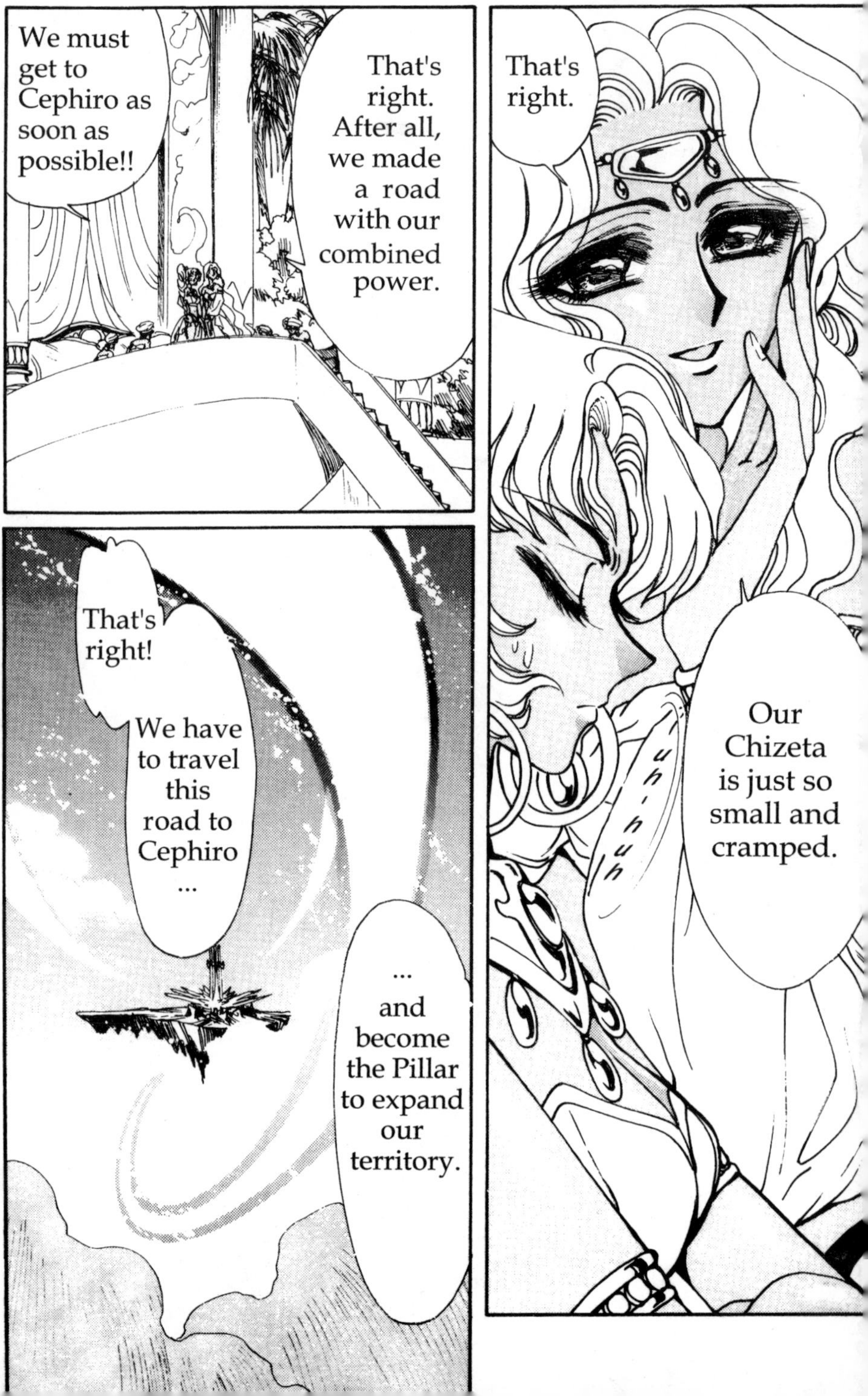
We must get to Cephiro as soon as possible!!
That's right. After all, we made a road with our combined power.
That's right.
Our Chizeta is just so small and cramped.
uh-huh
That's right!
We have to travel this road to Cephiro ...
... and become the Pillar to expand our territory.

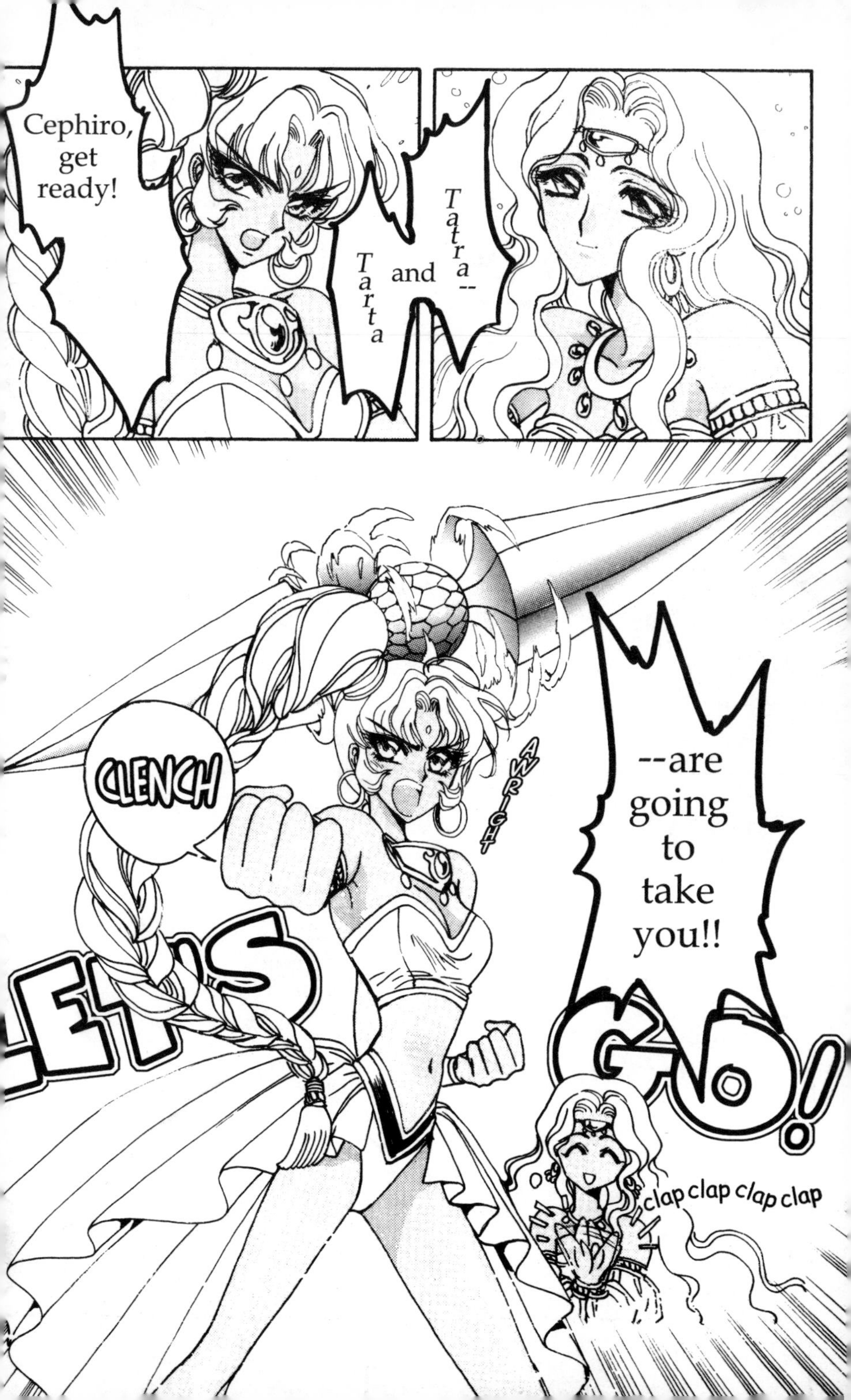
Cephiro, get ready!
Tatra and Tarta--
--are going to take you!!
CLENCH
AWRIGHT
LET'S GO!
clap clap clap clap

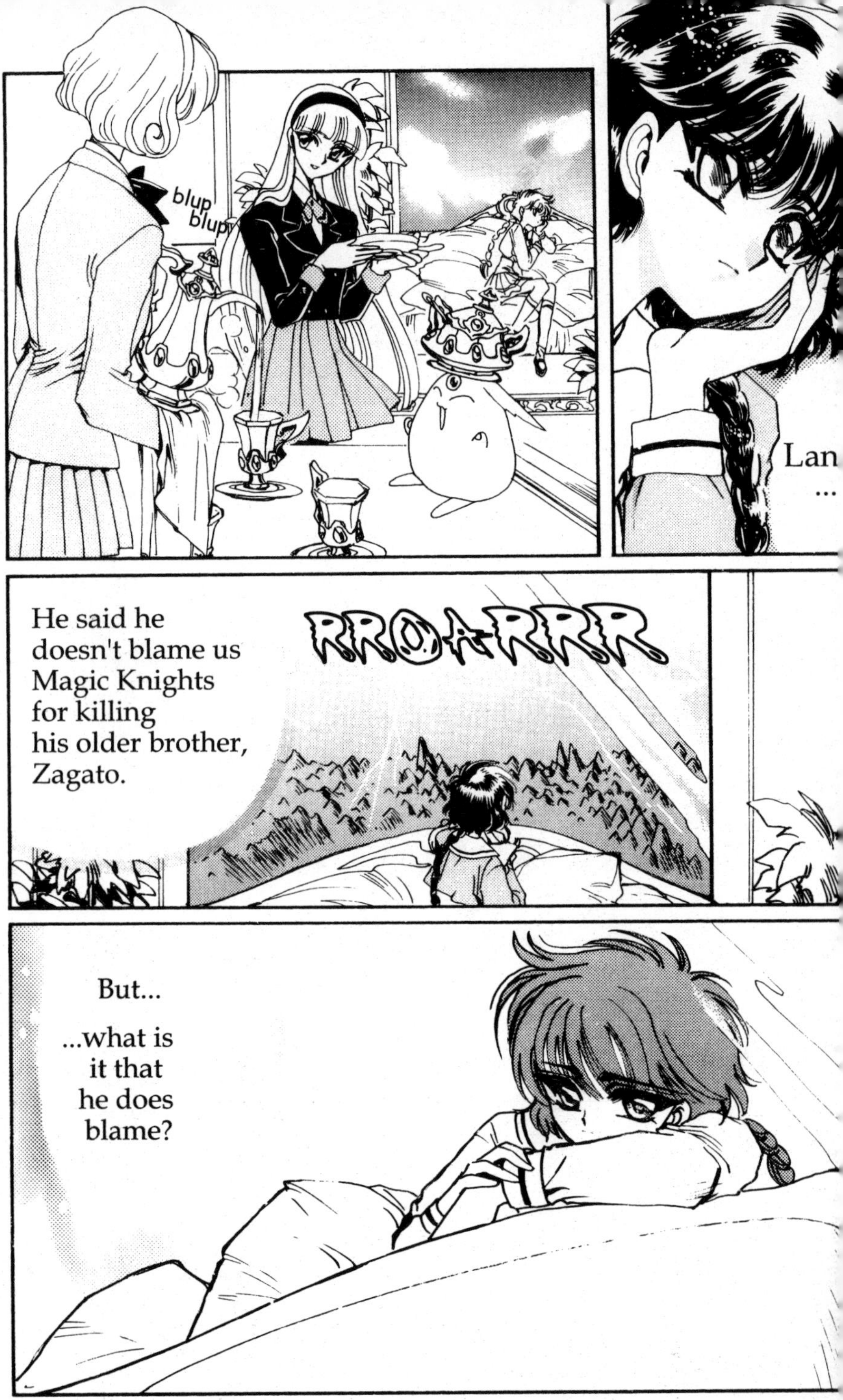
Lan
...
blup
blup
He said he doesn't blame us Magic Knights for killing his older brother, Zagato.
RROARRR
But...
...what is it that he does blame?

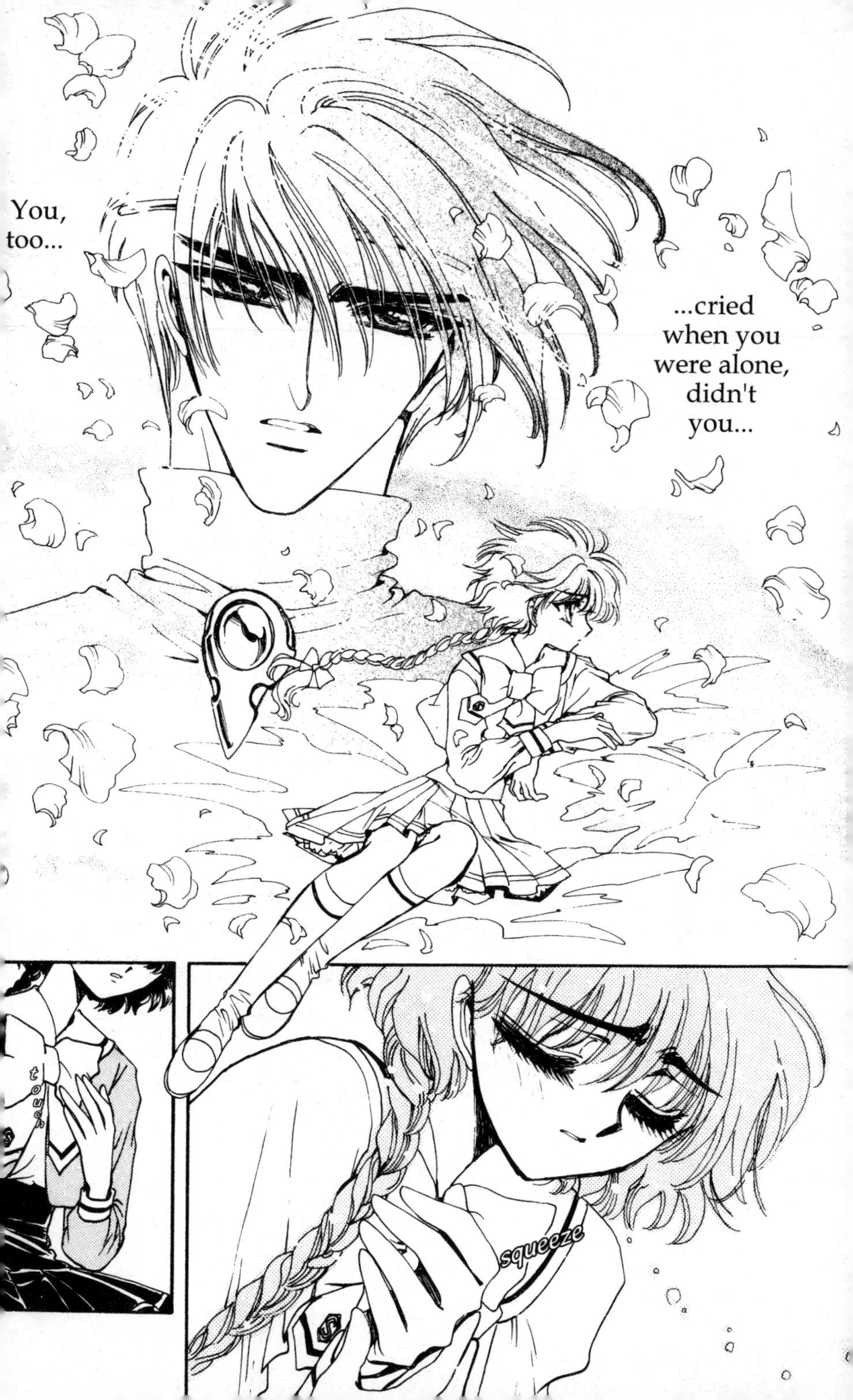
You, too...
...cried when you were alone, didn't you...
touch
squeeze

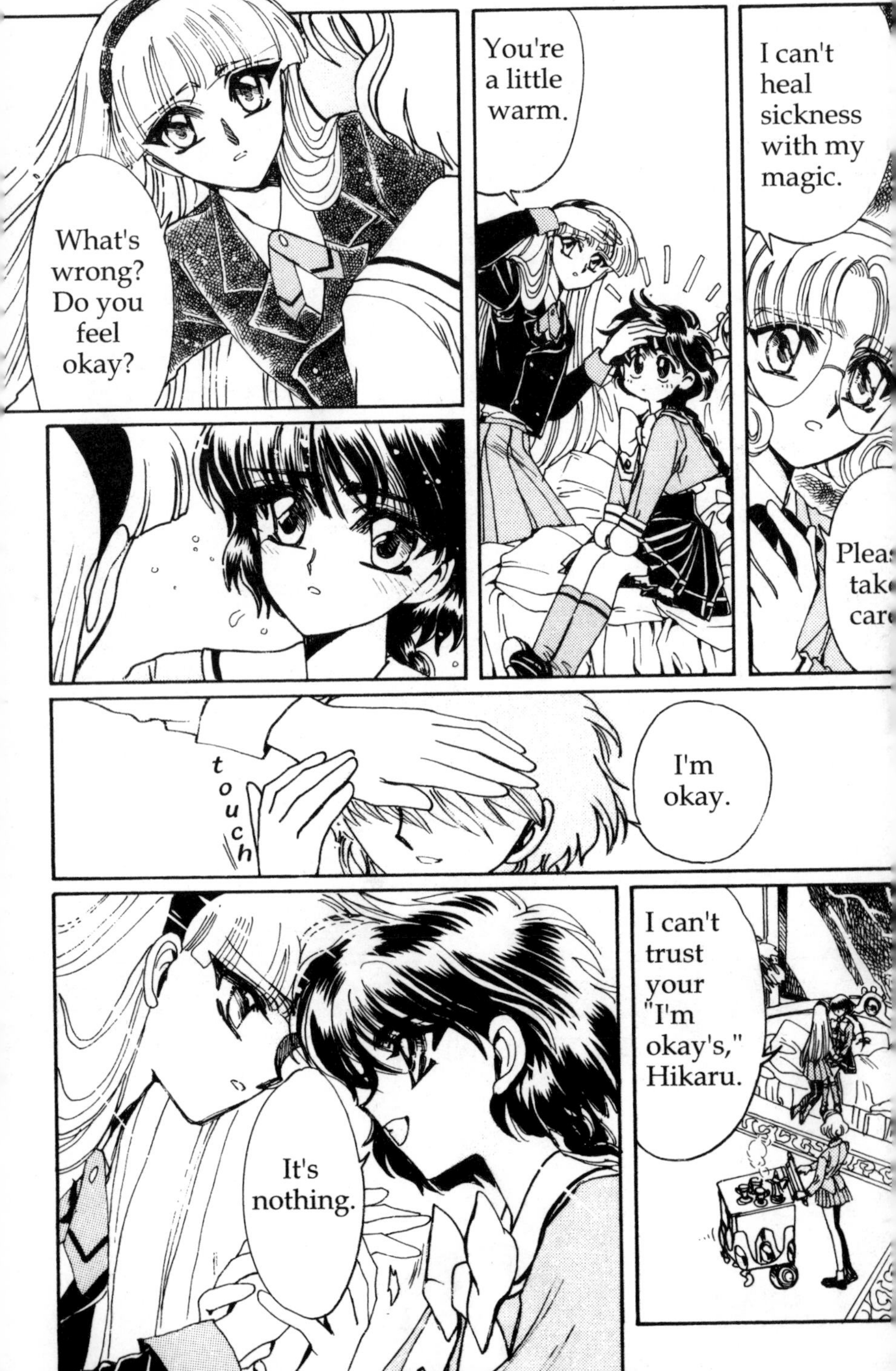

What's wrong? Do you feel okay?
You're a little warm.
I can't heal sickness with my magic.
touch
I'm okay.
It's nothing.
I can't trust your "I'm okay's," Hikaru.

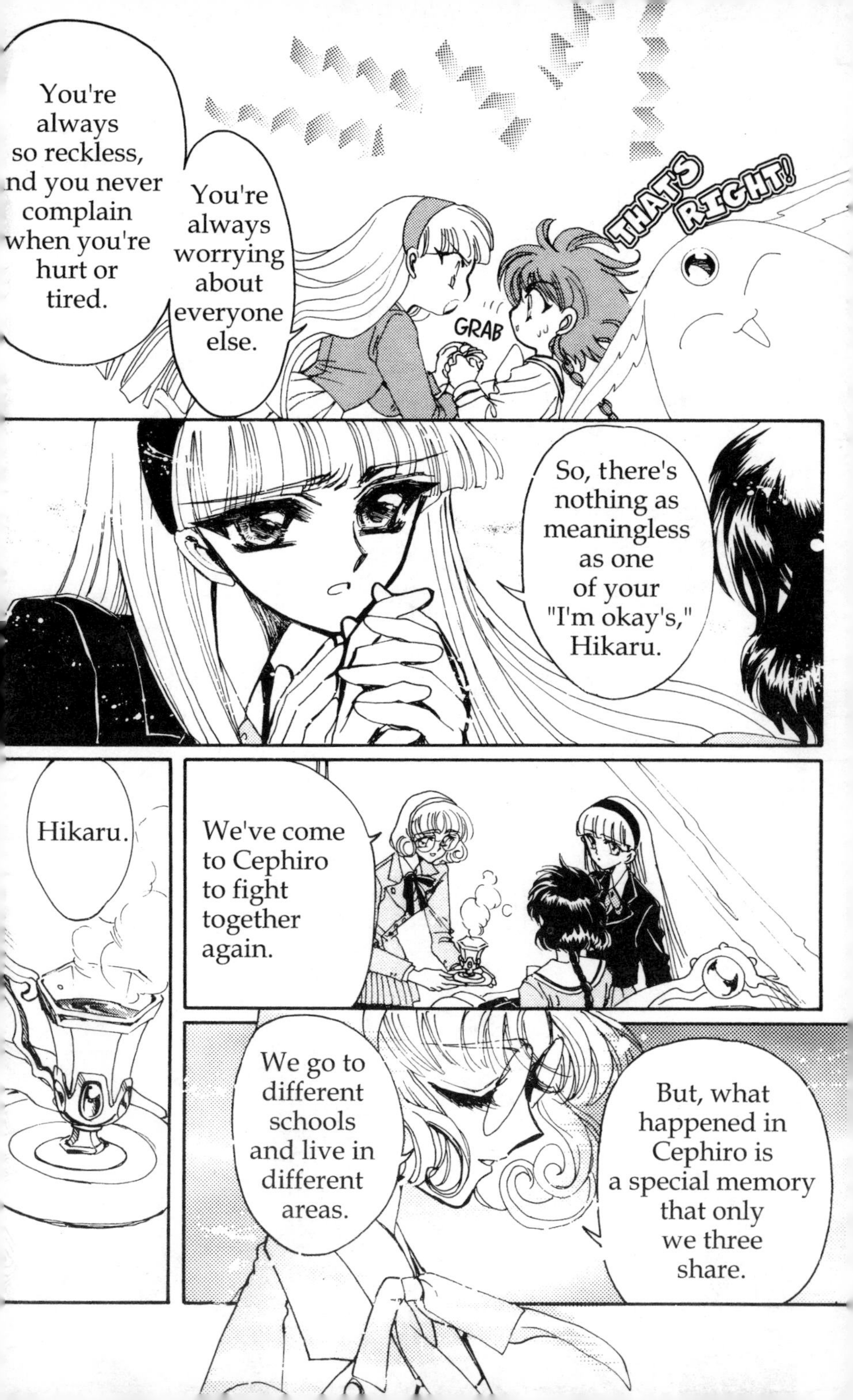

You're always so reckless, nd you never complain when you're hurt or tired.
You're always worrying about everyone else.
GRAB
THAT'S RIGHT!
So, there's nothing as meaningless as one of your "I'm okay's," Hikaru.
Hikaru.
We've come to Cephiro to fight together again.
We go to different schools and live in different areas.
But, what happened in Cephiro is a special memory that only we three share.

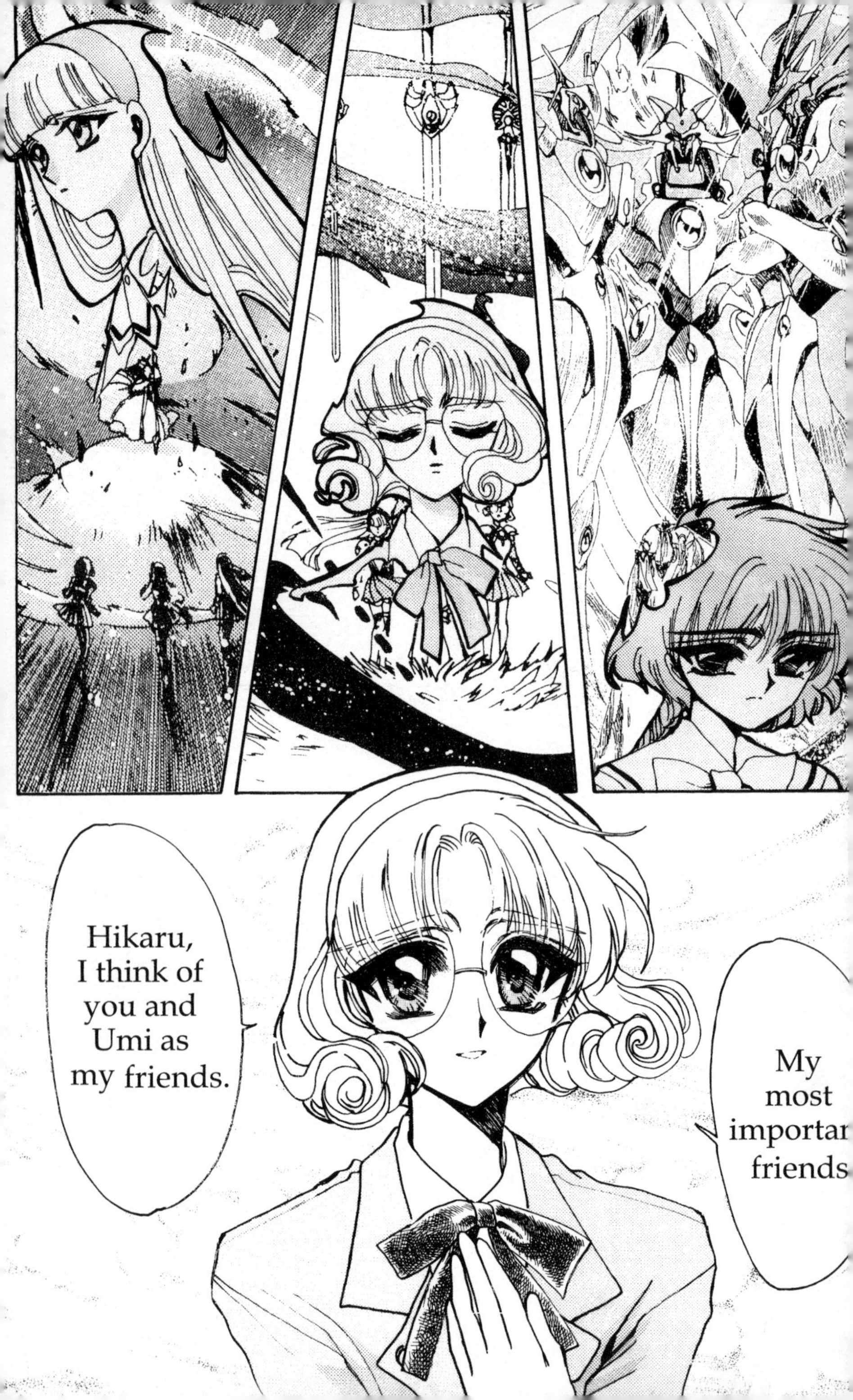
Hikaru, I think of you and Umi as my friends.
My most importar friends

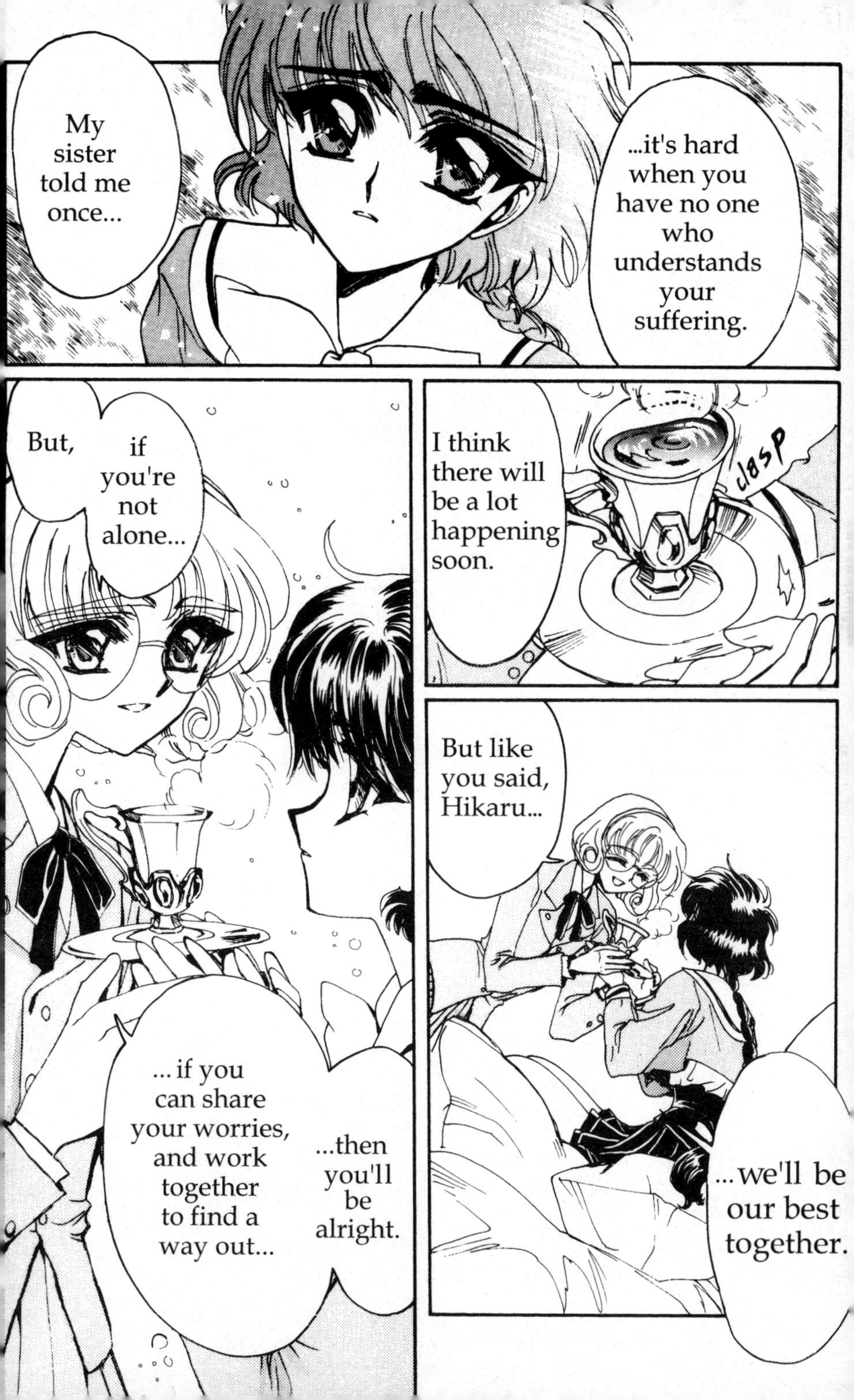
My sister told me once...
...it's hard when you have no one who understands your suffering.
But,
if you're not alone...
... if you can share your worries, and work together to find a way out...
...then you'll be alright.
I think there will be a lot happening soon.
clasp
But like you said, Hikaru...
...we'll be our best together.

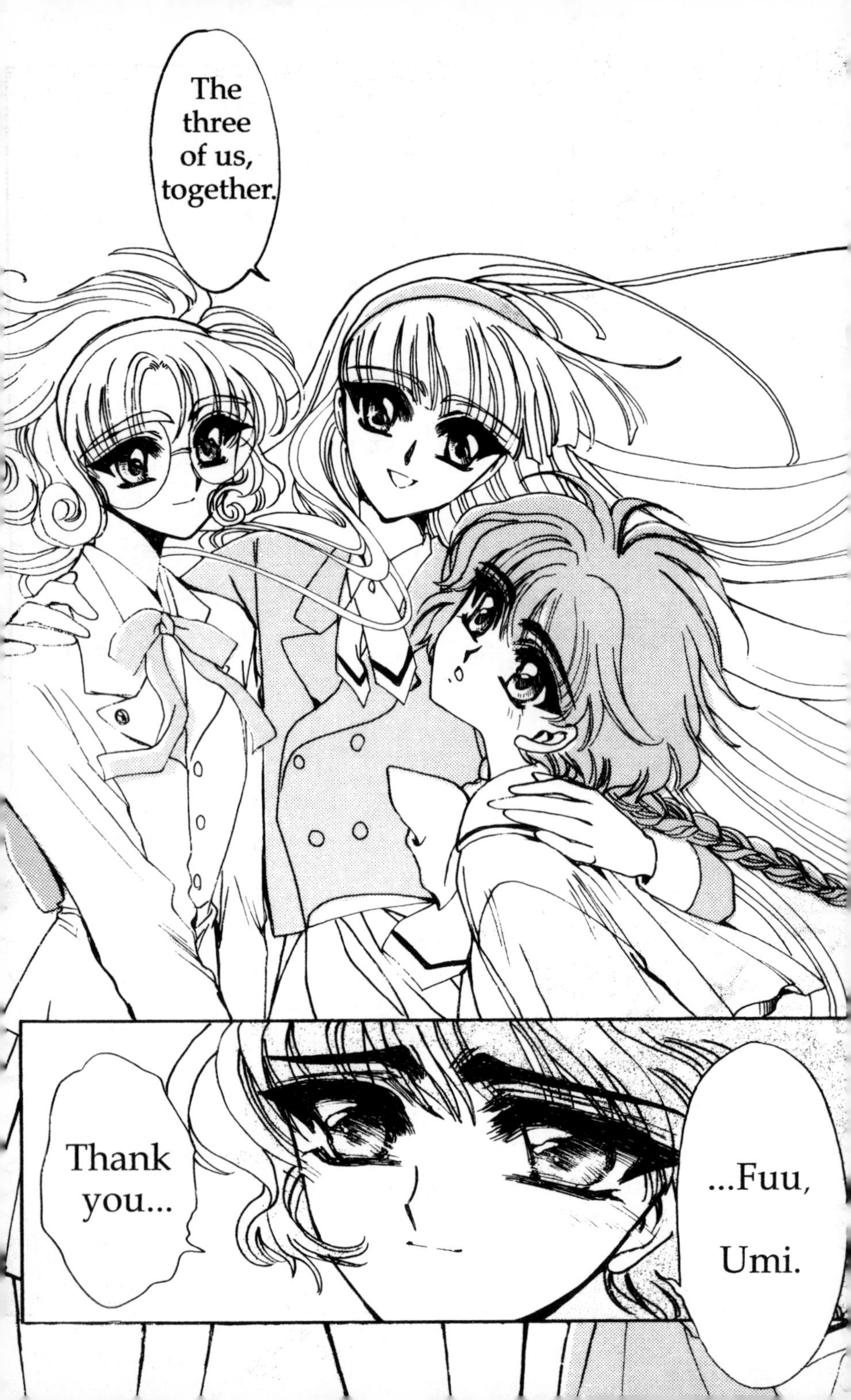
The three of us, together.
...Fuu, Umi.
Thank you...

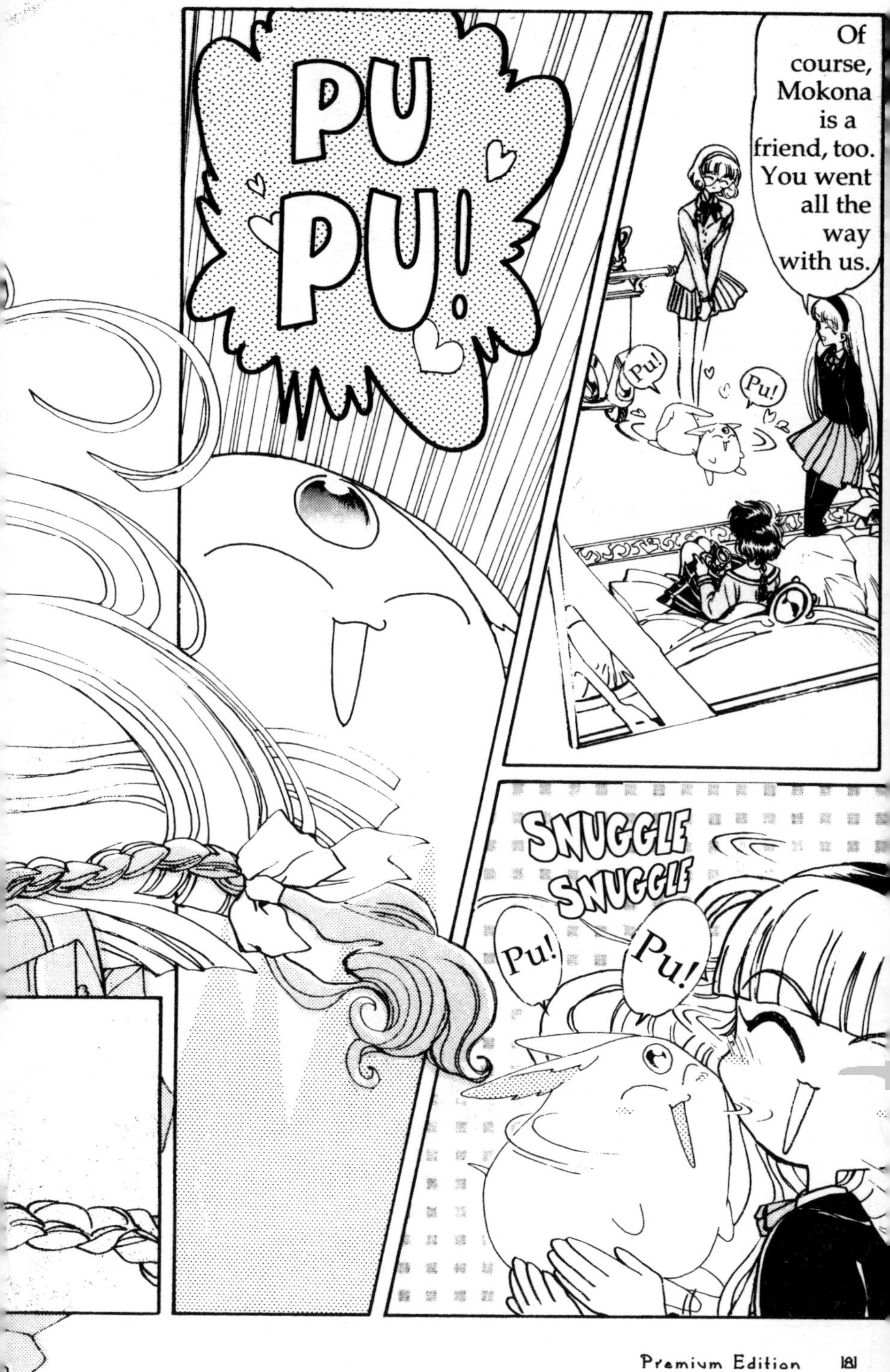
Of course, Mokona is a friend, too. You went all the way with us.
Pu!
Pu!
PU PU!
SNUGGLE SNUGGLE
Pu!
Pu!

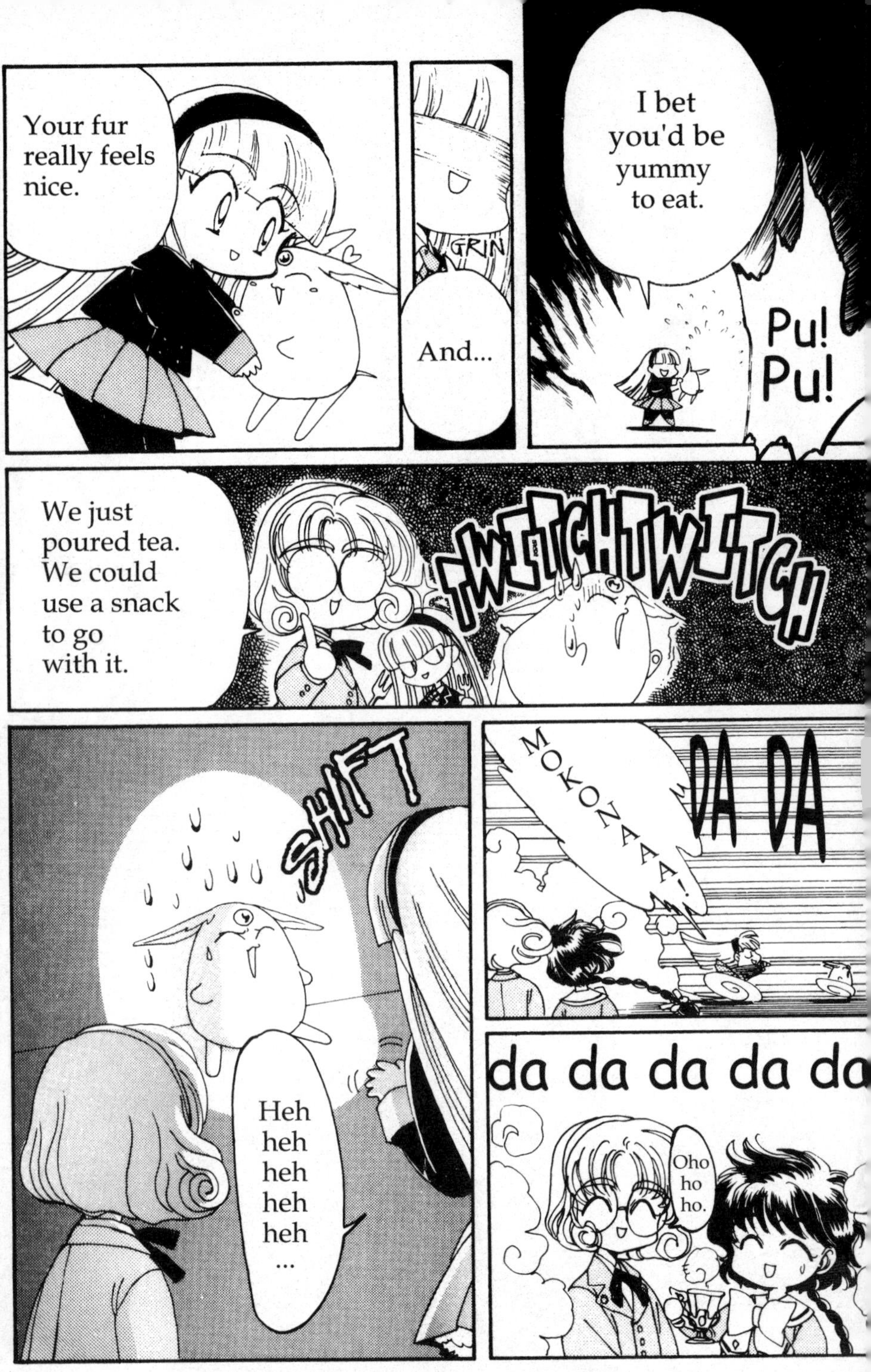
Your fur really feels nice.
GRIN
And...
I bet you'd be yummy to eat.
Pu! Pu!
We just poured tea. We could use a snack to go with it.
TWITCHTWITCH
SHIFT
Heh heh heh heh heh ...
MOKONAAAA!
DA DA
da da da da da
Oho ho ho.

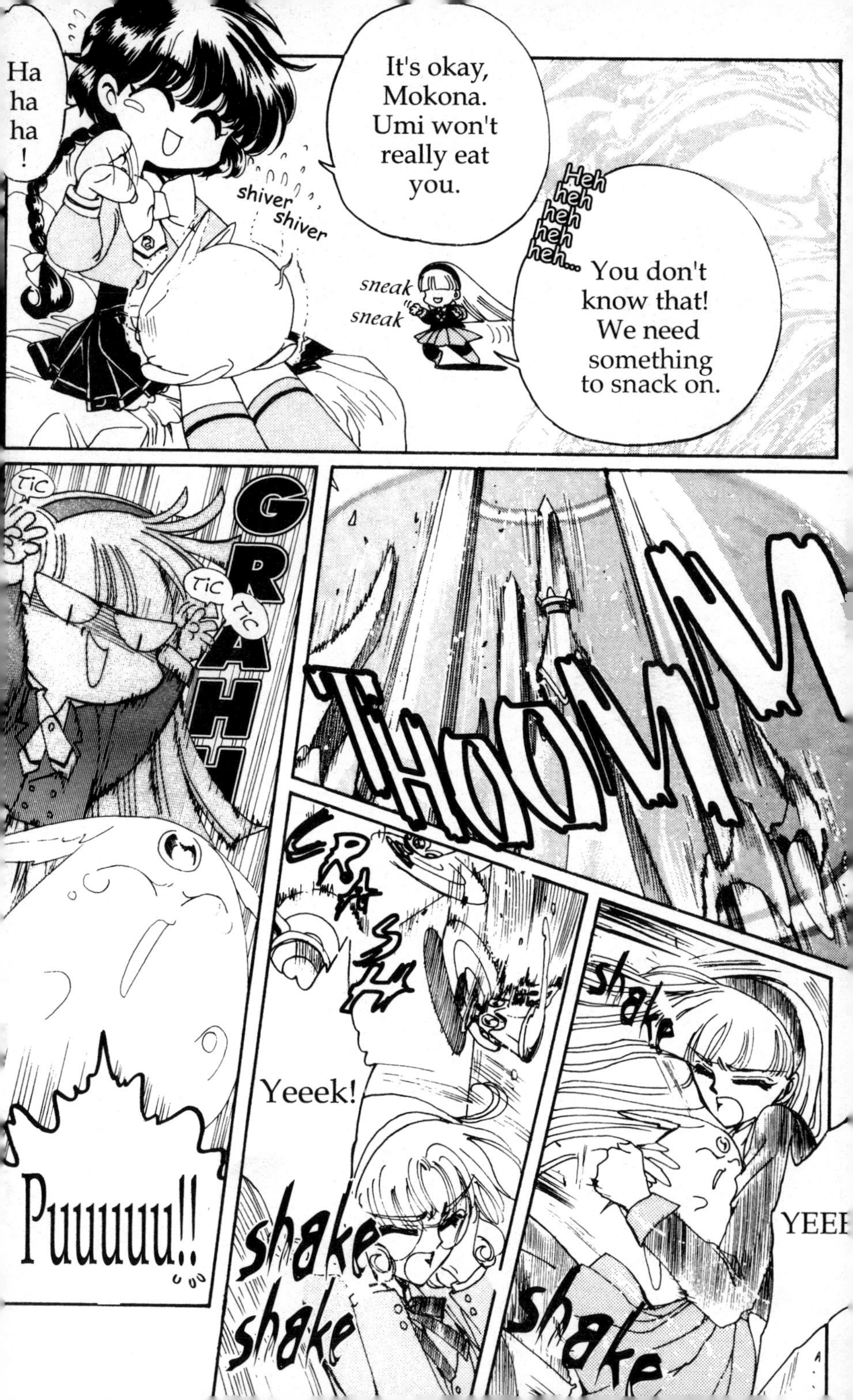

It's okay, Mokona. Umi won't really eat you.
Ha ha ha!
shiver shiver
Heh heh heh heh heh...
You don't know that! We need something to snack on.
sneak sneak
GRAHH
Tic
Tic
Tic
THOOM
Puuuuu!!
CRASH
Yeeek!
shake shake
shake
shake
YEEE

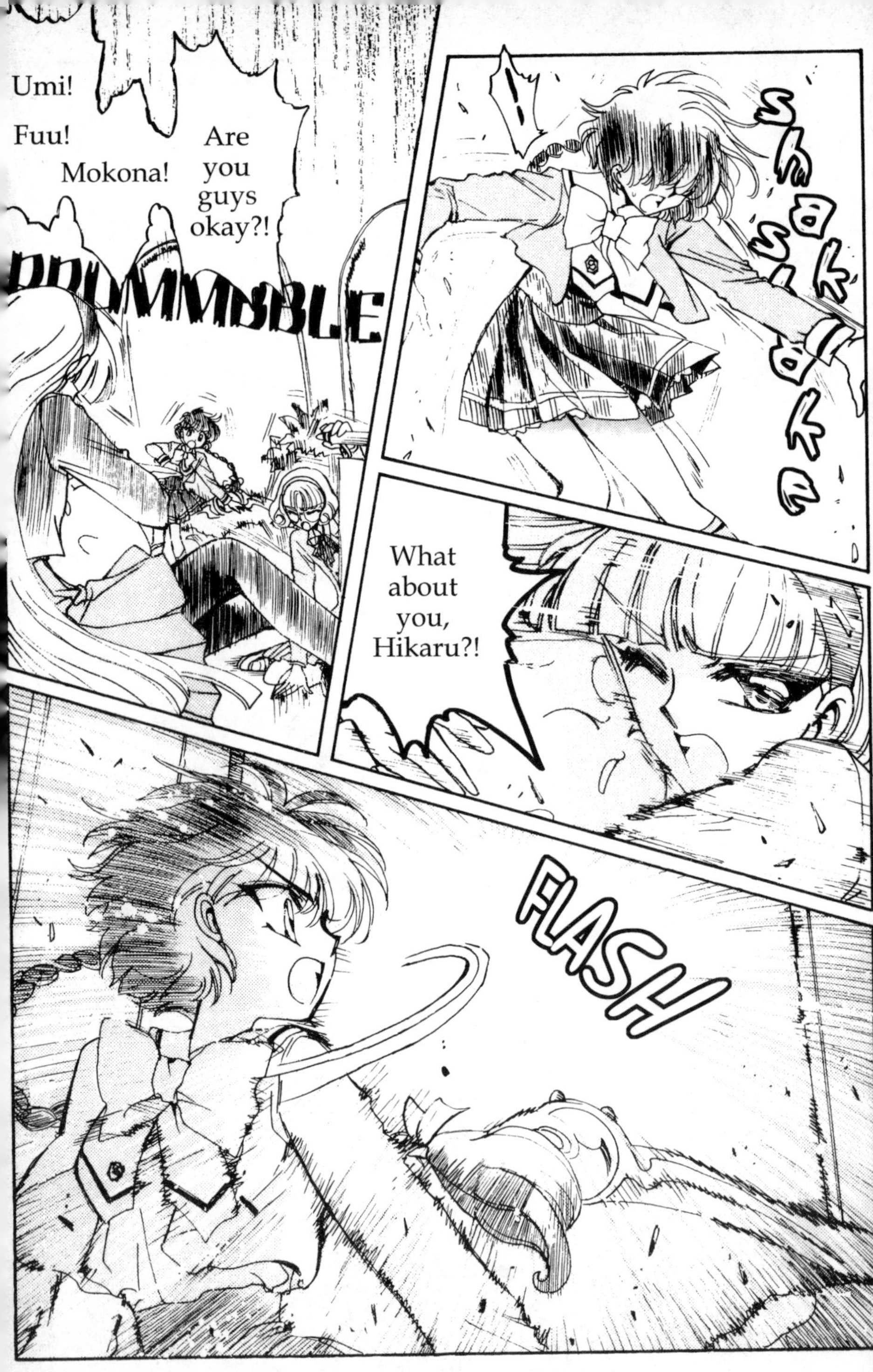
Umi!
Fuu!
Mokona!
Are you guys okay?!
What about you, Hikaru?!
FLASH

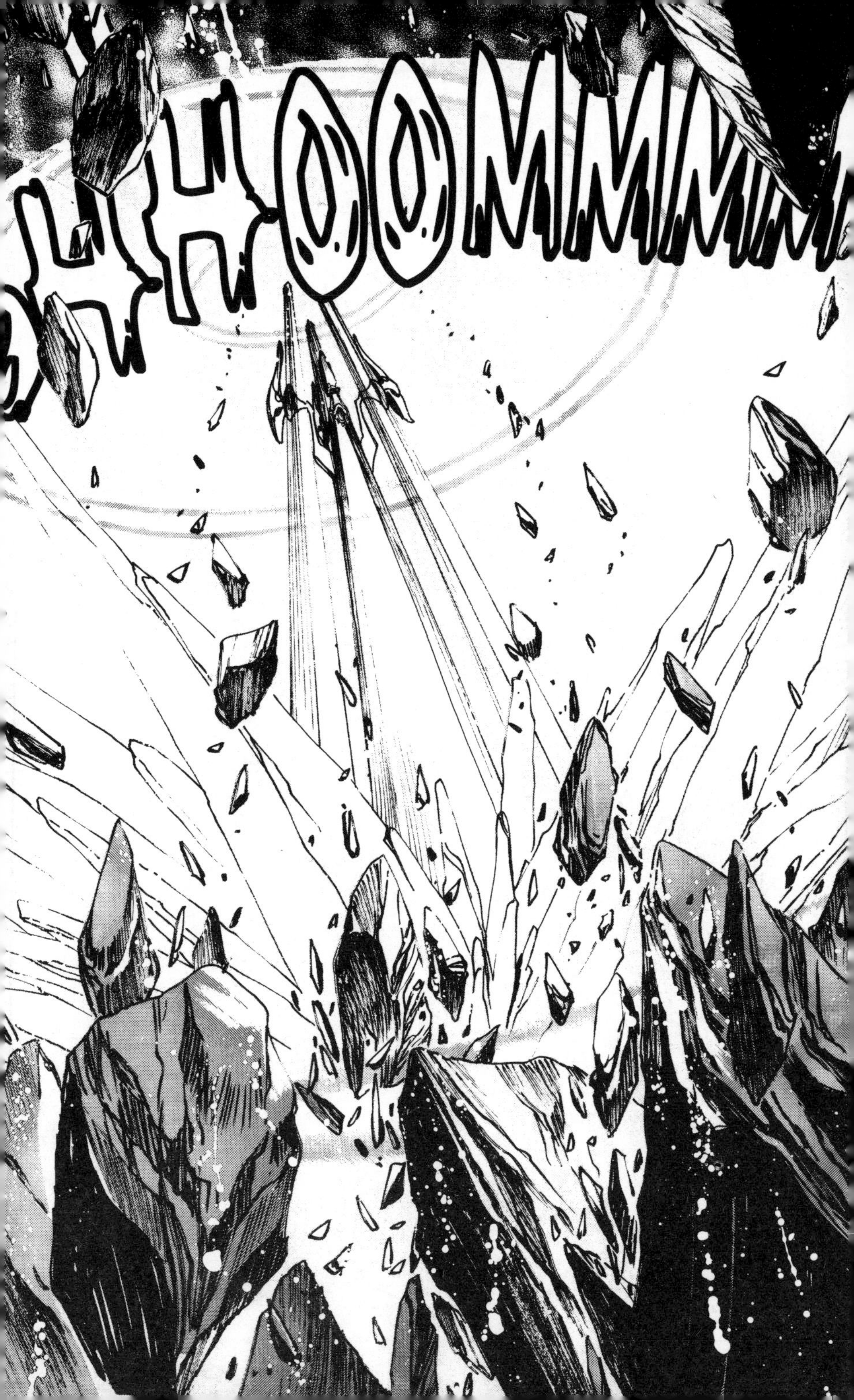
HHOOMMMMM

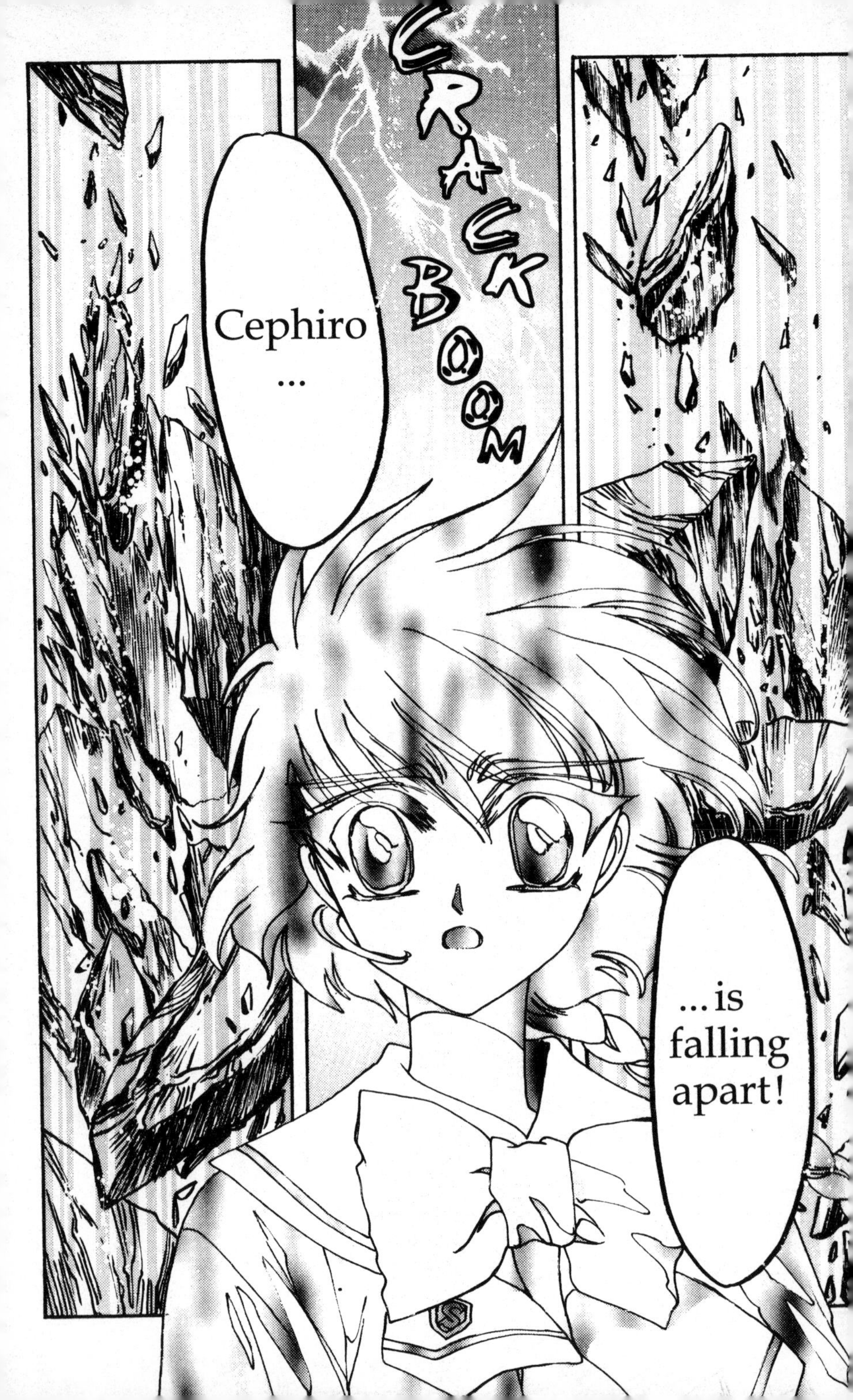
CRACK
BOOM
Cephiro
...
...is
falling
apart!

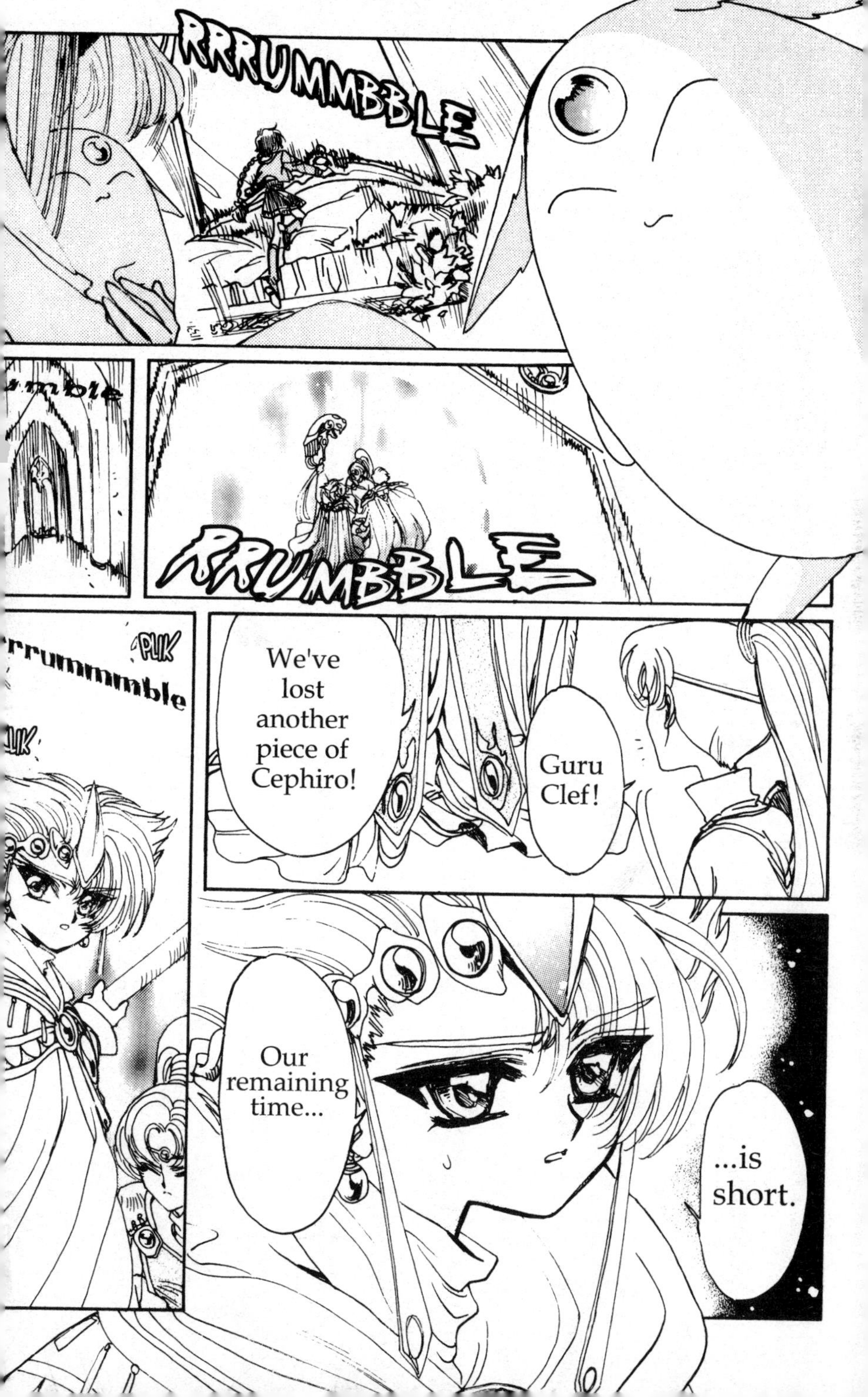
RRRUMMBBLE
rumble
RRUMBBLE
We've lost another piece of Cephiro!
Guru Clef!
rrrummmble
PLIK
PLIK
Our remaining time...
...is short.

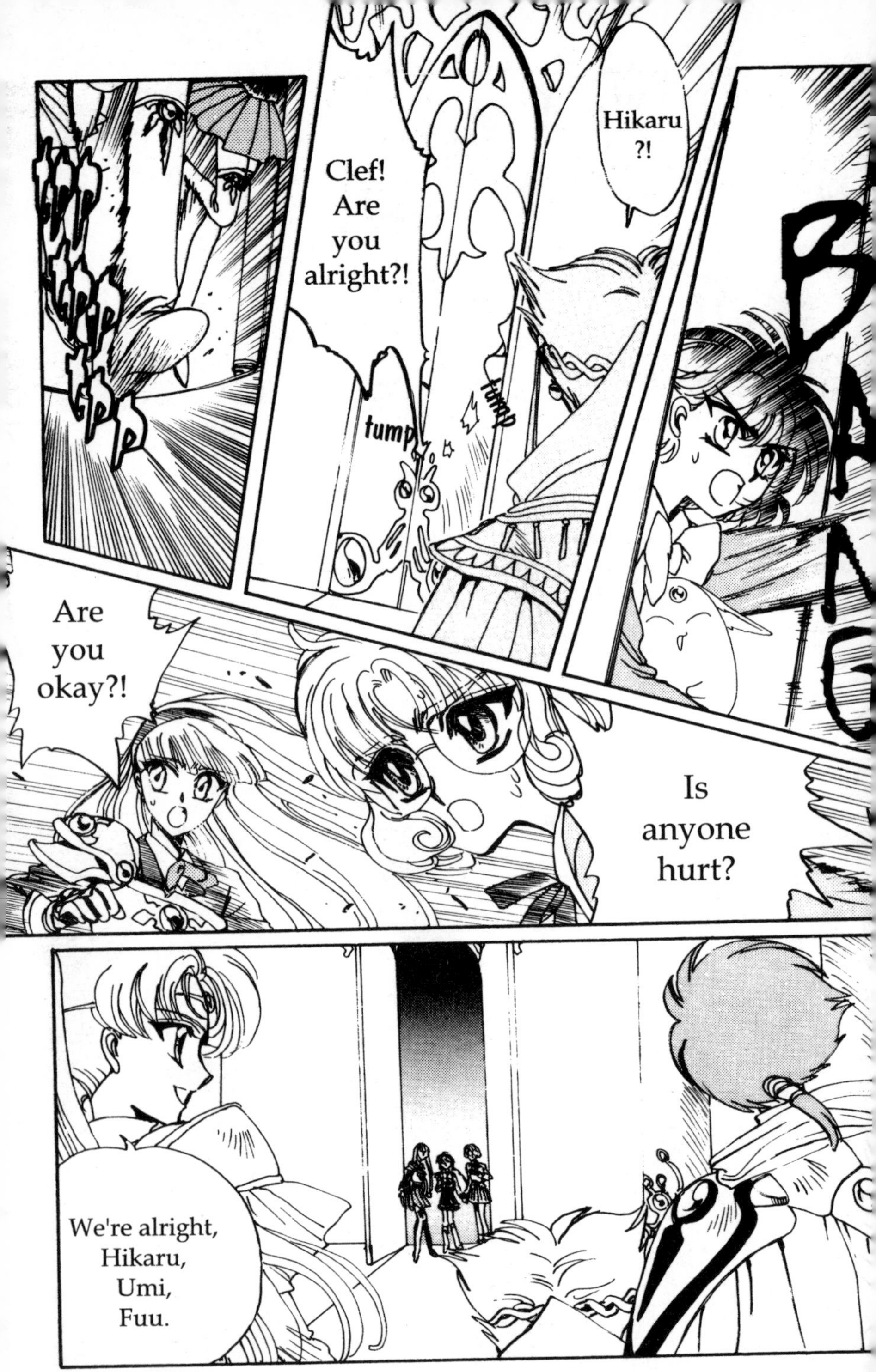
Hikaru ?!
Clef! Are you alright?!
tump
tump
Is anyone hurt?
Are you okay?!
We're alright, Hikaru, Umi, Fuu.

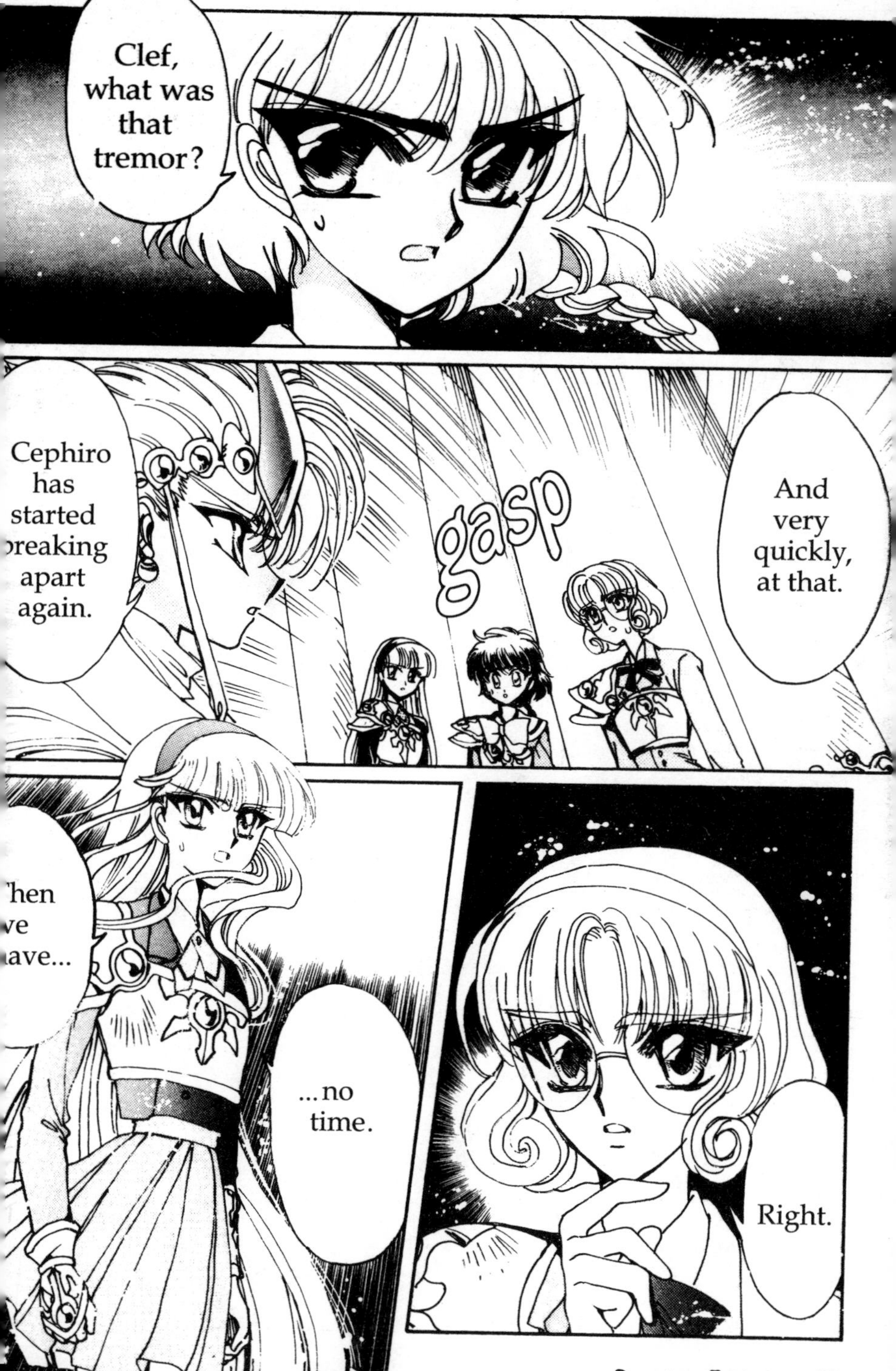
Clef, what was that tremor?
Cephiro has started reaking apart again.
gasp
And very quickly, at that.
hen ve ave...
...no time.
Right.

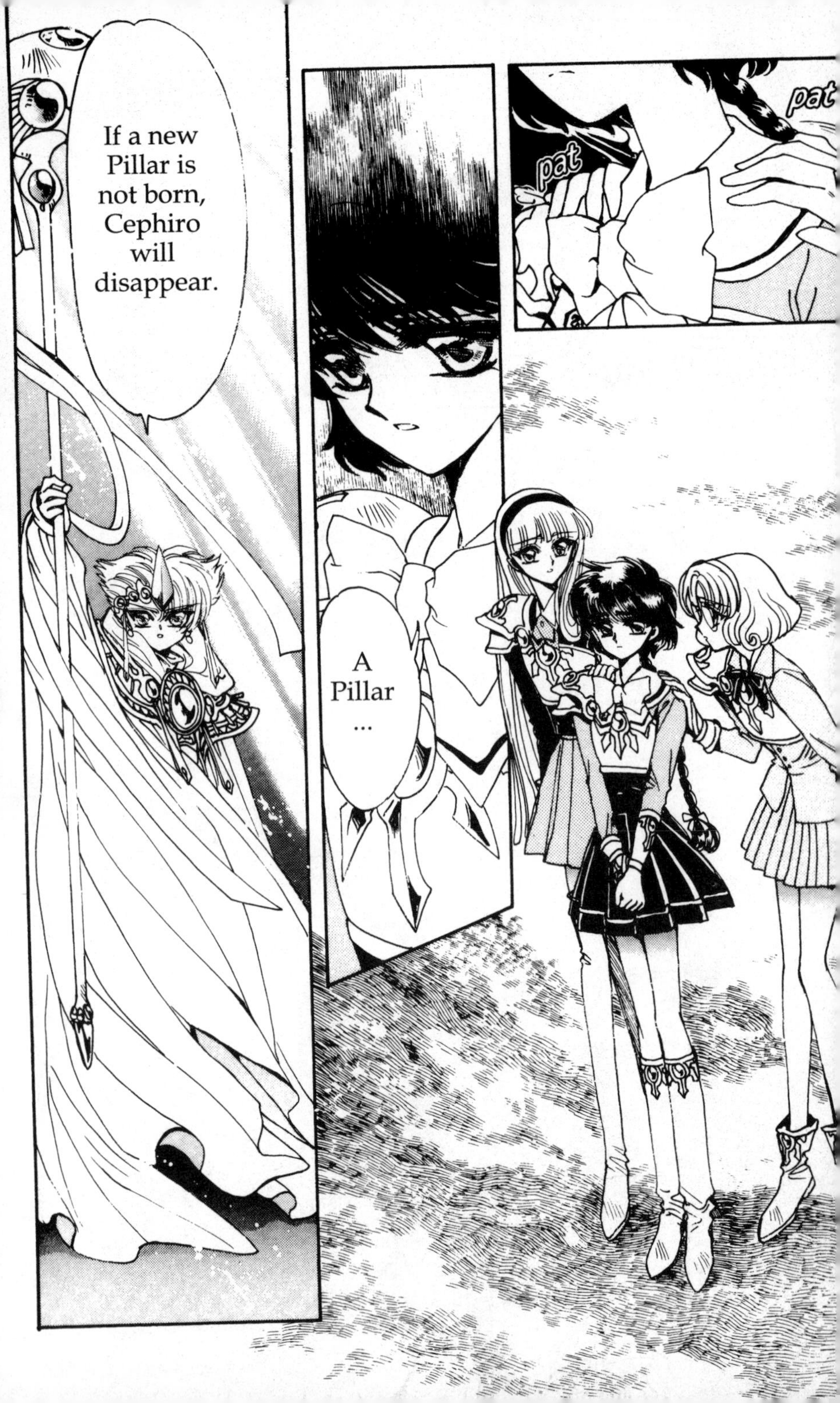
pat
pat
A Pillar ...
If a new Pillar is not born, Cephiro will disappear.

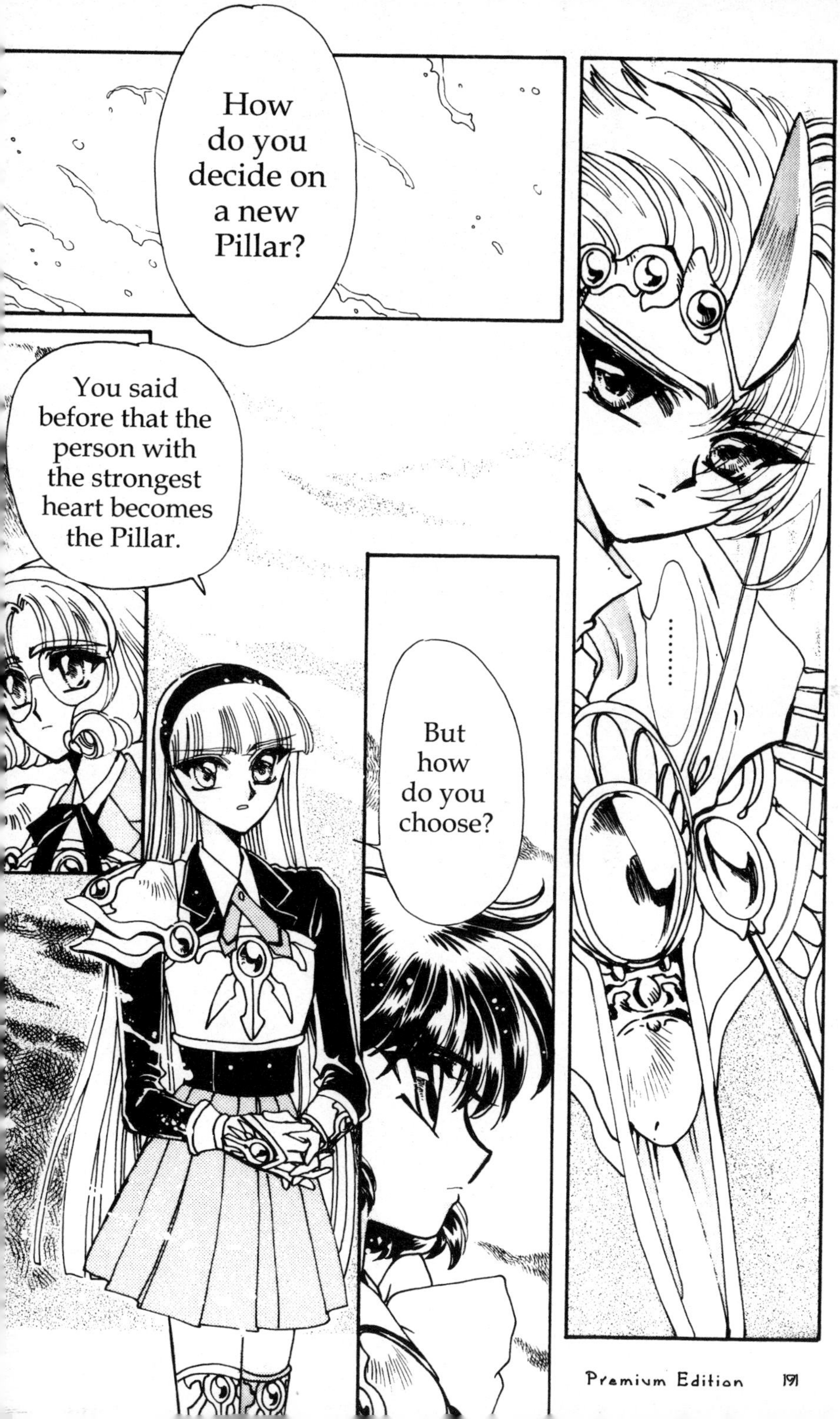
How do you decide on a new Pillar?
You said before that the person with the strongest heart becomes the Pillar.
But how do you choose?
......

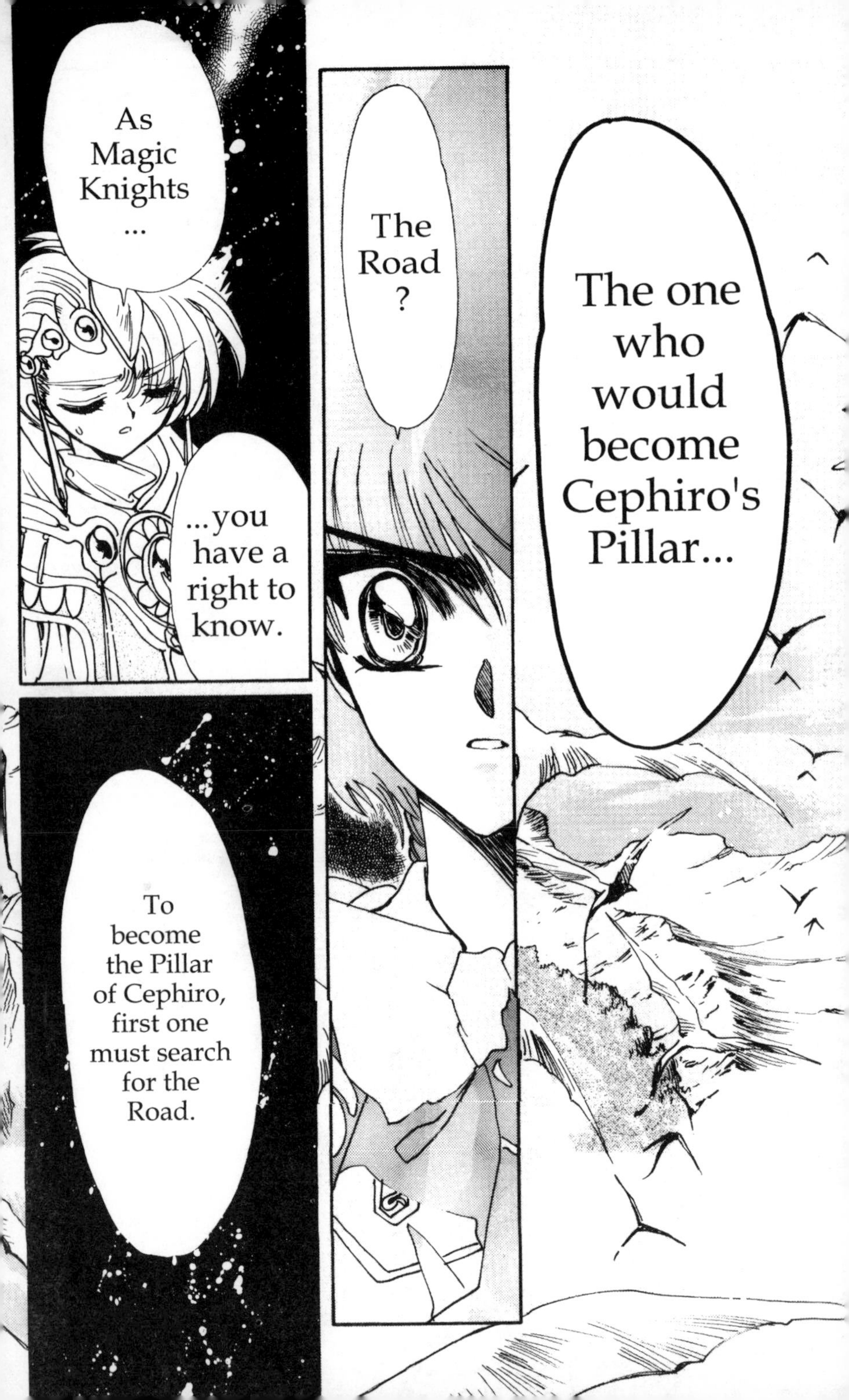
The one who would become Cephiro's Pillar...
The Road?
As Magic Knights...
...you have a right to know.
To become the Pillar of Cephiro, first one must search for the Road.

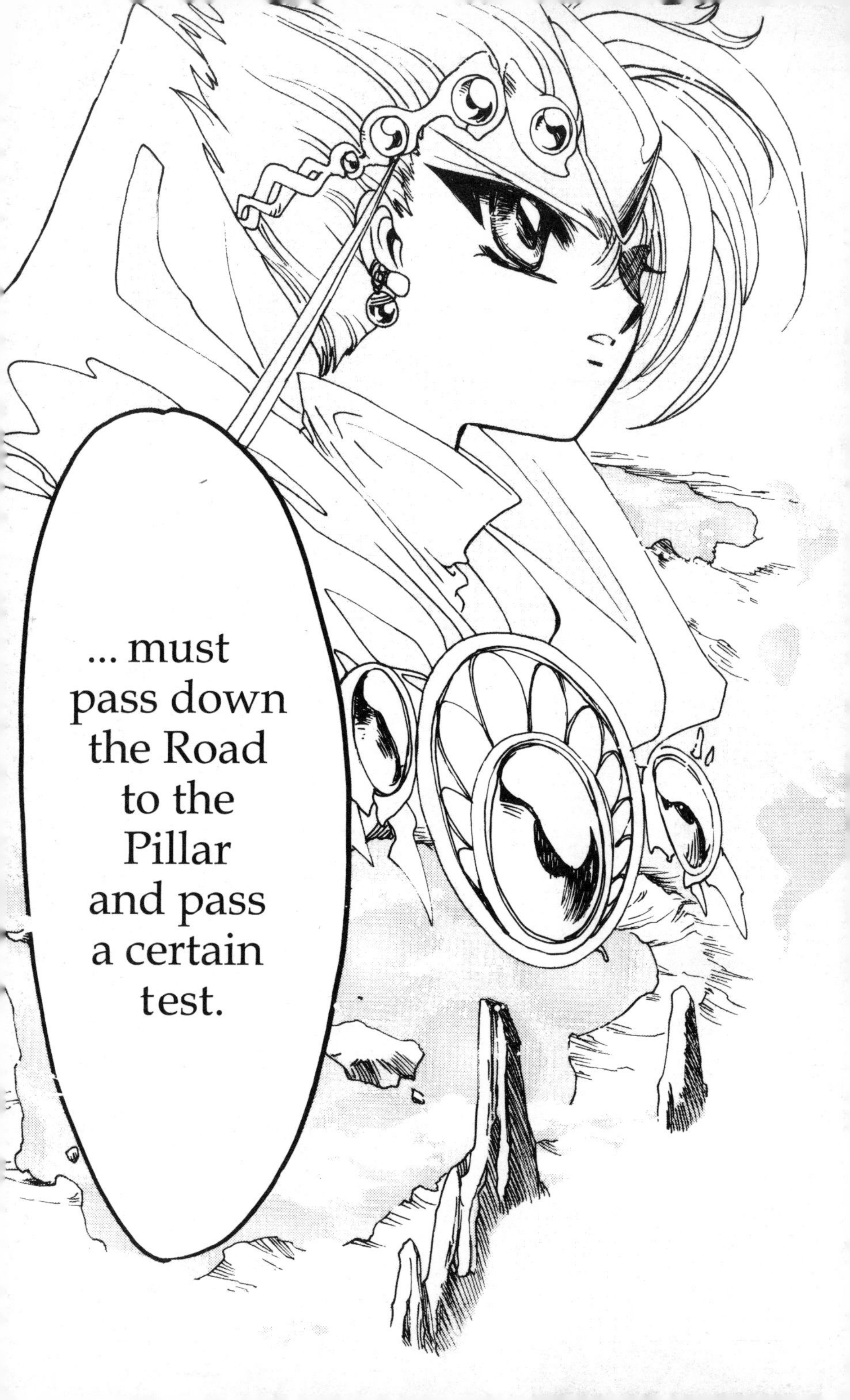
... must pass down the Road to the Pillar and pass a certain test.

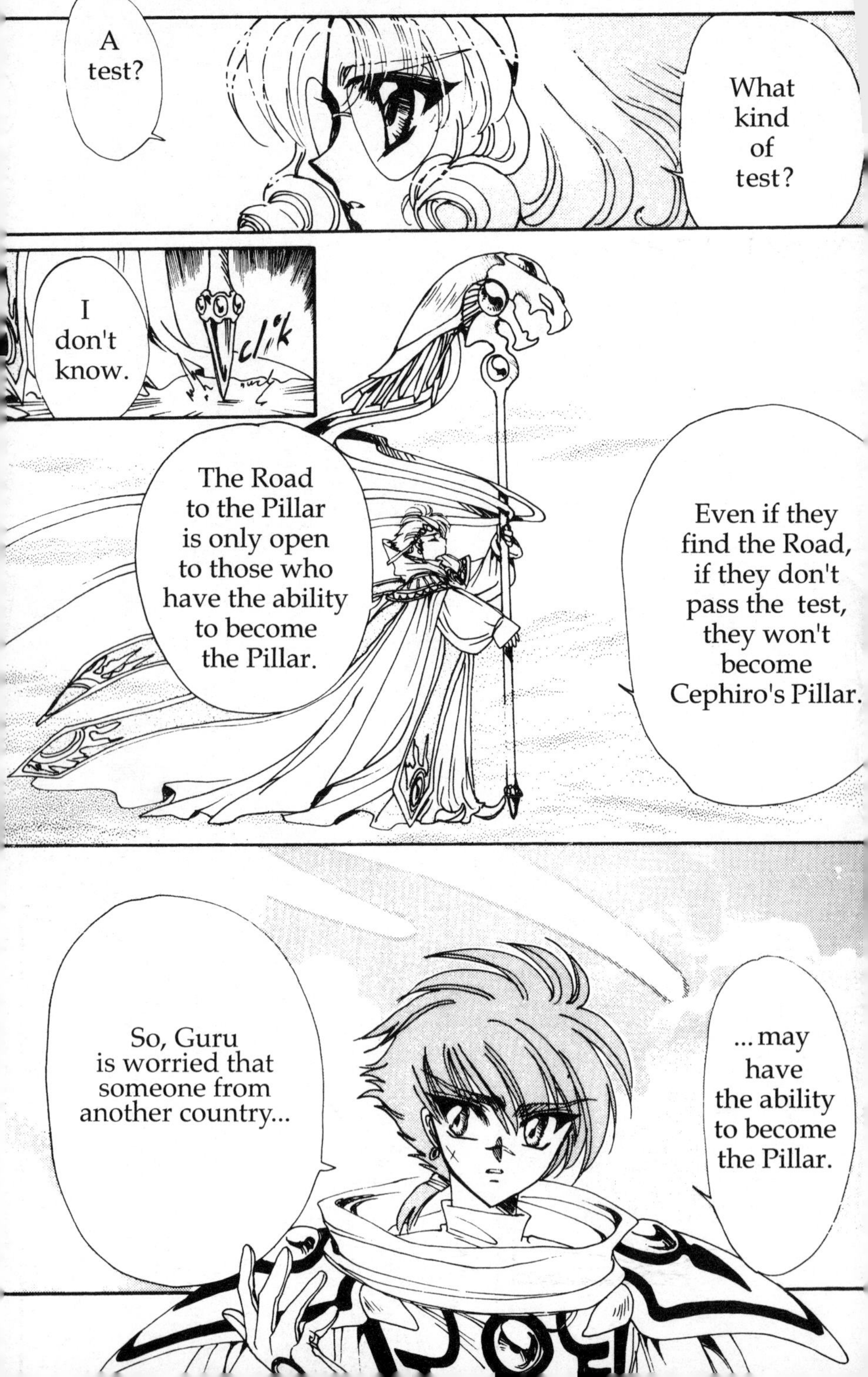

A test?
What kind of test?
I don't know.
clik
The Road to the Pillar is only open to those who have the ability to become the Pillar.
Even if they find the Road, if they don't pass the test, they won't become Cephiro's Pillar.
So, Guru is worried that someone from another country...
... may have the ability to become the Pillar.

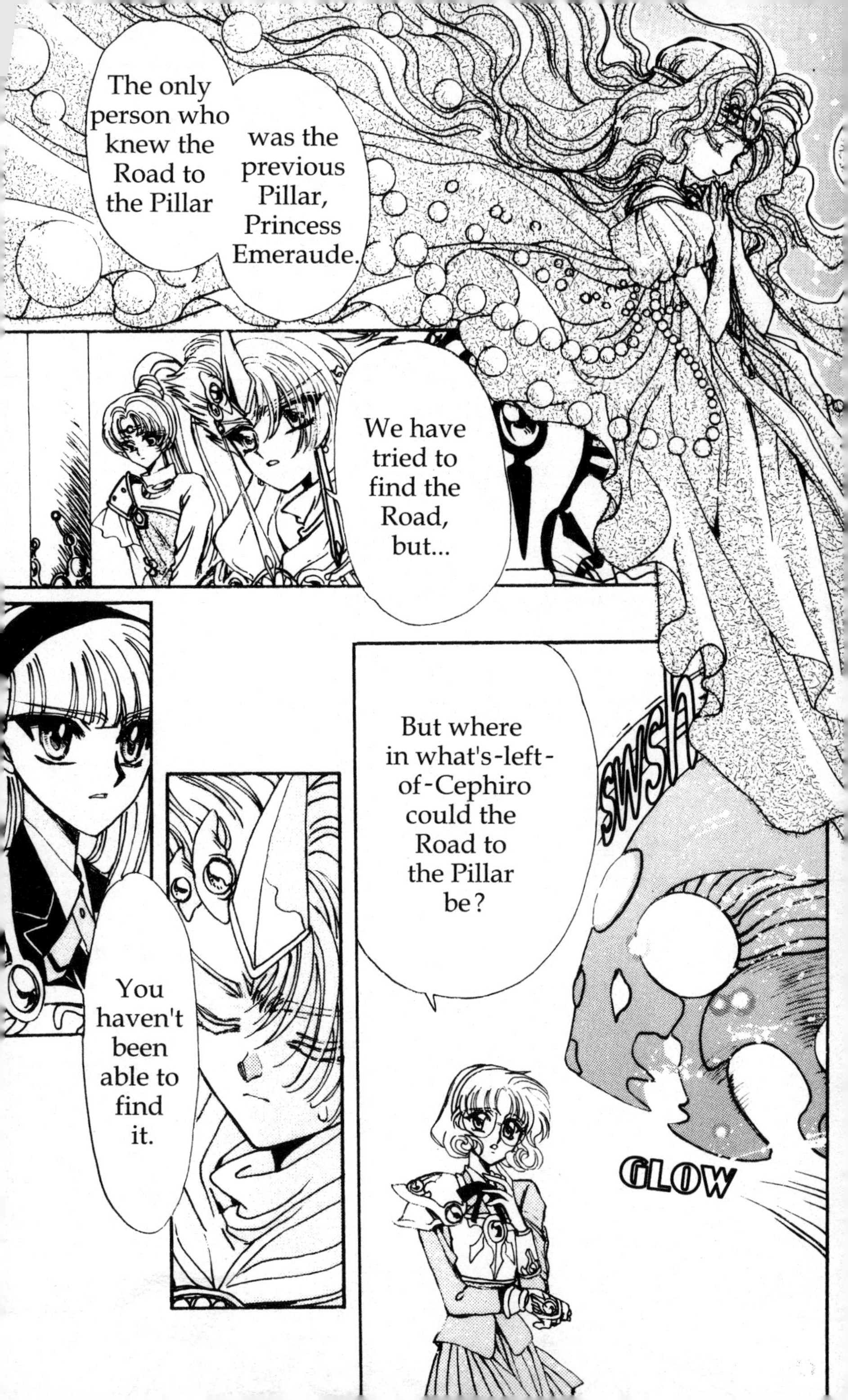
The only person who knew the Road to the Pillar
was the previous Pillar, Princess Emeraude.
We have tried to find the Road, but...
But where in what's-left-of-Cephiro could the Road to the Pillar be?
SWSH
You haven't been able to find it.
GLOW

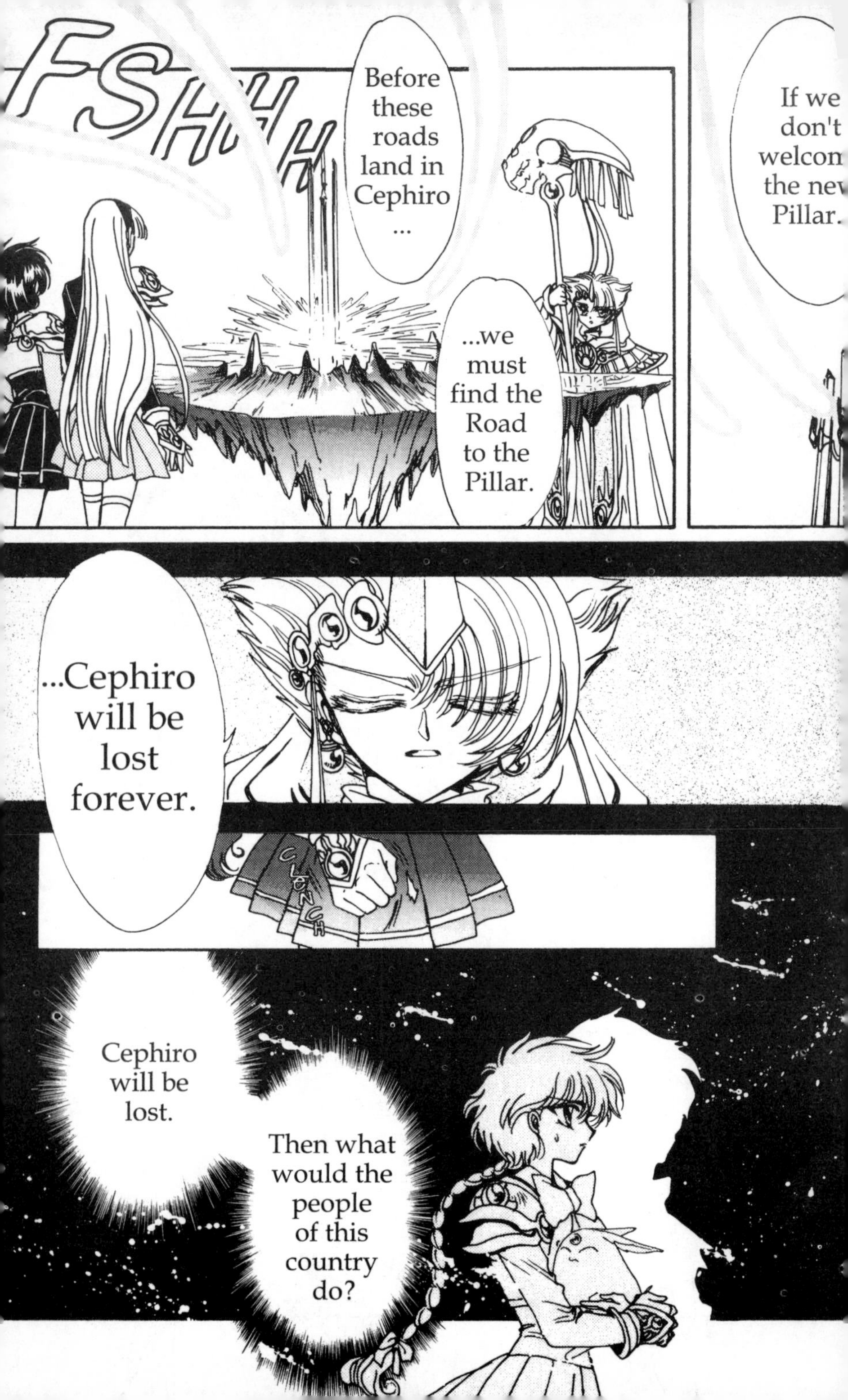
If we don't welcom the nev Pillar.
Before these roads land in Cephiro ...
...we must find the Road to the Pillar.
FSHHH
...Cephiro will be lost forever.
CLENCH
Cephiro will be lost.
Then what would the people of this country do?

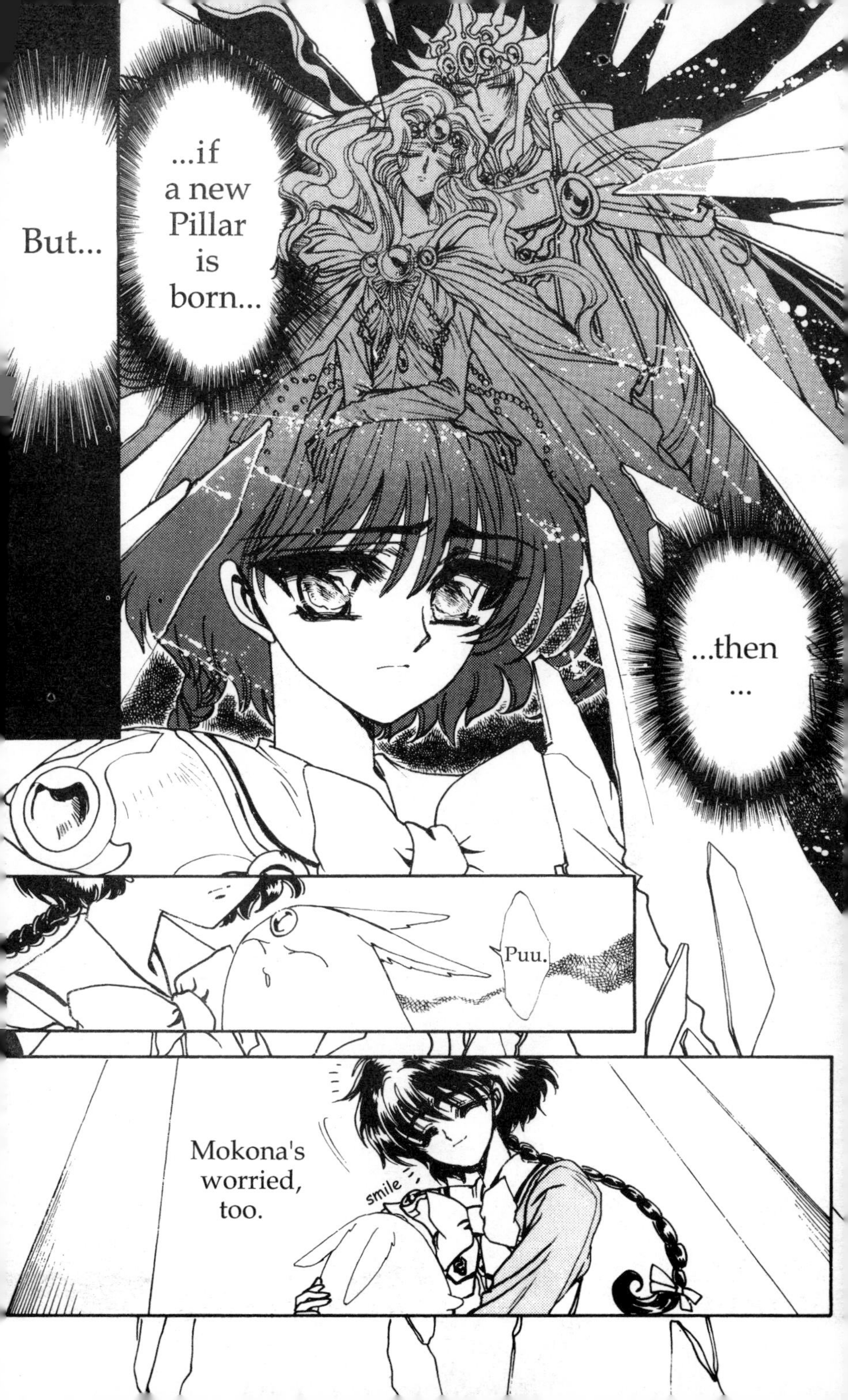

But...
...if a new Pillar is born...
...then ...
Puu.
Mokona's worried, too.
smile

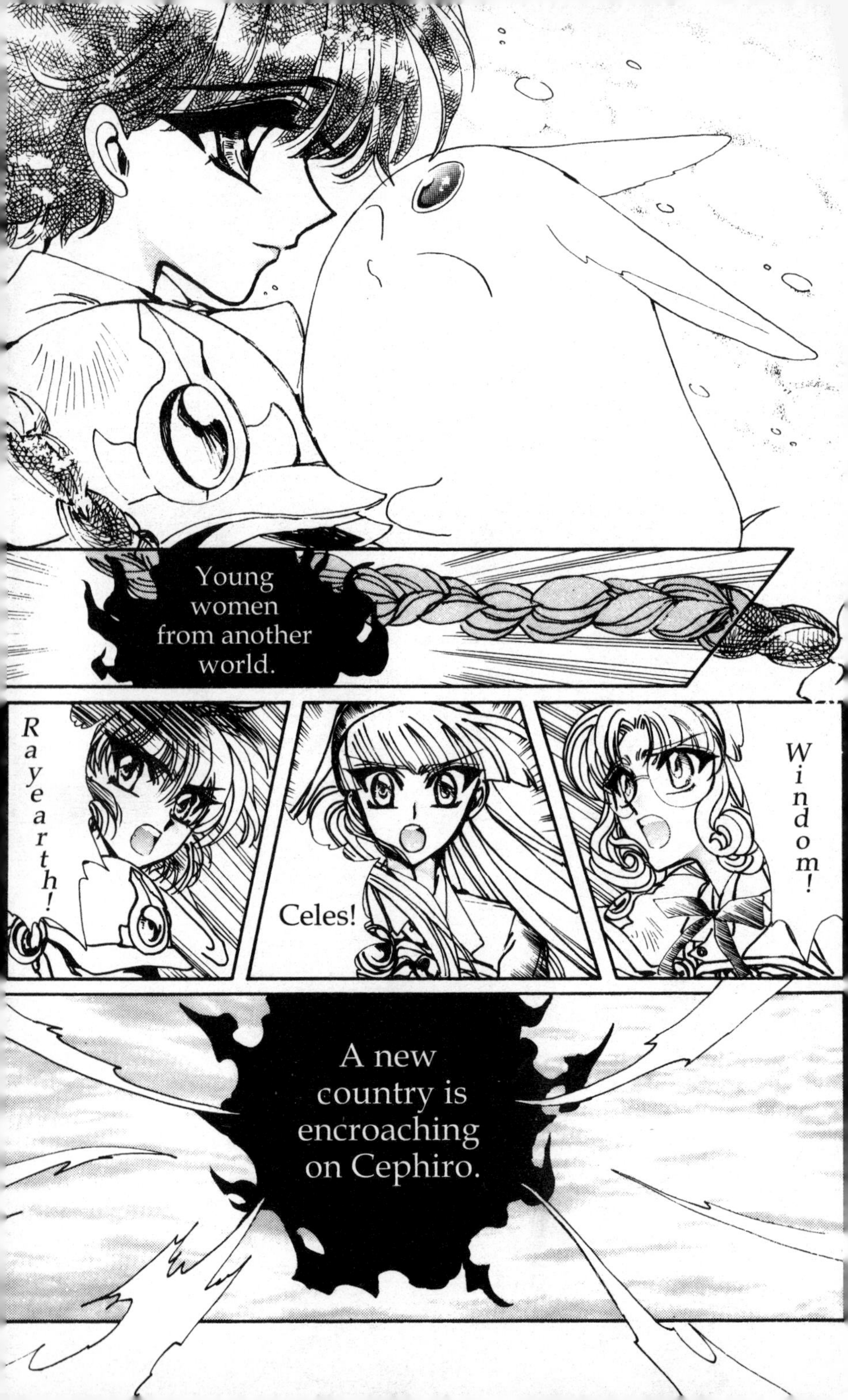
Young women from another world.
Rayearth!
Celes!
Windom!
A new country is encroaching on Cephiro.

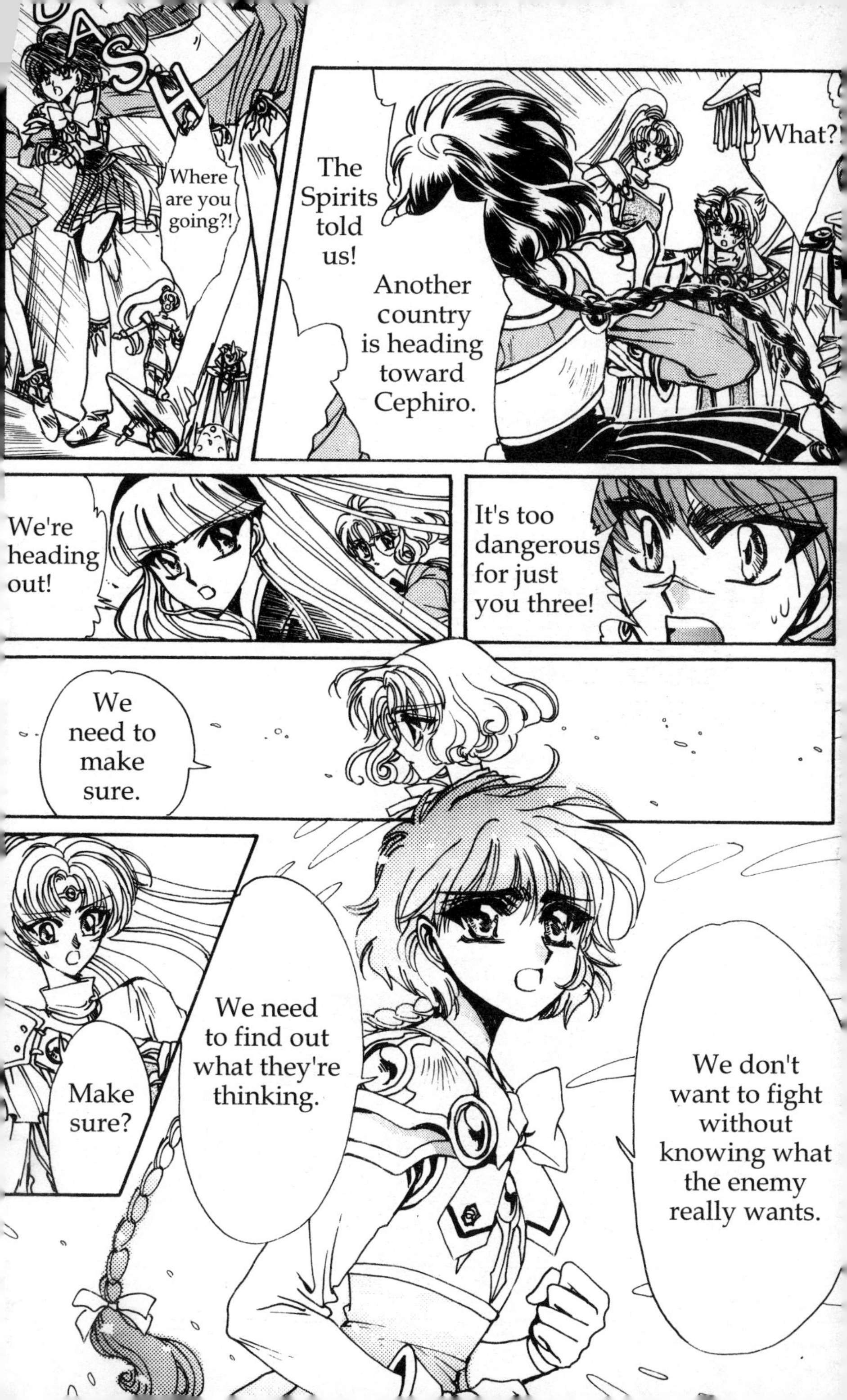
DASH
Where are you going?!
The Spirits told us!
Another country is heading toward Cephiro.
What?!
We're heading out!
It's too dangerous for just you three!
We need to make sure.
Make sure?
We need to find out what they're thinking.
We don't want to fight without knowing what the enemy really wants.

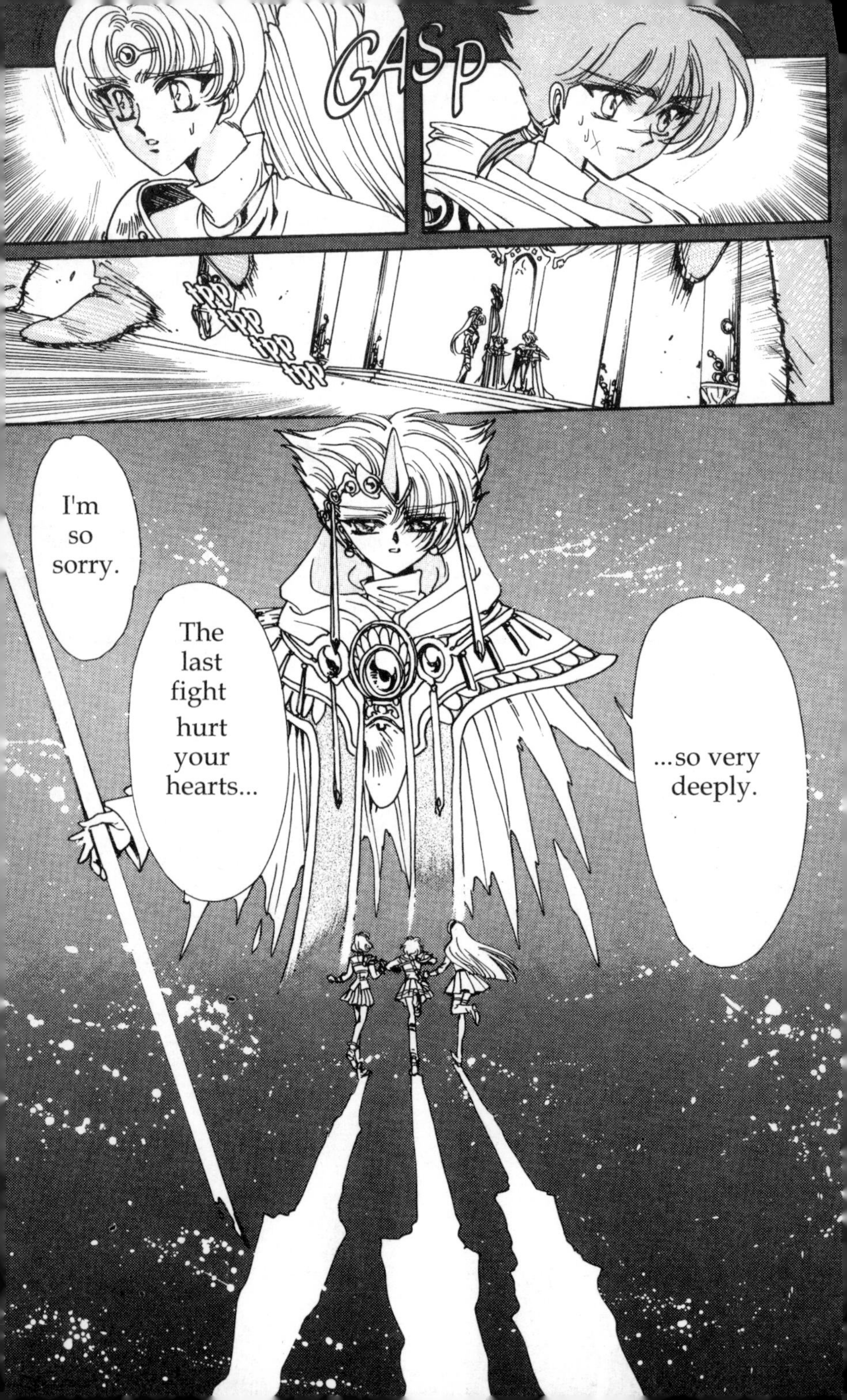
GASP
tpp tpp tpp tpp
I'm so sorry.
The last fight hurt your hearts...
...so very deeply.

FLASH

Cephiro.

It was such a peaceful and beautiful country.

But as soon as the Pillar is gone...

...it will turn ugly.

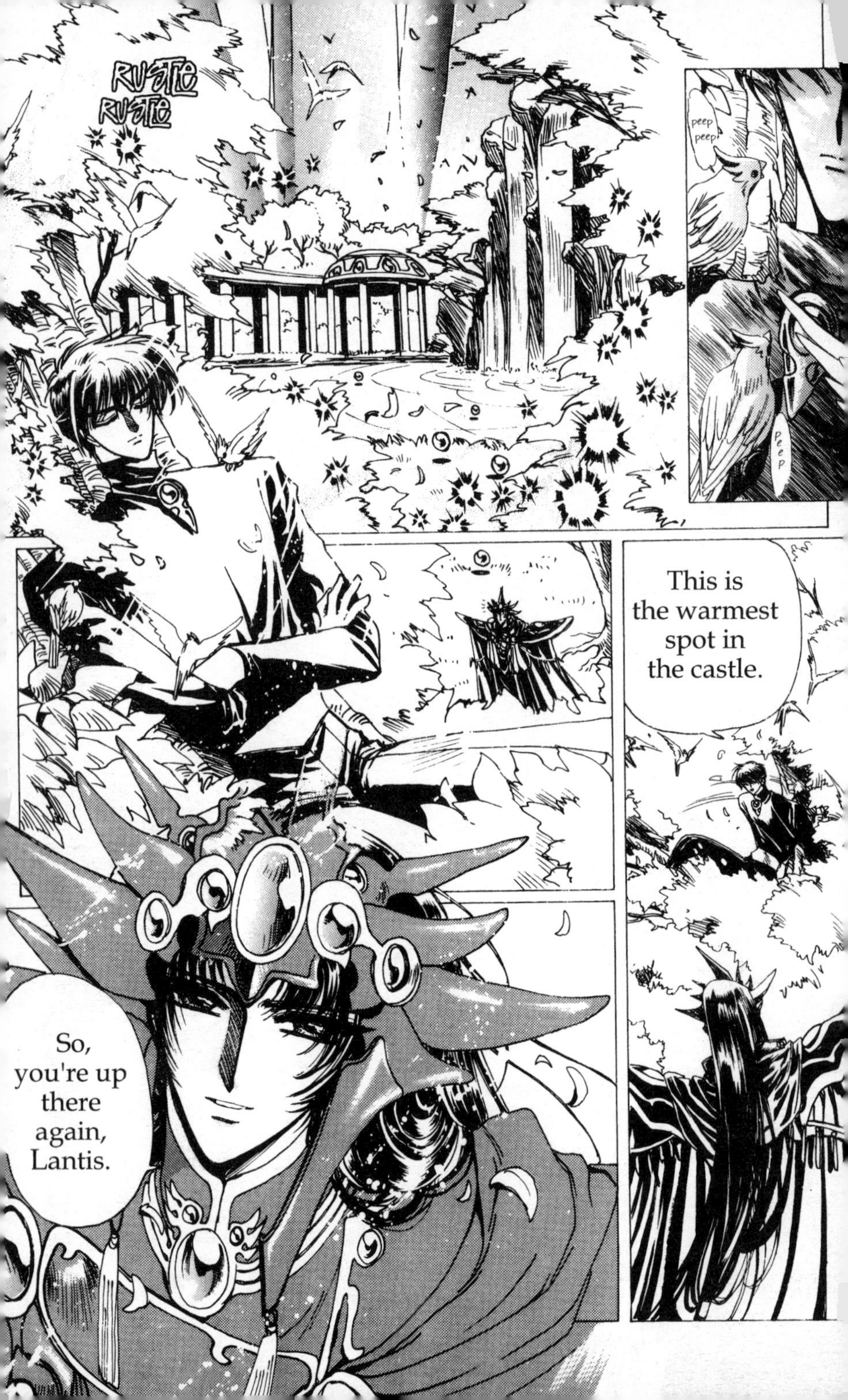
RUSTLE
RUSTLE
peep
peep
peep
So, you're up there again, Lantis.
This is the warmest spot in the castle.

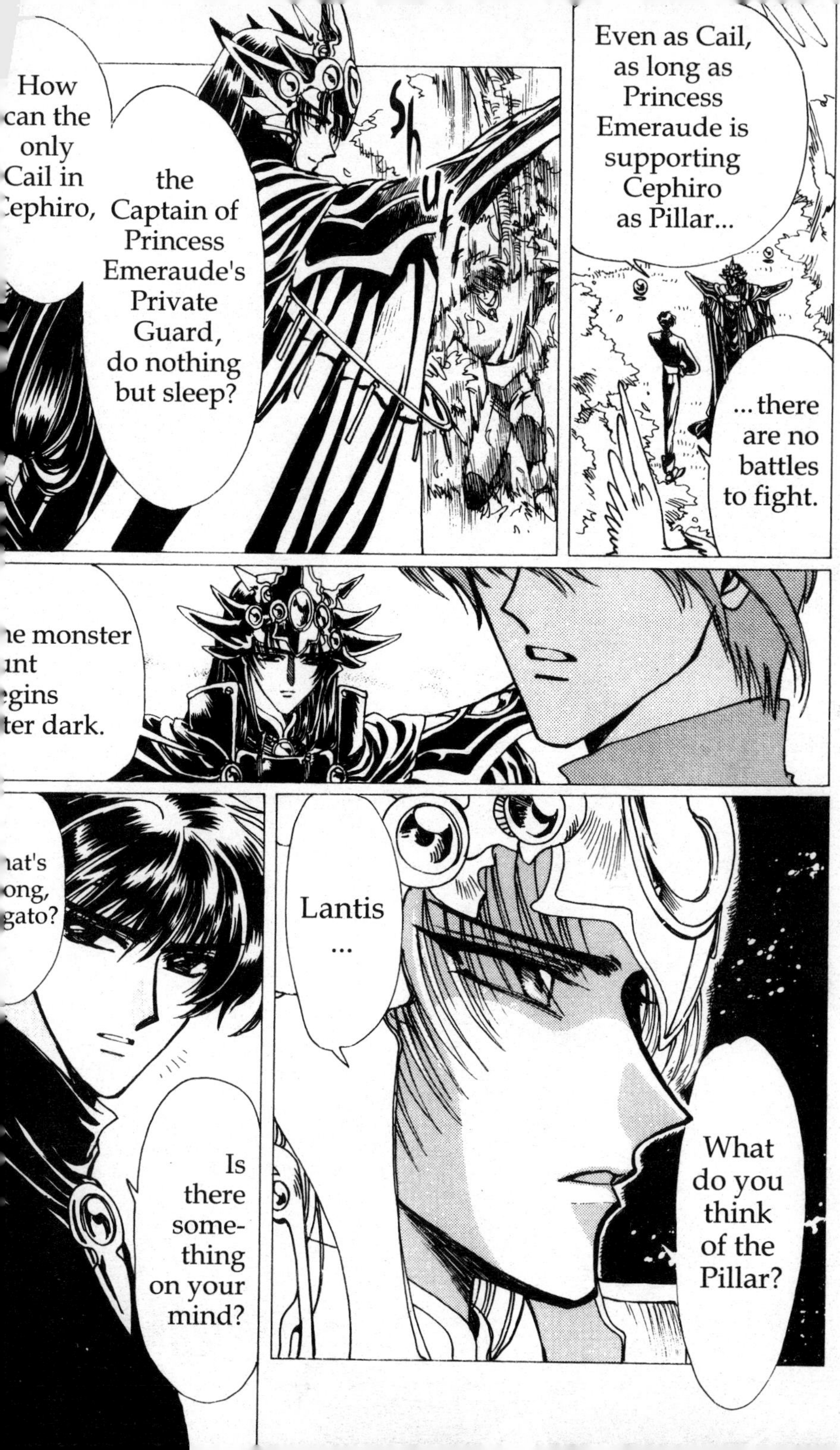

How can the only Cail in ɛephiro,
the Captain of Princess Emeraude's Private Guard, do nothing but sleep?
Sh
u
f
f
Even as Cail, as long as Princess Emeraude is supporting Cephiro as Pillar...
...there are no battles to fight.
ie monster unt gins ter dark.
nat's ong, gato?
Lantis ...
Is there some- thing on your mind?
What do you think of the Pillar?

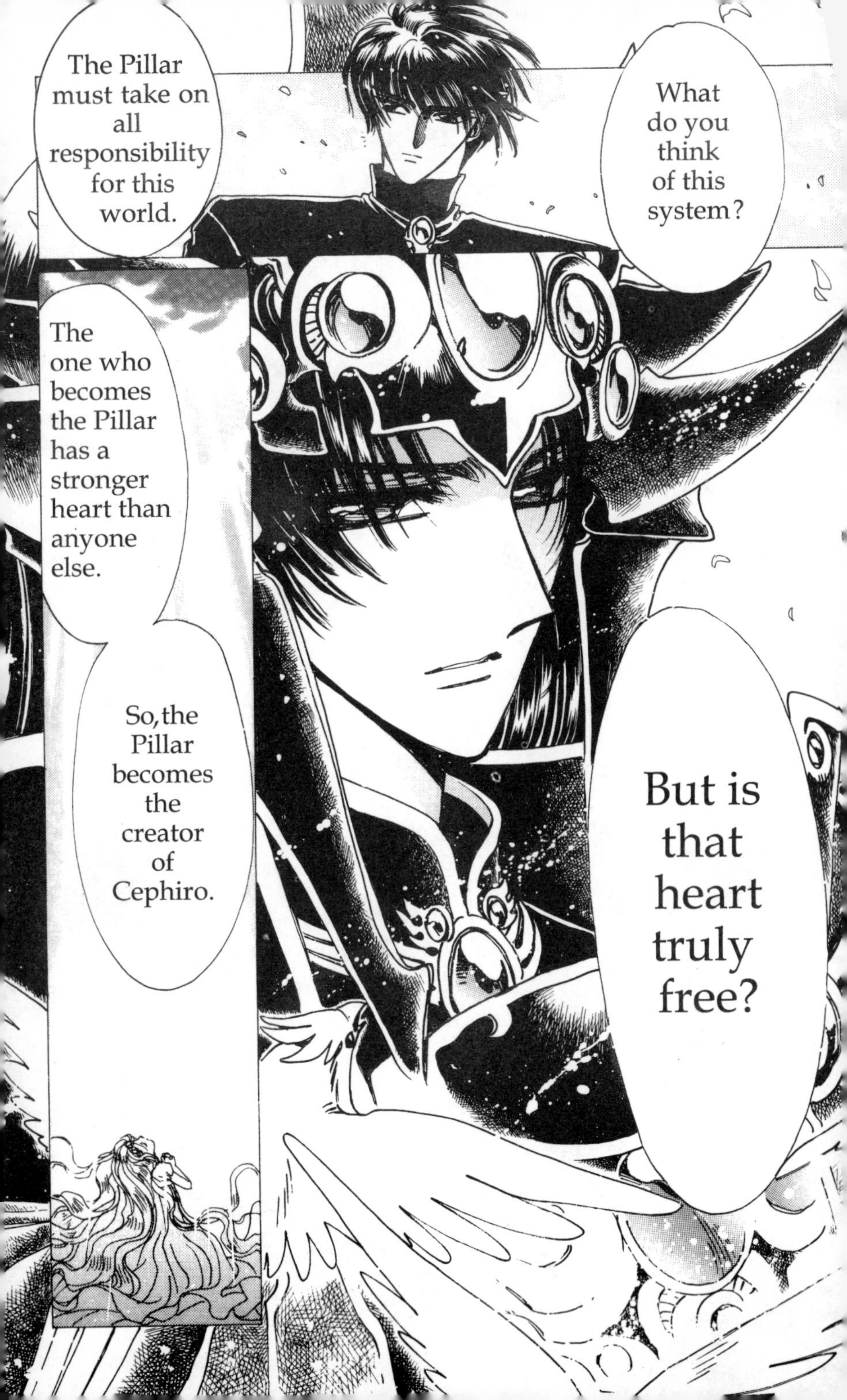
The Pillar must take on all responsibility for this world.
What do you think of this system?
The one who becomes the Pillar has a stronger heart than anyone else.
So, the Pillar becomes the creator of Cephiro.
But is that heart truly free?

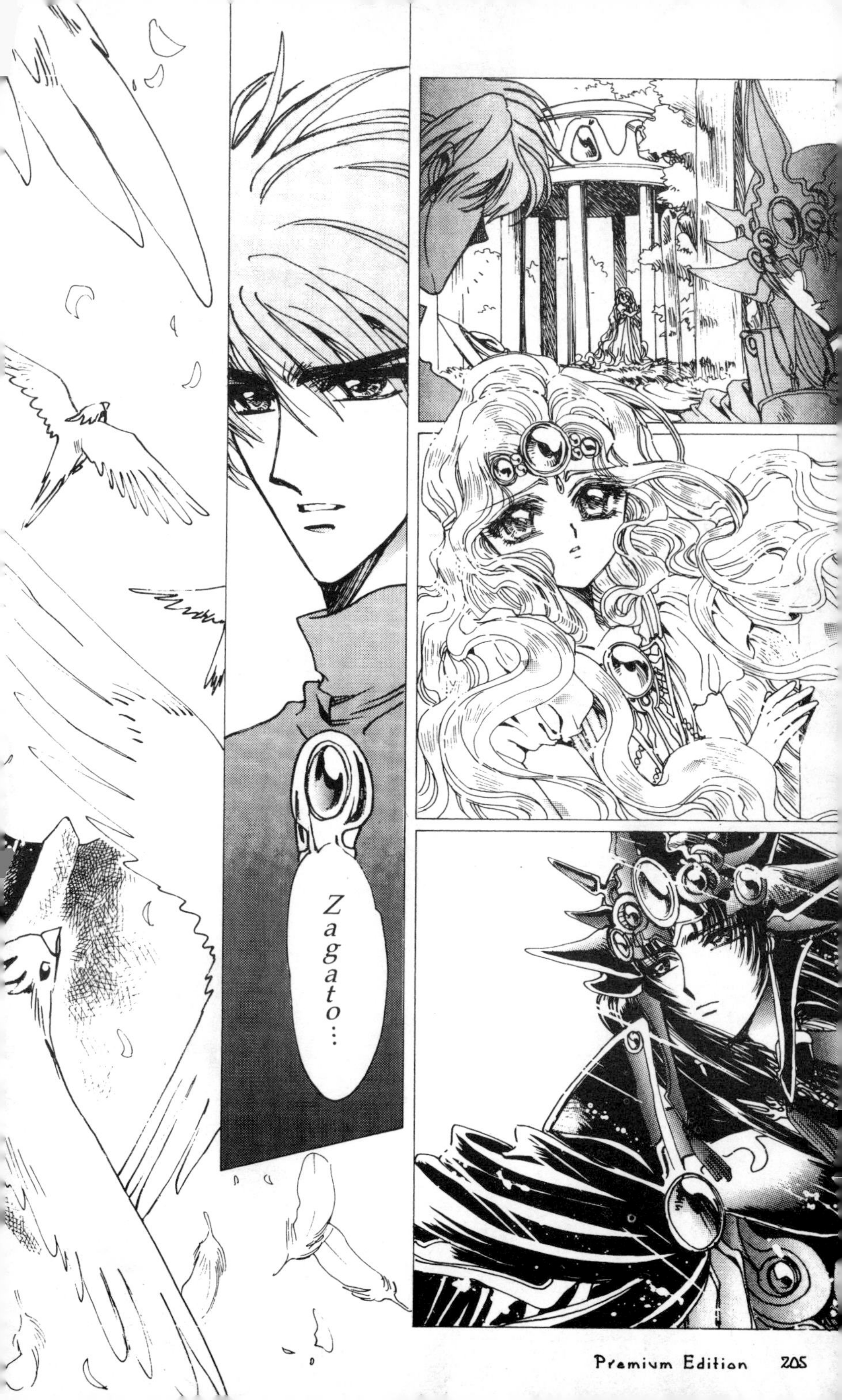
Zagato...

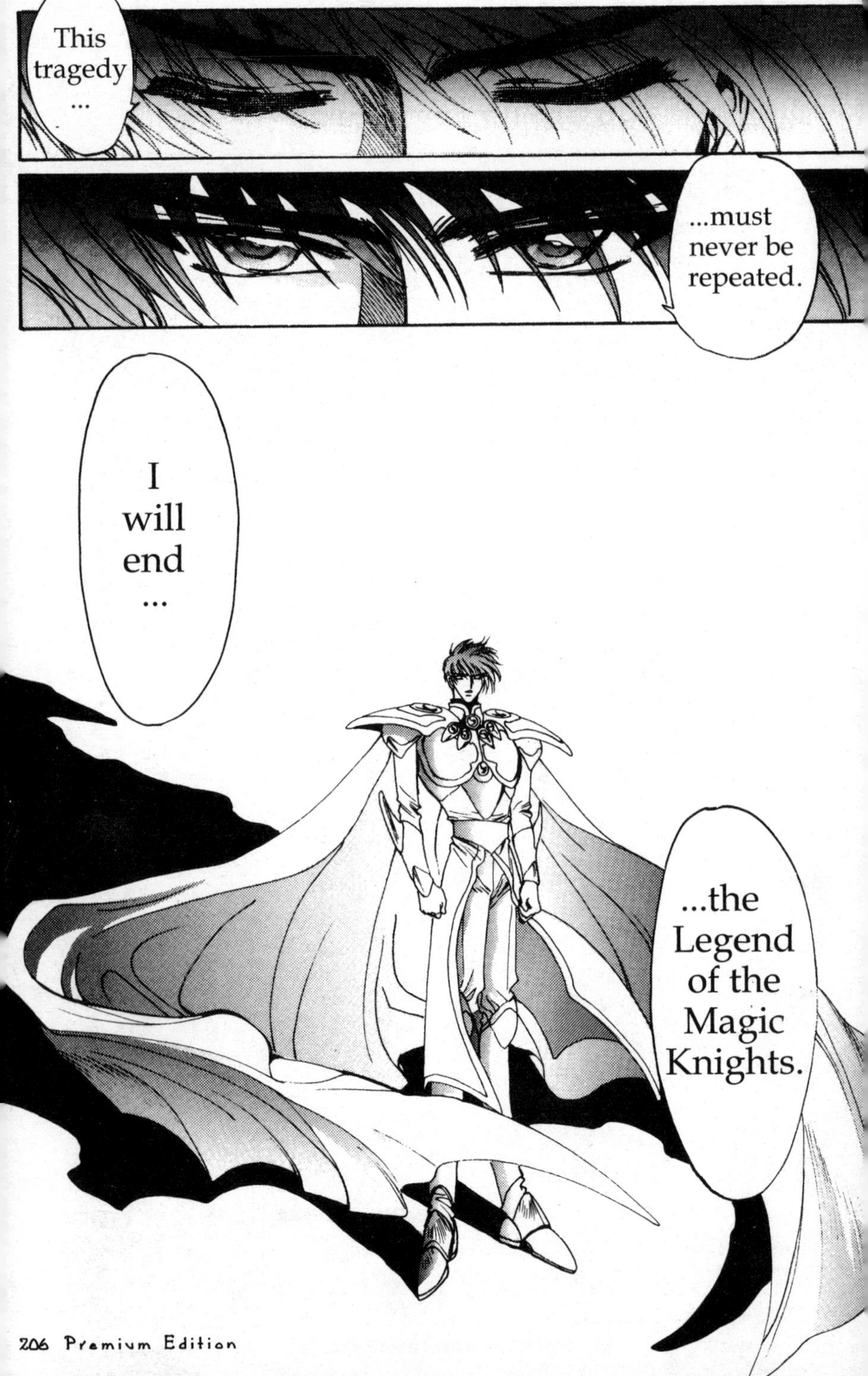
This tragedy ...
...must never be repeated.
I will end ...
...the Legend of the Magic Knights.

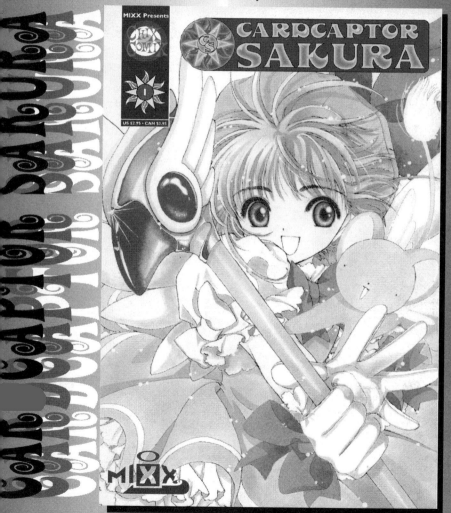